Rick Steves'

SNAPSHOT

Sevilla, Granada & Southern Spain

CONTENTS

INTRODUCTION

This Snapshot guide, excerpted from the latest edition of my guide-book *Rick Steves' Spain,* introduces you to southern Spain's two top cities—Sevilla and Granada—and the surrounding Spanish heartland. When Americans think of Spain, they often picture this region, with its massive cathedrals, Moorish palaces, vibrant folk life, whitewashed villages, bright sunshine, and captivating rat-a-tat-tat of flamenco.

Sevilla is the soulful cultural heart of southern Spain, with an atmospheric old quarter and riveting flamenco shows. Granada, formerly the Moorish capital, is home to the magnificent Alhambra palace. Córdoba features Spain's top surviving Moorish mosque, the Mezquita. Make time to delve into Andalucía's sleepy, white-washed hill towns: Arcos de la Frontera, Ronda, and Grazalema. Spain's south coast, the Costa del Sol, is a palm-tree jungle of beach resorts and concrete, but has some appealing destinations—Nerja, Tarifa, and Gibraltar—beyond the traffic jams. And since it's so easy, consider an eye-opening side-trip to another continent by hopping the ferry from Tarifa to Tangier, the newly revitalized gateway to Morocco (and to Africa).

To help you have the best trip possible, I've included the following topics in this book:

• **Planning Your Time,** with advice on how to make the most of your limited time

• **Orientation,** including tourist information (abbreviated as TI), tips on public transportation, local tour options, and helpful hints

• **Sights** with ratings:

    ▲▲▲—Don't miss

    ▲▲—Try hard to see

    ▲—Worthwhile if you can make it

    No rating—Worth knowing about

• **Sleeping** and **Eating,** with good-value recommendations in every price range

• **Connections,** with tips on trains, buses, and driving

• **Practicalities,** near the end of this book, has information on money, phoning, hotel reservations, transportation, and more, plus Spanish survival phrases.

To travel smartly, read this little book in its entirety before you go. It's my hope that this guide will make your trip more meaningful and rewarding. Traveling like a temporary local, you'll get the absolute most out of every mile, minute, and euro.

Buen viaje!

SEVILLA

Flamboyant Sevilla thrums with flamenco music, sizzles in the summer heat, and pulses with the passion of Don Juan and Carmen. It's a place where bullfighting is still politically correct and little girls still dream of growing up to become flamenco dancers. While Granada has the great Alhambra and Córdoba has the remarkable Mezquita, Sevilla has a soul. (Soul—or *duende*—is fundamental to flamenco.) It's a wonderful-to-be-alive-in kind of place.

The gateway to the New World in the 16th century, Sevilla boomed when Spain did. The explorers Amerigo Vespucci and Ferdinand Magellan sailed from its great river harbor, discovering new trade routes and abundant sources of gold, silver, cocoa, and tobacco. In the 17th century, Sevilla was Spain's largest and wealthiest city. Local artists Diego Velázquez, Bartolomé Murillo, and Francisco de Zurbarán made it a cultural center. Sevilla's Golden Age—and its New World riches—ended when the harbor silted up and the Spanish empire crumbled.

In the 19th century, Sevilla was a big stop on the Romantic "Grand Tour" of Europe. To build on this tourism and promote trade among Spanish-speaking nations, Sevilla planned a grand exposition in 1929. Bad year. The expo crashed along with the stock market. In 1992 Sevilla got a second chance at a world's fair. This expo was a success, leaving the city with an impressive infrastructure: a new airport, a train station, sleek bridges, and the super AVE bullet train (making Sevilla a 2.5-hour side-trip from Madrid). In 2007, the main boulevards—once thundering with noisy traffic and mercilessly cutting the city in two—were

Greater Sevilla

1 MILE
1 KM

TO ITÁLICA & MÉRIDA

ALAMILLO PARK

GUADALQUIVIR RIVER

ALAMILLO BRIDGE

TO A-4, AIRPORT & CÓRDOBA

LA CORTA BRIDGE

FORMER EXPO SITE

BASÍLICA DE LA MACARENA

CARR. DE CARMONA

LA CARTUJA

MUSEO DE BELLAS ARTES

GIRALDA TOWER

SANTA JUSTA TRAIN STN.

TO HUELVA

CORTA DE

ISABEL II BRIDGE

BULL-RING

MONTOTO

ANDALUCÍA

TRIANA

ALCÁZAR

TO A-92 & MÁLAGA

SAN TELMO BRIDGE

PLAZA DE ESPAÑA

APRIL FAIR FAIRGROUNDS

MARÍA LUISA PARK

AV. GARCIA MORATO

PASEO PALMERO

DCH

TO A-376 & RONDA

Bus Stations:
❶ El Prado
❷ Plaza de Armas

⬜ = HISTORIC CITY CENTER- SEE DETAIL MAP

pedestrianized, dramatically enhancing Sevilla's already substantial charm.

Today, Spain's fourth-largest city (pop. 704,000) is Andalucía's leading destination, buzzing with festivals, color, guitars, castanets, and street life, and enveloped in the fragrances of orange trees, jacaranda, and myrtle. James Michener wrote, "Sevilla doesn't *have* ambience, it *is* ambience." Sevilla also has its share of impressive sights. Its cathedral is Spain's largest. The Alcázar is a fantastic royal palace and garden ornamented with Mudejar (Islamic) flair. But the real magic is the city itself, with its tangled former Jewish Quarter, riveting flamenco shows, thriving bars, and teeming evening paseo.

Planning Your Time

On a three-week trip, spend two nights and two days here. On even the shortest Spanish trip, I'd zip here on the slick AVE train for a day trip from Madrid. With more time, if ever there was a Spanish city to linger in, it's Sevilla.

The major sights are few and simple for a city of this size. The cathedral and the Alcázar are worth about three hours, and a wander through the Santa Cruz district takes about an hour. You could spend half a day touring Sevilla's other sights. Stroll along the bank of the Guadalquivir River and cross Isabel II Bridge (also known as the Bridge of Triana) for a view of the cathedral and Torre del Oro. An evening here is essential for the paseo and a flamenco show. Stay up at least once until midnight (or later) to appreciate Sevilla on a warm night—one of its major charms.

Bullfights take place on most Sundays in May and June, on Easter and Corpus Christi, daily through the April Fair, and in late September. The Museo de Bellas Artes is closed on Monday. Tour groups clog the Alcázar and cathedral in the morning; go late in the day to avoid the lines.

Córdoba is a convenient and worthwhile side-trip from Sevilla, or a handy stopover if you're taking the AVE to or from Madrid.

Orientation to Sevilla

For the tourist, this big city is small. The bull's-eye on your map should be the cathedral and its Giralda Bell Tower, which can be seen from all over town. Nearby are Sevilla's other major sights, the Alcázar (palace and gardens) and the lively Santa Cruz district. The central north–south pedestrian boulevard, Avenida de la Constitución (with TIs, banks, a post office, and other services), stretches north a few blocks to Plaza Nueva, gateway to the shopping district. A few blocks west of the cathedral are the bullring and the Guadalquivir River, while Plaza de España is a few blocks south. Triana, the area on the west bank of the Guadalquivir River, is working-class and colorful, but lacks tourist sights. With most sights walkable, and taxis so friendly, easy, and affordable, I rarely bother with the bus.

Sevilla is an easy city to get turned around in. Be aware that city maps from the tourist office are oriented with north to the left, while this book's maps put north on top.

Tourist Information

Sevilla has tourist offices wherever you need them—at the **airport** (Mon-Fri 9:00-19:30, Sat-Sun 9:30-15:00, tel. 954-782-035), **train station** (overlooking tracks 6-7, Mon-Fri 9:00-19:30, Sat-Sun 9:30-15:00, tel. 954-782-003), and in three central locations near Avenida de la Constitución: near the river side of the **Alcázar** (Mon-Fri 9:00-19:30, Sat-Sun 9:30-15:00, Avenida de la Constitución 21, tel. 954-787-578); across the small square from the **cathedral** entrance (Mon-Sat 10:30-14:30 & 15:30-19:30, Sun 10:30-14:30, Plaza del Triunfo, tel. 954-210-005); and near **Plaza Nueva** (Mon-Fri 9:00-19:30, Sat-Sun 10:00-14:00, a block north of the square on Plaza San Francisco, tel. 954-595-288, free Internet access for one hour at certain times—see "Helpful Hints," later).

At any TI, ask for the city map, the English-language magazines *Welcome Olé* and *The Tourist*, and a current listing of sights with opening times. The free monthly events guide—*El Giraldillo*, written in Spanish basic enough to be understood by travelers—covers cultural events throughout Andalucía, with a focus on Sevilla. The Alcázar and airport TIs cover all of Andalucía as well as Sevilla; if you stop at one of these, ask for information you might need for elsewhere in the region (for example, if heading south, ask for the free *Route of the White Towns* brochure and a Jerez map). Helpful websites are www.turismosevilla.org and www.andalucia.org.

The **Sevilla Card** (sold at the ICONOS shop next to the Alcázar TI, Mon-Sat 10:00-20:30, Sun 11:00-19:00; or at the train station's hotel room–finding booth overlooking track 11) covers admission to most of Sevilla's sights (including the cathedral, Alcázar, Flamenco Dance Museum, Basílica de la Macarena, Bullfight Museum, and more), and gives discounts at some hotels and restaurants. It's doubtful whether any but the busiest sightseer would save much money using the card (€29/24 hours—includes choice of 2 museums and river cruise; €47/48 hours—includes all sights and choice of river cruise or bus tour; €60/72 hours or €80/120 hours—includes all sights plus cruise and bus tour; www.sevillacard.es). If you're over 65, keep in mind that even without the Sevilla Card, you'll get into the Alcázar free and into the cathedral almost free.

Arrival in Sevilla

By Train: Trains arrive at the sublime Santa Justa station, with banks, ATMs, and a TI. Baggage storage *(cosigna)* is below track 1 (€3-5/day depending on size of bag, security checkpoint). The TI overlooks tracks 6-7. If you don't have a hotel room reserved, the room-finding booth above track 11 can help; you can also get maps and other tourist information here if the TI line is long (Mon-Fri 10:00-20:30, Sat 10:00-14:30 & 16:30-20:30, Sun 9:30-14:30). The plush little AVE Sala Club, designed for business travelers, welcomes those with a first-class AVE ticket and reservation (across the main hall from track 1).

The town center is marked by the ornate Giralda Bell Tower, peeking above the apartment flats (visible from the front of the station—with your back to the tracks, it's at 1 o'clock). To get into the center, it's a flat and boring 25-minute walk (longer if you get lost) or a €5 taxi ride. By city bus, it's a short ride on #C1 to the El Prado bus station (€1.30, pay driver, find bus stop 100 yards in front of the train station), then a 10-minute walk.

By Bus: Sevilla's two major bus stations both have information offices, basic eateries, and baggage storage. The **El Prado station** covers most of Andalucía (daily 7:00-22:00, information tel. 954-417-111, no English spoken; baggage storage/*consigna* at the far end of station—€2/day, daily 9:00-21:00). From the bus station to downtown (and Barrio Santa Cruz hotels), it's about a 10-minute walk: Exit the station to the right, and cross the busy street at the big roundabout. Turn right and keep the fenced-in gardens on your left. At the end of the fence, duck left through the Murillo Gardens and into the heart of Barrio Santa Cruz (use the color map in the front of this book to navigate). To cut a few minutes off the walk—or to reach the hotels near Plaza Nueva—take the city's short tram from the El Prado station (€1.30, buy ticket at machine before boarding; ride it two stops to Archivo de Indias to reach the cathedral area, or three stops to Plaza Nueva).

The **Plaza de Armas station** (near the river, opposite the Expo '92 site) serves long-distance destinations such as Madrid, Barcelona, Lagos, and Lisbon. Ticket counters line one wall, an information kiosk is in the center, and at the end of the hall are luggage lockers (€3.50/day). As you exit onto the main road (Calle Arjona), the bus stop is to the left, in front of the taxi stand (bus #C4 goes downtown, €1.30, pay driver, get off at Puerta de Jerez near main TI). Taxis to downtown cost around €5.

By Car: To drive into Sevilla, follow *centro ciudad* (city center) signs and stay along the river. For short-term parking on the street, the riverside Paseo de Cristóbal Colón has two-hour meters and hardworking thieves. Ignore the bogus traffic wardens who direct you to an illegal spot, take a tip, and disappear later when your car gets towed. For long-term parking, hotels charge as much as a normal garage. For simplicity, I'd just park at a central garage (€15-20/day) and catch a taxi to my hotel. Try the big one under the bus station at Plaza de Armas, the Cristóbal Colón garage by the bullring and river, the Plaza Nueva garage on Albareda, or the one at Avenida Roma/Puerta de Jerez (cash only). For hotels in the Santa Cruz area, the handiest parking is the Cano y Cueto garage near the corner of Calle Santa María la Blanca and Menéndez Pelayo (open 24/7, at edge of big park, unsigned and underground).

By Plane: The Especial Aeropuerto (EA) bus connects the airport with the train station and town center, terminating south of the Alcázar gardens on Avenida del Cid (€2.40, 2/hour, 30 minutes, buy ticket from driver). If you're going from downtown Sevilla to the airport, ask your hotelier or the TI where to catch the bus; the stop is usually on Avenida del Cid by the Portugal Pavilion but can change because of religious processions, construction, and other factors. (The return bus also stops at the Santa Justa train station and the El Prado bus station.) To taxi into town, go to one of the airport's taxi stands to ensure a fixed rate (€22 by day, €24 at night and on weekends, €29 during Easter week, extra for luggage, confirm price with the driver before your journey). For flight information, call 954-449-000.

Getting Around Sevilla

Most visitors have a full and fun experience in Sevilla without ever riding public transportation. The city center is compact, and most of the major sights are within easy walking distance (the Basílica de la Macarena is a notable exception). On a hot day, air-conditioned buses can be a blessing.

By Taxi: Sevilla is a great taxi town. You can hail one anywhere, or find them parked by major intersections and sights (weekdays: €1.22 drop rate, €0.85/kilometer, €3.33 minimum; Sat-Sun, weekends, and nights between 21:00 and 7:00: €1.49 drop rate, €1.04/kilometer, €4.17 minimum; calling for a cab adds about €2-3. A quick daytime ride in town will be at or around the €3.33 minimum. Although I'm quick to take advantage of a taxi, thanks to one-way streets and traffic congestion it's often just as fast to hoof it between central points.

By Bus, Tram, and Metro: Due to ongoing construction projects in the city center, bus routes often change. It's best to check with your hotel or the TI for the latest updates.

A single trip on any form of city transit costs €1.30. You can also buy a Tarjeta Multiviajes card that's rechargeable and shareable (€6.40 for 10 trips without transfers, €7 with transfers, €1.50 deposit, buy at kiosks; for transit details, see www.tussam.es).

The various #C **buses,** which are handiest for tourists, make circular routes through town (note that all of them eventually wind up at Basílica de La Macarena). For all buses, buy your ticket from the driver. The #C3 stops at Murillo Gardens, Triana (district on the west bank of the river), then La Macarena. The #C4 goes the opposite direction without entering Triana. And the spunky little #C5 is a minibus that winds through the old center of town, including Plaza del Salvador, Plaza de San Francisco, the bullring, Plaza Nueva, the Museo de Bellas Artes, La Campana, and La Macarena, providing a fine and relaxing joyride that also connects some farther-flung sights.

A new **tram** *(tramvia)* makes just a few stops in the heart of the city, but can save you a bit of walking. Buy your ticket at the machine on the platform before you board (runs every 6-7 minutes until 1:45 in the morning). The handiest stops include (from south to north) Prado San Sebastián (El Prado Bus station), Puerta Jerez (the south end of Avenida de la Constitución), Archivo de Indias (next to the cathedral), and Plaza Nueva. Eventually the tram will reach the Santa Justa train station.

Sevilla also has a brand-new underground **metro,** but tourists won't need to use it. It's designed to connect the suburbs with the center and is only partially finished.

Helpful Hints

Festivals: Sevilla's peak season is April and May, and it has two one-week festival periods when the city is packed: Holy Week and April Fair.

While **Holy Week** (Semana Santa) is big all over Spain, it's biggest in Sevilla. It's held the week between Palm Sunday and Easter Sunday (April 1-8 in 2012). Locals start preparing for the big event up to a year in advance. What would normally be a five-minute walk can take an hour and a half if a procession crosses your path. But even these hassles seem irrelevant as you listen to the *saetas* (spontaneous devotional songs) and let the spirit of the festival take over.

Then, after Easter—after taking enough time off to catch its communal breath—Sevilla holds its **April Fair** (April 24-29 in 2012). This is a celebration of all things Andalusian, with plenty of eating, drinking, singing, and merrymaking (though most of the revelry takes place in private parties at a

Holy Week *(Semana Santa)* in Andalucía

Holy Week—the week between Palm Sunday and Easter (April 1-8 in 2012)—is a major holiday throughout the Christian world, but nowhere is it celebrated with as much fervor as in Andalucía, especially Sevilla. Holy Week is all about the events of the Passion of Jesus Christ: his entry into Jerusalem, his betrayal by Judas and arrest, his crucifixion, and his resurrection. In Sevilla, on each day throughout the week, 60 neighborhood groups (brotherhoods) parade from their neighborhood churches to the cathedral with floats depicting some aspect of the Passion story.

As the week approaches, the anticipation grows: Visitors pour into town, grandstands are erected along the parade routes, and TV stations anxiously monitor the weather report. The floats are so delicate that rain would force the processions (and live broadcasts) to be called off—a crushing disappointment.

By mid-afternoon of any day during Holy Week, thousands line the streets. The parade begins. First comes a line of "penitents" *(penitentes)*, carrying a big cross, candles, and incense. The penitents perform their penance publically but anonymously, their identities obscured by hooded robes. (The penitents' traditional hooded garb has been worn for centuries—long before such hoods became associated with racism in the American South.) Some processions are silent, but others are accompanied by beating drums, brass bands, or wailing singers.

A hush falls over the crowd as the floats approach. First comes a Passion float, showing Christ in some stage of the

large fairground).

Book rooms well in advance for these festival times. Prices can go sky-high, many hotels have four-night minimums, and food quality at touristy restaurants can plummet.

Internet Access: Almost every hotel in town has Wi-Fi, and many also have Internet terminals or loaner laptops for guests to use. Otherwise, try **Internetia,** a thriving-with-students Internet café with two dozen terminals (€2.30/hour, Wi-Fi, disc-burning, daily 10:00-23:00, about three blocks beyond the eastern edge of Santa Cruz at Avenida Menéndez Pelayo 43-45, tel. 954-534-003). The **TI at Plaza Nueva** (near Plaza San Francisco) offers up to one hour of free Internet access at eight terminals, as well as free Wi-Fi (Internet available only Mon-Fri 10:00-14:00 & 17:00-20:00, none Sat-Sun).

Post Office: The post office is at Avenida de la Constitución 32, drama—being whipped, appearing before Pilate, or carrying the cross to his execution. More penitents follow—with dozens or even hundreds of participants, a procession can stretch out over a half-mile. All this sets the stage for the finale—typically a float of the Virgin Mary, who represents the hope of resurrection.

The elaborate floats feature carved wooden religious sculptures, some embellished with gold leaf and silverwork. They can be adorned with fresh flowers, rows of candles, and even jewelry on loan from the congregation. Each float is carried by 30 to 50 men, who labor unseen (you might catch a glimpse of their shuffling feet). The bearers wear turban-like headbands to protect their heads and necks from the crushing weight (the floats can weigh as much as two tons). Two "shifts" of float carriers rotate every 20 minutes. As a sign of their faith, some men carry the float until they collapse.

As the procession nears the cathedral, it passes through the square called La Campana, south along Calle Sierpes, and through Plaza de San Francisco. (Some parades follow a parallel route a block or two east.) Grandstands and folding chairs are filled by VIPs and Sevilla's prominent families. Thousands of candles drip wax along the well-trod parade routes, forming a waxy buildup that causes car tires to squeal for days to come.

Being in Sevilla for Holy Week is both a blessing and a curse. It's a remarkable spectacle, but it's extremely crowded. Parade routes can block your sightseeing for hours. Check printed schedules if you want to avoid them. If you do find a procession blocking your way, look for a crossing point marked by a red-painted fence, or ask a guard. Regardless of your own faith, the intense devotion of the Andalusian people is reason enough to appreciate their Holy Week traditions.

across from the cathedral (Mon-Fri 8:30-20:30, Sat 9:30-14:00, closed Sun).

Laundry: Lavandería Roma offers quick and economical drop-off service (€6/load wash-and-dry, Mon-Fri 9:30-14:00 & 17:30-20:30, Sat 9:00-14:00, closed Sun, 2 blocks inland from bullring at Castelar 2, tel. 954-210-535). Near the recommended Santa Cruz hotels, **La Segunda Vera Tintorería** has two machines for self-service (€6/load wash-and-dry, €10/load drop-off service, Mon-Fri 9:30-13:45 & 17:30-20:00, closed Sat-Sun, about a block from the eastern edge of Santa Cruz at Avenida Menéndez Pelayo 11, tel. 954-534-219).

Train Tickets: For schedules and tickets, visit the RENFE Travel Center at the **train station** (daily 8:00-22:00, take a number and wait, tel. 902-320-320 for reservations and info) or the one near **Plaza Nueva** in the center (Mon-Fri 9:30-13:30 &

Sevilla at a Glance

▲▲▲Flamenco Flamboyant, riveting music-and-dance performances, offered at clubs throughout town. **Hours:** Shows start as early as 19:00. See page 49.

▲▲Cathedral and Giralda Bell Tower The world's largest Gothic church, with Columbus' tomb, a treasury, and climbable tower. **Hours:** July-Aug Mon-Sat 9:30-17:00, Sun 14:30-18:00; Sept-June Mon-Sat 11:00-17:00, Sun 14:30-18:00. See page 20.

▲▲Alcázar Palace built by the Moors in the 10th century, revamped in the 14th century, and still serving as royal digs. **Hours:** April-Sept daily 9:30-19:00, Oct-March daily 9:30-17:00. See page 28.

▲▲Basílica de la Macarena Church and museum with the much-venerated Weeping Virgin statue and two significant floats from Sevilla's Holy Week celebrations. **Hours:** Mon-Sat 9:00-14:00 & 17:00-21:00, Sun from 9:30. See page 43.

▲▲Bullfight Museum Guided tour of the bullring and its museum. **Hours:** Daily May-Oct 9:30-20:00, Nov-April 9:30-19:00, on fight days until 14:00. See page 46.

▲▲Evening Paseo Locals strolling in the cool of the evening, mainly along Avenida de la Constitución, Barrio Santa Cruz, the Calle Sierpes and Tetuán shopping pedestrian zone, and the Guadalquivir River. **Hours:** Spring through fall, until very late at night in summer. See page 51.

▲Museo Palacio de la Condesa de Lebrija A fascinating 18th-century aristocratic mansion. **Hours:** July-Aug Mon-Fri 9:00-15:00, Sat-Sun 10:00-14:00; Sept-June Mon-Fri 10:30-19:30, Sat-Sun 10:00-14:00. See page 38.

▲Flamenco Dance Museum High-tech museum explaining the history and art of Sevilla's favorite dance. **Hours:** Daily 9:30-19:00. See page 38.

▲Museo de Bellas Artes Andalucía's top paintings, including works by Spanish masters Murillo and Zurbarán. **Hours:** Tue-Sat 9:00-20:30, Sun 9:00-14:30, closed Mon. See page 39.

▲Bullfights Some of Spain's best bullfighting, held at Sevilla's arena. **Hours:** Fights generally at 18:30 on most Sundays in May and June, on Easter and Corpus Christi, and daily through the April Fair and in late September. Rookies fight small bulls on Thursdays in July. See page 45.

17:30-19:30, Sat 10:00-13:00, closed Sun, Calle Zaragoza 29, tel. 954-211-455). You can also check schedules at www.renfe .com. Many travel agencies sell train tickets; look for a train sticker in agency windows.

Warning: You may encounter women thrusting sprigs of rosemary into the hands of passersby, grunting, *"Toma! Es un regalo!"* ("Take it! It's a gift!"). If you take one of these sprigs, you'll be harassed for money in return. Just walk on by if you are approached.

Tours in Sevilla

Guided City Walks by Concepción—Concepción Delgado, an enthusiastic teacher who's a joy to listen to, takes small groups on English-language walks. Using me as her guinea pig, Concepción has designed a fine two-hour **Sevilla Cultural Show & Tell.**

This introduction to her hometown, sharing important insights the average visitor misses, is worthwhile even on a one-day visit (€15/person, minimum 4 people, Feb-July and Sept-Dec Mon-Sat at 10:30; Jan and Aug on Mon, Wed, and Fri only; meet at statue in Plaza Nueva).

For those wanting to really understand the city's two most important sights—which are tough to fully appreciate—Concepción also offers in-depth tours of the **cathedral** and the **Alcázar** (both tours last 1.25 hours, cost €7—not including entrance fees, €2 discount if you also take the Show & Tell tour; meet at 13:00 at statue in Plaza del Triunfo; minimum 4 people; cathedral tours—Mon, Wed, and Fri; Alcázar tours—Tue, Thu, and Sat; no Alcázar tours Jan and Aug).

Although you can just show up for Concepción's tours, it's smart to confirm the departure times and reserve a spot (tel. 902-158-226, mobile 616-501-100, www.sevillawalkingtours.com, info@sevillawalkingtours.com). Concepción does no tours on Sundays or holidays. Because she's a busy mom of two young kids, Concepción sometimes sends her colleague Alfonso (who's also excellent) to lead these tours.

Hop-on, Hop-off Bus Tours—Two competing city bus tours leave from the curb near the riverside Torre del Oro (Gold Tower). You'll see the parked buses and salespeople handing out fliers. Each tour does about an hour-long swing through the city with recorded narration (€16-17, daily 10:00-21:00, green route has shorter option). The tours, which allow hopping on and off at four

Sevilla

stops, are heavy on Expo '29 and Expo '92 neighborhoods—both zones of little interest in 2012. While the narration does its best, Sevilla is most interesting where buses can't go.

Horse and Buggy Tours—A carriage ride is a classic, popular way to survey the city and a relaxing way to enjoy María Luisa Park (€50 for a 45-minute clip-clop, find a likable English-speaking driver for better narration). Look for rigs at Plaza América, Plaza del Triunfo, Torre del Oro, Alfonso XIII Hotel, and Avenida Isabel la Católica.

Boat Cruises—Boring one-hour panoramic tours leave every 30 minutes from the dock behind Torre de Oro. The low-energy recorded narration is hard to follow, but there's little to see anyway (overpriced at €15, tel. 954-561-692).

More Tours—**Visitours,** a typical big-bus tour company, does

Barrio Santa Cruz Self-Guided Walk

€95 all-day trips to Córdoba (Tue, Thu, and Sat; tel. 955-999-760, mobile 686-413-413, www.visitours.es, visitours@visitours.es). For other guides, contact one of the **Guide Associations of Sevilla:** AUITS (tel. 699-494-204, www.auits.com, guias@auits.com) or APIT (tel. 954-210-037, www.apitsevilla.com, visitas@apitsevilla .com).

Self-Guided Walk

Barrio Santa Cruz

Of Sevilla's once-thriving Jewish Quarter, only the tangled street plan and a wistful Old World ambience survive. This classy maze of lanes (too slender for cars), small plazas, tile-covered patios, and whitewashed houses with wrought-iron latticework draped in flowers is a great refuge from the summer heat and bustle of Sevilla. The streets are narrow—some with buildings so close they're called "kissing lanes." A happy result of the narrowness is

S. MARIA
LA BLANCA

1 Plaza de la Virgen de los Reyes
2 Plaza del Triunfo
3 Patio de Banderas
4 Calle Agua
5 Plaza de la Santa Cruz
6 Plaza de Refinadores
7 Casa de Murillo
8 Monasterio de San José del Carmen
9 Plaza de los Venerables
10 Plaza de Doña Elvira
11 Plaza de la Alianza

PLAZA SANTA CRUZ

PLAZA DE REFINADORES

PLAZA DE ALFARO

MURILLO GARDENS

50 YARDS
50 METERS

◀ WALKING TOUR

DCH

shade: Locals claim the Barrio Santa Cruz is three degrees cooler than the rest of the city.

Orange trees abound—because they never lose their leaves, they provide constant shade. But forget about eating any of the oranges. They're bitter and used only to make vitamins, perfume, cat food, and that marmalade you can't avoid in British B&Bs. But when they blossom (for three weeks in spring, usually in March), the aroma is heavenly.

The Barrio is made for wandering. Getting lost is easy, and I recommend doing just that. But to get started, here's a plaza-to-plaza walk that loops you through the *corazón* (heart) of the neighborhood and back out again. Ideally, don't do the walk in the morning, when the Barrio's charm is trampled by tour groups.

Early evening (around 18:00) is ideal.

❶ Plaza de la Virgen de los Reyes: Start in the square in front of the cathedral, at the base of the Giralda Bell Tower. This square is dedicated to the Virgin of the Kings. See her tile on the white wall facing the cathedral. She is one of several different versions of Mary you'll see in Sevilla, each appealing to a different type of worshipper. This one is big here because the Spanish king reportedly carried her image with him when he retook the town from the Moors in 1248. The fountain dates from 1929. From this peaceful square, look up the street leading away from the cathedral and notice the characteristic (government-protected) 19th-century architecture. The ironwork is typical of Andalucía and the pride of Sevilla. You'll see it and the traditional color scheme of white-wash-and-goldenrod all over the town center.

Another symbol you'll see throughout Sevilla is the city insignia: "NO*8*DO," the letters "NODO" with a figure-eight-like shape at their center. *Nodo* meant "knot" in the old dialect, and this symbol evokes the strong ties between the citizens of Sevilla and King Alfonso X (during a succession dispute in the 13th century, the Sevillans remained loyal to their king).

• *Walk with the cathedral on your right into the...*

❷ Plaza del Triunfo: The "Plaza of Triumph" is named for the 1755 earthquake that destroyed Lisbon and rattled Sevilla, but left most of the city intact. Find the statue thanking the Virgin, located at the far end of the square, under a stone canopy. That Virgin faces another one (closer to you), atop a tall pillar honoring Sevillan artists, including the painter Murillo (see "Casa de Murillo," later).

• *Pass through the opening in the crenellated Alcázar wall under the arch. You'll emerge into a courtyard called the...*

❸ Patio de Banderas: Named for "flags," not Antonio, the Banderas Courtyard was once a kind of military parade ground for the royal guard. The barracks surrounding the square once housed the king's bodyguards. Today, the far end of this square is a favorite spot for a postcard view of the Giralda Bell Tower.

• *Exit the courtyard at the far corner, through the Judería arch. Go down the long, narrow passage. Emerging into the light, you'll be walking alongside the Alcázar wall. Take the first left, then right, through a small square and follow the narrow alleyway called...*

❹ Calle Agua: As you walk along the street, look to the left, peeking through iron gates for occasional glimpses of the flowersmothered patios of exclusive private residences. The patio at #2 is a delight—ringed with columns, filled with flowers, and colored with glazed tiles. The tiles are not only decorative; they keep buildings cooler in the summer heat. Emerging at the end of the street, turn around and look back at the openings of two old pipes built into the wall. These pipes once carried water to the Alcázar (and today give the street its name). You're standing at an entrance into the pleasant Murillo Gardens (to the right), formerly the fruit-and-vegetable gardens for the Alcázar.

• *Don't enter the gardens now, but instead cross the square diagonally and continue 20 yards down a lane to the...*

❺ **Plaza de la Santa Cruz:** Arguably the heart of the Barrio, this is a pleasant square of orange and olive trees and draping vines. It was once the site of a synagogue (the Barrio had three; now there are none), which Christians destroyed. They replaced the synagogue with a church, which the French (under Napoleon) then demolished. It's a bit of history that locals remember when they see the blue, white, and red French flag marking the French consulate, now overlooking this peaceful square. The Sevillan painter Murillo, who was buried in the now-gone church, lies somewhere below you. On the square you'll find the recommended Los Gallos flamenco bar, which combusts nightly after midnight with impromptu flamenco.

• *At the far end of the square, a one-block (optional) detour along Calle Mezquita leads to the nearby...*

❻ **Plaza de Refinadores:** Sevilla's most famous (if fictional) 17th-century citizen is honored here with a statue. Don Juan Tenorio—the original Don Juan—was a notorious sex addict and atheist who proudly thumbed his nose at the stifling Church-driven morals of his day.

• *Backtrack to Plaza de la Santa Cruz and turn right (north) on Calle Santa Teresa. At #8 (on the left) is...*

❼ **Casa de Murillo:** One of Sevilla's famous painters, Bartolomé Esteban Murillo (1618-1682), lived here, soaking in the ambience of street life and reproducing it in his paintings of cute beggar children.

• *Directly across from Casa de Murillo is the...*

❽ **Monasterio de San José del Carmen:** This is where St. Teresa stayed when she visited from her hometown of Ávila. The convent (closed to the public) keeps artifacts of the mystic nun, such as her spiritual manuscripts.

Continue north on Calle Santa Teresa, then take the first left on Calle Lope de Rueda, then left again, then right on **Calle Reinoso.** This street—so narrow that the buildings almost touch—is one of the Barrio's "kissing lanes." A popular explanation suggests the buildings were built so close together to provide

Sevilla's Jews

In the summer of 1391, smoldering anti-Jewish sentiment flared up in Sevilla. On June 6 Christian mobs ransacked the city's Jewish Quarter (Judería). Around 4,000 Jews were killed, and 5,000 Jewish families were driven from their homes. Synagogues were stripped and transformed into churches. The former Judería eventually became the neighborhood of the Holy Cross—Barrio Santa Cruz. Sevilla's uprising spread through Spain (and Europe), the first of many nasty pogroms during the next century.

Before the pogrom, Jews had lived in Sevilla for centuries as the city's respected merchants, doctors, and bankers. They flourished under the Muslim Moors. After Sevilla was "liberated" by King Ferdinand III (1248), Jews were given protection by Spain's kings and allowed a measure of self-government, though they were confined to the Jewish neighborhood.

But by the 14th century, Jews were increasingly accused of everything from poisoning wells to ritually sacrificing Christian babies. Mobs killed suspected Jews, and some of Sevilla's most respected Jewish citizens had their fortunes confiscated.

After 1391, Jews faced a choice: Be persecuted (even killed), relocate, or convert to Christianity. Those who converted—called *conversos*, New Christians, or *marranos* (swine)—were always under suspicion of practicing their old faith in private, undermining true Christianity. Longtime Christians were threatened by this new social class of converted Jews, who now had equal status, fanning the mistrust.

To root out the perceived problem of underground Judaism, the "Catholic Monarchs," Ferdinand and Isabel, established the Inquisition in Spain (1478). Under the direction of Grand Inquisitor Tomás de Torquemada, these religious courts arrested and interrogated *conversos* suspected of practicing Judaism. Using long solitary confinement and torture, they extracted confessions.

On February 6, 1481, Sevilla hosted Spain's first auto-da-fé ("act of faith"), a public confession and punishment for heresy. Six accused *conversos* were paraded barefoot into the cathedral, made to publicly confess their sins, then burned at the stake. Over the next three decades, thousands of *conversos* (some historians say hundreds, some say tens of thousands) were tried and killed in Spain.

In 1492, the same year the last Moors were driven from Spain, Ferdinand and Isabel decreed that all remaining Jews convert or be expelled (to Portugal and ultimately to Holland). Spain emerged as a nation unified under the banner of Christianity.

maximum shade. But remember this was the Jewish ghetto, where all the city's Jews were forced to live in a very small area. That's why the streets of Santa Cruz are so narrow.

• *The street spills onto the...*

❾ **Plaza de los Venerables:** This square is another candidate for "heart of the Barrio." The streets branching off it ooze local ambience. When the Jews were expelled from Spain in 1492, this area became deserted and run-down. But in 1929, for its world's fair, Sevilla turned the plaza into a showcase of Andalusian style, adding the railings, tile work, orange trees, and other too-cute Epcot-like adornments. A different generation of tourists enjoys the place today, likely unaware that what they're seeing in Santa Cruz is far from "authentic" (or, at least, not as old as they imagine).

The large, harmonious Baroque-style Hospital de los Venerables (1675), once a retirement home for old priests (the "venerables"), is now a cultural foundation and museum (€4.75, includes audioguide). The highlight is the church and courtyard, featuring a round, sunken fountain. The museum also has a small Velázquez painting of Santa Rufina, one of two patron saints protecting Sevilla. The painting was acquired at a 2007 auction for more than €12 million.

• *Continuing west on Calle Gloria, you soon reach the...*

❿ **Plaza de Doña Elvira:** This small square—with orange trees, tile benches, and a stone fountain—sums up our Barrio walk. Shops sell work by local artisans, such as ceramics, embroidery, and fans.

• *Cross the plaza and head north along Calle Rodrigo Caro into the...*

⓫ **Plaza de la Alianza:** Ever consider a career change? Gain inspiration at the site that once housed the painting studio of John Fulton (1932-1998; find the small plaque on the other side of the square), an American who pursued two dreams. Though born in Philadelphia, Fulton got hooked on bullfighting. He trained in the tacky bullrings of Mexico, then in 1956 he moved to Sevilla, the world capital of the sport. His career as matador was not top-notch, and the Spaniards were slow to warm to the Yankee, but his courage and persistence earned their grudging respect. After he put down the cape, he picked up a brush, making colorful paintings in his Sevilla studio.

• *From Plaza de la Alianza, you can return to the cathedral by turning left (west) on Calle Joaquin Romero Murube (along the wall). Or head northeast on Callejón de Rodrigo Caro, which intersects with Calle Mateos Gago, a street lined with tapas bars.*

Sights in Sevilla

▲▲Cathedral and Giralda Bell Tower

Sevilla's cathedral is the third-largest church in Europe (after St. Peter's at the Vatican and St. Paul's in London), and the largest Gothic church anywhere.

When they ripped down a mosque of brick on this site in 1401, the Reconquista Christians bragged, "We'll build a cathedral so huge that anyone who sees it will take us for madmen." They built for 120 years. Even today, the descendants of those madmen proudly display an enlarged photocopy of their *Guinness Book of Records* letter certifying, "Santa María de la Sede in Sevilla is the cathedral with the largest area: 126.18 meters x 82.60 meters x 30.48 meters high."

Cost and Hours: €8, €2 for those over age 65 (must show ID), kids under age 18 free, includes free entry to the Church of the Savior; July-Aug Mon-Sat 9:30-17:00, Sun 14:30-18:00; Sept-June Mon-Sat 11:00-17:00, Sun 14:30-18:00; last entry to cathedral one hour before closing, last entry to bell tower 30 minutes before closing; WC and drinking fountain just inside entrance and in courtyard near exit, tel. 954-214-971. Most of the website www .catedraldesevilla.es is in Spanish, but following the "vista virtual" links will take you to a virtual tour with an English option.

Crowd-Beating Tip: Though there's usually not much of a line to buy tickets, you can avoid it altogether by buying the €8 ticket at the Church of the Savior (Iglesia de Salvador), a few blocks north. See that church first, then come to the cathedral and waltz past the line to the turnstile.

Tours: My self-guided tour covers the basics. The €3 audio-guide explains each side chapel for anyone interested in all the old paintings and dry details. For €6 you can enjoy Concepción Delgado's tour instead (see "Tours in Sevilla," earlier).

◉ Self-Guided Tour: Enter the cathedral at the south end (closest to the Alcázar, with a full-size replica of the Giralda's weathervane statue in the patio).

• *First, you pass through the...*

❶ Art Pavilion: Just past the turnstile, you step into a room of paintings that once hung in the church, including works by Sevilla's two 17th-century masters—Bartolomé Murillo (*St. Ferdinand*—the king who freed Sevilla from the Moors) and Francisco de Zurbarán (*St. John the Baptist in the Desert*). Find a

Sevilla's Cathedral

1. Art Pavilion
2. High Altar
3. Choir
4. Tomb of Columbus
5. Antigua Chapel
6. Sacristy
7. Main Sacristy
8. Treasury
9. Royal Chapel
10. Chapel of St. Peter
11. View of Plateresque Ceiling
12. Altar de Plata
13. Chapel of St. Anthony
14. Pennant of Ferdinand III
15. Back of the Nave
16. MURILLO – Guardian Angel
17. Giralda Tower Climb Entrance
18. Court of the Orange Trees
19. Moorish-Style Doorway
20. To Nun-Baked Goodies

Bartolomé Murillo
(1617-1682)

The son of a barber of Seville, Bartolomé Murillo got his start selling paintings meant for export to the frontier churches of the Americas. In his 20s, he became famous after he painted a series of saints for Sevilla's Franciscan monastery. By about 1650, Murillo's sugary, simple, and accessible religious style was spreading through Spain and beyond.

Murillo painted street kids with cute smiles and grimy faces, and radiant young Marías with Ivory-soap complexions and rapturous poses (Immaculate Conceptions). His paintings view the world through a soft-focus lens, wrapping everything in warm colors and soft light, with a touch (too much, for some) of sentimentality.

Murillo became rich, popular, a family man, and the toast of Sevilla's high society. In 1664 his wife died, leaving him heartbroken, but his last 20 years were his most prolific. At age 65, Murillo died painting, after falling off a scaffold. His tomb is lost somewhere under the bricks of Plaza de la Santa Cruz.

painting showing two of Sevilla's patron saints—Santa Justa and Santa Rufina. Potters by trade, these two are easy to identify by their pots and palm branches, and the bell tower symbolizing the town they protect. As you tour the cathedral, keep track of how many depictions of this dynamic and saintly duo you spot. They're everywhere.

• *Walking past a rack of church maps and a WC, enter the actual church. In the center of the church, sit down in front of the...*

❷ **High Altar:** Look through the wrought-iron Renaissance grille at what's called the largest altarpiece *(retablo mayor)* ever made—65 feet tall, with 44 scenes from the life of Jesus carved from walnut and chestnut, blanketed by a staggering amount of

gold leaf (and dust). The work took three generations to complete (1481-1564). The story is told left to right, bottom to top. Find Baby Jesus in the manger, in the middle of the bottom row, then follow his story through the miracles, the

Passion, and the Pentecost. Crane your neck to look way up to the tippy-top, where a Crucifixion adorns the dizzying summit.

• *Turn around and check out the...*

❸ **Choir:** Facing the high altar, the choir features an organ of 7,000 pipes (played at the 10:00 Mass Mon-Fri, 10:00 & 13:00 Mass Sun, not in July-Aug, free for worshippers). A choir area like this one (an enclosure within the cathedral for more intimate services) is common in Spain and England, but rare in churches elsewhere. The big, spinnable book holder in the middle of the room held giant hymnals—large enough for all to chant from in a pre-Xerox age when there weren't enough books for everyone.

• *Now turn 90 degrees to the left and march to find the...*

❹ **Tomb of Columbus:** In front of the cathedral's entrance for pilgrims are four kings who carry the tomb of Christopher Columbus. His pallbearers rep-

resent the regions of Castile, Aragon, León, and Navarre (identify them by their team shirts). Columbus even traveled a lot posthumously. He was buried first in Spain, then in Santo Domingo in the Dominican Republic, then Cuba, and finally—when Cuba gained independence from Spain, around 1900—he sailed home again to Sevilla. Are the remains actually his? Sevillans like to think so. (Columbus died in 1506. Five hundred years later, to help celebrate the anniversary of his death, DNA samples gave Sevillans the evidence they needed to substantiate their claim.) On the left is a mural of St. Christopher—patron saint of travelers—from 1584. The clock above has been ticking since 1788.

• *Facing Columbus, turn right and duck into the first chapel (on your left) to find the...*

❺ **Antigua Chapel:** Within this chapel is the gilded fresco of the Virgin Antigua, the oldest art in the church. It was actually painted onto a horseshoe-shaped prayer niche of the mosque formerly on this site. After Sevilla was reconquered in 1248, the mosque served as a church for about 120 years—until it was torn down to make room for this huge cathedral. Builders, captivated by the beauty of the Virgin holding the rose and the Christ Child holding the bird (and knowing that she was considered the protector of sailors in this port city), decided to save the fresco.

• *Exiting the chapel, we'll tour the cathedral counterclockwise. As you explore, note that its many chapels are described in English, and many of the windows have their dates worked into the design. Just on the other side of Columbus, walk through the small chapel and into the...*

❻ **Sacristy:** This space is where the priests get ready each morning before Mass. The Goya painting above the altar features Justa and Rufina—patron saints of Sevilla who were martyred in ancient Roman times. They're always shown with their trademark attributes: the town bell tower, pots, and palm leaves. I say they're each holding a bowl of gazpacho (particularly refreshing on hot summer days) and sprigs of rosemary from local Gypsies (an annoyance even back then). Art historians claim that since they were potters, they are shown with earthenware, and the sprigs are palm leaves—symbolic of their martyrdom. Whatever.

• *Two chapels down is the entrance to the...*

❼ **Main Sacristy:** Marvel at the ornate, 16th-century Plateresque dome of the main room, a grand souvenir from Sevilla's Golden Age. The intricate masonry resembles lacy silverwork (it's named for *plata*—silver). God is way up in the cupola. The three layers of figures below him show the heavenly host; relatives in purgatory—hands folded—looking to heaven in hope of help; and the wretched in hell, including a topless sinner engulfed in flames and teased cruelly by pitchfork-wielding monsters. Locals use the 110-pound silver religious float that dominates this room to parade the holy host (communion wafer) through town during Corpus Christi festivities.

• *At the far end of the main sacristy, at the left-hand corner, is a door leading to our next stop. (If it's closed, you can backtrack to the main part of the church and head next door.)*

❽ **Treasury:** The *tesoro* fills several rooms in the corner of the church. Wander deeper into the treasury to find a unique oval dome. It's in the 16th-century chapter room *(sala capitular),* where monthly meetings take place with the bishop (he gets the throne, while the others share the bench). The paintings here are by

Murillo: a fine *Immaculate Conception* (1668, high above the bishop's throne) and portraits of saints important to Sevillans.

The wood-paneled "room of ornaments" shows off gold and silver reliquaries, which hold hundreds of holy body parts, as well as Spain's most valuable crown. The jeweled crown by Manuel de la Torres (the Corona de la Virgen de los Reyes) sparkles with 11,000 precious stones and the world's largest pearl—used as the torso of an angel. Opposite the crown is a reliquary featuring what is said to be a

Immaculate Conception

Throughout Sevilla and Spain you'll see paintings titled *The Immaculate Conception,* all looking quite similar (see example on page 22). Young, lovely, and beaming radiantly, these virgins look pure, untainted...you might even say "immaculate." According to Catholic doctrine, Mary, the future mother of Jesus, entered the world free from the original sin that other mortals share. When she died, her purity allowed her to be taken up directly to heaven (the Assumption).

The doctrine of Immaculate Conception can be confusing, even to Catholics. It does not mean that the Virgin Mary herself was born of a virgin. Rather, Mary's mother and father conceived her in the natural way. But at the moment Mary's soul animated her flesh, God granted her a special exemption from original sin. The doctrine of Immaculate Conception had been popular since medieval times, though it was not codified until 1854. It was Sevilla's own Bartolomé Murillo (1617-1682) who painted the model of this goddess-like Mary, copied by so many lesser artists. In Counter-Reformation times (when Murillo lived), paintings of a fresh-faced, ecstatic Mary made abstract doctrines like the Immaculate Conception and the Assumption tangible and accessible to all.

Most images of the Immaculate Conception show Mary wearing a radiant crown and with a crescent moon at her feet; she often steps on the heads of cherubs. Paintings by Murillo frequently portray Mary in a blue robe with long, wavy hair— young and innocent.

piece of the "true cross"—the cross to which Christ was nailed.

• *Leave the treasury and cross through the church to see...*

More Church Sights: First you'll pass the closed-to-tourists ❾ **Royal Chapel,** the burial place of several of the kings of Castile (open for worship only—access from outside), then the ❿ **Chapel of St. Peter,** which is dark but filled with paintings by Francisco de Zurbarán (showing scenes from the life of St. Peter). At the far corner—past the glass case displaying the *Guinness* certificate declaring that this is indeed the world's largest church by area—is the entry to the Giralda Bell Tower. You'll finish your visit here. But for now, continue your counterclockwise circuit. Near the middle (and high) altar, crane your neck skyward to admire the ⓫ **Plateresque tracery** on the ceiling, and take in the enormous ⓬ **Altar de Plata** rising up in a side chapel. The gleaming silver altarpiece adorned with statues looks like a big monstrance, those vessels for displaying the communion wafer.

The ⓭ **Chapel of St. Anthony** (Capilla de San Antonio), the last chapel on the right, is used for baptisms. The Renaissance baptismal font has delightful carved angels dancing along its base.

In Murillo's painting, *Vision of St. Anthony* (1656), the saint kneels in wonder as a Baby Jesus comes down surrounded by a choir of angels. Anthony is one of Iberia's most popular saints. As he is the patron saint of lost things, people come here to pray for Anthony's help in finding jobs, car keys, and life partners. Above the *Vision* is *The Baptism of* *Christ*, also by Murillo. You don't need to be an art historian to know that the stained glass dates from 1685. And by now you must know who the women are....

Nearby, a glass case displays the ⓮ **pennant of Ferdinand III,** which was raised over the minaret of the mosque on November 23, 1248, as Christian forces finally expelled the Moors from Sevilla. For centuries, it was paraded through the city on special days.

Continuing on, stand at the ⓯ **back of the nave** (behind the choir) and appreciate the ornate immensity of the church. Can you see the angels trumpeting on their Cuban mahogany? Any birds?

Turn around. The massive candlestick holder dates from 1560. To the left is a niche with ⓰ **Murillo's** *Guardian Angel* pointing to the light and showing an astonished child the way.

• *Backtrack the length of the church toward the Giralda Bell Tower, and notice the back of the choir's Baroque pipe organ. The* exit *sign leads to the Court of the Orange Trees and the exit. But first, some exercise.*

⓱ **Giralda Tower Climb:** Your church admission includes entry to the bell tower. Notice the beautiful Moorish simplicity as you climb to its top, 330 feet up, for a grand city view. The spiraling ramp was designed to accommodate riders on horseback, who galloped up five times a day to give the Muslim call to prayer.

• *Go back down into the cathedral interior, then visit the...*

⓲ **Court of the Orange Trees:** Today's cloister was once the mosque's Court of the Orange Trees (Patio de los Naranjos).

Twelfth-century Muslims stopped at the fountain in the middle to wash their hands, face, and feet before praying. The ankle-breaking lanes between the bricks were once irrigation streams—a reminder that the Moors introduced irrigation to Iberia. The mosque was made of bricks; the church is built of stone. The only remnants of the mosque today are the Court of the Orange Trees, the Giralda Bell Tower, and the site itself.

• *You'll exit the cathedral through the Court of the Orange Trees (if you need to use the WCs, they're at the far end of the courtyard, downstairs). As you leave, look back from the outside and notice the arch over the...*

⓳ Moorish-Style Doorway: As with much of the Moorish-looking art in town, it's actually Christian—the two coats of arms are a giveaway. The relief above the door shows the Bible story of Jesus ridding the temple of the merchants...a reminder to contemporary merchants that there will be no retail activity in the church. The plaque on the right honors Miguel de Cervantes, the great 16th-century Spanish writer. It's one of many plaques scattered throughout town showing places mentioned in his books. (In this case, the topic was pickpockets.) The huge green doors predate the church. They are a bit of the surviving pre-1248 mosque—wood covered with bronze. Study the fine workmanship.

Giralda Tower Exterior: Step across the street from the exit gate and look at the bell tower. Formerly a Moorish minaret from which Muslims were called to prayer, it became the cathedral's bell tower after the Reconquista. A 4,500-pound bronze statue symbolizing the Triumph of Faith (specifically, the Christian faith over the Muslim one) caps the tower and serves as a weather vane (in Spanish, *girar* means "to rotate"—so a *giraldillo* is something that rotates). Locals actually use it to predict the weather. (If the wind is blowing from the southwest, it means moist ocean air will soon bring rain.) In 1356, the original top of the tower fell. You're looking at a 16th-century Christian-built top with a ribbon of letters proclaiming, "The strongest tower is the name of God" (you can see *Fortísima*—"strongest"—from this vantage point).

Now circle around for a close look at the corner of the tower at ground level. Needing more strength than their bricks could provide for the lowest section of the tower, the Moors used Roman-cut stones. You can actually read the Latin chiseled onto one of the stones 2,000 years ago. The tower offers a brief recap of the city's history—sitting on a Roman foundation, a long Moorish period capped by our Christian age. Today, by law, no building can be higher than the statue atop the tower.

• *Your cathedral tour is finished. If you've worked up an appetite, get out your map and make your way a few blocks for some...*

⓴ Nun-Baked Goodies: Stop by the El Torno Pasteleria de Conventos, a co-op where the various orders of cloistered nuns send their handicrafts (such as babies' baptismal dresses) and baked goods to be sold. "El Torno" is the lazy Susan that the cloistered nuns spin to sell their cakes and cookies without being seen. You won't actually see the *torno* (this shop is staffed by non-nuns), but this humble little hole-in-the-wall shop is worth a peek, and definitely serves the best cookies, bar nun. It's located through the passageway at 24 Avenida de la Constitución, immediately in front of the cathedral's biggest door: Go through the doorway marked *Plaza del Cabildo* into the quiet courtyard (Sept-July Mon-Fri 10:00-13:30 & 17:00-19:30, Sat-Sun 10:30-14:00, closed Aug, Plaza del Cabildo 2, tel. 954-219-190).

▲▲ Alcázar

Originally a 10th-century palace built for the governors of the local Moorish state, this building still functions as a royal pal-

ace—the oldest in use in Europe. The core of the palace features an extensive 14th-century rebuild, done by Muslim workmen for the Christian king, Pedro I (1334-1369). Pedro was nicknamed either "the Cruel" or "the Just," depending on which end of his sword you were on. Pedro's palace embraces both cultural traditions.

Today, visitors can enjoy several sections of the Alcázar. Spectacularly decorated halls and courtyards have distinctive Islamic-style flourishes. Exhibits call up the era of Columbus and Spain's New World dominance. The lush, sprawling gardens invite exploration. Even the palatial rooms used by today's king and queen can be visited (reservations required).

Cost and Hours: €8.50; €2 for students and seniors over 65—must show ID, free for children under 16; ticket also includes Antiquarium at Plaza de la Encarnación, April-Sept daily 9:30-19:00, Oct-March daily 9:30-17:00; tel. 954-502-323, www .patronato-alcazarsevilla.es.

Crowd-Beating Tips: Tour groups clog the palace and rob it of any mystery in the morning (especially on Tue); come as late as possible.

Tours: The fast-moving €3.60 audioguide gives you an hour of information as you wander. My self-guided tour hits the highlights, or consider Concepción Delgado's Alcázar tour.

The **Upper Royal Apartments** can only be visited with a separate tour, reserved in advance (€4.20, includes audioguide, must check bags in provided lockers.) Groups leave every half-hour from 10:00 to 13:30—if interested, book a spot as soon as you arrive at the Alcázar. You tour in a small group of 15 people, escorted by a

Alcázar

50 YARDS
50 METERS

GARDENS

WALLS

DCH

KING
PEDRO I's
PALACE

DEÁN MIRANDA

⑨

⑧

⑦

④   ⑤

⑥

PATIO
DEL
CRUCIERO

③

WC

⑩

①

ADMIRAL'S
APARTMENTS

VIDA

JUDERÍA

SHOP

⑪

GATE

②

CALLE

EXIT

PATIO
DEL
LEÓN

PATIO
DE
BANDERAS

SHOP

C. MANARA

TO 🛈→

PUERTA
DE LEÓN

ENTER

ROM. MUR.

WALLS

PLAZA DEL
TRIUNFO

BARRIO
SANTA CRUZ

TO
CATHEDRAL ↘

① Patio de la Montería
② Admiral's Room
③ Palace Facade
④ Courtyard of the Maidens
⑤ Hall of the Ambassadors
⑥ Courtyard of the Dolls
⑦ Charles V Ceiling Room
⑧ Banquet Hall &
  Hall of Tapestries
⑨ The Gardens
⑩ To Upper Royal Apts.
⑪ To Exit

security guard, following a 25-minute audioguide. For some it's worth it just to escape the mobs in the rest of the palace.

◉ Self-Guided Tour: This royal palace is decorated with a mix of Islamic and Christian elements—a style called Mudejar. It's a thought-provoking glimpse of a graceful Al-Andalus (Moorish) world that might have survived its Castilian conquerors...but didn't. The floor plan is intentionally confusing, to make experiencing the place more exciting and surprising. While Granada's Alhambra was built by Moors for Moorish rulers, what you see here is essentially a Christian ruler's palace, built in the Moorish style.

• *Buy your ticket and enter through the turnstiles. Pass through the garden-like Patio of the Lions and through the arch into a courtyard called the . . .*

❶ Patio de la Montería (Courtyard of the Hunt): Get oriented. The palace's main entrance is directly ahead, through the elaborately decorated facade. WCs are in the far-left corner. In the far-right corner is the staircase (and ticket booth) for the Upper Royal Apartments—reserve an entry time now, if you're interested (see details at the end of this tour).

The palace complex was built over many centuries. It has rooms and decorations from the many rulers who've lived here. Moorish caliphs built the original 10th-century palace and gardens. After Sevilla was Christianized, King Pedro I built the most famous part of the complex. During Spain's Golden Age, Ferdinand and Isabel and, later, their grandson Charles V lived here; they all left their mark. Successive monarchs added still more luxury. And today's king and queen still use the palace's upper floor as one of their royal residences.

• *Before entering the heart of the palace, start in the wing to the right of the courtyard. Step inside.*

❷ Admiral's Room (Cuarto del Almirante): When Queen Isabel debriefed Columbus at the Alcázar after his New World discoveries, she realized this could be big business. She created this wing in 1503 to administer Spain's New World ventures. In these halls, Columbus recounted his travels, Ferdinand Magellan planned his around-the-world cruise, and mapmaker Amerigo Vespucci tried to come up with a catchy moniker for that newly discovered continent.

In the pink-and-red Audience Chamber (once a chapel), the **altarpiece painting** is of St. Mary of the Navigators (*Santa María de los Navegantes*, by Alejo Fernández, 1530s). The Virgin—the

Christopher Columbus
(1451-1506)

This Italian wool-weaver ran off to sea, was shipwrecked in Portugal, married a captain's daughter, learned Portuguese and Spanish, and convinced Spain's monarchs to finance his bold scheme to trade with the East by sailing west. On August 3, 1492, Columbus set sail from Palos (near Huelva, 60 miles west of Sevilla) with 3 ships and 90 men, hoping to land in Asia, which Columbus estimated was 3,000 miles away. Three thousand miles later—with the superstitious crew ready to mutiny, having seen evil omens like a falling meteor and a jittery compass—Columbus landed on an island in the Bahamas (October 12, 1492), convinced he'd reached Asia. They traded with the "Indians" and returned home to Palos harbor, where they were received as heroes.

Columbus made three more voyages to the New World and became rich with gold. He gained a bad reputation among the colonists, was arrested, and returned to Spain in chains. Though pardoned, Columbus fell out of favor with the court. On May 20, 1506, he died in Valladolid. His son said he was felled by "gout and by grief at seeing himself fallen from his high estate," but historians speculate that diabetes or syphilis may have contributed. Columbus died thinking he'd visited Asia, unaware he'd opened up Europe to a New World.

patron saint of sailors and a favorite of Columbus—keeps watch over the puny ships beneath her. Her cape seems to protect everyone under it—even the Native Americans in the dark background (the first time "Indians" were painted in Europe).

Standing beside the Virgin (on the right, dressed in gold, joining his hands together in prayer) is none other than Christopher Columbus. He stands on a cloud, because he's now in heaven (as this was painted a few decades after his death). Notice that Columbus is blond. Columbus' son said of his dad: "In his youth his hair was blond, but when he reached 30, it all turned white." Many historians believe this to be the earliest known portrait of Columbus. If so, it also might be the most accurate. On the left side of the painting, the man with the gold cape is King Ferdinand.

Left of the painting is a **model** of Columbus' *Santa María*, his flagship and the only one of his three ships not to survive the 1492 voyage. Columbus complained that the *Santa María*—a big cargo ship, different from the sleek *Niña* and *Pinta* caravels—was too slow. On Christmas Day it ran aground off present-day Haiti and tore a hole in its hull. The ship was dismantled to build the first permanent structure in America, a fort for 39 colonists. (After Columbus left, the natives burned the fort and killed the colonists.) Opposite the altarpiece (in the center of the back wall) is the family **coat of arms** of Columbus' descendants, who now live in Spain and Puerto Rico. Using Columbus' Spanish name, it reads: "To Castile and to León, Colón gave a new world."

Return to the still-used reception room, filled with big canvases. The **biggest painting** (and most melodramatic) shows the turning point in Sevilla's history: King Ferdinand III humbly kneels before the bishop, giving thanks to God for helping him liberate the city from the Muslims (in 1248). Ferdinand promptly turned the Alcázar of the caliphs into the royal palace of Christian kings.

Pop into the room beyond the grand piano for a look at ornate **fans** (mostly foreign and well-described in English). A long painting shows 17th-century Sevilla during Holy Week. Follow the procession, which is much like today's, with traditional floats carried by teams of men and followed by a retinue of penitents.

• *Return to the Patio de la Montería. Face the impressive entrance façade of the...*

❸ **Palace of King Pedro I (Palacio del Rey Pedro I):** This is the entrance to the 14th-century nucleus of the complex. The façade's elaborate blend of Islamic tracery and Gothic Christian elements introduces us to the Mudejar style seen throughout Pedro's part of the palace.

• *Enter the palace. Pass through the Vestibule (impressive, yes, but we'll see better), and continue through the maze of rooms and passageways until you emerge into the big courtyard with a long pool in the center. This is the...*

❹ **Courtyard of the Maidens (Patio de las Doncellas):** You've reached the center of King Pedro's palace. It's an open-air courtyard, surrounded by rooms. In the center is a long, rectangular reflecting pool. Like the Moors who preceded him, Pedro built his palace around water. The pool has four (covered) cisterns, two at each end. They distribute water to the four quadrants of the palace and—symbolically—to the four corners of the world.

King Pedro cruelly abandoned his wife and moved into the Alcázar with his mistress, then hired Muslim workers from

Granada to re-create the romance of that city's Alhambra in Sevilla's stark Alcázar. The designers created a microclimate engineered for coolness: water, plants, pottery, thick walls, and darkness. This palace is considered Spain's best example of the Mudejar style. Stucco panels with elaborate designs, colorful ceramic tiles, coffered wooden ceilings, and lobed arches atop slender columns create a refined, pleasing environment. The elegant proportions and symmetry of this courtyard are a photographer's delight.

• *Explore the rooms branching off the courtyard. Through the door at the end of the long reflecting pool is the palace's most important room, called the...*

❺ Hall of the Ambassadors (Salón de Embajadores): Here, in his throne room, Pedro received guests and caroused in luxury.

The room is a cube topped with a half-dome, like many important Islamic buildings. In Islam, the cube represents the earth, and the dome is the starry heavens. In Pedro's world, the symbolism proclaimed that he controlled heaven and earth. Islamic horseshoe arches stand atop columns with golden capitals. Lattice windows (a favorite of Pedro's) are above those.

The stucco on the walls is molded with interlacing plants, geometrical shapes, and Arabic writing. Imagine, here in a Christian palace, that the walls are inscribed with unapologetically Muslim sayings: "None but Allah conquers" and "Happiness and prosperity are benefits of Allah, who nourishes all creatures." The artisans added propaganda phrases such as "Dedicated to the magnificent Sultan Pedro—thanks to God!"

The Mudejar style also includes Christian motifs. Find the row of kings, high up at the base of the dome, chronicling all of Spain's ruler from the 600s to the 1600s. Throughout the palace, you'll see coats of arms—including the castle of Castile and the lion of León. There are also natural objects (shells and birds) you wouldn't normally find in Islamic decor, which traditionally avoids realistic images of nature.

Wander through adjoining rooms. Straight ahead from the Hall of the Ambassadors, in the **Philip II Ceiling Room** (Salón del Techo de Felipe II), look above the arches to find peacocks, falcons, and other birds amid interlacing vines. Imagine day-to-day life in the palace—with VIP guests tripping on the tiny but jolting steps.

• *Make your way to the second courtyard, nearby (in the Hall of the Ambassadors, face the Courtyard of the Maidens, then walk to the left). This smaller courtyard is the...*

❻ Courtyard of the Dolls (Patio de las Muñecas): This delicate courtyard was for the king's private and family life. Originally, the center of the courtyard had a pool, cooling the residents and reflecting the decorative patterns once brightly painted on the walls. The columns are different colors—alternating white, black, and pink marble. (Pedro's original courtyard was a single story. The upper floors and skylight were added centuries later.) The courtyard's name comes from the tiny doll faces found at the base of one of the arches. Circle the room and try to find them.

• *The long adjoining room with the gilded ceiling, the **Prince's Room** (Cuarto del Príncipe), was Queen Isabel's bedroom, where she gave birth to a son, Prince Juan.*

Return to the Courtyard of the Maidens. Look up and notice the second story. Isabel's grandson, Charles V, added it in the 16th century. See the difference in styles: Mudejar below (lobed arches and elaborate tracery), and Renaissance above (round arches and less decoration).

As you stand in the courtyard with your back to the Hall of the Ambassadors, the door in the middle of the right side leads to the...

❼ Charles V Ceiling Room (Salón del Techo del Carlos V): Emperor Charles V, who ruled Spain at its peak of New World wealth, expanded the palace. The reason? His marriage to his beloved Isabel, which took place in this room. Devoutly Christian, Charles celebrated his wedding night with a midnight Mass, and later ordered the Mudejar ceiling in this room to be replaced with a less Islamic (but no less impressive) one.

• *We've seen the core of King Pedro's palace, with the additions by his successors. Return to the Courtyard of the Maidens, turn right, and find the staircase in the corner. This leads up to rooms decorated with bright ceramic tiles. Pass through the chapel and into two big, long, parallel rooms, the...*

❽ Banquet Hall (Salón Gótico) and **Hall of Tapestries (Salón Tapices):** Charles and Isabel's wedding reception was held in this big, airy banquet hall. Tiles of yellow, blue, green, and orange line the room, some decorated with whimsical human figures with vase-like bodies. The windows open onto views of the gardens.

Next door, the walls are hung with large Brussels-made tapestries showing the conquests, trade, and industriousness of Charles' prosperous reign. (The highlights are described in Spanish along the top and in Latin along the bottom.) The map tapestry of the Mediterranean world has south pointing up. Find Genova, Italy, on the bottom; Africa on top;

Lisbon on the far right; and the large city of Barcelona in between. The artist included himself holding the legend—with a scale in both leagues and miles.

• *At the far end of the Banquet Hall, head outside to...*

❾ **The Gardens:** This space is full of tropical flowers, feral cats, cool fountains, and hot tourists. The intimate geometric

zone nearest the palace is the Moorish garden. The far-flung garden beyond that was the backyard of the Christian ruler. The **elevated walkway** (Galería del Grutesco—the Grotto Gallery) along the left side of the gardens provides fine views. (Enter it from the palace end.)

Descending to the lower garden, find the entrance to the **Baths of María de Padilla**—an underground rainwater cistern named for Pedro's mistress.

Garden lovers could linger here for hours. Even aborophobes will find it fascinating. Here in the gardens, the Christian and Islamic traditions merge. Both cultures used water and nature as essential parts of their architecture. The garden's pavilions and fountains only enhance this. Wander among palm trees, myrtle hedges, and fragrant roses, and experience a small sample of the heavenly paradise that both cultures believed lay beyond.

• *If you'd like to see more, return to the Patio de la Montería and go upstairs to visit the Upper Royal Apartments (requires reservation and separate entry fee). Otherwise, skip to the conclusion of this tour, below.*

❿ **Upper Royal Apartments (Cuarto Real Alto):** This is the royal palace of today's monarchs. Fifteen public reception rooms are open to visitors: the official dining room, Audience Hall, and so on. The rooms are amply decorated with Versailles-like furniture, chandeliers, carpets, and portraits of 19th-century nobility. The highlight is the Audience Room, a Mudejar-style room overlooking the Patio de la Montería. You don't get to see the actual living quarters of the present king and queen, but they're just down the hall.

• *When you're ready to go, head for the exit, through the **Patio de Banderas**—enjoying a classic Giralda Bell Tower view as you leave. In former times, this courtyard was the entrance for those arriving by horse carriage.*

Your Royal Alcázar tour is over. From Moors to Pedro the Cruel to Isabel and Charles to King Juan Carlos and Queen Sofia, we've seen the home of a millennium of kings and queens. After digesting all those names, I need some Alcaseltzer.

Near the Cathedral and Alcázar

Archivo de Indias—The Lonja Palace, across the street from the Alcázar, was designed by royal architect Juan de Herrera, the same person who planned El Escorial. Originally a market for traders, this is the top building from Sevilla's 16th-century glory days. Today, it houses the archive of documents from the discovery and conquest of the New World, which are shown in rotating exhibits. This could be fascinating, but generally little of importance makes it on display (old maps of Havana, anyone?). The displays are in Spanish, with limited English information.

Cost and Hours: Free, Mon-Sat 9:30-17:00, Sun 10:00-14:00, Avenida de la Constitución 3, tel. 954-500-528.

Avenida de la Constitución—Old Sevilla is bisected by this grand boulevard. Its name celebrates the country's 1978 adoption of a democratic constitution, as the Spanish people moved quickly to re-establish their government after the 1975 death of longtime dictator Francisco Franco. Long a commercial street, the avenue was converted into a pedestrian boulevard in 2007. Overnight, the city's paseo route took on a new dimension. And suddenly cafés and shops here had fresh appeal. (Two Starbucks moved in, strategically bookending the boulevard, but they're having a tough time winning over locals who like small €1 coffees rather than mammoth €4 ones.) The new tram line (infamously short at only three-quarters of a mile) is controversial, as it violates what might have been a more purely pedestrian zone.

Between the River and the Cathedral

Hospital de la Caridad—This Charity Hospital was founded by a nobleman in the 17th century. Peek into the fine courtyard. On the left, the chapel has some gruesome art (above both doors) illustrating that death is the great equalizer, and an altar so sweet only a Spaniard could enjoy it. The Dutch tiles depicting scenes of the Old and New Testament are a reminder that the Netherlands was under Spanish rule in the mid-16th century.

Cost and Hours: €5, includes slightly interesting audio-guide, erratic hours, but typically Mon-Sat 9:00-13:00 & 15:30-19:00, Sun 9:00-12:30, last entry 30 minutes before closing, tel. 954-223-232.

Torre del Oro (Gold Tower) and Naval Museum—Sevilla's historic riverside Gold Tower was the starting and ending point for all shipping to the New World. It's named for the golden tiles that once covered it—not for all the New World booty that landed here. Since the Moors built it in the 13th century, it has been part of the city's fortifications, with a heavy chain draped across the river to protect the harbor. Today it houses a dreary little naval museum. Looking past the dried fish and charts of knots, find the mural showing the world-spanning journeys of Vasco da Gama, the model of Columbus' *Santa María* (the first ship to land in the New World), and an interesting mural of Sevilla in 1740. Enjoy the view from the balconies upstairs. The Guadalquivir River is now just a trickle of its former self, after canals built in the 1920s siphoned off most of its water to feed ports downstream.

Cost and Hours: €2, includes audioguide, Tue-Fri 9:30-13:30, Sat-Sun 10:30-13:30, closed Mon and Aug, tel. 954-222-419.

North of the Cathedral

Plaza Nueva—This "New Square" is marked by a statue of King Ferdinand III, who liberated Sevilla from the Moors in the 13th century and was later sainted. This is the end of the line for Sevilla's short tram system (which zips down Avenida de la Constitución to the El Prado bus station). Running along the top of the square is the relatively modern **City Hall.** For a more interesting look at this building, circle around to the other end (on the smaller square, called Plaza San Francisco) where you can see how the structure has expanded right along with the city it governs: architectural styles evolve, from left to right, along the facade. The newest, right part of the facade is more or less undecorated—a blank canvas for future artists to leave their mark. This square has been used for executions, bullfights, and (today) big city events.

▲**Church of the Savior (Iglesia del Salvador)**—Sevilla's second-biggest church after its cathedral was built on the site of a mosque dating from the ninth century. (In the courtyard next to the church, you can still see the remains of the mosque's patio and the foot of the former minaret.) The spacious interior, which was recently renovated, now gleams with freshly scrubbed Baroque pride. Explore its 14 richly decorated altarpieces, many from the 18th century. You'll also find sculptures by some of Sevilla's most celebrated Baroque artists, such as *Jesus of the Passion* by Martinez Montañés and *Christ of Love* by Juan de Mena. Plaza del Salvador, the pleasant square in front of the church, is cozy and intimate—a favorite meeting point for locals.

Cost and Hours: €3, free with €8 cathedral ticket, audioguide-€2.50; Mon-Sat July-Aug 10:00-17:00, Sept-June 11:30-18:00; Sun 15:00-19:00 year-round; Plaza del Salvador, tel. 954-211-679. If you plan to visit this church and later go to the cathedral, avoid possible lines there by buying your cathedral ticket here.

▲Museo Palacio de la Condesa de Lebrija—This aristocratic mansion takes you back into the 18th century like no other place in town. The Countess of Lebrija was a passionate collector of antiquities. Her home's ground floor is paved with Roman mosaics (that you can actually walk on) and lined with musty old cases of Phoenician, Greek, Roman, and Moorish artifacts—mostly pottery. To see a plush world from a time when the nobility had a private priest and their own chapel, take a quickie tour (in both English and Spanish) of the upstairs, which shows the palace as the countess left it when she died in 1938.

Cost and Hours: €5 for unescorted visit of ground floor, €8 includes tour of "lived-in" upstairs offered every 45 minutes; July-Aug Mon-Fri 9:00-15:00, Sat-Sun 10:00-14:00; Sept-June Mon-Fri 10:30-19:30, Sat-Sun 10:00-14:00; free and obligatory bag check, Calle Cuna 8, tel. 954-227-802, www.palaciodelebrija.com.

Plaza de la Encarnación—This formerly nondescript square recently underwent a dramatic renovation and now makes a bold architectural statement in the heart of old Sevilla. A gigantic undulating canopy of five waffle-patterned, mushroom-shaped, hundred-foot-tall structures provides shade to the formerly sun-baked square. Under the canopy is a gazebo for performances, and in the concrete structure below are

a food market and an *antiquarium* (a museum displaying Roman ruins found during the excavation of the site). The canopy, named the Metropol Parasol, was designed by German architect Jürgen Mayer H., who won a contest to create a new iconic structure for Sevilla (trendy-to-the-max Jürgen shifted his middle initial to become his last name). The dynamic vaulting is intended to echo the interior of Sevilla's vast cathedral. The wooden structure, unbelievably, is held together with glue. And—as you might guess for a cutting-edge architectural work with a hefty price tag (reportedly €86 million) completed several years behind deadline—it has been controversial. Architecture critics greeted its March 2011 unveiling with a mix of appreciation and puzzlement, and the structure has yet to win over the hearts of most Sevillans. Fans of modern architecture (or experimental civic projects) will find it worth the short walk from Plaza Nueva to take a peek (especially handy if you're visiting the Museo Palacio de la Condesa de Lebrija, just a block away).

▲Flamenco Dance Museum (Museo del Baile Flamenco)—If you want to understand more about the dance that embodies the spirit of southern Spain, this small but good museum—overpriced at €10—does the trick. The grande dame of flamenco, Cristina Hoyos, has collected a few artifacts and costumes and put together a series of well-produced videos explaining the art of flamenco. Ride the red elevator to floor 1 to tour the main exhibition, with videos, flamenco dresses and other objects, and posters celebrating notable flamenco artists over time. The place is heavy on evocative video clips, but a bit light on actual information. One particularly interesting film illustrates the key elements of the dance form: pain, joy, elegance, seduction, soul, and—I believe—love of ham. Floor 2 and the basement (-1) feature temporary exhibits—mostly artwork relating to flamenco. On the ground floor and in the basement, you can watch flamenco lessons in progress—or even take one yourself.

Cost and Hours: €10, 10 percent discount with this book in 2012, daily 9:30-19:00, last entry 30 minutes before closing, Manuel Rojas Marcos 3, about 3 blocks east of Plaza Nueva, tel. 954-340-311, www.museoflamenco.com.

Classes: You can participate in a one-hour lesson and take a little *olé* home (up to €60/person, prices go down with more people, shoes not provided).

Performances: Regular dance shows run Sun-Thu at 19:00 (€15) and Fri-Sat at 19:30 (€23). A combo-ticket includes the museum and a show (€20 weekday or €28 weekend; 10 percent discount off museum, show, or combo-ticket with this book in 2012).

▲Museo de Bellas Artes

Sevilla's passion for religious art is preserved and displayed in its Museum of Fine Arts. While most Americans go for El Greco,

Goya, and Velázquez (not a forte of this collection), this museum gives a fine look at other, less-appreciated Spanish masters: Zurbarán and Murillo. Rather than exhausting, the museum is pleasantly enjoyable.

Cost and Hours: €1.50, Tue-Sat 9:00-20:30, Sun 9:00-14:30, closed Mon, last entry 15 minutes before closing, tel. 954-786-500, www.juntadeandalucia.es/cultura /museos.

Getting There: The museum is at Plaza Museo 9; it's a 15-minute walk from the cathedral, or a short ride on bus #C5 from Plaza Nueva. If coming from the Basílica de La Macarena, take bus #C4 to the Torneo stop and walk inland four blocks. Pick up the English-language floor plan, which explains the theme of each room.

SEVILLA

Background: Sevilla was Spain's wealthy commercial capital, similar to New York City, whereas Madrid was a newly built center of government, like Washington, D.C. In the early 1800s, Spain's liberal government was disbanding convents and monasteries, and secular fanatics were looting churches. Thankfully, the region's religious art was rescued and hung safely here in this convent-turned-museum.

Spain's economic Golden Age (the 1500s) blossomed into the Golden Age of Spanish painting (the 1600s). Several of Spain's top artists—Zurbarán, Murillo, and Velázquez—lived in Sevilla during the 1600s. Artists labored to make the spiritual world tangible, and forged the gritty realism that marks Spanish painting. You'll see balding saints and monks with wrinkled faces and sunburned hands. The style suited Spain's spiritual climate, as the Catholic Church used this art in its Counter-Reformation battle against the Protestant rebellion.

◑ Self-Guided Tour: The permanent collection features 20 rooms in neat chronological order. It's easy to breeze through once with my tour, then backtrack to what appeals to you.

• *Enter and follow signs to the permanent collection, which begins in Sala I (Room 1).*

Rooms 1-4: Medieval altarpieces of gold-backed saints, Virgin-and-babes, and Crucifixion scenes attest to the religiosity that nurtured Spain's early art. Spain's penchant for unflinching realism culminates in Room 2 with Pedro Torrigiano's 1525 statue of an emaciated San Jerónimo, and in Room 3 with the painted clay head of St. John the Baptist—complete with severed neck muscles, throat, and windpipe. This kind of warts-and-all naturalism would influence the great Sevillan painter Velázquez (whose few works are often displayed in Room 4).

• *Continue through the pleasant outdoor courtyard to the former church that is now Room 5.*

Room 5—Murillo: The works of another hometown boy, Bartolomé Murillo (mur-EE-oh, 1617-1682), are displayed here. His signature subject is the Immaculate Conception, the doc-

trine that holds that Mary was exempt from original sin. Several *Inmaculadas* may be on display. Typically, Mary is depicted as young, dressed in white and blue, standing atop the moon (crescent or full). She clutches her breast and gazes up rapturously, surrounded by tumbling winged babies. Murillo's tiny *Madonna and Child (Virgen de la Servilleta,*

1665; at the end of the room in the center, where the church's altar would have been) shows the warmth and appeal of his work.

Murillo's sweetness is quite different from the harsh realism of his fellow artists, but his work was understandably popular. For many Spaniards, Mary is their main connection to heaven. They pray directly to her, asking her to intercede on their behalf with God. Murillo's Marys are always receptive and ready to help.

Besides his *Inmaculadas*, Murillo painted popular saints. They often carry sprigs of plants, and cock their heads upward, caught up in a heavenly vision of sweet Baby Jesus. Murillo is also known for his "genre" paintings—scenes of common folk and rascally street urchins—but the museum has few of these.

• *Now head upstairs to the first floor.*

Rooms 6-9: In rooms 6 and 7, you'll see more Murillos and Murillo imitators. Room 8 is dedicated to yet another native Sevillan (and friend of Murillo), Juan de Valdés Leal (1622-1690). He adds Baroque motion and drama to religious subjects. His surreal colors and feverish, unfinished style create a mood of urgency.

Room 10—Zurbarán: Francisco de Zurbarán (thoor-bar-AHN, 1598-1664) painted saints and monks, and the miraculous things they experienced, with an unblinking, crystal-clear, brightly lit, highly detailed realism. Monks and nuns could meditate upon Zurbarán's meticulous paintings for hours, finding God in the details.

In Zurbarán's *St. Hugo Visiting the Refectory (San Hugo en el Refectorio)*, white-robed Carthusian monks gather together for their

simple meal in a communal dining hall. Above them hangs a painting of Mary, Baby Jesus, and John the Baptist. Zurbarán created paintings for monks' dining halls like this. His audience: celibate men and women who lived in isolation, as in this former convent, devoting their time to quiet meditation, prayer, and Bible study. Zurbarán shines a harsh spotlight on many of his subjects, creating strong shadows. Zurbarán's people often stand starkly isolated against a single-color background—a dark room or the gray-white of a cloudy sky. He was the ideal painter of the austere religion of 17th-century Spain.

Find *The Virgin of the Caves (La Virgen de las Cuevas)* and study the piety and faith in the monks' weathered faces. Zurbarán's Mary is protective, with her hands placed on the heads of two monks. Note the loving detail on the cape embroidery, the brooch, and the flowers at her feet. But also note the angel babies holding the cape, with their painfully double-jointed arms. Zurbarán was no Leonardo.

The Apotheosis of St. Thomas Aquinas (*Apteosis de Santo Tomás de Aquino*, may be displayed on ground level, Room 5) is considered Zurbarán's most important work. It was done at the height of his career, when stark realism was all the rage. In a believable, down-to-earth way, Zurbarán presents the pivotal moment when the great saint-theologian experiences his spiritual awakening.

The Rest of the Museum: Spain's subsequent art, from the 18th century on, generally followed the trends of the rest of Europe. Room 12 has creamy Romanticism and hazy Impressionism. You'll see typical Sevillan motifs such as matadors, cigar-factory girls, and river landscapes. Enjoy these painted slices of Sevilla, then exit to experience similar scenes today.

South of the Cathedral, near Plaza de España

University—Today's university was yesterday's *fábrica de tabacos* (tobacco factory), which employed 10,000 young female *cigareras*—including the saucy femme fatale of Bizet's opera *Carmen*. In the 18th century, it was the second-largest building in Spain, after El Escorial. Wander through its halls as you walk to Plaza de España. The university's bustling café is a good place for cheap tapas, beer, wine, and conversation (Mon-Fri 8:00-21:00, Sat 9:00-13:00, closed Sun).

Plaza de España—This square, the surrounding buildings, and the nearby María Luisa Park are the remains of the 1929 inter-

national fair, where for a year the Spanish-speaking countries of the world enjoyed a mutual-admiration fiesta. When they finish the restoration work here (it's taking years), this delightful area—the epitome of world's fair–style architecture—will once again be great for people-watching (especially during the 19:00-20:00 peak paseo hour). The park's highlight is the former Spanish Pavilion. Its tiles (a trademark of Sevilla) show historic scenes and maps from every province of Spain (arranged in alphabetical order, from Álava to Zaragoza). Climb to one of the balconies for a fine view. Beware: This is a classic haunt of thieves and con artists. Believe no one here. Thieves, posing as lost tourists, will come at you with a map unfolded to hide their speedy, greedy fingers.

Away from the Center

▲▲Basílica de la Macarena

Sevilla's Holy Week (Semana Santa) celebrations are Spain's grandest. During the week leading up to Easter, the city is packed

with pilgrims witnessing 60 processions carrying about 100 religious floats. If you miss the actual event, you can get a sense of it by visiting the Basílica de la Macarena and its accompanying museum to see the two most impressive floats and the darling of Holy Week, the statue of the Virgen de la Macarena.

Cost and Hours: Church-free, treasury museum-€5, audioguide-€1, Mon-Sat 9:00-14:00 & 17:00-21:00, Sun from 9:30. Although far from the city center, it's located on Sevilla's ring road and easy to reach. Wave down a taxi and say "Basilica Macarena" (about €7 from city center). All the #C buses go there, including bus #C3 or #C4 from Puerta de Jerez (near the Torre de Oro) or Menéndez Pelayo (the ring road east of the cathedral), tel. 954-901-800, www.hermandad delamacarena.es.

➍ Self-Guided Tour: Despite the long history of the Macarena statue, the Neo-Baroque church was only built in 1949 to give the oft-moved sculpture a permanent home.

• *Grab a pew and study the...*

Weeping Virgin: La Macarena is known as the "Weeping Virgin" for the five crystal teardrops trickling down her cheeks. She's like a Baroque doll with human hair and articulated arms, and is even dressed in underclothes. Sculpted in the late 17th century (probably by Pedro Roldán), she's become Sevilla's most popular image of Mary.

Her beautiful expression—halfway between smiling and crying—is ambiguous, letting worshippers project their own emotions onto her. Her weeping can be contagious—look around you. She's also known as La Esperanza, the Virgin of Hope, and she promises better times after the sorrow.

Installed in a side chapel (on the left) is the **Christ of the**

Judgment (from 1654), showing Jesus on the day he was con-
demned. This statue and La Macarena stand atop the two most
important floats of the Holy Week parades.

• *To see the floats and learn more, visit the treasury museum to the left
of the church.*

Tesoro (Treasury Museum): This small three-floor museum
tells the history of the Virgin statue and the Holy Week parades.
Though rooted in medieval times, the current traditions developed
around 1600, with the formation of various fraternities (*herman-
dades*). During Holy Week, they demonstrate their dedication to
God by parading themed floats throughout Sevilla to retell the
story of the Crucifixion and Resurrection of Christ. The museum
displays ceremonial banners, scepters, and costumed mannequins;
videos show the parades in action (some displays in English).

The three-ton float that carries the Christ of the Judgment
is slathered in gold leaf and shows a commotion of figures acting
out the sentencing of Jesus. (The statue of Christ—the one you
saw in the church—is placed before this crowd for the Holy Week
procession.) Pontius Pilate is about to wash his hands. Pilate's wife
cries as a man reads the death sentence. During the Holy Week
procession, pious Sevillan women wail in the streets while relays
of 48 men carry this float on the backs of their necks—only their
feet showing under the drapes—as they shuffle through the streets
from midnight until 14:00 in the afternoon every Good Friday. The
men rehearse for months in advance to get their choreographed
footwork in sync.

La Macarena follows the Christ of the Judgment in the procession. Mary's smaller 1.5-ton float seems all silver and candles—
"strong enough to support the roof, but tender enough to quiver in
the soft night breeze." Mary has a wardrobe of three huge mantles,
worn in successive years. They are about 100 years old. Her six-
pound gold crown/halo is from 1913. This float has a mesmeriz-
ing effect on the local crowds. They line up for hours, clapping,
weeping, and throwing roses as it slowly sways along the streets,
working its way through town. My Sevillan friend explained,
"She knows all the problems of Sevilla and its people. We've
been confiding in her for centuries. To us, she is hope. That's her
name—Esperanza."

The museum collection also contains some matador parapher-
nalia. La Macarena is the patron saint of bullfighters, and they
give thanks for her protection. Copies of her image are popular in
bullring chapels. In 1912 the bullfighter José Ortega, hoping for
protection, gave La Macarena the five emerald brooches she wears.
It worked for eight years...until he was gored to death in the ring.
For a month, La Macarena was dressed in widow's black—the only
time that has happened.

• *Exit the church into the...*

Macarena Neighborhood: Outside, notice the best surviving bit of Sevilla's old walls. Originally Roman, what remains today was built by the Moors in the 12th century to (unsuccessfully) keep the Christians out. And yes, it's from this city that a local dance band (Los del Río) changed the world by giving us the popular 1990s song "The Macarena." He-e-y-y, Macarena!

Near Sevilla

Itálica—One of Spain's most impressive Roman ruins is found outside the sleepy town of Santiponce, about six miles north-west of Sevilla. Founded in 206 B.C. for wounded soldiers recu-perating from the Second Punic War, Itálica became a thriving town of great agricultural and military importance. It was the birthplace of famous Roman emperors Trajan and Hadrian. Today its best-preserved ruin is its amphitheater—one of the largest in the Roman Empire—with a capacity for 30,000 spectators. Other highlights include beautiful floor mosaics, such as the one in Casa de los Pájaros (House of the Birds) that shows more than 30 species of birds. To avoid the midday heat in summer, plan your visit to arrive early or late, and definitely bring water.

Cost and Hours: €1.50; April-Sept Tue-Sat 8:30-21:00, Sun 9:00-15:00; Oct-March Tue-Sat 9:00-18:30, Sun 10:00-15:00; closed Mon year-round; last entry 30 minutes before closing; tel. 955-622-266, www.juntadeandalucia.es/cultura/italica.

Getting There: You can get to Itálica on bus #M-172A (30-minute trip, frequent departures from Sevilla's Plaza de Armas station). If you're driving, head west out of Sevilla in the direc-tion of Huelva; after you cross the second branch of the river, turn north on SE-30/A-66, and after a few miles, get off at Santiponce. Drive past pottery warehouses and through the town to the ruins at the far (west) end.

Experiences in Sevilla

Bullfighting

▲**Bullfights**—Some of Spain's best bullfighting is done in Sevilla's 14,000-seat bullring, Plaza de Toros. Fights are held (generally at 18:30) on most Sundays in May and June; on Easter and Corpus Christi; daily during the April Fair (April 24-29 in 2012); and at the end of September (during the Feria de San Miguel). These serious fights, with adult matadors, are called *corrida de toros* and often sell out in advance. On many Thursday evenings in July, there are *novillada* fights, with teenage novices doing the killing and smaller bulls doing the dying. *Corrida de toros* seats range from €25 for high seats looking into the sun to €150 for the first three rows in the shade under the royal box; *novillada* seats are half that—and easy to buy at the arena a few minutes before show time (ignore scalpers outside; get information at a TI, your hotel, by phone, or online; tel. 954-210-315, www.lamaestranza.es).

▲▲**Bullring (Plaza de Toros) and Bullfight Museum (Museo Taurino)**—Follow a bilingual (Spanish and English) 40-minute guided tour through the bullring's strangely quiet and empty arena, its museum, and the chapel where the matador prays before the fight. (Thanks to readily available blood transfusions, there have been no deaths in nearly three decades.) The two most revered figures of Sevilla, the Virgen de la Macarena and the Jesús del Gran Poder (Christ of All Power), are represented in the chapel. In the museum, you'll see great classic scenes and the heads of a few bulls—awarded the bovine equivalent of an Oscar for a particularly good fight. The city was so appalled when the famous matador Manolete was killed in 1947 that even the mother of the bull that gored him was destroyed. Matadors—dressed to kill—are heartthrobs in their "suits of light." Many girls have their bedrooms wallpapered with posters of cute bullfighters.

Cost and Hours: €6.50, entrance with escorted tour only— no free time inside, 3/hour, daily May-Oct 9:30-20:00, Nov-April 9:30-19:00, until 14:00 on fight days, when chapel and horse room are closed. The last tour departs 15 minutes before closing. While they take groups of up to 50, it's still wise to call or drop by to reserve a spot in the busy season (tel. 954-210-315, www.realmaestranza.com).

The April Fair

For a seven-day period that falls a week or two after Easter, much of Sevilla is packed into its vast fairgrounds for a grand party (April 24-29 in 2012). The fair, seeming to bring all that's Andalusian together, feels friendly, spontaneous, and very real. The local passion for horses, flamenco, and sherry is clear—riders are ramrod straight, colorfully clad girls ride sidesaddle, and everyone's drinking sherry spritzers. Women sport outlandish dresses that would look clownish elsewhere, but are somehow brilliant here en masse. Horses clog the streets in an endless parade until about 20:00, when they clear out and the streets fill with exuberant locals. The party goes for literally 24 hours a day for the entire week.

Countless private party tents, or *casetas*, line the lanes. Each tent is the private party zone of a family, club, or association. You need to know someone in the group—or make friends quickly—to get in. Because of the exclusivity, it has a real family-affair feeling. In each *caseta*, everyone knows everyone. It seems like a thousand wedding parties being celebrated at the same time.

Any tourist can have a fun and memorable evening by simply crashing the party. The city's entire fleet of taxis (who'll try to charge double) and buses seems dedicated to shuttling people from downtown to the fairgrounds. Given the traffic jams and inflated prices, you may be better off hiking: From the Torre del Oro, cross the San Telmo Bridge to Plaza de Cuba and hike down Calle Asunción. You'll see the towering gate to the fairgrounds in the distance. Just follow the crowds (there's no admission charge). Arrive before 20:00 to see the horses, but stay later, as the ambience improves after the *caballos* giddy-up on out. Some of the larger tents are sponsored by the city and open to the public, but the best action is in the streets, where party-goers from the livelier *casetas* spill out. Although private tents have bouncers, everyone is so happy that it's not tough to strike up an impromptu friendship, become a "special guest," and be invited in. The drink flows freely, and the food is fun and cheap.

Shopping in Sevilla

For the best local shopping experience, follow my shopping stroll (described next). The popular pedestrian streets Sierpes and

Tetuán/Velázquez—along with the surrounding lanes near Plaza Nueva—are packed with people and shops. Small shops close between 13:30 and 16:00 or 17:00 on weekdays, as well as on Saturday afternoons and all day Sunday. But big ones such as El Corte Inglés stay open (and air-conditioned) right through the siesta. El Corte Inglés also has a supermarket downstairs and a good but expensive restaurant (Mon-Sat 10:00-22:00, closed Sun). Popular souvenir items include ladies' fans, shawls, *mantillas*, other items related to flamenco (castanets, guitars, costumes), ceramics, and bullfighting posters.

Collectors' markets hop on Sunday: stamps and coins at Plaza del Cabildo (near the cathedral) and art on Plaza del Museo (by the Museo de Bellas Artes).

Mercado del Arenal, the covered fish-and-produce market, is perfect for hungry photographers (Mon-Sat 9:00-14:30, closed Sun, least lively on Mon, on Calle Pastor y Landero at Calle Arenal, just beyond bullring).

▲▲Shopping Paseo Tour

Although many tourists never get beyond the cathedral and the Santa Cruz neighborhood, it's important to wander west into the lively pedestrian shopping center of town. These streets—Calle Tetuán (which becomes Velázquez), Calle Sierpes, and Calle Cuna—also happen to be part of the oldest section of Sevilla. A walk here is a chance to join one of Spain's liveliest paseos—that bustling celebration of life that takes place before dinner each evening, when everyone is out strolling, showing off their fancy shoes and making the scene. This walk (if done between 18:00 and 20:00) gives you a look at the paseo scene and the town's most popular shops. You'll pass windows displaying the best in both traditional and trendy fashion. The walk ends at a plush mansion of a local countess (open to the public).

Start on the pedestrianized **Plaza Nueva,** a 19th-century square facing the ornate city hall, which features a statue of Ferdinand III, a local favorite because he freed Sevilla from the Moors in 1248. From here wander the length of **Calle Tetuán** (notice the latest in outrageous shoes). Calle Tetuán becomes **Velázquez,** and ends at La Campana (a big intersection and popular meeting point, with the super department store, El Corte Inglés, just beyond, on Plaza del Duque de la Victoria). At La Campana, tempt yourself with sweets at the venerable Confitería La Campana.

Next, take two rights to get to **Calle Sierpes,** great for shopping and strolling. Calle Sierpes is the main street of the Holy Week processions—imagine it packed with celebrants and its balconies bulging with spectators. At the corner of Sierpes and Jovellanos/Sagasta, you're near several fine shops featuring Andalusian accessories. Drop in to see how serious local women are about their fans, shawls, *mantillas* (ornate head scarves), and *peinetas* (combs designed to secure and prop up the *mantilla*). The most valuable *mantillas* are silk, and the top-quality combs are made of tortoise shell (though most women opt for much more affordable polyester and plastic). Andalusian women have various fans to match different dresses—they are considered an accessory. The *mantilla* comes in black (worn only on Good Friday and by the mother of the groom at weddings) and white (worn at bull-fights during the April Fair).

From here turn left down **Calle Sagasta.** Notice that the street has two names—the modern version and a medieval one: Antigua Calle de Gallegos ("Ancient Street of the Galicians"). With the Christian victory in 1248, the Muslims were given one month to evacuate. To consolidate Christian control, settlers from the northwest corner of Iberia were planted here. This street was home to the Galicians.

Finally, you'll arrive at the charming Plaza del Salvador. It's teeming with life again, now that the Church of the Savior is completely restored. Backtrack left along **Calle Cuna,** famous for its exuberant flamenco dresses and classic wedding dresses. Local women save up to have flamenco dresses custom-made for the April Fair: They're considered an important status symbol. (Flamenco miniskirts have been popular in recent years, but now hemlines are falling again.) If all this shopping makes you feel like a countess, Calle Cuna leads to the Museo Palacio de la Condesa de Lebrija, and nearby is the super-modern Metropol Parasol structure towering over Plaza de la Encarnación.

Nightlife in Sevilla

▲▲▲Flamenco

This music-and-dance art form has its roots in the Roma (Gypsy) and Moorish cultures. Even at a packaged "flamenco evening," sparks fly. The men do most of the flamboyant machine-gun footwork. The women often concentrate on the graceful turns and

smooth, shuffling step of the *soléa* version of the dance. Watch the musicians. Flamenco guitarists, with their lightning-fast finger-roll strums, are among the best in the world. The intricate rhythms are set by castanets or the hand-clapping (called *palmas*) of those who aren't dancing at the moment. In the raspy-voiced wails of the singers, you'll hear echoes of the Muslim call to prayer.

Like jazz, flamenco thrives on improvisation. Also like jazz, good flamenco is more than just technical proficiency. A singer or dancer with "soul" is said to have *duende*. Flamenco is a happening, with bystanders clapping along and egging on the dancers with whoops and shouts. Get into it. For a tourist-oriented flamenco show, your hotel can get you nightclub show tickets (happily, since they snare a hefty commission for each sale). But it's easy to book a place on your own. Aficionados will likely enjoy the Flamenco Dance Museum as well, which also has performances.

You basically have three options: serious—yet still touristy—flamenco shows, where the singing and dancing take center stage; even more touristy shows that have a bar and/or food (scurrying waiters can distract from the performers); and casual bars—the least touristy—where you can catch impromptu or semi-impromptu musicians at play.

Serious Flamenco Shows—Touristy flamenco shows give you all the clichés; at **Casa de la Memoria de Al-Andalus** (House of the Memory of Al-Andalus) you'll enjoy an elegant and classy musical experience with a small cast and classic solos. In an alcohol-free atmosphere, 90 tourists sit on 3 rows of folding chairs circling a small stage for an intimate concert featuring flamenco and other Andalusian music. It's all acoustic, and the nightly musical mix varies according to the personalities of the performers. It's also a perfect place to practice your Spanish fan (*abanico*) skills on warm nights. One-hour concerts are nightly all year at 21:00; with demand, shows are added at 19:30 and/or 22:30 (€15, reservations smart, box office open Mon-Sat 10:00-14:00 and daily 18:00-22:00. Same-day tickets generally available but better to buy tickets a day or more beforehand, arrive early for front-row seats, in Barrio Santa Cruz, adjacent to Hotel Alcántara at Ximénez de Enciso 28, tel. 954-560-670, www.casadelamemoria .es, memorias@terra.es).

Auditorio Álvarez Quintero, another good option just a block from the cathedral, fills a small atrium with 85 folding chairs and good performers that change each evening (€17, nightly at 21:00, doors open at 20:30—worth arriving early to get a good seat, Álvarez Quintero 48, tel. 954-293-949, www.alvarezquintero .com).

Shows with Drinks and/or Food—These packaged shows can be a bit sterile, and an audience of tourists doesn't help, but I find both Los Gallos and El Arenal entertaining and riveting. While El Arenal may have a slight edge on talent and feels slicker, Los Gallos has a cozier setting, with cushy rather than hard chairs—and it's cheaper.

Los Gallos presents nightly two-hour shows at 20:00 and 22:30 (€30 ticket includes a drink, €3/person discount with this book in 2012—but limited to two admissions, arrive 30 minutes early for best seats, noisy bar but no food served, Plaza de la Santa Cruz 11, tel. 954-216-981, www.tablaolosgallos.com, owners José and Nuria promise goose bumps).

Tablao El Arenal has arguably more professional performers and a classier setting for its show—but dinner customers get the preferred seating, and waiters are working throughout the performance (€37 ticket includes a drink, €59 includes tapas, €72 includes dinner, shows at 20:00 and 22:00, near bullring at Calle Rodó 7, tel. 954-216-492, www.tablaoelarenal.com).

El Patio Sevillano is more of a variety show, with flamenco as well as other forms of song and dance. At this venue, in a big hall with hard chairs, diners have the worst seats rather than the best (€38 ticket includes a drink, €60 with tapas, €72 with dinner, 1.5-hour shows at 19:00 and 21:30, next to bullring on busy riverfront road at Paseo de Cristóbal Colón, tel. 954-214-120, www.elpatiosevillano.com).

Impromptu Flamenco in Bars—Spirited flamenco singing still erupts spontaneously in bars throughout the old town after midnight. Head across the river to Triana and just follow your ears as you wander down Calle Betis, the riverfront street leading off Plaza de Cuba across the bridge. The **Lo Nuestro** and **Rejoneo** bars are local favorites (at Calle Betis 31A and 31B).

Or try **La Carbonería Bar,** the sangria equivalent of a beer garden. It's a sprawling place with a variety of rooms leading to a big, open tented area filled with young locals, casual guitar strummers, and nearly nightly flamenco music after about 23:00 (no dancing). Located just a few blocks from most of my recommended hotels, this is worth finding if you're not quite ready to end the day (no cover, €2.50 sangria, daily 20:00-3:00 in the morning; near Plaza Santa María—find Hotel Fernando III, the side alley Céspedes dead-ends at Levies, head left to Levies 18, unsigned door).

▲▲Evening Paseo

Sevilla is meant for strolling. The paseo thrives every non-winter evening in these areas: along either side of the river between the San Telmo and Isabel II bridges (Paseo de Cristóbal Colón and Triana district), up Avenida de la Constitución, around Plaza Nueva, at Plaza de España, and throughout the Barrio Santa Cruz. On hot summer nights, even families with toddlers are out and about past midnight. Spend some time rafting through this sea of humanity. Savor the view of floodlit Sevilla by night from the far side of the river—perhaps over dinner.

Sleeping in Sevilla

All of my listings are centrally located, mostly within a five-minute walk of the cathedral. The first are near the charming but touristy Santa Cruz neighborhood. The last group is just as central but closer to the river, across the boulevard in a more workaday, less touristy zone.

Sleep Code

(€1 = about $1.40, country code: 34)
S = Single, **D** = Double/Twin, **T** = Triple, **Q** = Quad, **b** = bathroom, **s** = shower only. Unless otherwise noted, credit cards are accepted, hoteliers speak enough English, tax is usually included, and breakfast generally costs extra.

To help you easily sort through these listings, I've divided the accommodations into three categories based on the price for a double room with bath during high season:

$$$ Higher Priced—Most rooms €110 or more.
 $$ Moderately Priced—Most rooms between €60-110.
  $ Lower Priced—Most rooms €60 or less.

Prices can change without notice; verify the hotel's current rates online or by email. For other updates, see www .ricksteves.com/update.

Room rates as much as double during the two Sevilla fiestas (Holy Week; and the weeklong April Fair, held a week or two after Easter). In general, the busiest and most expensive months are April, May, September, and October. Hotels put rooms on the discounted push list in July and August—when people with good sense avoid this furnace—and from November through February. Prices generally include the IVA hotel tax. A price range indicates low- to high-season prices (but I have not listed festival prices).

If you do visit in July or August, the best values are central business-class places. They offer summer discounts and provide a (necessary) cool, air-conditioned refuge. But be warned that Spain's air-conditioning often isn't the icebox you're used to, especially in Sevilla.

Santa Cruz Neighborhood

These places are off Calle Santa María la Blanca and Plaza Santa María. The most convenient parking lot is the underground Cano y Cueto garage near the corner of Calle Santa María la Blanca and Menéndez Pelayo (about €18/day, open 24/7, at edge of big park, unsigned). A fine Internet café and self-service launderette are a couple of blocks away up Menéndez Pelayo.

$$$ Hotel Casa 1800, well-priced for its elegance, is worth the extra euros. Located dead-center in Santa Cruz (facing a boisterous tapas bar that quiets down after midnight), its 24 rooms circle an elegant chandeliered patio lounge that hosts a daily free afternoon tea for guests. With a rooftop terrace offering an impressive cathedral view and elegantly appointed rooms with high, beamed ceilings, it's a winner (standard Db-€138, superior Db with private patio-€150, deluxe Db with patio and Jacuzzi-€184, "grand deluxe" Db with all of the above and more-€220, breakfast-€12, air-con, elevator, free Internet access and Wi-Fi, Rodrigo Caro 6, tel. 954-561-800, www.hotelcasa1800.com, info@hotelcasa1800.com).

$$$ Hotel Las Casas de la Judería has 178 quiet, elegant rooms and suites, many of them tastefully decorated with hardwood floors and a Spanish flair. The rooms, which surround a series of peaceful courtyards, are a romantic splurge. Ask for one of the newer rooms to avoid the dated ones. The service can be stiff and stuffy (Sb-€100-160, Db-€120-200, extra bed-€45; low-season prices—July-Aug and late-Nov-Feb—are discounted a further 10 percent to those with this book who ask in 2012, but check their website for even better rates; expensive but great buffet breakfast-€19, air-con, elevator, free Wi-Fi in lobby, pool in summer, valet parking-€19/day, Plaza Santa María 5, tel. 954-415-150, fax 954-422-170, www.casasypalacios.com, juderia@casasypalacios.com).

$$ Hotel Amadeus is a little gem that music lovers will appreciate (it even has a couple of soundproof rooms with pianos—something I've never seen anywhere else in Europe). It's lovingly decorated with a music motif around small courtyards, with elevators that take you to your choice of two roof terraces (one with an under-the-stars Jacuzzi). Though small, this 24-room place is classy and comfortable, with welcoming public spaces and a very charming staff. The €8.50 breakfast comes on a trolley—enjoy it in your room, in the lounge, or on a terrace (Sb-€85, Db-€98, big Db-€115, suites-€165-195, cheaper July-Aug, air-con, elevator, free Internet access and Wi-Fi, laundry-€15, parking-€16, Calle Farnesio 6, tel. 954-501-443, fax 954-500-019, www.hotelamadeus sevilla.com, reservas@hotelamadeussevilla.com, wonderfully run by María Luisa and her staff—Zaida and Cristina). They'll even loan you a free laptop to access Wi-Fi in your room. Their next-door annex is every bit as charming and a similarly good value: **$$$ La Música de Sevilla** offers six additional, beautifully appointed rooms; three rooms face the interior patio, and three are streetside with small balconies (patio Db-€110, exterior Db-€130, air-con, reserve and check in at Hotel Amadeus).

$$ El Rey Moro encircles its spacious, colorful patio (which tourists routinely duck into for a peek) with 19 rooms. Colorful and dripping with quirky Andalusian character, and thoughtful about including extras (such as free loaner bikes), it's a class act (Sb-€39-79, Db-€69-100, breakfast-€9—or free if you reserve on their website, check their site for other specials, air-con, elevator,

Santa Cruz Hotels,

free Internet access and Wi-Fi, Lope de Rueda 14, tel. 954-563-468, www.hotelelreymoro.com, hotel@elreymoro.com).

$$ YH Giralda, once an 18th-century abbots' house, is now a charming 14-room hotel tucked away on a little street right off Mateo Gagos, just a couple of blocks from the cathedral. The exterior rooms have windows onto a pedestrian street, and a few of the interior rooms have small windows that look into the inner courtyard; all rooms are neatly appointed (Sb-€50-84, Db-€50-94, Tb-€75-115, Qb-€85-135, higher rates are for weekends, no breakfast, air-con, pay Wi-Fi, Calle Abades 30, tel. 954-228-324, fax 954-227-019, www.yh-hoteles.com, yhgiralda@yh-hoteles.com).

$$ Hotel Alcántara offers more no-nonsense comfort than character. Well-located but strangely out of place in the midst of the Santa Cruz jumble, it rents 21 slick rooms at a good price (Sb-€71, small Db-€82, bigger Db twin-€93, fancy Db-€117, 10 percent discount or a free breakfast—your choice—if you book direct, pay cash, and show this book in 2012—not valid during Holy Week

Restaurants, & Flamenco

SEVILLA

50 YARDS
50 METERS

S. MARIA LA BLANCA

SANTA MARIA LA BLANCA
CISO
PL. S. MARIA
CRUCES

PLAZA DE REFINADORES

P

MURILLO GARDENS

PLAZA DE ALFARO

AV DE MENÉNDEZ

TO 20

❶ Hotel Casa 1800
❷ Hotel Las Casas de la Judería
❸ Hotel Amadeus, La Música de Sevilla & Pensión Córdoba
❹ El Rey Moro
❺ YH Giralda
❻ Hotel Alcántara & Casa de la Memoria de Al-Andalus (Flamenco, Music)
❼ Hotel Murillo
❽ Pensión San Benito Abad
❾ To Samay Hostel, Internet Café & Launderette
❿ Bodega Santa Cruz
⓫ Las Teresas Bar
⓬ Cervecería Giralda
⓭ Corral del Agua Restaurante
⓮ Restaurante Modesto (2)
⓯ Freiduría Puerta de la Carne
⓰ Bar Restaurante El 3 de Oro
⓱ Restaurante San Marco
⓲ Café Bar Carmela
⓳ Los Gallos (Flamenco)
⓴ To La Carbonería Bar

or April Fair, breakfast-€6, air-con, elevator, free Wi-Fi, rentable laptop, outdoor patio, Ximénez de Enciso 28, tel. 954-500-595, fax 954-500-604, www.hotelalcantara.net, info@hotelalcantara.net). The hotel is adjacent to Casa de la Memoria de Al-Andalus, which offers concerts (described earlier under "Flamenco").

$$ Hotel Murillo enjoys one of the most appealing locations in Santa Cruz, along one of the very narrow "kissing lanes." Above its elegant, antiques-filled lobby are 57 nondescript rooms with marble floors (Sb-€65-90, Db-€80-105, about €25 more for "superior" rooms with fancier decor, breakfast-€8.50, air-con, elevator, free Wi-Fi in lobby, bar across the street closes at midnight, Lope de Rueda 7, tel. 954-216-095, www.hotelmurillo.com, reservas @hotelmurillo.com). They also rent apartments with kitchens (Db-€90-120, see website for details).

$ Pensión Córdoba, a homier and cheaper option, has 12 tidy, quiet rooms, solid modern furniture, and a showpiece tiled courtyard (S-€30-40, Sb-€40-50, D-€45-55, Db-€60-70, no breakfast, cash only, air-con, free Internet access and Wi-Fi in

SEVILLA

Sevilla Hotels,

TO MUSEO DE BELLAS ARTES

LA MAGDALENA

TO ARMAS BUS STN.

TO April Fair Fairgrounds

Hotels

1 Hotel Alminar & Auditorio Álvarez Quintero

2 Hotel San Francisco

3 Hotel Vincci La Rábida & Laundry

4 Hotel Taberna del Alabardero

5 Hotel Maestranza

6 To Oasis Backpackers Hostel

Restaurants & Flamenco

7 Bar Bistec & Taberna La Plazuela

8 Bar Santa Ana

9 Restaurante Río Grande

10 El Faro de Triana & La Taberna del Pescador

11 Bodega Restaurante La María

Restaurants, & Flamenco

12 Horno San Buenaventura
13 Bodega Morales & Freiduría La Isla
14 Bodega Paco Góngora
15 Cafetería Mesón Serranito
16 Marisquería Arenal Sevilla & Mercado del Arenal
17 Bar Restaurante Pepe Hillo
18 La Societé
19 Restaurante Enrique Becerra
20 Taberna del Alabardero
21 Tablao El Arenal (Flamenco)
22 El Patio Sevillano (Flamenco)
23 Lo Nuestro & Rejoneo Bars
24 El Torno Pastelería de Conventos

lobby, on a tiny lane off Calle Santa María la Blanca at Farnesio 12, tel. 954-227-498, www.pensioncordoba.com, reservas@pension cordoba.com, Ana and María).

$ Pensión San Benito Abad, with eight humble rooms, faces a traditional Sevilla courtyard buried at the end of a dead-end lane just off Plaza Santa María. The rooms are dark, with windows that open onto an inner courtyard. The hardworking owners don't speak English, but offer some of the most conveniently located cheap rooms in town (S-€25, D-€40, Db-€50, slightly cheaper if you don't use the air-con or heat, no breakfast, parking-€15, on a tiny lane next to Cano y Cueto garage at Calle Canarios 4, tel. 954-415-255, www.hostalsanbenito.com, hostalsanbenito@gmail .com, Charo and Tomás).

$ Samay Hostel, on a busy street a block from the edge of the Barrio Santa Cruz, is a youthful, well-run slumbermill with 90 beds in 23 rooms (Db-€25-32/person, bunk in 4- to 10-bed dorm-€15-18, includes linens, no breakfast but shared kitchen, air-con, elevator, free Internet access and Wi-Fi, laundry service, 24-hour reception, rooftop terrace, Menéndez Pelayo 13, tel. 955-100-160, www.samayhostels.com, Pablo).

Near the Cathedral

$$$ Hotel Alminar, plush and elegant, rents 12 fresh, slick, minimalist rooms (Sb-€60-95, Db-€95-125, superior Db with terrace-€115-155, extra bed-€25, breakfast-€6, air-con, elevator, free Internet access and Wi-Fi, just 100 yards from the cathedral at Álvarez Quintero 52, tel. 954-293-913, fax 954-212-197, www.hotel alminar.com, reservas@hotelalminar.com, run by well-dressed, never-stressed Francisco).

$$ Hotel San Francisco may have a classy facade, but inside its 17 rooms are sparsely decorated, with metal doors. It's centrally located, clean, and quiet, except for the noisy ground-floor room next to the TV and reception (Sb-€40-55, Db-€50-68, Tb-€62-80, no breakfast, air-con, elevator, small rooftop terrace with cathedral view, free Wi-Fi in lobby with loaner netbook, located on pedestrian street at Álvarez Quintero 38, tel. 954-501-541, www.san franciscoh.com, info@sanfranciscoh.com, Carlos).

West of Avenida de la Constitución

$$$ Hotel Vincci La Rábida, part of a big, impersonal hotel chain, offers four-star comfort with its 113 rooms, huge and inviting courtyard lounge, and powerful air-conditioning. Its pricing is dictated by a magical computer that has perfect price discrimination down to a science (see website for prices—rates can spike to €400 with high demand and dip to €80 during slow times, when that air-con is most welcome; elevator, pay Wi-Fi, Castelar 24, tel.

954-501-280, fax 954-216-600, www.vinccihoteles.com, larabida @vinccihoteles.com).

$$$ Hotel Taberna del Alabardero is unique, with only seven rooms occupying the top floor of a poet's mansion (above the recommended classy restaurant, Taberna del Alabardero). It's nicely located, a great value, and the ambience is perfectly circa 1900 (Db-€130-160, Db suite-€200-250, tax not included, 10 percent discount with this book in 2012, includes breakfast, air-con, elevator, free Wi-Fi, parking-€20, closed in Aug, Zaragoza 20, tel. 954-502-721, fax 954-563-666, www.tabernadelalabardero.es, hotel.alabardero@esh.es).

$$ Hotel Maestranza, sparkling with loving care and charm, has 18 small, clean, simple rooms well-located on a street just off Plaza Nueva. It feels elegant for the price. To escape the noise from the tapas bars below, ask for an interior room, especially on weekends (Sb-€41-53, Db-€57-87, family suite-€104-135, extra bed-€20, 5 percent cash discount, no breakfast, air-con, elevator, free Wi-Fi, Gamazo 12, tel. 954-561-070, fax 954-214-404, www.hotel maestranza.es, sevilla@hotelmaestranza.es, Antonio).

North of Plaza Nueva, Between Plaza de la Encarnación and Plaza de la Alfalfa

$ Oasis Backpackers Hostel is a good place for cheap beds and for hanging out and connecting with young backpackers. Each of the eight rooms, with four double bunks, comes with a modern bathroom and individual lockers. The rooftop terrace—with lounge chairs, a small pool, and adjacent kitchen—is well-used (€15-20/bed, includes breakfast, free Internet access, just off Plaza de la Encarnación behind the church at #29 1/2 on the tiny and quiet lane, tel. 954-293-777, www.hostelsoasis.com, sevilla @hostelsoasis.com). They also have popular branches in Granada, Málaga, and Lisbon.

Eating in Sevilla

Local soups, such as *salmorejo* (Córdoba-style super-thick gazpacho) and *ajo blanco* (almond-based with garlic), are tasty. A popular Andalusian meal is fried fish, particularly marinated *adobo*. I like *taquitos de merluza* (hake fish), but for a mix of fish, ask for *frito variado*.

Restaurants generally serve lunch from 13:00 to 16:00 and dinner from 20:00 until very late (Spaniards don't start dinner until about 21:00). If you're hungry for dinner before the locals are, do the tapas tango. Wash down your tapas with *fino* (chilled dry sherry) or the more refreshing *tinto de verano* ("summer red wine"), an Andalusian red wine with soda, like a mild sangria. A good, light white wine is *barbadillo.* And for a heavy red, always go for the Rioja.

Across the River in Triana

The colorful Triana district—on the west bank of the river, between the San Telmo and Isabel II bridges—is filled with rustic and fun eateries. The riverside and traffic-free Calle Betis is lined with a variety of places to eat, from fine riverside restaurants to sloppy fish joints. It also comes with good picnic and take-out opportunities for romantics.

Tapas in a Triana Neighborhood Joint

Bars along the river and the parallel street one block inland are good for tapas. Before sitting down, walk to the Santa Ana church (midway between the bridges, two blocks off the river), where tables spill onto the square behind the church (Plazuela de Santa Ana) in the shadow of the floodlit spire. It feels like the whole neighborhood is out celebrating.

Bar Bistec, with most of the square's tables, does grilled fish with gusto. They're enthusiastic about their cod fritters and calamari, and brag about their pigeon, quail, and snails in sauce. Consider the indoor seating and the fun at the bar before sitting out on the square (€8 half-*raciones,* €14 *raciones,* daily 11:30-16:00 & 20:00-24:00, Plazuela de Santa Ana, tel. 954-274-759).

Taberna La Plazuela is self-service, doing simpler fare with enticing €10 *tostones* (giant fancy Andalusian bruschetta, good for 3-4 people) and €2.30 *montaditos* (little sandwiches). Get what you want and grab a table on the leafy square. Ignore the printed menu and read the daily specials board (same hours and owners as Bar Bistec, above).

Bar Santa Ana, just a block away alongside the church, is a rustic neighborhood sports-and-bull bar with great seating on the street. Peruse the interior, draped in bullfighting and Weeping Virgin memorabilia. It's always busy with the neighborhood gang enjoying fun tapas like *delicia de solomillo* (tenderloin) and the bar's willingness to serve even cheap tapas at the outdoor tables. If you stand at the bar, they'll keep track of your bill by chalking it directly on the counter in front of you (long hours, typically closed one day per week—closed Sun during April Fair, facing the side of the church at Pureza 82, tel. 954-272-102).

Riverside Dinners in Triana

Restaurante Río Grande is your stuffy, candlelit-fancy option—*the* place for a restaurant dinner with properly attired waiters and a full menu rather than tapas. Dining on the terrace is less expensive and more casual (€10-20 starters, €15-25 main dishes, daily

13:00-16:00 & 20:00-24:00, air-con, 2-person minimum for house specialties—paella and rice dishes, also lots of seafood, next to the San Telmo Bridge, tel. 954-273-956).

El Faro de Triana is actually the old yellow bridge tower overlooking the Isabel II Bridge. While professional, it's less formal and quirkier than Río Grande. They offer inexpensive tapas, €7-9 half-*raciones*, €12-18 *raciones*, and grand views over the river from the top floor (the views are better than the food; some diners object to strong river aroma). Choose from four dining zones: rooftop, outdoor terrace just below the rooftop (perhaps the best), riverside metal tables on the sidewalk, and the bar. There's no cover charge, but they don't serve tapas on the roof or riverside (open daily, bar—8:00-24:00, restaurant—13:00-16:30 & 20:15-24:00, tel. 954-336-192).

La Taberna del Pescador, with tablecloths on its riverside tables, is a fancy dining option (€6-10 half-*raciones*, €12-15 *raciones*, daily 8:00-24:00, 50 yards from Puente de Isabel II on Calle Betis, tel. 954-330-069).

Bodega Restaurante La María also offers fine tablecloth-type restaurant seating on the riverside, but with a formal menu focusing on fresh fish and grilled meat rather than tapas (€5-10 half-*raciones*, €9-16 *raciones*, Wed-Mon 13:00-16:00 & 20:00-24:00, closed Tue, Calle Betis 12, tel. 954-338-461).

Near Recommended Hotels in Barrio Santa Cruz

These eateries—for tapas, dining, and cheaper eats—are handy to my recommended Barrio Santa Cruz accommodations.

Tapas

For tapas, the Barrio Santa Cruz is trendy and *romántico*. Plenty of atmospheric-but-touristy restaurants fill the neighborhood near the cathedral and along Calle Santa María la Blanca. From the cathedral, walk up Mateos Gago, where several classic old bars—with the day's tapas scrawled on chalkboards—keep tourists and locals well fed and watered. (Turn right at Mesón del Moro for several more.)

A block farther, you'll find **Bodega Santa Cruz** (a.k.a. **Las Columnas**), a popular, user-friendly standby with cheap, unpretentious tapas. You're not coming here for the food (which is basic), but for the bustling atmosphere, as locals and tourists alike crowd the place, inside and out, for hours on end. You can keep an eye on the busy kitchen from the bar, or hang out like a cowboy at the tiny stand-up tables out front. Separate chalkboards list €2 tapas and €2 *montaditos* (little sandwiches served on a bun).

SEVILLA

Las Teresas is a characteristic small bar draped in fun photos. It serves good tapas from a tight little menu. Prices at the bar and outside tables (for fun tourist-watching) are the same, but they serve tapas only at the bar. The hams (with little upside-down umbrellas that catch the dripping fat) are a reminder that the Spanish are enthusiastic about their cured-meat dishes (€3-4 tapas, €8-10 half-*raciones*, €14-19 *raciones*, open daily but sometimes closed during siesta, Calle Santa Teresa 2, tel. 954-213-069).

Cervecería Giralda is a long-established meeting place for locals. With an almost genteel tiled setting and stiff waiters, it has an upscale air. It's famous for its fine tapas, but feels particularly touristy (confirm prices, stick with straight items on menu rather than expensive trick specials proposed by waiters; daily 9:00-24:00, Mateos Gago 1).

Dining

Corral del Agua Restaurante, a romantic pink-tablecloth place with a smart interior and charming courtyard seating, serves fine Andalusian cuisine deep in the Barrio Santa Cruz (€7-12 starters, €16-23 main dishes, three-course lunch special with a glass of wine—€20, Mon-Sat 12:00-16:00 & 20:00-24:00, closed Sun, arrive early or reserve ahead, Calle Agua 6, tel. 954-224-841).

Restaurante Modesto is a local favorite serving pricey but top-notch Andalusian fare—especially fish—with a comfortable dining room and atmospheric outdoor seating in the bright, bustling square just outside the Barrio Santa Cruz. They offer creative, fun meals—look around before ordering—and a good €20 fixed-price lunch or dinner served by energetic, occasionally pushy waiters. Their €9 house salad is a meal, and their €15.10 *fritura modesto* (fried seafood plate) is popular (€7-15 starters, €12-20 main dishes, inside open daily 12:00-17:00 & 20:00-24:00, outside tables open daily 12:00-24:00, near Santa María la Blanca at Cano y Cueto 5, tel. 954-416-811). Across the street is the related **Modesto Tapas,** with stand-up tables and a more basic all-tapas menu (also with outdoor seating; at Cano y Cueto 2).

Eating Casually in Barrio Santa Cruz and Plaza Santa María la Blanca

Freiduría Puerta de la Carne and **Bar Restaurante El 3 de Oro** are a two-for-one operation. Freiduría is a fried-fish-to-go place, with great outdoor seating, while El 3 de Oro is a fancier restaurant across the street that serves fine wine or beer to the fry shop's outdoor tables. First go into the fry shop and order a cheap cone of tasty fried fish with a tomato salad. Study the photos of the various kinds of seafood available; *un quarto* (250 grams for €5-7) serves one person. Then head out front and flag down a server to order a drink (technically from the restaurant), all while enjoying a great outdoor setting—almost dining for the cost of a picnic (Freiduría open Mon-Sat 13:00-24:00, Sun lunch only; El 3 de Oro open Mon-Sat 13:00-16:30 & 19:30-24:00, Sun lunch only; Santa María la Blanca 34, tel. 954-426-820).

Restaurante San Marco offers reasonably priced pizza and fun, basic Italian cuisine under the arches of what was a Moorish bath in the Middle Ages (and a disco in the 1990s). The air-conditioned atmosphere feels upscale but is easygoing and family-friendly (€7-9 salads, pizza, and pasta; €10-17 meat dishes; daily 13:00-16:15 & 20:00-24:00, Calle Mesón del Moro 6, tel. 954-564-390).

Breakfast on Plaza Santa María la Blanca: Several nondescript places seem to keep travelers happy at breakfast time on the sunny main square near most of my recommended hotels. I like **Café Bar Carmela.** For the cost of a continental breakfast at your hotel (€5.50-7.50), you can have a hearty American-style breakfast on the square (easy menus, open from 9:30, Calle Santa María la Blanca 6, tel. 954-540-590).

Between the Cathedral and the River

I don't like the restaurants surrounding the cathedral, but many good places are just across Avenida de la Constitución. In the area between the cathedral and the river, you can find tapas, cheap eats, and fine dining.

Tapas

Calle García de Vinuesa leads past several colorful and cheap tapas places to a busy corner surrounded with happy eateries.

Horno San Buenaventura, across from the cathedral on the corner of García de Vinuesa and the Avenida, is a big, venerable bakery with a quiet dining room upstairs. Its slick, chrome-filled, spacious main floor is lined with long display cases of sandwiches and desserts. The tapas bar upstairs has table service only (open daily, light meals are posted by the door, avoid the frozen paella).

Bodega Morales, farther up Calle García de Vinuesa (at #11), oozes old Sevilla ambience. The front area is more of a drinking bar; for food, go in the back section (if it's crowded, use the separate entrance around the corner). Here, sitting among huge adobe jugs, you can munch tiny sandwiches *(montaditos)* and tapas. Both are the same price (€2 *montaditos,* €2 tapas, €6 half-*raciones*—order at the bar, Mon-Sat 12:00-16:00 & 20:00-24:00, closed Sun, tel. 954-22-1242).

Freiduría La Isla, across the street, has been frying fish since 1938 (they renovated a few years ago...and changed the oil). Along with *pescado frito* (€5.50-7.50), they also sell wonderful homemade potato chips and fried almonds. It's family-friendly, with an easy English menu. Try their €5.50 *adobo* (marinated shark) or *frito variado* for a fish sampler. It's pretty much all fried fish, except for a tomato and pepper dish and their €1.20 gazpacho, offered only in the summer (Mon 20:00-23:00, Tue-Sat 13:00-15:30 & 20:00-23:00, closed Sun).

Bodega Paco Góngora is colorful and a bit classier than most tapas bars, with a tight dining area and delightful tapas served at the bar. Its sit-down meals are well presented and reasonably priced (€2-5 tapas, €8-10 half-*raciones*, daily 12:00-16:00 & 20:00-24:00, ask for the English menu, off Plaza Nueva at Calle Padre Marchena 1, tel. 954-214-139).

Mesón Serranito has a long hall with a mural-tile bar and ham hocks on one side, and bulls' heads over tables on the other. It's relatively spacious and typically full of happily munching locals (€8-9 *platos combinados,* daily 12:00-24:00, Antonia Díaz 11, tel. 954-211-243).

Cheap Eats at the Market Hall

Mercado del Arenal, the covered fish-and-produce market, is ideal for both snapping photos and grabbing a cheap lunch. As with most markets, you'll find characteristic little diners with prices designed to lure in savvy shoppers, not to mention a crispy fresh world of picnic goodies—and a riverside promenade with benches just a block away (Mon-Sat 9:00-14:30, closed Sun, sleepy on Mon, on Calle Pastor y Landero at Calle Arenal, just beyond bullring). There's also a fancier fish restaurant in the market with a great lunch deal (see Taberna del Alabardero, in next section).

Dining Between the Cathedral, Plaza Nueva, and the River

Marisquería Arenal Sevilla is a popular fish restaurant that thrives in the middle of the Arenal Market. When the market closes (daily at 14:30), this eatery stays open. You'll be eating in the empty Industrial Age market with workers dragging their crates around. It's a great family-friendly, finger-licking-good scene much appreciated by its enthusiastic local following. Fish is priced by weight, so be careful when ordering, and always double-check the bill (€6-18 fish plates, generally open 13:00-17:00 & 21:00-24:00, closed Sun night and all day Mon, reservations smart for dinner, Mercado del Arenal, enter on Calle Pastor y Landero 9, tel. 954-220-881).

Bar Restaurante Pepe Hillo is an appealing, trendy-yet-accessible hangout serving upscale bar food with a bull motif, across from the bullring (and, therefore, riotous after fights). One side is a youthful tapas bar, while the other side is a delightful, relatively calm oasis. Both share the same inviting menu (in English), with big €8 half-*raciones*, €10-13 *raciones*, creative house specialties, and a good wine list—but no tapas (daily 12:00-24:00 but dining room closes in mid-afternoon, enter on Calle Pastor y Landero, Adriano 24, tel. 954-215-390).

La Societé is an antidote for the same old variations-on-a-theme Sevillan tapas bars. With a sleek, Ikea-mod ambience and a long chalkboard menu of €3 *montaditos* (sandwiches), it's a welcome break (€3-5 tapas, €6-9 half-*raciones*, €10-12 *raciones*, daily 12:00-17:00 & 20:00-24:00, Adriano 8).

Restaurante Enrique Becerra is a fancy little 10-table place popular with local foodies. It's well known for its gourmet Andalusian cuisine and fine wine. Muscle past the well-dressed locals at the tapas bar for gourmet snacks and wine by the glass, or head to the quieter upstairs dining room. While the restaurant satisfies its guests with quality food, given the tight seating and its popularity with tourists, it can feel like a trap (€3-4 tapas available only at the bar, otherwise €11-18 starters and €18-26 main dishes, Mon-Sat 13:00-16:30 & 20:00-24:00, closed Sun, reservations essential, Gamazo 2, tel. 954-213-049).

Taberna del Alabardero, one of Sevilla's finest restaurants, serves refined Spanish cuisine in chandeliered elegance just a couple of blocks from the cathedral. If you order à la carte, it adds up to about €45 a meal, but for €48 (or €58 with wine) you can have a fun seven-course fixed-price meal with lots of little surprises from the chef. Or consider their €18/person (no sharing) starter sampler, followed by an entrée. The service in the fancy upstairs dining rooms gets mixed reviews (carefully read and understand your bill)...but the setting is stunning (daily 13:00-16:30 & 20:00-24:00, closed Aug, air-con, reservations smart, Zaragoza 20, tel. 954-502-721).

Taberna del Alabardero Student-Served Lunch: The ground-floor dining rooms (elegant but nothing like upstairs) are popular with local office workers for a great-value, student-chef-prepared, fixed-price lunch sampler (three delightful courses-€13 Mon-Fri, €18 Sat-Sun; €20 dinner available daily, drinks not included, open daily 13:00-16:30 & 20:00-23:30). To avoid a wait, arrive before 14:00 (no reservations possible).

Sevilla Connections

Note that many destinations are well served by both trains and buses.

By Train
From Sevilla by AVE Train to Madrid: The AVE express train is expensive (€81, €8 cheaper during off-peak times, minimum

€10.35 reservation fee with railpass) but fast (2.5 hours to Madrid; hourly departures 7:00-23:00). Departures between 16:00 and 19:00 can book up far in advance, but surprise holidays and long weekends can totally jam up trains as well—reserve as far ahead as possible.

From Sevilla by Train to Córdoba: There are three options for this journey: slow and cheap **regional** trains (8/day, 80 minutes, €11), fast and cheap regional high-speed **Avant** trains (9/day, 45 minutes, €17, requires reservation), and fast and expensive **AVE** trains en route to Madrid (19/day, 45 minutes, €34, requires reservation). Unless you must be on a particular departure, there's no reason to pay double for AVE; Avant is just as quick and half the price. (If you have a railpasss, you still must buy a reservation: €6.50 for Avant or €10.35 for AVE.)

Other Trains from Sevilla to: Málaga (6/day, 2 hours on AVE or Avant; 6/day, 2.5 hours on slower regional trains), **Ronda** (2/day, 4 hours, transfer in Bobadilla), **Granada** (4/day, 3 hours), **Jerez** (12/day, 1.25 hours), **Barcelona** (2/day, 5.5 hours; plus one slow train, 12 hours), **Algeciras** (3/day, 5 hours, transfer at Córdoba, Antequera, or Bobadilla). Trains run to **Lisbon,** Portugal, but they take a long time, since they go through Madrid; buses to Lisbon are far better (see later). Train info: toll tel. 902-320-320, www.renfe.com.

By Bus

Sevilla has two bus stations: The El Prado station, just south of the Alcázar, primarily serves regional destinations; the Plaza de Armas station, farther north (near the bullring), handles most long-distance buses. Bus info: tel. 954-908-040 but rarely answered, go to TI for latest schedule info.

From Sevilla's El Prado station to Andalucía and the South Coast: Regional buses are operated by Comes (www.tgcomes.es), Los Amarillos (www.losamarillos.es), and Linesur (www.linesur.com). Connections to **Jerez** are frequent, as many southbound buses head there first (7-10/day, 1.5 hours, run by all three companies; note that train is also possible—see above). Los Amarillos runs buses to some of Andalucía's hill towns, including **Ronda** (3 *directo* buses/day take 2 hours, 5 others go via Villamartín and take 2.5 hours) and **Arcos** (2/day, 2 hours; many more departures possible with a transfer in Jerez). For the South Coast, a handy Comes bus departs Sevilla four times a day and heads for **Tarifa** (2.5-3.25 hours), **Algeciras** (3.5-4 hours), and **La Línea/Gibraltar** (4-4.5 hours). However, if **Algeciras** is your goal, Linesur has a much faster direct connection (7-8/day, 2.5 hours). There's also one bus a day from this station to **Granada** (2.5 hours); the rest depart from the Plaza de Armas station.

From Sevilla's Plaza de Armas station to: Madrid (departures generally on the hour, 6 hours, €20, tel. 902-229-292), **Córdoba** (7/day, 2.5 hours), **Granada** (9/day, 3.5 hours *directo, ruta* buses take about 10 minutes more), **Málaga** (6/day direct, 2.5-3 hours, connects to Nerja), **Nerja** (2/day, 4.75 hours), **Barcelona** (2/day, 16.5 hours, including one overnight bus). Information: tel. 902-450-550.

By Bus to Portugal: The best way to get to **Lisbon,** Portugal, is by bus (Alsa and Eurolines share a twice-daily service, departures at 15:00 and 24:00, 7 hours, €35, departs Plaza de Armas station, tel. 954-905-102, www.alsa.es). The midnight departure continues past Lisbon to **Coimbra** (arriving 10:30) and **Porto** (arriving 12:15). Sevilla also has direct bus service to **Lagos,** Portugal, on the Algarve (4/day in summer, 2/day off-season, about 6 hours, €20, buy ticket a day or two in advance May-Oct, tel. 954-907-737, www.damas-sa.es). The bus departs from Sevilla's Plaza de Armas bus station and arrives at the Lagos bus station. If you'd like to visit Tavira on the way to Lagos, purchase a bus ticket to Tavira, have lunch there, then take the train to Lagos.

GRANADA

For a time, Granada was the grandest city in Spain. But after the tumult that came with the change from Moorish to Christian rule, it lost its power and settled into a long slumber. Today, Granada seems to specialize in evocative history and good living. Settle down in the old center and explore monuments of the Moorish civilization and its conquest. Taste the treats of a North African–flavored culture that survives here today.

Compared to other Spanish cities its size, Granada is delightfully cosmopolitan—it's worked hard to accept a range of cultures, and you'll see far more ethnic restaurants here than elsewhere in Andalucía. Its large student population (70,000 students, including more than 10,000 from abroad) also lends it a youthful zest. The Grenadine people are serious about hospitality, and have earned a reputation among travelers for being particularly friendly and eager to help you enjoy their historic city.

Granada's magnificent Alhambra fortress was the last stronghold of the Moorish kingdom in Spain. The city's exotically tangled Moorish quarter, the Albayzín, invites exploration. From its viewpoints, romantics can enjoy the sunset and evening views of the grand, floodlit Alhambra.

An old Spanish saying goes, "Give him a coin, woman, for there is nothing worse in this life than to be blind in Granada." This city has much to see, yet it reveals itself in unpredictable ways; it takes a poet to sort through and assemble the jumbled shards of Granada. Peer through the intricate lattice of a Moorish window. Hear water burbling unseen among the labyrinthine hedges of the Generalife Gardens. Listen to a flute trilling deep in the swirl of alleys around the cathedral. Don't be blind in Granada—open all your senses.

Planning Your Time

Granada is worth two days and two nights, but you could conceivably hit its highlights in one very busy day. No matter what, reserve in advance for the Alhambra—at least several days, or, better, several weeks ahead.

If you only have one full day here, you could fit in the top sights by following this intense plan: In the morning, stroll the Pescadería market streets and follow my self-guided walk of the old town (or catch the 10:30 Cicerone walking tour), including a visit to the cathedral and its Royal Chapel. After a quick lunch, do the Alhambra in the afternoon (reservation essential). Hike the hippie lane into the Albayzín Moorish quarter (or catch minibus #31 or #32) to the San Nicolás viewpoint for the magic hour before sunset, then find the right place for a suitably late dinner (taxi home for safety if in the Albayzín late). This is an extremely ambitious one-day plan; if you can spread it over two days, you'll be able to slow down and smell the incense (or make the most of one and a half days—e.g., if you're arriving in the early afternoon, do the self-guided walk before dinner).

When you're ready to move on, consider heading to nearby Nerja, the Costa del Sol's best beach town (1.5 hours by car, 2-2.5 hours by bus). You can also get to White Hill Towns such as Ronda (2.5 hours by train). Sevilla is an easy 2.5-hour train ride away. The Madrid–Granada train service is slow (5 hours), but passes through beautiful countryside.

Orientation to Granada

Modern Granada sprawls (300,000 people), but its sights are all within a 20-minute walk of Plaza Nueva, where dogs wag their
tails to the rhythm of modern hippies and street musicians. Most of my recommended hotels are within a few blocks of Plaza Nueva. Make this the hub of your Granada visit.

Plaza Nueva was a main square back when kings called Granada home. This historic center is in the Darro River Valley, which separates two hills (the river now flows under the square). On one hill is the great Moorish palace, the Alhambra, and on the other is the best-preserved Moorish quarter in Spain, the Albayzín. To the southwest are the cathedral,

Greater Granada

TO BUS STN.

TO AIRPORT

TO CARTHUSIAN MONASTERY

¼ MILE

.5 KM

AV. CONSTITUCIÓN

ANCHA DE CAPUCHINOS

REAL DE CARTUJA

VIEW

TRAIN STATION

PLAZA TRIUNFO

MURCIA

PAGES

PLAZA LARGA

SACRO-MONTE

GRAN VÍA DE COLÓN

ALHACABA

PAN.

CUESTA DEL

OLD WALL

SAN NICOLÁS

CAMINO DEL SACRO-MONTE

A L B A Y Z Í N

CHAPIN

CALD NUEVA SAN GREG.

PASEO DE LOS TRISTES

DARRO RIVER

CATHEDRAL & ROYAL CHAPEL

CALD VIEJA

C. DEL DARRO

PALACIOS NAZARIES

PLAZA DE BIB-RAMBLA

GOMÉREZ

ALHAMBRA

GENERA-LIFE

PLAZA DEL CARMEN

PLAZA NUEVA

JUSTICE GATE ENTRANCE

PUERTA REAL

PLAZA ISABEL LA CATÓLICA

MAIN ENTRANCE

RECOGIDAS

PCH

TO FREEWAY

= HISTORIC CITY CENTER-SEE DETAIL MAPS

Royal Chapel, and Alcaicería (Moorish market), where the city's two main drags—Gran Vía de Colón (often just called "Gran Vía" by locals) and Calle Reyes Católicos—lead away into the modern city.

Tourist Information

The main TI is tucked away just above Plaza Nueva on Santa Ana (Mon-Fri 9:00-19:30, Sat-Sun 9:30-15:00, above the church, tel. 958-575-202). Another TI is at the entrance of the Alhambra, inside the ticket office (mid-March-mid-Oct Mon-Fri 8:00-20:00, Sat 8:00-19:00, Sun 8:00-13:30, off-season closes at 18:00 on weekdays, tel. 958-544-002). Get a free city map and the *Pocket Guía* magazine in easy Spanish, and verify your Alhambra plans. To save yourself a trip to the train or bus stations, get schedule information here; both TIs post all departures on their walls. These TIs cover not only Granada, but also Andalucía (pick up good, free maps for wherever else you're going in the region). A municipal TI, which covers only Granada, is inside City Hall on Plaza del Carmen, a short walk from the cathedral; they also sell the Bono Turístico city pass described later (Mon-Sat 10:00-19:00, Sun 10:00-14:00, tel. 958-248-280).

Alhambra Info: While any TI has information on the town's top sight, the very helpful info desk just inside the door of the official Alhambra bookstore (Tienda Librería de la Alhambra) is your best resource, as it's run by the Alhambra administration and is located right in the heart of town. The counter sells Alhambra tickets for future dates (no same-day sales) and has a ServiCaixa machine for printing pre-booked tickets (daily 9:30-20:30, between Plaza Isabel La Católica and Plaza Nueva at Calle Reyes Católicos 40, tel. 958-227-846).

Arrival in Granada

By Train: Granada's modest train station is connected to the center by frequent buses, a €7 taxi ride, or a 30-minute walk down Avenida de la Constitución and Gran Vía. The train station does not have luggage storage. If your itinerary is set, reserve your train out upon arrival.

Taxis wait out front, and it's a three-minute walk to reach the bus stop: Exiting the train station, walk straight ahead down the tree-lined Avenida Andaluces. At the first major intersection, turn right onto Avenida de la Constitución, and within a block you'll see a series of bus stops with routes marked on the signposts. Most of these buses stop at the cathedral (Gran Vía 1), which is four stops from the train station and the nearest stop to Plaza Nueva. Check the easy-to-read routes for the "Gran Vía 1" stop (your options include buses #1, #3, #4, #5, #6, #7, #8, #9, and others). An electronic board shows how long the wait is for each bus. When you board, buy a €1.20 ticket from the driver. For Plaza Nueva and most of my recommended hotels, get off at the cathedral (ask, "¿Catedral?"—kah-tay-DRAHL); cross the busy Gran Vía and walk three short blocks to Plaza Nueva.

By Bus: Located on the city outskirts, Granada's bus station (estación de autobuses) has a good and cheap cafeteria, ATMs, luggage lockers (€3.50), coin-op Internet access, and a privately run tourist agency masquerading as a TI—all of these are downstairs, where you exit the buses. Upstairs is the main arrivals hall with ticket windows, automated ticket machines, and a helpful information counter in the main hall that hands out printed schedules for each route. All buses are operated by Alsa (tel. 902-422-242, www.alsa.es).

To get from the bus station to the city center, either take a 10-minute taxi ride (€8) or bus #3 or #33 (€1.20, pay driver). It's about a 20-minute bus ride; nearing the center, the bus goes up Gran Vía. For Plaza Nueva, get off at the "Gran Vía 1" stop near the cathedral (cathedral not visible from bus, ask, "¿Catedral?"—

kah-tay-DRAHL), a half-block before the grand square called Plaza Isabel La Católica. From here, it's a short three-block walk to Plaza Nueva and most of my recommended hotels.

By Car: Driving in Granada's historic center is restricted to buses, taxis, and (technically) tourists with hotel reservations. Signs

are posted to this effect, and entrances are strictly controlled—but generally not by an officer. Hidden cameras snap a photo of your license plate as soon as you enter the restricted zone. Getting into the old center and finding your hotel or a parking garage is a major frustration because of these strict controls and the many one-way streets. Many hoteliers recommend simply not driving in the historic center. However, if you choose to drive, here's what to do: Contact your hotelier in advance with your license-plate number (usually a couple of days is enough), and they'll contact the police department to register your car, preventing a nasty surprise when you return your rental car. Be sure to ask your hotelier for detailed driving instructions into the historic center, then follow them exactly. Each hotel district has a strict route that their guests must follow; any deviations are caught by cameras and result in fines. Some hoteliers have deals with nearby garages and provide directions to those spots.

If, upon arrival in Granada, you're driving directly to the Alhambra, you can easily avoid the historic center.

By Plane: Granada's sleepy airport, which serves only a dozen or so planes a day, is about 10 miles west of the city center. To get between the airport and downtown, you can take a taxi (€25) or, much cheaper, the airport bus, timed to leave when flights arrive and depart (€3, 12/day, 40 minutes). If you're leaving from the town center, use the bus stop at Gran Vía del Colón, nearly across from the cathedral. Airport info: tel. 958-245-223 (press "9" for English).

Helpful Hints

Theft Alert: Roma (Gypsy) women, usually hanging out near the cathedral and Alcaicería, will accost you with sprigs of rosemary. The twig is free...and then they grab your hand and read your fortune for a tip. Coins are "bad luck," so the minimum payment they'll accept is €5. Don't make eye contact, don't accept a sprig, and say firmly but politely, *"No, gracias."* Though aggressive (especially in the morning), these Spanish Roma are harmless. Locals warn that Gypsies from Romania (who tend to have gold teeth) are more likely to be pickpockets. In general, be on guard for pickpockets, especially late at night in the Albayzín. Your biggest threat is being conned while enjoying drinks and music in Sacromonte.

City Pass: The **Bono Turístico** city pass covers the Alhambra, cathedral, Royal Chapel, Carthusian Monastery, and several trips on city buses, plus minor sights and discounts on others (€25/3 days, €30/5 days—this version also includes CitySightseeing bus, www.bonoturisticogranada.com). When you buy your pass, the vendor schedules a time for your Alhambra visit. Note that 300 Alhambra reservations each day are allotted to Bono Turístico buyers; if all 300 have already been claimed—which is very rare—it's possible that you won't get a time. Be sure that slots are available before you buy the pass.

Passes are sold at the TI in City Hall on Plaza del Carmen, at the Caja Granada Bank branch in Plaza Isabel La Católica, and at the "This is Granada" kiosk on Plaza Nueva. You can also buy a pass and book your Alhambra palace visit in advance online (http://caja.caja-granada.es; click "Inform. y Compra Bono Turístico"). Fancier hotels provide one free pass per room for stays of two or more nights; check with your hotel before buying a pass yourself.

The local TI is working on creating a **new combo-ticket** that will allow you to pick and choose which specific sights are included (for details, ask at the TI).

Festivals and Concerts: From late June to early July, the **International Festival of Music and Dance** offers classical music, ballet, flamenco, and zarzuela (light opera) nightly in the Alhambra at reasonable prices. The ticket office is located in the Corral del Carbón (open mid-April-Oct). Beginning in February, you can also book tickets online at www.granadafestival.org. This festival is one of the most respected and popular in Spain, and tickets for major performers typically sell out months in advance. During the festival, flamenco is free every night at midnight; ask the ticket office or TI for the venue.

From fall through spring, the **City of Granada Orchestra** offers popular concerts—mostly on weekends—that generally sell out quickly (€6-23, late Sept-mid-May only, Auditorio Manuel de Falla, ticket office in Corral del Carbón, Mon-Fri 12:00-14:00 & 17:00-19:00, Sat 12:00-14:00, closed Sun, tel. 958-221-144, www.orquestaciudadgranada.es).

Internet Access: Almost all Granada hotels have Wi-Fi for their guests, and some have computers for use as well. Many

Internet points are scattered throughout Granada, often part of *locutorios* (call centers).

Laundry: Tintorería-Lavandería Duquesa, a few blocks west of the cathedral area, offers a pricey service to wash, dry, and fold your clothes (€10/small load, same-day service possible if you bring it in the morning, no self-service, Mon-Fri 9:30-14:00 & 17:00-21:00, Sat 9:30-14:00, closed Sun, Duquesa 24, tel. 958-280-685).

Post Office: It's on Puerta Real (Mon-Fri 8:30-20:30, Sat 9:30-14:00, closed Sun, tel. 958-221-138).

Travel Agencies: All travel agencies book flights, and many also sell long-distance bus and train tickets. Mega-chain **El Corte Inglés** sells plane, train, and bus tickets (Mon-Sat 10:00-22:00, closed Sun, Acera del Darro, floor 2, tel. 958-282-612).

Getting Around Granada

With cheap taxis, frisky minibuses, good city buses, and nearly all points of interest an easy walk from Plaza Nueva, you'll get around Granada easily.

Tickets for minibuses and city buses cost €1.20 per ride (buy from driver). Credibus magnetic cards save you money if you'll be riding often—or, since they're shareable, if you're part of a group (€5/7 trips, €10/16 trips, plus €2 for each card issued). You can buy these from the driver as well. To get a €5 card, ask for *"un bono de cinco euros."* For a €10 card, request *"un bono de diez euros."* These are valid on minibuses and city buses (no fee for connecting bus if you transfer within 45 minutes).

By Minibus: Handy little made-for-tourists red minibuses, which cover the city center, depart every few minutes from Plaza Nueva and Plaza Isabel La Católica until late in the evening (about 22:00 or 23:00). Here are several handy minibus routes to look for:

Bus #32 is the best for a trip up to the Alhambra, connecting the Alhambra and Albayzín (from Plaza Isabel La Católica, the bus goes up to the Alhambra, returns to Plaza Isabel La Católica, then loops through Plaza Nueva on its way up to the Albayzín and back down Gran Vía del Colón).

Bus #31 does the Albayzín loop, departing from Plaza Nueva.

Bus #35 follows the same route as #31, but also makes a side-trip into Sacromonte. It runs less frequently (every 30-40 minutes).

By City Bus: These are handy if you're visiting the Carthusian Monastery (bus #8) or going to the bus station (#3 or #33) or train station (#3-#9).

Granada at a Glance

▲▲▲**The Alhambra** The last and greatest Moorish palace, highlighting the splendor of that civilization in the 13th and 14th centuries. Reservations are a must if you plan to visit during the day. **Hours:** The entire complex is open daily mid-March-mid-Oct 8:30-20:00, off-season 8:30-18:00. Palacios Nazaries and Generalife Gardens are open for nighttime visits mid-March-mid-Oct Tue-Sat 22:00-23:30, closed Sun-Mon; off-season Fri-Sat 20:00-21:30, closed Sun-Thu. See page 87.

▲▲**Royal Chapel** Lavish 16th-century Plateresque Gothic chapel with the tombs of Queen Isabel and King Ferdinand. **Hours:** March-Oct daily 10:15-13:30 & 16:00-19:30 except opens at 11:00 on Sun; in Nov-Feb daily 10:15-13:30 & 15:30-18:30 but opens at 11:00 on Sun. See page 104.

▲▲**San Nicolás Viewpoint** Breathtaking vista over the Alhambra and the Albayzín. **Hours:** Always open; best at sunset. See page 112.

▲**Cathedral** The second-largest cathedral in Spain, unusual for its bright Renaissance interior. **Hours:** April-Oct Mon-Sat 10:45-13:30 & 16:00-20:00, Sun 16:00-20:00; Nov-March until 19:00. See page 108.

▲**The Albayzín** Spain's best old Moorish quarter. **Hours:** Always open, but use caution after dark. See page 109.

▲**Cave Museum of Sacromonte** A center with caves and displays on Roma cave building, crafts, food, and music. **Hours:** April-Oct Tue-Sun 10:00-14:00 & 17:00-20:30, Nov-March Tue-Sun 10:00-14:00 & 16:00-19:00, closed Mon. See page 115.

Tours in Granada

Walking Tours—Cicerone, run by María and Rosa, offers informative 2.5-hour city tours. Their excellent guides describe the fitful and fascinating changes the city underwent as it morphed from a Moorish capital to a Christian one 500 years ago. While the tour doesn't enter any actual sights, it weaves together bits of the Moorish heritage that survive around the cathedral and the Albayzín. Tours start on Plaza de Bib-Rambla and finish on Plaza Nueva. Groups are small (may cancel if less than five show up, although you have the option of paying more for it to go); to help them gauge if there's enough interest, reservations are encouraged (though not required). Visits are generally only in English, but may

Alcaicería Tiny shopping lanes filled with tacky tourist shops. **Hours:** Always open, with shops open long hours. See page 82.

Corral del Carbón Granada's only surviving caravanserai (inn for traveling merchants), with impressive Moorish door. **Hours:** Always viewable. See page 80.

Paseo de los Tristes A prime strolling strip above the Darro River lined with eateries and peppered with Moorish history. **Hours:** Always open; best in the evenings. See page 85.

Hammam El Bañuelo 11th-century ruins of Moorish baths. **Hours:** Unreliably Tue-Sat 10:00-14:00, April-Sept opens at 9:00, closed Sun-Mon year-round. See page 86.

Great Mosque of Granada Islamic house of worship featuring a minaret with a live call to prayer, an information center for the Muslim perspective on Granada history, and a courtyard with commanding views. **Hours:** Daily 11:00-14:00 & 18:00-20:30. See page 113.

Hammam Baños Árabes Tranquil spot for soaks and massages in Arab baths. **Hours:** Daily 10:00-24:00. See page 109.

Zambra Dance Touristy flamenco-like dance performance in Sacromonte district. **Hours:** Shows generally daily at 22:00. See page 116.

Carthusian Monastery Lavish Baroque monastery on the outskirts of town. **Hours:** Daily April-Oct 10:00-13:00 & 16:00-20:00, Nov-March 10:00-13:00 & 15:00-18:00. See page 117.

be in both English and Spanish on slow days (€12, show this book to save €2, kids under 14 free, March-Oct Sun-Fri at 10:30, Nov-Feb Sun-Fri at 11:00, Sat tours are generally in Spanish only; to book a tour, visit the kiosk labeled *Meeting Point* on Plaza de Bib-Rambla—staffed by cheerful Alma, or call mobile 607-691-676, 670-541-669, or 600-412-051; www.ciceronegranada.com, reservas @ciceronegranada.com). They also offer tours of the Alhambra that include an entry time to Palacios Nazaries—handy if you have trouble getting a reservation on your own (€45-47, try to book at least 3-4 days ahead).

Local Guides—**Margarita Ortiz de Landazuri,** an English-speaking guide, is a charming and effective teacher (tel. 958-221-406, www.alhambratours.com, info@alhambratours.com).

GRANADA

Getting Tickets for the Alhambra's Palacios Nazaries

The Alhambra fortress's top sight is Palacios Nazaries, the Moorish palace. Sadly, many tourists never get to see it, because they didn't make reservations. Since only 300 visitors are allowed to enter per half-hour (in 50-person spurts every five minutes), it's critical to make a reservation as soon as you're ready to commit to a time (especially if you're visiting during Holy Week, on weekends, or on major holidays). During the off-season (July-Aug and winter), you might be able to walk right in—but it's not worth the risk. Getting a reservation is easy.

Get the **General Daytime Visit** ticket (described on page 87). Be careful not to accidentally buy a different type of ticket—this is the only one that lets you in Palacios Nazaries by day. It comes with a reservation to enter the palace at a certain time; for advice on timing your visit, see the sidebar on page 92.

Reserving in Advance: You can reserve up to three months in advance of your visit, in one of four ways: online, by phone, through your hotelier, and by buying a city pass. The first three ways come with a surcharge of about €1.30 (well worth it). If you order online or by phone, you'll still need to pick up a printed ticket once you're in Spain—it's not difficult, but make sure you bring both the same credit card that you used to book the reservation and its PIN code (every credit card has one; ask your bank if you don't know yours). If you run into trouble retrieving your ticket, your passport will come in handy—yet another reason to always keep it with you (tucked safely in a money belt).

Here are details on your reservation options:

• Order online at www.alhambra-tickets.es. This is easy and just takes a few minutes. On the first page, select "Buy Ticket" under the "General Daytime Visit" category. On the next page, select your date and time period—morning (De 8:30h a 14h) or afternoon (De 14h a 20h)—then the exact half-hour time window for entry into Palacios Nazaries (*Agotado* means "sold out"). Unless you're traveling with a child under 12 (*Niños menos 12 a*), ignore the "special offers" options and simply hit "Continue."

• Order by phone. Within Spain, dial 934-923-750 (or toll tel. 902-888-001; from the US, dial 011-34-934-923-750; phone answered Mon-Fri 8:00-21:00 Spanish time, not answered Sat-Sun; while you wait for an operator, a recording tells you the date of the next available tickets).

• When you book your room, ask if your hotelier can reserve Alhambra tickets; if so, request a time slot.

• Get a Bono Turístico pass, which covers the Alhambra (and most other sights—worthwhile for a two-day visit); book your Palacios Nazaries appointment when you buy it (see page 170).

Picking Up Tickets: If you bought your tickets online, you can print them anytime at one of Spain's many yellow ATM-like **ServiCaixa machines.** In downtown Granada, you'll find one inside the official Alhambra bookstore (between Plaza Isabel

La Católica and Plaza Nueva) and another at the La Caixa bank just a couple of blocks around the corner, across from the cathedral (at the corner of Gran Vía de Colón and Calle Carcel Baja). If your card isn't accepted by the machine, go to the downtown Alhambra bookstore's information desk, where they can print your tickets for you. Printing your tickets before arriving at the Alhambra saves time (see next) and walking (see "Justice Gate Shortcut Entrance," page 90).

If you arrive at the Alhambra without printed tickets, go to the main entrance about an hour before your Palacios Nazaríes appointment, since the line to pick up tickets may require a wait of up to 20 minutes, and walking from the ticket office to the palace takes 15 minutes. Don't forget to bring the right credit card, its PIN number, and (to be safe) your passport. If you reserved your tickets online, follow *Bookings collection with credit card* signs (after passing the bookstore on your right and café on your left, you'll see a series of yellow ServiCaixa machines; English-speaking staff are usually on hand to help). Otherwise, wait in line to pick up your reserved tickets at the windows marked *Retirada de Reservas* (next to the much longer *Venta Directa* line).

If You're in Granada Without a Palace Reservation: You still have a number of options.

• Ask your hotel if they can book a reservation for you.

• Check www.alhambra-tickets.es, and cross your fingers.

• Drop by the downtown Alhambra bookstore at least a day ahead of your palace visit (they can't sell same-day tickets).

• Buy a Bono Turístico city pass, which comes with a reservation for the palace (same-day reservations may be available; for details, see "Helpful Hints," page 73).

• Wake up early and stand in line. The Alhambra admits about 7,700 visitors a day. While the vast majority of tickets are sold in advance, some same-day tickets are sold each day at the Alhambra ticket office (the number changes daily). The window labeled *Venta Directa,* for cash-only, same-day tickets, is where most early-risers line up. Smart visitors avoid the line by using the yellow ServiCaixa machines (beyond the bookstore and café), which issue same-day tickets (starting at the same time the ticket windows open). Go as early as you can. During the busy months, if you're in line by about 7:30, you'll likely get an entry time, probably for later that day. On a slow day, you'll get in right away. On an extremely busy day, however (such as over Easter weekend), lining up at 5:30 still doesn't guarantee you a ticket. A PA system and screens above the ticket-office door provide periodic updates on how many tickets are left for the day—which can help you judge whether it's worth waiting in line.

• Take a tour of the Alhambra (see "Tours," pages 76 and 90).

• See the Generalife Gardens and Alcazaba fort by day (these don't sell out), then return to visit Palacios Nazaríes at night (see "The Alhambra by Moonlight" on page 93).

If Margarita is busy, her partner, Miguel Ángel, and her cousin, Patricia Ortiz de Landazuri Quero (patlandazuri@yahoo.es, tel. 619-053-972), are also very good. Guide rates are standard (€130/2.5 hours, €260/day).

Hop-On, Hop-Off Bus Tour—CitySightseeing operates a route with 11 stops around the city, including Gran Vía de Colón (in front of the cathedral), at the Alhambra, and at the Carthusian Monastery. However, the bus concentrates on far-flung areas that are far less interesting than the easy-to-walk city center (€18, 9:30-20:00 in summer, 9:30-18:00 in winter, tel. 958-535-028).

This is Granada Audio Tour—You can rent an MP3 player pre-loaded with four different walking-tour itineraries around the city, including the Alhambra. Two people get the system for up to three days for €15 (maybe longer off-season; rent from "This is Granada" kiosk on Plaza Nueva, includes map, tel. 958-210-239).

Olive Oil Tour—This company helps you explore Granada's countryside and taste some local olive oil. Choose between a three-hour tour that departs in the morning or afternoon (€38) or a six-hour tour that includes lunch (€55). Tours are in English, and a driver will pick you up at your hotel (tel. 958-559-643, mobile 651-147-504, www.oliveoiltour.com, reservas@oliveoiltour.com).

Self-Guided Walk

▲▲The Transition from Moorish to Christian

This short walk serves as an orientation to the old town, and covers all the essential sights beyond the Alhambra. Along the way, we'll see vivid evidence of the dramatic changes brought about by the Reconquista, the long and ultimately successful battle to retake Spain from the Moors and re-establish Christian rule.

• *Start at Corral del Carbón, near Plaza del Carmen.*

❶ **Corral del Carbón:** A caravanserai (of Silk Road fame) was a protected place for merchants to rest their camels, spend the night, get a bite to eat, and spin yarns. This, the only surviving caravanserai of Granada's original 14, was just a block away from the silk market (Alcaicería; the next stop on this walk). Stepping through the caravanserai's grand Moorish door, you find a square with 14th-century Moorish brick- work surrounding a water fountain. This plain-yet-elegant struc- ture evokes the times when traders would gather here with exotic goods and swap tales from across the Muslim world.

It's a common mistake to think of the Muslim Moors as

Granada's Old Town Walk

(B) **Bus Stop** w/ #s
#32 To Alhambra
#31 & #35 To Albayzín

P **Parking**

(T) **Taxi Stand**

→ **Entry Point to Sights**

To Train & Bus Stations

100 YARDS
100 METERS

ALBAYZÍN
MOORISH QUARTER

MERCADO SAN AGUSTÍN

GRAN VIA DE COLÓN

CALLE

VAL

CALD. NUEVA

S. GREGORIO

To San Nicolás Viewpoint & Plaza Larga

To Sacramonte

CATHEDRAL & ROYAL CHAPEL

PL. PESC.

CETTI

ELVIRA

COSTA

CALD. VIEJA

CARCEL ALTA

AIRE

DARRO

ALMIR.

PLAZA NUEVA

PL. S. ANA

OFICIOS

LA MADRAZA

ABER

PAN.

PLAZA DE BIB-RAMBLA

ERMITA ZACATIN

PLAZA ISABEL LA CATÓLICA

CUCH.

S. ANA

CUESTA GOMÉREZ

ARAB BATHS

REYES CATÓLICOS

#32 (B)

ANIMAS

PAVANERAS

CALLE

PLAZA DEL CARMEN

NAVAS

CITY HALL

PANERA

To Alhambra

PUERTA REAL

#31 & #35 (B)

START

Walk

1 Corral del Carbón
2 Alcaicería
3 Plaza de Bib-Rambla
4 Cathedral
5 Royal Chapel Square
6 Plaza Isabel La Católica
7 Plaza Nueva
8 To Paseo de los Tristes & Moorish Baths

Other

9 Alhambra Bookstore, Info & Servi-Caixa Machine (Alhambra Tickets)
10 ServiCaixa Machine
11 Bus from Train & Bus Stations
12 Bus to Train & Bus Stations; Airport

GRANADA

somehow not Spanish. They lived here for seven centuries and were really just as "indigenous" as the Romans, Goths, and Celts. While the Moors were Muslim, they were no more connected to Arabia than they were to France.

After the Reconquista, this space was used as a coal storage facility (hence "del Carbón"). These days it houses two offices where you can buy tickets for musical events.

• *From the caravanserai, exit straight ahead and walk down Puente del Carbón to the big street named Calle Reyes Católicos (for the*

"Catholic Monarchs" Ferdinand and Isabel, who finally conquered the Moors). The street covers a river that once ran openly here, with a series of bridges (like the "Coal Bridge," Puente del Carbón) lacing together the two parts of town. Continue one block farther to the yellow gate marked Alcaicería. The pedestrian street you're crossing, Zacatín, was the main drag, which ran parallel to the river before it was covered. Today it's a favorite paseo destination, busy each evening with strollers. Pass through the Alcaicería gate and walk 20 yards into the old market to the first intersection.

❷ **Alcaicería:** Originally a Moorish silk market with 200 shops, the Alcaicería (al-kai-thay-REE-ah) was filled with precious

salt, silver, spices, and silk. It had 10 armed gates and its own guards. Silk was huge in Moorish times, and silkworm-friendly mulberry trees flourished in the countryside. It was such an important product that the sultans controlled and guarded it by constructing this fine, fortified market. After the Reconquista, the Christians realized this market was good for business and didn't mess with it. Later, the more zealous Philip II had it shut down. A terrible fire in 1850 destroyed what was left. Today's Alcaicería was rebuilt in the late 1800s as a tourist souk (marketplace) to complement the romantic image of Granada popularized by the writings of Washington Irving.

Explore the mesh of tiny shopping lanes: overpriced trinkets, popcorn machines popping, men selling balloons, leather goods spread out on streets, kids playing soccer, barking dogs, dogged shoe-shine boys, and the whirring grind of bicycle-powered knife sharpeners. You'll invariably meet obnoxious and persistent Gypsy women pushing their sprigs on innocents in order to extort money. Be strong.

• *Turn left down Ermita lane. After 50 yards, leave the market via another fortified gate and enter a big square. The Neptune fountain marks the center of the...*

❸ **Plaza de Bib-Rambla:** This exuberant square, just two blocks behind the cathedral (from the fountain you can see its blocky spire peeking above the big orange building) was once the center of Moorish Granada. While Moorish rule of Spain lasted 700 years, the last couple of those centuries were a period of decline as Muslim culture split under weak leadership and Christian forces grew more determined. The last remnants of the Moorish kingdom united and ruled from Granada. As Muslims fled south from reconquered lands, Granada was flooded with refugees. By 1400 Granada had 120,000 people—huge for medieval Europe. This was the main square, the focal point of market and festivals, but it was much smaller then than now, pushed in by the jam-packed city.

Under Christian rule, Moors and Jews were initially tolerated (as they were considered good for business), and this area became the Moorish ghetto. Then, with the Inquisition (under Philip II, c. 1550), ideology trumped pragmatism, and Jews and Muslims were evicted or forced to convert. The elegant square you see today was built, and built big. In-your-face Catholic processions started here. To assert Christian rule, all the trappings of Christian power were layered upon what had been the trappings of Moorish power. Between here and the cathedral were the Christian University (the big orange building) and the adjacent archbishop's palace.

Today Plaza de Bib-Rambla is good for coffee or a meal amid the color and fragrance of flower stalls and the burbling of its Neptune-topped fountain. It remains a multigenerational hangout, where it seems everyone is enjoying a peaceful retirement. A block away (Neptune would get there if he could just turn 180 degrees and walk 100 yards), the Pescadería square is a smaller, similarly lively version of Bib-Rambla.

• *Leave the square by walking toward the cathedral, heading down the lane between the big orange building and Bar Manolo. In a block you come to a small square fronting a very big church.*

❹ **Cathedral:** Wow, the cathedral facade just screams triumph. That's partly because its design is based on a triumphal arch,

built over a destroyed mosque. Five hundred yards away, there was once open space outside the city wall with good soil for a foundation. But the Christian conquerors said, "No way." Instead, they destroyed the mosque and built their cathedral right here on difficult, sandy soil. This was the place where the people of Granada traditionally worshipped—and now they would worship as Christians.

The church has a Gothic foundation and was built mostly in the Renaissance style. Hometown artist Alonso Cano finished it, at the king's request, in Baroque. Accentuating the power of the Roman Catholic Church, the emphasis here is on Mary rather than Christ. The facade declares *Ave Maria*. (This was Counter-Reformation time and the Church was threatened by Protestant Christians. Mary was also more palatable to Muslim converts, as she is revered in the Quran.)

• *Walk around to the right, popping into the Baroque chapel if it's open. (The entrance to the cathedral itself is on the far side of the church; we'll pass it soon.) Then circle around the cathedral, keeping it to your left, until you reach the small square facing the Royal Chapel.*

❺ **Royal Chapel Square:** This square was once ringed by important Moorish buildings. A hammam (public bath), a madrassa (school), a caravanserai (Day's Inn), the silk market, and the leading mosque were all right here. With Christian rule, the madrassa (the faux-gray-stone building with the walls painted in 3-D Baroque style) became Granada's first City Hall. The royal coffins were moved from the Alhambra's parador to the oval Royal Chapel in 1521.

• *Continue up the cobbled, stepped lane to the big street, Gran Vía de Colón. With the arrival of cars and the modern age, the people of Granada wanted a Parisian-style boulevard. In the early 20th century they mercilessly cut through the old town and created Gran Vía and its French-style buildings—in the process destroying everything in its path, including many historic convents.*

From here you could enter the cathedral, catch minibus #32 to the Alhambra, or go left two blocks, cross the street, and walk up Calle Cárcel Baja into the Albayzín. But for now let's continue our orientation tour. Cross the busy street, turn right, and walk down Gran Vía to the big square ahead. Face the statue above the fountain from across the busy intersection.

❻ **Plaza Isabel La Católica:** Granada's two grand boulevards, Gran Vía and Calle Reyes Católicos, meet a block off Plaza Nueva at Plaza Isabel La Católica. Above the fountain, a

beautiful statue shows Columbus unfurling a long contract with Isabel. It lists the terms of Columbus' *mcccclxxxxii* voyage: "For as much as you, Columbus, are going by our command to discover and subdue some Islands and Continents in the ocean...." The two reliefs show the big events in Granada of 1492: Isabel and Ferdinand accepting Columbus' proposal and a stirring battle scene (which never happened) at the walls of the Alhambra.

Isabel was driven by her desire to spread Catholicism. Columbus was driven by his desire for money. As a reward for adding territory to Spain's Catholic empire, Isabel promised Columbus the ranks of Admiral of the Oceans and Governor of the New World. To sweeten the pie, she tossed in one-eighth of all the riches he brought home. Isabel died thinking that Columbus had found India or China. Columbus died poor and disillusioned.

Calle Reyes Católicos leads from this square to the busy intersection with Puerta Real. From there, Acera del Darro takes you through modern Granada to the river via the huge El Corte Inglés department store and lots of modern commerce. This area erupts with locals out strolling each night. For the best Granada paseo, wander the streets here around 19:00.

• *Follow Calle Reyes Católicos a couple of blocks to the left where you'll find another square.*

❼ Plaza Nueva: Long a leading square in Granada, Plaza Nueva is dominated by the Palace of Justice (grand Baroque facade with green Andalusian flag). The fountain is capped by a stylized pomegranate—the symbol of the city, always open and fertile. The main action here is the comings and goings of the busy little shuttle buses serving the Alhambra and Albayzín. The local hippie community, nicknamed the *pies negros* (black feet) for obvious reasons, hangs out here and on Calle de Elvira. They squat—with their dogs and guitars—in abandoned caves above those the Gypsies occupy in Sacromonte. Many are the children of rich Spanish families from the north, hell-bent on disappointing their high-achieving parents.

• *Our tour continues with a stroll up Paseo de los Tristes. Leave Plaza Nueva opposite where you entered (via the street to the left of the church) and walk up the Darro River Valley. This is particularly enjoyable in the cool of the evening. If you're tired, note that minibuses #31 and #32 run from Plaza Nueva, up this lane, and then hook into and through the Albayzín quarter.*

❽ Paseo de los Tristes: This "Walk of the Sad Ones" was once the route of funeral processions to the cemetery at the edge of town. Leaving Plaza Nueva, pass the Church of Santa Ana

on your right. This was originally a mosque—the church tower replaced a minaret. Notice the ceramic brickwork. This is Mudejar art by Moorish craftsmen, whose techniques were later employed by Christians. Inside you'll see a fine Alhambra-style cedar ceiling.

Follow Carrera del Darro high above the River Darro, which flows along the base of the Alhambra (look down by the river for a glimpse of feral cats). Six miles upstream, part of the Darro is diverted to provide water for the Alhambra's many fountains—a remarkable feat of Moorish engineering that allowed the grand fortress complex to be resistant to siege.

After passing two small, picturesque bridges, you'll see the broken nub of a once-grand 11th-century bridge over the river, leading to the Alhambra. Notice two slits in the column: One held an iron portcullis to keep bad guys from entering the town via the river. The second held a solid door that was lowered to build up water, then released to flush out the riverbed and keep it clean.

• *Across from the remains of the bridge (and the stop for minibuses #31 and #35) is the brick facade of an evocative Moorish bath, the Hammam El Bañuelo.*

❾ Hammam El Bañuelo (Moorish Baths): In Moorish times, hammams were a big part of the community (working-class homes didn't have bathrooms). Baths were strictly segregated (as they are today) and functioned as more than a place to wash: Business was done here, and it was a social meeting point. In Christian times it was assumed that conspiracies brewed in these baths—therefore, only a few of them survive. This place gives you the chance to explore the stark but evocative ruins of an 11th-century Moorish public bath (free, unreliably Tue-Sat 10:00-14:30, April-Sept opens at 9:00, closed Sun-Mon year-round, borrow the English description at the door).

Entering the baths, you pass the house of the keeper and the foyer, then visit the cold room, the warm room (where services like massage were offered), and finally the hot or steam room. Beyond that, you can see the oven that generated the heat, which flowed under the hypocaust-style floor tiles (the ones closest to the oven were the hottest). The romantic little holes in the ceiling once had stained-glass louvers that attendants opened and closed with sticks to regulate the heat and steaminess. Whereas Romans soaked in their pools, Muslims just doused. Rather than being totally immersed, people scooped and splashed water over themselves. Imagine attendants stoking the fires under the metal boiler...while people in towels and wooden slippers (to protect their feet from the heated floors) enjoyed all the spa services you can imagine as beams of light slashed through the mist.

This was a great social mixer. As all were naked, class distinctions disappeared—elites learned the latest from commoners. Mothers found matches for their kids. A popular Muslim phrase sums up the attraction of the baths: "This is where anyone would spend their last coin."

• *Continuing straight ahead, on your right is the Church of San Pedro, the parish church of Sacromonte's Gypsy community (across from the Mudejar Art Museum). Within its rich interior is an ornate oxcart used to carry the host on the annual pilgrimage to Rocio, a town near the Portuguese border. Just past this, on your left, is Santa Catalina de Zafra, a convent of cloistered nuns (they worship behind a screen that divides the church's rich interior in half).*

This walk ends at Paseo de los Tristes—with its restaurant tables spilling out under the floodlit Alhambra. From here, the road arcs up into Sacromonte. If you've worked up a hunger, you can backtrack a few blocks to Calle de Gloria where the Convento de San Bernardo sells cookies and monastic wine. Look for the Venta de Dulces *sign; goods are sold from behind a lazy Susan.*

Sights in Granada

▲▲▲The Alhambra

This last and greatest Moorish palace is one of Europe's top sights. Attracting up to 8,000 visitors a day, it's the reason most tourists

come to Granada. Nowhere else does the splendor of Moorish civilization shine so beautifully.

The last Moorish stronghold in Europe is, with all due respect, really a symbol of retreat. For centuries, Granada was merely a regional capital. Gradually the Christian Reconquista moved south, taking Córdoba (1237) and Sevilla (1248). The Nazarids, one of the many diverse ethnic groups of Spanish Muslims, held together the last Moorish kingdom, which they ruled from Granada until 1492. As you tour their grand palace, remember that while Europe slumbered through the Dark Ages, Moorish magnificence blossomed—ornate stucco, plaster "stalactites," colors galore, scalloped windows framing Granada views, exuberant gardens, and water, water everywhere. Water—so rare and precious in most of the Islamic world—was the purest symbol of life to the Moors. The Alhambra is decorated with water: standing still, cascading, masking secret conversations, and drip-dropping playfully.

Cost: Various tickets cover the sights of the Alhambra. The one you want is the €13 **"General Daytime Visit"** *(visita diurna general)* ticket, which covers the Alcazaba fort, Palacios Nazaries, and Generalife Gardens. This ticket is the only one that allows you to see Palacios Nazaries during the day. Note that same-day tickets are virtually never available—reservations are essential. If you don't bother to make a reservation, you deserve the frustration of not seeing this great sight.

The Alhambra

ALBAYZÍN ↑

PALACIOS NAZARIES

ALCAZABA (FORT)

BAR

PLAZA ALJIBES

④

③

②

CHA·PA·

① (T) Taxi Stand

CUESTA DE GOMÉREZ

TO PLAZA NUEVA & MOST HOTELS

GRANADA GATE

(B)

JUSTICE GATE

JUSTICE GATE STOP

TORRES BERMEJAS

N

TO CITY

(B) BUS STOP   ⅄ VIEW   (T) TAXI STAND

--- FOOTPATH   → ONE-WAY STREET

⬅ 15-MIN. WALK FROM MAIN ENTRANCE TO PALACIOS NAZARIES

GRANADA

Other, less-ideal tickets are available for people who've waited too long to get the General Daytime Visit ticket:

- Daytime ticket for just the Alcazaba and Generalife Gardens—€7
- Nighttime ticket for just Palacios Nazaries—€8
- Nighttime ticket for just the Generalife Gardens—€5
- "Circular Azul" ticket, which allows a nighttime visit of the Palacio Nazaries, then (the next morning) the Alcazaba and Generalife Gardens—€15

The Alhambra grounds are free to visit, as is Charles V's Palace (and the Alhambra Museum inside it).

GRANADA

Alhambra
1. Main Entrance
2. Justice Gate Entrance (Ticketholder Shortcut)
3. Wine Gate (WC, ATM, Guidebooks)
4. Palacios Nazaries Entrance
5. ServiCaixa Ticket Machines

Sleeping & Eating
6. Parador de Granada San Francisco & Restaurante
7. Hotel América & Restaurante
8. Hotel Guadalupe & Restaurante La Yedra Real
9. Restaurante Jardines Alberto

Hours: The whole Alhambra complex is open daily mid-March–mid-Oct 8:30-20:00, off-season 8:30-18:00 (ticket office opens at 8:00, last entry one hour before closing, toll tel. 902-441-221).

Palacios Nazaries and Generalife Gardens are also open most **evenings** mid-March–mid-Oct Tue-Sat 22:00-23:30 (ticket office open 21:30-22:30), closed Sun-Mon; and off-season Fri-Sat 20:00-21:30 (ticket office open 19:30-20:30), closed Sun-Thu.

Getting There: You have four options for getting to the Alhambra.

1. On foot: From Plaza Nueva, hike 30 minutes up the street

called Cuesta de Gomérez. Keep going straight—you'll see the Alhambra high on your left. (Along the way, after about 10-15 minutes, look for the Justice Gate shortcut, described below.) The ticket pavilion is on the far side of the Alhambra, near the Generalife Gardens.

2. **By bus:** From Plaza Isabel La Católica, catch a red #32 minibus, marked *Alhambra* (€1.20, runs every 10-15 minutes). There are three Alhambra stops: Justice Gate (best if you have a printed ticket—see next), Charles V, and Generalife (main ticket office and the gardens).

3. **By taxi:** It's a €5 ride from the taxi stand on Plaza Nueva.

4. **By car:** If you're coming from outside the city by car, you can drive to the Alhambra without passing through Granada's historic center. From the freeway, take the exit marked *Ronda Sur–Alhambra*. Signs will lead you to the Alhambra parking lot, conveniently located near the entrance of the Alhambra (€1.50/hour). When you leave, be careful to go out the same way you came in, avoiding the driving ban in Granada's historic center.

Justice Gate Shortcut Entrance: If you already have your printed ticket in hand (i.e., you picked it up from a ServiCaixa machine in town), you can take a shortcut to the core of the complex by entering through the Justice Gate, downhill from the main entrance (if you're walking, this saves about 15 minutes of uphill climbing; you can also get off the minibus here). But if you want to go to the Generalife Gardens first, or don't yet have a ticket in hand, use the upper, main entrance.

Tours: Various companies run tours for about €45-50 that include transportation to the Alhambra and a guided tour of Palacios Nazaries (for example, GranaVisión has a tour for €49, tel. 958-535-875, www.visitargranada.com; Cicerone also has tours for €45-57).

Audioguides: The €6 "complete" audioguide brings the palace to life, with 33 stops throughout the complex. The €4 "garden" audioguide covers just 15 stops, mostly outside the buildings (rent it at the entrance or at Charles V's Palace, leave €20 cash deposit or your ID—you'll need to return the audioguide where you picked it up). If you want to use headphones with these audioguides, you must bring your own. Audioguides are not available for night visits.

Guidebooks: Consider getting a guidebook in town and reading it the night before to understand the layout and history of this remarkable sight before entering. Official Alhambra bookstores (including the one in town, and those up at the grounds) push the €18 *Official Guide,* a well-produced scholarly tome loaded with history, photos, maps, and practical information—but it weighs a ton. Unofficial bookstores sell other options. Of these, I enjoy the slick *Alhambra and Generalife in Focus,* which has vibrant color photos and a visually pleasing layout (€8); the thinner *The Alhambra and the Generalife* has less information and mostly photos (also €8).

Photography: Photos are permitted.

Eating: Within the Alhambra walls, your food options are somewhat limited. Choose between the restaurant at the **parador** (*cafetería*: €7-12 sandwiches, €12-20 light meals; restaurant—get a table on the terrace: €10-15 starters, €18-27 main dishes, €34 fixed-price meal); the courtyard of the **Hotel América** (with pricey €15-20 meals but affordable €6 sandwiches and a great peaceful ambience, Sun-Fri 12:30-16:30, closed Sat); a small **bar-café kiosk** in front of the Alcazaba fort (€3 basic sandwiches and other snacks); and **vending machines** (at the WC) next to the Wine Gate, near Charles V's Palace. You're welcome to bring in a **picnic** as long as you eat it in a public area.

For better-value (but touristy) options, head outside to the area around the parking lot and ticket booth at the top of the complex. **Restaurante La Yedra Real,** a short walk up from the gate, is pleasantly efficient and your best economical sit-down eatery (€3 sandwiches, €5-7 salads, €8-14 main dishes, Tue-Sun 9:30-17:00, closed Mon, easy photo menu, air-con, over the Alhambra parking lot at Paseo de la Sabica 28, tel. 958-229-145). **Restaurante Jardines Alberto,** closer to the main entrance and across from the breezy Restaurante La Mimbre, has a nice courtyard, offers a more formal menu, and feels a little more dignified (€5 sandwiches, €8-12 salads, €12-22 main dishes, €14 fixed-price lunch, daily 9:00-20:00).

Nearby: If you're going to the Albayzín afterward, catch minibus #32, which goes from the three Alhambra stops back through Plaza Isabel La Católica and then up into the Albayzín. Or, for a delightful "Back Door" escape, walk back into town along the Cuesta de los Chinos. (It starts near the ticket booth, by Restaurante La Mimbre and the minibus stop.) You'll walk on a desolate lane downhill along a stream, beneath the Alhambra ramparts, and past the sultan's cobbled horse lane leading up to Generalife Gardens. In 10 minutes you're back in town at Paseo de los Tristes. You can't get lost.

⊙ **Self-Guided Tour:** I've listed these sights in the order you're likely to visit them. The first three sights cluster at the bottom/far end of the complex, while the Generalife Gardens are about a 15-minute walk away, at the top (main entrance). If you have a long time to wait for your Palacios Nazaries appointment, you could do the gardens first, then head down to the other three; otherwise it makes sense to start on the lower end of the hill.

Planning Your Time at the Alhambra

The Alhambra consists of four sights clustered together atop a hill:

▲▲▲**Palacios Nazaries**—Exquisite Moorish palace, the one must-see sight. To see it during the day, advance reservations are a must.

▲▲**Charles V's Palace**—Christian Renaissance palace plopped on top of the Alhambra after the Reconquista, with the fine Alhambra Museum (free entry).

▲**Generalife Gardens**—Fancy, manicured gardens with small summer palace.

Alcazaba—Empty old fort with tower and views.

When to Go

Daytime tickets for Palacios Nazaries come stamped with a 30-minute time slot. Time your visit around that appointment, as your reservation is only good if you enter the palace within that 30-minute window. (Once inside the palace, you can linger as long as you like.)

How best to see the rest of the Alhambra complex depends on whether your Palacios Nazaries reservation is for a time before or after 14:00. If your entry time for Palacios Nazaries is before 14:00, you can visit the other Alhambra sights (the Alcazaba, Generalife Gardens, and Charles V's Palace) anytime in the morning, see Palacios Nazaries at your appointed time, and leave the Alhambra by 14:00 (although you can get away with staying longer in the fort, gardens, or Palacios Nazaries, you won't be allowed to *enter* any of these sites after 14:00). If your ticket is stamped for 14:00 or later, you cannot enter the Alhambra sights any earlier than 14:00. For instance, if you have a reservation to visit Palacios Nazaries at 16:30, you can enter the Alhambra sights any time after 14:00 and see the fort and Generalife Gardens before Palacios Nazaries.

Because of the time restriction on afternoon visits, morning tickets sell out the quickest. But for most travelers, an afternoon is ample time to see the site—the light is perfect, and there are fewer tour groups.

If you're picking up your tickets at the main entrance (at the top end), or just want to start with the gardens, be aware that you're a 15-minute walk away from Palacios Nazaries at the other end. Be sure to arrive at the Alhambra with enough time to make it to the palace before your allotted half-hour entry time slot ends. The ticket-checkers at Palacios Nazaries are strict.

Your Route

To minimize walking, see Charles V's Palace and the Alcazaba fort before your visit to Palacios Nazaries. When you finish touring the palace, you'll leave through the Partal Gardens, a pleasant 15-to-20-minute walk from the Generalife Gardens. Depending on the time, you can visit the Generalife Gardens before or after seeing Palacios Nazaries. If you have any time to kill before your palace appoint-

ment, do it luxuriously on the breezy view terrace of the parador bar (actually within the Alhambra walls; for other options see "Eating," page 123). Drinks, WCs, and guidebooks are available at the Wine Gate, near the entrance of Palacios Nazaries, but not inside the palace.

The Alhambra by Moonlight

If you prefer doing things after dark, you can avoid the reservation hassle. Late-night visits to the Alhambra are easy (separate

nighttime tickets are sold for Palacio Nazaries and the Generalife Gardens; see "Cost," page 87)—just buy your ticket upon arrival, as night-visit tickets hardly ever sell out. Keep in mind that two separate tickets (Alcazaba and Generalife Gardens by day, Palacios

Nazaries by night) cost the same as the Circular Azul ticket, and offer more flexibility, as you're not locked into the Circular Azul's next-morning stipulation.

You can't see the Alcazaba fort or Charles V's Palace at night, but, hey, Palacios Nazaries provides 80 percent of the Alhambra's thrills anyway. Although a few small sections of both the palace and the gardens are closed at night, you'll see most of what the daytime visitors see. While some find the Alhambra disappointing at night, others find it even more magical (less crowded and beautifully lit); either way, it's better than not seeing it at all (for exact times see "Hours," page 89).

▲▲Charles V's Palace and the Alhambra Museum

It's only natural for a conquering king to build his own palace over his foe's palace, and that's exactly what the Christian king Charles V did. Palacios Nazaries wasn't good enough for Charles, so he built this new home, which was financed by a salt-in-the-wound tax on Granada's defeated Muslim population. With a unique circle-within-a-square design by Pedro Machuca, a pupil of Michelangelo, this is Spain's most impressive Renaissance building. Stand in the circular courtyard

surrounded by mottled marble columns, then climb the stairs. Perhaps Charles' palace was designed to have a dome, but it was never finished—his son, Philip II, abandoned it to build his own much more massive palace outside Madrid, El Escorial (the final and most austere example of Spanish Renaissance architecture). Even without the dome, acoustics are perfect in the center—stand in the middle and sing your best aria. The palace doubles as one of the venues for the popular International Festival of Music and Dance.

The **Alhambra Museum** (Museo de la Alhambra, on the ground floor of Charles V's Palace) shows off some of the Alhambra's best surviving Moorish art. While modest compared to the other Alhambra sights, the museum's artifacts—including tiles, pottery, pieces of fountains, and a beautiful carved-wood door—help humanize the Alhambra. Everything is well-described in English (free, Tue-Sun 8:30-14:30, closed Mon). The **Fine Arts Museum** (Museo de Bellas Artes, upstairs, also free) is of little interest to most.

If you have an early-morning reservation to Palacios Nazaries, you'll notice that other tourists with reservations line up immediately for that sight. While they're in line, you can take a few minutes to pop into Charles V's Palace, and have it all to yourself.

• *From the front of Charles V's palace (as you face the Alcazaba fort), the entrance to Palacios Nazaries is to the right (look for the line snaking along the outside edge of the garden), while the Alcazaba is across a moat straight ahead (to get there, bear left through the keyhole-shaped Wine Gate, then hook right and walk up to the open area in front of the fort).*

Alcazaba

This fort—the original "red castle" ("Alhambra")—is the oldest and most ruined part of the complex, offering exercise and fine city views. What you see is from the mid-13th century, but

GRANADA

there was probably a fort here in Roman times. Once upon a time, this tower defended a medina (town) of 2,000 Muslims living within the Alhambra walls. It's a huge, sprawling complex—wind your way through passages and courtyards, over uneven terrain, to reach the biggest tower at the tip of the complex. Then climb stairs steeply up to the very top. From there (looking north), find Plaza Nueva and the San Nicolás viewpoint (in the Albayzín). To the south are the Sierra Nevada Mountains. Is anybody skiing today? Notice the tower's four flags: the blue of the European Union, the green and white of Andalucía, the red and yellow of Spain, and the red and green of Granada.

Speaking of flags, imagine that day in 1492 when the Christian cross and the flags of Aragon and Castile were raised on this tower, and the fleeing Moorish king Boabdil (Abu Abdullah, in Arabic) looked back and wept. His mom chewed him out, saying, "You weep like a woman for what you couldn't defend like a man." With this defeat, more than seven centuries of Muslim rule in Spain came to an end. Much later, Napoleon stationed his troops at the Alhambra, contributing substantially to its ruin when he left.

• *If you're going from the Alcazaba to Palacios Nazaries, you'll have to backtrack through the Wine Gate, then look for the people lined up along the gardens in front of Charles V's Palace.*

▲▲▲Palacios Nazaries

During the 30-minute entry time slot stamped on your ticket, enter the jewel of the Alhambra: the Moorish royal palace. Once you're in, you can relax—you're no longer under any time constraints. You'll walk through three basic sections: royal offices, ceremonial rooms, and private quarters. Built mostly in the 14th century, this palace offers your best possible look at the refined, elegant Moorish civilization of Al-Andalus (the Arabic word for the Iberian Peninsula).

You'll visit rooms decorated from top to bottom with carved wood ceilings, stucco "stalactites," ceramic tiles, molded-plaster walls, and filigree windows. Open-air courtyards feature fountains with bubbling water, which give the palace a desert-oasis feel. A garden enlivened by lush vegetation and peaceful pools is the

GRANADA

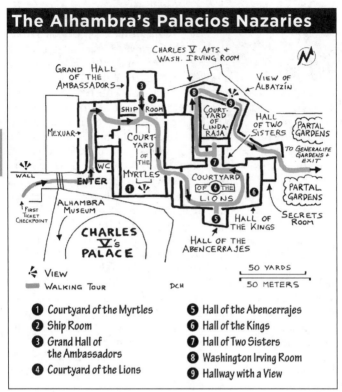

The Alhambra's Palacios Nazaries

CHARLES V APTS. +
WASH. IRVING ROOM

VIEW OF
ALBAYZÍN

GRAND HALL
OF THE
AMBASSADORS→

SHIP ROOM

COURT-YARD OF
LINDA-RAJA

HALL
OF TWO
SISTERS

PARTAL
GARDENS

MEXUAR→

COURT-YARD
OF
THE
MYRTLES

TO GENERALIFE
GARDENS +
EXIT

WC

WALL

ENTER

COURTYARD
OF THE
LIONS

PARTAL
GARDENS

FIRST
TICKET
CHECKPOINT

ALHAMBRA
MUSEUM

HALL OF
THE KINGS

SECRETS
ROOM

CHARLES
V's
PALACE

HALL OF THE
ABENCERRAJES

VIEW

WALKING TOUR   DCH

50 YARDS

50 METERS

① Courtyard of the Myrtles

② Ship Room

③ Grand Hall of the Ambassadors

④ Courtyard of the Lions

⑤ Hall of the Abencerrajes

⑥ Hall of the Kings

⑦ Hall of Two Sisters

⑧ Washington Irving Room

⑨ Hallway with a View

Quran's symbol of heaven. The palace is well-preserved, but the trick to fully appreciating it is to imagine it furnished and filled with Moorish life...sultans with hookah pipes lounging on pillows upon Persian carpets, heavy curtains on the windows, and ivory-studded wooden furniture. The whole place was painted with bright colors, many suggested by the Quran—red (blood), blue (heaven), green (oasis), and gold (wealth). Throughout the palace, walls, ceilings, vases, carpets, and tiles were covered with decorative patterns, mostly poems and verses of praise from the Quran written in calligraphy. Much of what is known about the Alhambra is known simply from reading the inscriptions that decorate its walls.

As you wander, keep the palace themes in mind: water, a near absence of figural images (forbidden by the Quran), "stalactite" ceilings—and few signs telling you where you are. As tempting as it might be to touch the stucco, don't—it is very susceptible to the oils from your hand. Use the map above to locate the essential stops listed below.

• Begin by walking through a few administrative rooms (the mexuar) with a stunning Mecca-oriented prayer room (the oratorio, with a niche *on the right facing Mecca) and a small courtyard with a round fountain, until you hit the big rectangular courtyard with a fish pond lined by a myrtle-bush hedge.*

❶ Courtyard of the Myrtles

Moors loved their patios—with a garden and water, under the sky. In accordance with medieval Moorish mores, women rarely

went out, so they stayed in touch with nature in courtyards like the Courtyard of the Myrtles (Patio de los Arrayanes)—named for the two fragrant myrtle hedges that added to the courtyard's charm. Notice the wooden screens (erected by jealous husbands) that allowed the cloistered women to look out without being clearly seen. The upstairs was likely for win-

ter use, and the cooler ground level was probably used in summer.

If the Courtyard of the Lions and the Hall of the Kings (described later) are still being renovated—likely through early 2012—you may see, at the right end of this courtyard, a temporary exhibit displaying those newly restored lion statues, with videos about the archaeologists' work.

• *Head left from the entry through gigantic wooden doors into the long narrow antechamber to the throne room, called the...*

❷ Ship Room

It's understandable that many think the Ship Room (Sala de la Barca) is named for the upside-down-hull shape of its fine cedar ceiling. But the name is actually derived from the Arab word *baraka*, meaning "divine blessing and luck" (which was corrupted to *barca*, the Spanish word for "ship" or "boat"). As you passed through this room, blessings and luck are exactly what you'd need—because in the next room, you'd be face-to-face with the sultan.

• *Oh, it's your turn. Enter the ornate throne room.*

❸ Grand Hall of the Ambassadors

The palace's largest room, the Gran Salón de los Embajadores (also known as the Salón de Comares), functioned as the throne room. It was here that the sultan, seated on a throne opposite the entrance, received foreign emissaries. Ogle the room—a perfect cube—from top to bottom. The star-studded, domed wooden ceiling (made from 8,017 inlaid pieces like a giant jigsaw puzzle) suggests the complexity of Allah's infinite universe. Wooden "stalactites" form the cornice, running around the entire base of the ceiling. The

GRANADA

Islamic Art

Rather than making paintings and statues, Islamic artists expressed themselves with beautiful but functional objects.

Ceramics (most of them blue and white, or green and white), carpets, glazed tile panels, stucco-work ceilings, and glass tableware are covered with complex patterns. The intricate interweaving, repetition, and unending lines suggest the complex, infinite nature of God, known to Muslims as Allah.

You'll see only a few pictures of humans or animals, since Islamic doctrine is wary of any "graven images" or idols forbidden by God. However, secular art by Muslims for their homes and palaces was not bound by this restriction; you'll get an occasional glimpse of realistic art featuring men and women enjoying a garden paradise, a symbol of the Muslim heaven.

Look for floral patterns (twining vines, flowers, and arabesques) and geometric designs (stars and diamonds). The most common pattern is calligraphy—elaborate lettering of an inscription in Arabic, the language of the Quran. A quote from the Quran on a vase or lamp combines the power of the message with the beauty of the calligraphy.

stucco walls, even without their original paint and gilding, are still glorious, decorated with ornamental flowers made by pressing a mold into the wet plaster. The filigree windows once held stained glass and had heavy drapes to block out the heat. Some precious 16th-century tiles survive in the center of the floor.

A visitor here would have stepped from the glaring Courtyard of the Myrtles into this dim, cool, incense-filled world, to meet the silhouetted sultan. Imagine the alcoves functioning busily as work stations, and the light at sunrise or sunset, rich and warm, filling the room.

Let your eyes trace the finely carved Arabic script. Muslims avoided making images of living creatures—that was God's work. But they could carve decorative religious messages. One phrase—

"only Allah is victorious"—is repeated 9,000 times throughout the palace. Find the character for "Allah"—it looks like a cursive W with a nose on its left side. The swoopy toboggan blades underneath are a kind of artistic punctuation used to set off one phrase.

In 1492, two historic events likely took place in this room. Culminating a 700-year-long battle, the Reconquista was completed here as the last Moorish king, Boabdil, signed the terms of his surrender before eventually leaving for Africa.

And it was here that Columbus made one of his final pitches to Isabel and Ferdinand to finance a sea voyage to the Orient. Imagine the scene: The king, the queen, and the greatest minds from the University of Salamanca gathered here while Columbus produced maps and pie charts to make his case that he could sail west to reach the East. Ferdinand and the professors laughed and called Columbus mad—not because they thought the world was flat (most educated people knew otherwise), but because they thought Columbus had underestimated the size of the globe, and thus the length and cost of the journey.

But Isabel said, *"Sí, señor."* Columbus fell to his knees (promising to pack light, wear a money belt, and use the most current guidebook available).

Opposite the Ship Room entrance, photographers pause for a picture-perfect view of the tower reflected in the Courtyard of the Myrtles pool. This was the original palace entrance (before Charles V's Palace was built).

• *Continue deeper into the palace, to a courtyard where, 600 years ago, only the royal family and their servants could enter. It's the much-photographed...*

❹ Courtyard of the Lions

The Patio de los Leones features a fountain that's usually ringed with 12 lions; however, they've been missing for the past several years as they undergo restoration (they should be back in place by early 2012).

Why did the fountain have 12 lions? Since the fountain was a gift from a Jewish leader celebrating good relations with the sultan (Granada had a big Jewish community), the lions probably represent the 12 tribes of Israel. During Moorish times, the fountain functioned as a clock, with a different lion spouting water each hour. (Conquering Christians disassembled the fountain to see how it worked, and it's never worked since.) From the center, four streams went out—figuratively to the corners of the earth and literally to various apartments of the royal family. Notice how the court, with its 124 columns, resembles the cloister of a Catholic monastery. The craftsmanship is first-class. For example, the lead fittings between the pre-cut sections of the columns allow things to flex during an earthquake, preventing destruction during shakes.

Six hundred years ago, the Muslim Moors could read the Quranic poetry that ornaments this court, and they could understand the symbolism of this lush, enclosed garden, considered the embodiment of paradise or truth. ("How beautiful is this garden / where the flowers of Earth rival the stars of Heaven. / What can compare with this alabaster fountain, gushing crystal-clear water? / Nothing except the fullest moon, pouring light from an unclouded sky.") Imagine—they appreciated this part of the palace even more than we do today.

• *On the right, off the courtyard, is a square room called the...*

❺ Hall of the Abencerrajes

This was the sultan's living room, with an exquisite ceiling based on the eight-sided Muslim star. The room has a sad history. The father

of Boabdil took a new wife and wanted to disinherit the children of his first marriage—one of whom was Boabdil. In order to deny power to Boabdil and his siblings, the sultan killed nearly all of the pre-Boabdil Abencerraje family members. He thought this would pave the way for the son of his new wife to be the next sultan. He stacked 36 Abencerraje heads in the pool, under the sumptuous honeycombed stucco ceiling in this hall, called the Sala de los Abencerrajes. But his scheme failed, and Boabdil ultimately assumed the throne. Bloody power struggles like this were the norm here in the Alhambra.

• *At the end of the court opposite where you entered is the . . .*

❻ Hall of the Kings

Notice the ceilings of the three chambers branching off this gallery, the Sala de los Reyes. Breaking from the tradition of imageless art, paintings on the goat-leather ceiling depict scenes of the sultan and his family. The center room's group portrait shows the first 10 of the Alhambra's 22 sultans. The scene is a fantasy, since these people lived over a span of many generations. The two end rooms display scenes of princely pastimes, such as hunting and

GRANADA

shooting skeet. In a palace otherwise devoid of figures, these offer a rare look at royal life in the palace.

• *As you exit, you'll pass doors leading right and left to a 14th-century WC plumbed by running water and stairs up to the harem. Next is the...*

❼ Hall of Two Sisters

The Sala de Dos Hermanas—nicknamed for the giant twin slabs of white marble on the floor flanking the fountain—has another oh-wow stucco ceiling lit from below by clerestory windows. The room features geometric patterns and stylized Arabic script quoting verses from the Quran. If the inlaid color tiles look "Escheresque," you've got it backward: Escher is Alhambra-esque. M. C. Escher was inspired by these very patterns on his visit. Study the patterns—they remind us of the Moorish expertise in math. The sitting room (farthest from the entry) has low windows, because Moorish people sat on the floor. Some rare stained glass survives in the ceiling. From here the sultana enjoyed a grand view of the medieval city (before the 16th-century wing was added that blocks the view today).

• *That's about it for the palace. From here, wander past the domed roofs of the old baths down a hallway to a pair of rooms decorated with a mahogany ceiling. Marked with a large plaque is the...*

❽ Washington Irving Room

Washington Irving wrote *Tales of the Alhambra* in this room. While living in Spain in 1829, Irving stayed in the Alhambra. It was a romantic time, when the palace was home to Gypsies and donkeys. His "tales" kindled interest in the Alhambra, causing it to become recognized as a national treasure. A plaque on the wall thanks Irving, who later served as the US ambassador to Spain (1842-1846). Here's a quote from Irving's *The Alhambra by Moonlight:* "On such heavenly nights I would sit for hours at my window inhaling the sweetness of the garden, and musing on the checkered fortunes of those whose history was dimly shadowed out in the elegant memorials around."

• *As you leave, stop at the open-air...*

❾ Hallway with a View

Here you'll enjoy the best-in-the-palace view of the labyrinthine Albayzín—the old Moorish town on the opposite hillside. Find the famous San Nicolás viewpoint (below where the white San Nicolás church tower breaks the horizon). Creeping into the mountains on the right are the Gypsy neighborhoods of Sacromonte. Still circling old Granada is the Moorish wall (built in the 1400s to protect the city's population, swollen by Muslim refugees driven south by the Reconquista).

The Patio de Lindaraja (with its maze-like hedge pattern garden) marks the end of the palace visit. Before exiting, you can detour right into the adjacent "Secrets Room"— stark brick rooms of the former bath with fun acoustics. Whisper into a corner, and your friend—with an ear to the wall—can hear you in the opposite corner. Try talking in the exact center.

• *Leaving the palace, you enter the Partal Gardens (El Partal), where you can enjoy the reflecting pond of the Partal Palace. Climb a few stairs, continue through the gardens, and follow signs directing you left to the Generalife Gardens or right to the Alcazaba (and the rest of the Alhambra grounds). If you're interested in poking around the Alhambra grounds, exit and do it now before entering the Generalife (because you can't easily backtrack into the Alhambra grounds after leaving the gardens).*

If you do go from the Partal Gardens to the Generalife Gardens, it's a delightful 15-to-20-minute stroll through lesser (but still pleasant) gardens, along a row of fortified towers—just follow signs for Torres Generalife. *Just before reaching Generalife, you'll cross over a bridge and look down on the dusty lane called Cuesta de los Chinos (a handy shortcut for returning to downtown later).*

▲Generalife Gardens

If you have a long wait before your entry to Palacios Nazaries, tour these gardens first, then the Alcazaba fort and Charles V's Palace.

The sultan's vegetable and fruit garden and summer palace, called the Generalife (hen-eh-raw-LEEF-ay), are a short hike uphill past the ticket office. The 2,000 residents of the Alhambra enjoyed the fresh fruit and veggies grown here. But most importantly, this little palace provided the sultan with a cool and quiet summer escape.

Follow the simple one-way path through the sprawling gardens (planted only in the 1930s—in Moorish times, there were no cypress trees here). The sleek, modern amphitheater has been renovated and continues to be an important concert venue for Granada. It sees most activity during the International Festival of Music

The Alhambra Grounds

As you wander the grounds, remember that the Alhambra was once a city of 2,000 people fortified by a 1.5-mile rampart and

30 towers. The zone within the walls was the medina, a town with a general urban scene. As you stroll from the ticket booth down the garden-like Calle Real de la Alhambra to the palace, you're walking through the ruins of the medina (destroyed by the French in 1812).

The Palacios Nazaries, Alcazaba fort, and Generalife Gardens all have turnstiles. But the medina—with Charles V's Palace, a line of shops showing off traditional woodworking techniques, and the fancy Alhambra parador—is wide open to anyone with an Alhambra ticket.

It's especially fun to snoop around the historic **Parador de Granada San Francisco,** which—as a national monument—is legally required to be open to the public. Once a Moorish palace within the Alhambra, it was later converted into a Franciscan monastery, with a historic claim to fame: Its church is where the Catholic Monarchs (Ferdinand and Isabel) chose to be buried. For a peek, step in through the arch leading to a small garden area and reception. Enter to see the tomb, located in the open-air ruins of the church (just before the reception desk and the guests-only-beyond-this-point sign). The slab on the ground near the altar—a surviving bit from the mosque that was here before the church—marks the place where the greatest king and queen of Spain were buried until 1521 (when they were moved to the Royal Chapel—see page 104). The next room is a delightful former cloister. Now a hotel, the parador has a restaurant and café open to non-guests.

The medina's main road dead-ended at the **Wine Gate** (Puerta del Vino), which protected the fortress. When you pass through the Wine Gate, you enter a courtyard that was originally a moat, then a reservoir (in Christian times). The well—now encased in a bar-kiosk—is still a place for cold drinks. If you're done with your Alhambra visit, you can exit down to the city from the Wine Gate.

and Dance. Many of the world's greatest artists have performed here, including Arthur Rubenstein, Rudolf Nureyev, and Margot Fonteyn. Head for the top of the amphitheater, then walk through the manicured hedge gardens, along delightful ponds and fountains, to the palace.

At the small palace, pass through the dismounting room (imagine dismounting onto the helpful stone ledge, and letting your horse drink in the trough here). Show your ticket and enter the most exceptional Arabian garden in Andalucía.

Here in the summer home of the Moorish kings, this garden is the closest thing on earth to the Quran's description of heaven. It was planted more than 600 years ago—that's remarkable longevity for a European garden. Five-hundred-year-old paintings show it looking essentially the same as it does today. The flowers, herbs, aromas, and water are exquisite...even for a sultan. Up the Darro River, the royal aqueduct diverted a life-giving stream of water into the Alhambra. It was channeled through this extralong decorative fountain to irrigate the bigger garden outside, then along an aqueduct into the Alhambra for its 2,000 thirsty residents. And though the splashing fountains are a delight, they are a 19th-century addition. The Moors liked a peaceful pond instead.

At the end of the pond you enter the sultan's tiny three-room summer palace. From the end, climb 10 steps into the Christian Renaissance gardens. The ancient decrepit tree rising over the pond inspired Washington Irving, who wrote that this must be the "only surviving witness to the wonders of that age of Al-Andalus."

Climbing up and going through the turnstile, you have two options for where to head next. If you're exhausted, just head to the right and follow *salida* signs toward the gardens' exit (next to the Alhambra's main entrance). But if you want a little more exercise (and views), turn left and huff up the staircase called Escalera del Agua, whose banisters double as little water canals. From the top, you'll have a chance to enter the "Romantic Viewpoint"—climb up the stairs for a top-floor view over the gardens (pleasant enough, but less impressive than other views at the Alhambra). Then hike back down through the garden and follow *salida* signs to the exit.

Your visit to the Alhambra is complete, and you've earned your reward. "Surely Allah will make those who believe and do good deeds enter gardens beneath which rivers flow; they shall be adorned therein with bracelets of gold and pearls, and their garments therein shall be of silk" (Quran 22.23).

▲▲Royal Chapel (Capilla Real)

Without a doubt Granada's top Christian sight, this lavish chapel holds the dreams—and bodies—of Queen Isabel and King Ferdinand. The "Catholic Monarchs" were all about the

Reconquista. Their marriage united the Aragon and Castile king-doms, allowing an acceleration of the Christian and Spanish push south. In its last 10 years, the Reconquista snowballed. This last Moorish capital—symbolic of their victory—was their chosen burial place. While smaller and less architecturally striking than the cathedral (described next), the chapel is far more historically significant.

Cost and Hours: €3.50; March-Oct daily 10:15-13:30 & 16:00-19:30 except opens at 11:00 on Sun; in Nov-Feb daily 10:15-13:30 & 15:30-18:30 except opens at 11:00 on Sun; no photos, entrance on Calle Oficios, just off Gran Vía del Colón—go through iron gate, tel. 958-227-848.

GRANADA

◆ **Self-Guided Tour:** In the lobby, before you show your ticket and enter the chapel, notice the **painting of Boabdil** (on the black horse) giving the key of Granada to the conquering King Ferdinand. Boabdil wanted to fall to his knees, but the Spanish king, who had great respect for his Moorish foe, embraced him instead. They fought a long and noble war (for instance, respect-fully returning the bodies of dead soldiers). Ferdinand is in red, and Isabel is behind him wearing a crown. The painting is flanked high on the wall by portraits of Ferdinand and Isabel. Two small exhibits celebrate the 500th anniversaries of the death of Isabel in 2004 and of Philip the Fair (her son-in-law) in 2006.

Isabel decided to make Granada the capital of Spain (and burial place for Spanish royalty) for three reasons: 1) With the conquest of this city, Christianity had finally overcome Islam in Europe; 2) her marriage with Ferdinand, followed by the conquest of Granada, had marked the beginning of a united Spain; and 3) in Granada, she agreed to sponsor Columbus.

Show your ticket and step into the **chapel.** It's Plateresque Gothic—light and lacy silver-filigree style, named for and inspired by the fine silverwork of the Moors. The chapel's interior was orig-inally austere, with fancy touches added later by Ferdinand and Isabel's grandson Charles V. Five hundred years ago, this was the most lavish interior money could buy. Ferdinand and Isabel spent a quarter of their wealth on it. Because of its speedy completion

(1506-1521), the architecture is unusually harmonious.

In the center of the cha-pel (in front of the main altar), the **four royal tombs** are Renaissance-style. Carved in Italy in 1521 out of Carrara marble, they were sent by ship to Spain. The faces—based on death masks—are considered accurate. If you're looking at the altar, **Ferdinand** and **Isabel** are on the right. (Isabel fans attribute the bigger dent she puts in the pillow to her larger brain.) Isabel's contemporaries described the queen as being of medium height, with auburn hair and blue eyes, and possessing a serious, modest, and gentle personality. (Compare Ferdinand and Isabel's tomb statues with the painted and gilded wood statues of them kneeling in prayer, flanking the altarpiece.)

Philip the Fair and **Juana the Mad** (who succeeded Ferdinand and Isabel) lie on the left. Philip was so "Fair" that it drove the insanely jealous Juana "Mad." Philip died young, and for two years Juana kept his casket at her bedside, kissing his embalmed body good night. Philip and Juana's son, Charles V (known as Carlos I in Spain), was a key figure in European history, as his coronation merged the Holy Roman Empire (Philip the Fair's Habsburg domain) with Juana's Spanish empire. Europe's top king, Charles V ruled a vast empire stretching from Holland to Sicily, from Bohemia to Bolivia (1519-1556).

When Philip II, the son of Charles V, decided to build El Escorial (his palace outside Madrid) and establish Madrid as the single capital of a single Spain, Granada lost power and importance. More importantly, Spain began to decline. After the reign of Charles V, Spain squandered her vast wealth trying to maintain this impossibly huge empire. The country's rulers did it not only for material riches, but to defend the romantic, quixotic dream of a Catholic empire—ruled by one divinely ordained Catholic monarch—against an irrepressible tide of nationalism and Protestantism that was sweeping across the vast Habsburg holdings in Central and Eastern Europe. Spain's relatively poor modern history can be blamed, in part, on its people's stubborn unwillingness to accept the end of this old-regime notion. Even Franco borrowed symbols from the Catholic Monarchs to legitimize his dictatorship and keep the 500-year-old legacy alive. Today's Spaniards reflect that the momentous marriage that created their country also sucked them into centuries of European squabbling, eventually leaving Spain impoverished.

Look at the intricate carving on the tombs. It's a humanistic statement, with these healthy, organic, realistic figures rising out of the Gothic age.

From the feet of the marble tombs, step downstairs to see the actual **coffins.** They are plain. Ferdinand and Isabel were originally buried in the Franciscan monastery (in what is today the parador, up at the Alhambra). You're standing in front of the two people who created Spain. The fifth coffin (on right, marked *PM*) belongs to a young Prince Michael, who would have been king of a united Spain and Portugal. (A sad—but too long—story....)

The **high altar** is one of the finest Renaissance works in Spain. It's dedicated to two Johns: the Baptist and the Evangelist. In the center you can see the Baptist and the Evangelist chatting as if over tapas—an appropriately humanistic scene. Scenes from the Baptist's life are on the left: John beheaded after Salomé's fine dancing, and (below) John baptizing Jesus. Scenes from the Evangelist's life are on the right: John's martyrdom (a failed attempt to boil him alive in oil), and, below, John on Patmos (where he may have written the last book of the Bible, Revelation). John is talking to the eagle that, according to tradition, flew him to heaven. A colorful series of reliefs at the bottom level recalls the Christian conquest of the Moors (left to right): Ferdinand, Boabdil with army and key to Alhambra, Moors expelled from Alhambra (right of altar table), conversion of Muslims by tonsured monks, and Ferdinand again.

A finely carved Plateresque arch, with the royal initials *F* and *Y,* leads to a small glass pyramid in the **treasury.** This holds Queen Isabel's silver crown ringed with pomegranates (symbolizing

Granada), her scepter, and King Ferdinand's sword. Do a counterclockwise spin around the room to see it all, starting to the right of the entry arch. There you'll see the devout Isabel's prayer book, in which she followed the Mass. The book and its sturdy box date from 1496. According to legend, the fancy box on the other side of the door is supposedly the one that Isabel filled with jewels and gave to Columbus (her military expenses had made her cash-poor). Columbus sold these to finance his journey. In the corner (and also behind glass) is the ornate silver-and-gold cross that Cardinal Mendoza, staunch supporter of Queen Isabel, carried into the Alhambra on that historic day in 1492. Next, the big silver-and-gold silk tapestry is the altar banner for the mobile campaign chapel of Ferdinand and Isabel, who always traveled with their army. In the case to its left, you'll see the original Christian army flags raised over the Alhambra in 1492.

The next zone of this grand hall holds the first great art collection ever established by a woman. Queen Isabel amassed more than 200 important paintings. After Napoleon's visit, only 30 remained. Even so, this is a fine collection, all on wood, featuring works by Sandro Botticelli, Pietro Perugino, the Flemish master Hans Memling, and some less-famous Spanish masters.

Finally, at the end of the room, the two carved sculptures of Ferdinand and Isabel were the originals from the high altar. Charles V considered these primitive and replaced them with the ones you saw earlier.

To reach the cathedral (described next), exit behind Isabel, out through one iron gate and then immediately through the neighboring iron gate.

▲Cathedral

One of only two Renaissance churches in Spain (the other is in Córdoba), Granada's cathedral is the second-largest in Spain after Sevilla's. While it was started as a Gothic church, it was built using Renaissance elements, and then decorated in Baroque style.

Cost and Hours: €3.50; April-Oct Mon-Sat 10:45-13:30 & 16:00-20:00, Sun 16:00-20:00; Nov-March until 19:00; 45-minute audioguide-€3, entrance off Gran Vía del Colón through the iron gateway next to the "Gran Vía 1" bus stop, tel. 958-222-959.

◒ Self-Guided Tour: Your visit starts in the priests' wardrobe room (after the ticket checker, step right). It's lush and wide-open; the gilded ceilings, mirrors, and wooden cabinets give this room a light, airy feel. Two grandfather clocks made in London (one with Asian motifs) ensured that everyone got dressed on time. The highlight of this room: the small, delicate painted wood statue of the *Immaculate Conception* by Granada's own Alonso Cano (1601-1667).

Wandering out, you'll be behind the main altar. A fine series of paintings by Cano, moved from under arches high above, now encircle the back of the altar. Their distortion was intentional, since the paintings were designed to look natural when viewed from floor level. As you walk around the pews and gigantic Baroque organs, you'll see the cathedral at its most beautiful.

Standing in front of the high altar, look up at the spread of vacant niches (with squares now filled with paintings). These were intended to hold the royal coffins. But Phillip II changed focus, abandoning Granada for El Escorial, and these sit empty to this day. Only four royals are buried in Granada (at the Royal Chapel). The cathedral's cool, spacious, bright interior is a refreshing break from the dark Gothic of so many Spanish churches. In a move that was modern back in the 18th century, the walls of the choir (the big, heavy wooden box that dominates the center of most Spanish churches) were taken out so that people could be involved in the worship. At about the same time, a bishop ordered the interior painted with lime (for hygienic reasons, during a time of disease). The people liked it, and it stayed white. As you explore, remember that the abundance of Marys is all part of the Counter-

Reformation. Most of the side chapels are decorated in Baroque style. On the outer wall, directly to the right of the high altar, is a politically incorrect version of St. James the Moor-Slayer, with his sword raised high and an armored Moor trampled under his horse's hooves.

Wander back through the pews toward the cathedral's main doors. A small sacristy museum is tucked away in the right corner (as you face the doors). There may be no detailed descriptions for any of the items, but a beautiful bust of St. Pablo (Paul, with a flowing beard) by Cano is worth seeking out. As you head out, look for the music sheets behind the main altar; they're mostly 16th-century Gregorian chants. Notice the sliding C clef. Rather than a fixed G or F clef, the monks knew that this clef—which could be located wherever worked best on the staff—marked middle C, and they chanted to notes relative to that. Go ahead—try singing a few verses of the Latin.

Immediately in front of the cathedral is the stop for minibus #32 to the Alhambra. And four blocks away (if you head left up the busy street, then turn right) is the Albayzín.

Near Plaza Nueva

Hammam Baños Árabes (Arab Baths)—For an intimate and subdued experience, consider some serious relaxation at the Arab Baths, where you can enjoy the three different-temperature pools and a steam room. A maximum of 30 people are allowed in the baths at one time.

Cost and Hours: If you just want a 90-minute soak in the baths, the cost is €22; it costs more to add a 15-minute massage: a regular massage is €32, a traditional scrubbing massage is €39, and to have both costs €49. Daily 10:00-24:00, appointments scheduled every even-numbered hour, co-ed with mandatory swimsuits, quiet atmosphere encouraged, free lockers and towels available, no loaner swimsuits but you can buy one for €12, just off Plaza Nueva and a few doors down from the TI at Santa Ana 16, 50 percent paid reservation required, tel. 958-229-978, www.hammamspain .com/granada.

▲The Albayzín

Explore Spain's best old Moorish quarter, with countless colorful corners, flowery patios, and shady lanes. While the city center of Granada—which is pleasant enough—feels more or less like many other Spanish cities, the Albayzín is unique. You can't say you've really seen Granada until you've at least strolled a few of its twisty lanes. It's an odd mix of very touristy and gritty—with very little in between. Climb high to the San Nicolás church for the best view of the Alhambra. Then wander through the mysterious back streets. (I've listed these sights roughly in order from the San Nicolás viewpoint.)

Getting to the Albayzín: A handy city **minibus** threads its way around the Albayzín from Plaza Nueva (see "Albayzín Circular Bus Tour," next), getting you scenically and sweatlessly to the San Nicolás viewpoint. You can also **taxi** to the San Nicolás church and explore from there. (Consider having your cabbie take you on a detour to the Sacromonte enclave of cave-dwelling Gypsies, described later.)

It's a steep but fascinating 20-minute walk up: Leave the west end of Plaza Nueva on Calle de Elvira. After about 50 yards, at the pharmacy and newsstand, bear right on Calle Calderería Vieja. Follow this stepped street past Moroccan eateries and pastry shops, vendors of imported North African goods, halal butchers, and *teterías* (Moorish tea rooms). The lane bears right, then passes to the left of the church (becoming Cuesta de San Gregorio), and slants, winds, and zigzags uphill. Cuesta de San Gregorio eventually curves left and is regularly signposted. When you reach the Moorish-style house, La Media Luna (with the tall trees and keyhole-style doorway), stop for a photo and a breather, then follow the wall, continuing uphill. At the next intersection (with the black cats), turn right on Aljibe del Gato. Farther on, this street takes a 90-degree turn to the right; at this point, turn left onto Calle Atarasana Vieja. It's confusing, but keep going up, up, up. At the crest (and the dead-end), turn right on Camino Nuevo de San Nicolás, then walk 200 yards to the street that curves up left (look for a bus-stop sign—this is where the minibus would have dropped you off). Continue up the curve and soon you'll see feet hanging from the plaza wall. Steps lead up to the church's viewpoint. Whew! You made it!

Albayzín Circular Bus Tour—The handy Albayzín minibus #31 gallops the 15-minute loop as if in a race, departing from Plaza Nueva about every 15 minutes (pay driver €1.20, minibus #32 does the same loop, but—depending on where you catch it—goes to the Alhambra first). While good for a lift to the top of the Albayzín (buzz when you want to get off), I'd stay on for an entire circle and return to the Albayzín later for dinner—either on foot or by bus again. (Note: The less frequent minibus #35, departing every 40 minutes, does same trip with a side-trip up into Sacromonte.)

Here's the route: Go along up above the Darro River, past the ruins of a bridge and gate and the Paseo de los Tristes square. Turning uphill, pass Sacromonte on the right (entrance to the

Albayzín Neighborhood

STREET WIDTH IS EXAGGERATED FOR CLARITY

PL. DE FATIMA

MURCIA

CALLE

ALHABACA

PARDO

PLAZA APANADEROS

OLD WALL

PLAZA LARGA

Plaza San Miguel el Bajo

Puerta Nueva

ISABEL

NUEVO SAN

SAN NICOLÁS

ABAD

SALVADOR

ELVIRA

TOMASAS

CHORROHUMO STATUE

NUEVA

VIEJA

SAN GREGORIO

ALJIBE TRILLO

CAMINO DEL SACROMONTE

SAN JUAN DE

MOORISH BATHS

LOS REYES

CHAPIN

PLAZA NUEVA

PL. S. ANA

C. DARRO

PASEO DE LOS TRISTES

To CATHEDRAL

GOMEREZ

Arab Baths

RIO DARRO

TO

ALHAMBRA

VIEW

DCH

NOTE: NOT TO SCALE

20 MIN. UPHILL WALK FROM PLAZA NUEVA TO SAN NICOLÁS

1 Hotel Santa Isabel la Real

2 El Numero 8 "Casa de Rafa" (Apts.)

3 Makuto Guesthouse

4 Plaza S. Miguel el Bajo Eateries

5 Casa Torcuato (2 locations)

6 Restaurante El Ladrillo

7 Rest. Estrellas de S. Nicolás & Great Mosque of Granada

8 Bar Kiki

9 Paseo de los Tristes Bars

10 Carmen Mirador de Aixa & Carmen de las Tomasas Rests.

11 Carmen de Aben Humeya Rest.

12 Carmen de la Media Luna (Landmark)

13 Hammam El Bañuelo (Moorish Baths)

14 Hammam Baños Árabes (Arab Baths)

15 To Cave Museum of Sacromonte, Roma Caves & Zambra Dance Clubs

neighborhood marked by a statue of a popular Gypsy guide). Then, turning left, enter the actual Albayzín. After stopping at the church of San Salvador, plunge into the thick of it, with stops below the San Nicolás church (famous viewpoint, and the jumping-off point for my suggested "Exploring the Albayzín" stroll, described later) and at Plaza San Miguel Bajo (cute square with recommended eateries and another viewpoint). Then descend, enjoying a commanding view of Granada on the left as you swing through the modern city. Hitting the city's main drag, Gran Vía del Colón,

GRANADA

Safety in the Albayzín

With tough economic times, young ruffians are hanging out in the dark back lanes of the labyrinthine Albayzín quarter. While this charming Moorish district is certainly safe by day, it can be edgy after dark. Most of the area is fine to wander, though many streets are poorly lit, and the maze of lanes can make it easy to get lost and wind up somewhere you don't want to be. Some nervous travelers choose to avoid the neighborhood entirely after dark, but I recommend venturing into the Albayzín to enjoy its restaurants, ideal sunset views, and charming ambience. Just be sure to exercise normal precautions: Leave your valuables at your hotel, stick to better-lit streets, and take a minibus or taxi home if you're unsure of your route. Violent crime is rare, but pickpocketing is epidemic. Keep a very close eye on your stuff. Some visitors mistakenly think that the danger in this historic "Moorish" district is from Arabs, but the real crooks can be Northern and Eastern European hippies loitering in the squares.

Locals say the biggest hazard when walking in the Albayzín are the many deposits left by its animal inhabitants (and not cleaned up by their poorly trained owners). If you bury your nose in a guidebook while you walk, you'll likely wind up burying your shoe in something else.

make a U-turn at the Gardens of the Triumph, celebrating the Immaculate Conception of the Virgin Mary (notice her statue atop a column). Behind Mary stands the old Royal Hospital—built in the 16th century for Granada's poor by the Catholic kings after the Reconquista, in hopes of winning the favor of the city's conquered residents. From here, zip back into town, stopping at the cathedral, and back home to Plaza Nueva.

▲▲San Nicolás Viewpoint (Mirador de San Nicolás)—For one of Europe's most romantic viewpoints, be here at sunset, when

the Alhambra glows red and the Albayzín widows share the benches with local lovers, hippies, and tourists (free, always open). In 1997 President Clinton made a point to bring his family here—a favorite spot from a trip he made as a student. But this was hardly an original idea; generations of visitors have been drawn here. For an affordable (€3-6) drink with the same million-euro view, step into the El Huerto de Juan Ranas Bar (just below and to the left, at Calle de Atarazana 8).

Great Mosque of Granada—Granada's Muslim population is on the rebound, and now numbers 8 percent of the city's residents. A striking and inviting mosque is just next to the San Nicolás view-point

(to your left as you face the Alhambra). Local Muslims write, "The Great Mosque of Granada signals, after a hiatus of 500 years, the restoration of a missing link with a rich and fecund Islamic contribution to all spheres of human enterprise and activity." Built in 2003 (with money from the local community and Islamic Arab nations), it has a peaceful view courtyard and a minaret that comes with a live call to prayer five times a day (printed schedule inside). It's stirring to see the muezzin holler "God is Great" from the minaret without amplification (locals didn't want it amplified). Visitors are welcome in the courtyard, which offers Alhambra views without the hedonistic ambience of the more famous San Nicolás viewpoint.

Cost and Hours: Free, daily 11:00-14:00 & 18:00-20:30.

Background: While tourists come to Granada to learn about the expulsion of the Moors in 1492, local Muslims are frustrated by what a flier at the mosque calls the "errors, non-sense, and lies local guides perpetuate without knowledge nor shame which flocks of passive tourists accept without questioning." The flier tries to set the record straight, from the Muslim perspective: Muslims were as indigenous as any other group. After living here for seven centuries, the Muslims of Granada and Andalucía were as Iberian as the modern Spaniards of today. Islam is not a religion of immigrants; Islam is not a culture of the Orient and Arabs. "Muslim" and "Arab" are not interchangeable terms. The Muslims of Al-Andalus were not hedonistic. The Reconquista did not "liberate" Spain. Harems were not just full of sexy women. (For more on the Muslim perspective, visit the info desk at the mosque.)

The European Union sees Granada as a center for Muslim-Christian integration—or, at least, co-existence. To Muslims, the city is a symbol of the "holocaust" of the Reconquista, when 135,000 of their people were brutally expelled and many more suffered "forced conversion" in the 16th century. Today there are about 700,000 Muslims in Spain (and about 5 million in France).

Exploring the Albayzín—From the San Nicolás viewpoint and the Great Mosque, you're at the edge of a hilltop neighborhood even the people of Granada recognize as a world apart. Each of the district's 20 churches sits on a spot once occupied by a mosque. When the Reconquista arrived in Granada, the Christians attempted to coexist with the Muslims. But after seven years, this idealistic attempt ended in failure, and the Christians forced the Muslims to convert. In 1567 Muslims were expelled, leading to 200 years of economic depression for the city. Eventually, large walled noble manor houses with private gardens were built here in the depopulated Albayzín. These survive today in the form of the characteristic *carmen* restaurants so popular with visitors.

From the San Nicolás viewpoint, turn your back to the Alhambra and walk north (passing the church on your right and the Biblioteca Municipal on your left). A lane leads past a white stone arch (on your right)—now a chapel built into the old Moorish wall. You're walking past the scant remains of the pre-Alhambra fortress of Granada. At the end of the lane, step down to the right through the 11th-century "New Gate" (Puerta Nueva—older than the Alhambra) and into **Plaza Larga.** In medieval times this tiny square (called "long," because back then it was) served as the local marketplace. It still is a busy market each morning. Casa Pasteles, at the near end of the square, serves good coffee and cakes.

Leave Plaza Larga on **Calle Agua de Albayzín** (as you face Casa Pasteles, it's to your right). The street, named for the public baths that used to line it, shows evidence of the Moorish plumbing system: gutters. Back when Europe's streets were filled with muck, Granada actually had Roman Empire–style gutters with drains leading to clay and lead pipes.

You're in the heart of the Albayzín. Explore. Poke into an old church. They're plain by design to go easy on the Muslim converts, who weren't used to being surrounded by images as they worshipped. You'll see lots of real Muslim culture living in the streets, including many recent Spanish converts.

Sacromonte

The Sacromonte district is home to Granada's thriving Roma community. Marking the entrance to Sacromonte is a statue of Chorrohumo (literally, "exudes smoke," and a play on the slang word for "thief": *chorro*). He was a Roma from Granada, popular in the 1950s for guiding people around the city.

While the neighboring Albayzín is a sprawling zone blanketing a hilltop, Sacromonte is much smaller—very compact and very steep. Most houses are burrowed into the wall of a cliff. Sacromonte has one main street: Camino del Sacromonte, which is lined with caves primed for tourists and restaurants ready to

Granada's Roma (Gypsies)

Both the English word "Gypsy" and its Spanish counterpart, *gitano,* come from the word "Egypt"—where Europeans once believed these nomadic people had originated. Today the preferred term is "Roma," since "Gypsy" has acquired negative connotations (though for clarity's sake, I've used both terms throughout this book).

After migrating from India in the 14th century, the Roma people settled mostly in the Muslim-occupied lands in southern Europe (such as the Balkan Peninsula, then controlled by the Ottoman Turks). Under medieval Muslims, the Roma enjoyed relative tolerance. They were traditionally good with crafts and animals.

The first Roma arrived in Granada in the 15th century—and they've remained tight-knit ever since. Today 50,000 Roma call Granada home, many of them in the district called Sacromonte. In most of Spain, Roma are more assimilated into the general population, but Sacromonte is a large, distinct Roma community. (After the difficult Civil War era, they were joined by many farmers who, like the Roma, appreciated Sacromonte's affordable, practical cave dwellings—warm in the winter and cool in the summer.)

Spaniards, who generally consider themselves to be tolerant and not racist, claim that in maintaining such a tight community, the Roma segregate themselves. The Roma call Spaniards *payos* ("whites"). Recent mixing of Roma and *payos* has given birth to the term *gallipavo* (rooster-duck), although who's who depends upon whom you ask.

Are Roma thieves? Sure, some of them are. But others are honest citizens, trying to make their way in the world just like anyone else. Because of the high incidence of theft, it's wise to be cautious when dealing with a Roma person—but it's also important to keep an open mind.

fight over the bill. (Don't come here expecting to get a deal on anything.) Intriguing lanes run above and below this main drag—a steep hike above Camino del Sacromonte is the cliff-hanging, parallel secondary street, Vereda de Enmedio, which is less touristy, with an authentically residential vibe.

▲**Cave Museum of Sacromonte (Museo Cuevas del Sacromonte)** —This hilltop complex, also known as the Center for the Interpretation of Sacromonte (Centro de Interpretación del Sacromonte), is a kind of open-air folk museum about Granada's unique Roma cave-dwelling tradition (though doesn't have much on the Gypsies themselves). The exhibits, with good English descriptions, are spread through a series of whitewashed caves along a ridge, with spectacular views to the Alhambra. As you stroll from cave to cave, you'll learn about the local geology (rocks, flora, and fauna); crafts (basket-weaving, pottery-making, metalworking, and weaving); and lifestyles (including a look into a typical home and kitchen). There's also an exhibit about other cave-dwelling cultures from around the "troglodyte world," and one about Sacromonte's vital role in the development of Granada's local brand of flamenco. As you wander, imagine this in the 1950s, when it was still a bustling community of Roma cave-dwellers. Today, hippies squat in abandoned caves higher up.

Cost and Hours: €5; April-Oct Tue-Sun 10:00-14:00 & 17:00-20:30, Nov-March Tue-Sun 10:00-14:00 & 16:00-19:00, closed Mon year-round; Barranco de los Negros, tel. 958-215-120, www.sacromontegranada .com.

Getting There: You can ride minibus #35 from Plaza Nueva (ask driver, "*¿Museo Cuevas?*," departs only every 40 minutes) or a taxi. You'll get off at the "Sacromonte 2" bus stop, next to the Venta El Gallo restaurant, at the bottom of the hill along the main road. From there, it's a very steep but interesting 10-minute hike past cave dwellings up to the top of the hill—follow the signs. If you don't want to wait for minibus #35, you can ride #31 or #32 to the entrance of Sacromonte, and walk from there—giving you a good look at the whole area.

Performances: In summer (July-Aug), the center also features flamenco shows and classical guitar concerts in its wonderfully scenic setting (prices and schedules vary—see website above for details).

Zambra Dance—A long flamenco tradition exists in Granada, and the Gypsies of Sacromonte are credited with developing this city's unique flavor of this Andalusian art form. Sacromonte is a good place to see *zambra,* a flamenco variation with a more Oriental feel in which the singer also dances. A half-dozen cave-bars offering *zambra* in the evenings line Sacromonte's main drag. Two well-established venues are Zambra Cueva de la Rocío (€25, includes a drink and a bus ride from hotel, €20 without transport, daily show at 22:00, 1 hour, Camino del Sacromonte 70, tel. 958-227-129) and María la Canastera (€25, includes a drink and transportation from hotel, €17 without transport, daily show at 22:00, 1 hour, Camino del Sacromonte 89, tel. 958-121-183, www.granadainfo.com /canastera). The biggest operation here is the restaurant Venta El Gallo, which has performances of more straightforward flamenco (not specifically *zambra*). Or consider the summer performances at the museum (explained earlier). I'd just go and explore late at night (with no wallet and €30 in my pocket) rather than book an evening through my hotel (they'll likely offer to reserve for you).

Near Granada

Carthusian Monastery (La Cartuja)—A church with an interior that looks as if it squirted out of a can of whipped cream, La Cartuja is nicknamed the "Christian Alhambra" for its elaborate white Baroque stucco work. In the rooms just off the cloister, notice the gruesome paintings of martyrs placidly meeting their grisly fates.

Cost and Hours: €3.50, daily April-Oct 10:00-13:00 & 16:00-20:00, Nov-March 10:00-13:00 & 15:00-18:00, catch bus #8 from Gran Vía del Colón, tel. 958-161-932. The monastery is a mile north of town on the way to Madrid; drivers take the *Méndez Núñez* exit from the A-44 expressway and follow signs.

Sleeping in Granada

In July and August, when Granada's streets are littered with sunstroke victims, rooms are plentiful and prices soft. In the crowded months of April, May, September, and October, prices can spike up 20 percent. (If you see a price range below, it indicates low- to high-season rates—though I've excluded Holy Week and other inflated prices.) Except for the hotels in the Albayzín and near the Alhambra, most of my listings are within a 5-to-10-minute walk of Plaza Nueva.

Given all the restrictions, it's difficult to drive into Granada even when you know the system. While few hotels have parking facilities, any of them can direct you to a garage (such as Parking San Agustín, just off Gran Vía del Colón, €25/day).

On or near Plaza Nueva

Each of these (except the hostel) is big, professional, plenty comfortable, and perfectly located. Prices vary with demand.

$$$ Casa del Capitel Nazarí, just off the church end of Plaza Nueva, is a restored 16th-century Renaissance palace transformed into 18 small but tastefully decorated rooms, all facing a courtyard that hosts changing art exhibits (Sb-€60-88, Db-€75-118, extra bed-€35-38, breakfast-€9, includes afternoon tea/coffee, aircon, free Internet access and Wi-Fi, parking-€18.50/day, Cuesta Aceituneros 6, tel. 958-215-260, fax 958-215-806, www.hotelcasa capitel.com, info@hotelcasacapitel.com).

$$$ Hotel Casa 1800 Granada, with 25 rooms around a beautiful, airy old courtyard in the lower part of the Albayzín

Sleep Code

(€1 = about $1.40, country code: 34)
S = Single, **D** = Double/Twin, **T** = Triple, **Q** = Quad, **b** = bathroom, **s** = shower only. Unless otherwise noted, credit cards are accepted and English is spoken. Prices include the IVA hotel tax. Breakfast may or may not be included.

    To help you easily sort through these listings, I've divided the accommodations into three categories based on the price for a standard double room with bath during high season:

$$$ Higher Priced—Most rooms €100 or more.
  $$ Moderately Priced—Most rooms between €50-100.
    $ Lower Priced—Most rooms €50 or less.

Prices can change without notice; verify the hotel's current rates online or by email. For other updates, see www.ricksteves.com/update.

(just steps above the Paseo de los Tristes), sets the bar for affordable class. It's tidy and well-run, and offers special extras, such as a complimentary tea and coffee bar each afternoon (standard Db-€135, pricier "superior" and "deluxe" rooms are available but not much different, big buffet breakfast-€11, air-con, elevator, free Wi-Fi, Benalúa 11, tel. 958-210-700, www.hotelcasa1800granada.com, info@hotelcasa1800granada.com).

$$$ Hotel Maciá Plaza, right on the colorful Plaza Nueva, has 44 smallish, clean, modern, and classy rooms. Choose between an on-the-square view or a quieter interior room (Sb-€60-75, Db-€120, €20 extra for a square view, extra bed-€15, 10 percent discount in 2012 when you show this book at check-in—but you must book direct, good buffet breakfast-€7.50, air-con, elevator, free Wi-Fi, Plaza Nueva 5, tel. 958-227-536, fax 958-227-533, www.maciahoteles.com, maciaplaza@maciahoteles.com).

$$ Hotel Anacapri is a bright, cool marble oasis with 49 modern rooms and a quiet lounge (Sb-€55-65, Db-€75-97, Tb-€95-117, extra bed-€20, includes breakfast with direct bookings in 2012 except with promotional rates, air-con, elevator, free limited Internet access and free Wi-Fi in lobby with this book, parking-€15, 2 blocks toward Gran Vía from Plaza Nueva at Calle Joaquín Costa 7, just a block from cathedral bus stop, tel. 958-227-477, fax 958-228-909, www.hotelanacapri.com, reservas@hotelanacapri.com, helpful Kathy speaks Iowan).

$$ NH Hotel Inglaterra is a modern and peaceful chain hotel, with 36 rooms offering all the comforts (Db-€55-90, extra bed-€20-30, buffet breakfast-€13, air-con, elevator to third floor

Granada Hotels & Restaurants

B BUS STOP w/#s
#32 TO ALHAMBRA
#31 + #35 TO
ALBAYZÍN

P PARKING

MERCADO SAN AGUSTÍN

CATHEDRAL + ROYAL CHAPEL

ALBAYZÍN
MOORISH QUARTER

TO SAN NICOLÁS VIEWPOINT + PLAZA LARGA

TO TRAIN + BUS STATIONS

TO SACRAMONTE

PLAZA NUEVA

PLAZA DE BIB-RAMBLA

PLAZA ISABEL LA CATÓLICA

PLAZA DEL CARMEN

PUERTA REAL

ARAB BATHS

TO ALHAMBRA

100 YARDS
100 METERS

DCH

❶ Casa del Capitel Nazarí
❷ Hotel Casa 1800 Granada
❸ Hotel Maciá Plaza
❹ Hotel Anacapri
❺ NH Hotel Inglaterra
❻ Oasis Hostel Granada
❼ Hotel Puerta de las Granadas
❽ Pensión Landazuri
❾ Hostal Residencia Britz
❿ Hostal Navarro Ramos

⓫ Hostal Austria
⓬ Hotel Los Tilos
⓭ To Hotel Reina Cristina, Hostals Lima & Rodri & Zurita Pensión
⓮ Bodegas Castañeda
⓯ Restaurante Sevilla
⓰ La Cueva de 1900
⓱ Arrayanes Restaurante
⓲ Calle Calderería Nueva Tea Shops
⓳ Los Italianos Ice Cream
⓴ Mercado San Agustín
㉑ Pescadería Market Stalls

only, free Wi-Fi in lobby, parking-€14, Cetti Merien 6, tel. 958-221-559, fax 958-227-100, www.nh-hotels.com, nhinglaterra@nh -hotels.com).

$ Oasis Hostel Granada offers 90 beds in 11 rooms (all with bathrooms) and lots of backpacker bonding, just a block above the lively Moorish-flavored tourist drag (6-10 bunks per room, €16-20 per person, includes breakfast and sheets, free Internet access and Wi-Fi, shared kitchen, Placeta Correo Viejo 3, tel. 958-215-848, www.hostelsoasis.com).

Cheap Sleeps on Cuesta de Gomérez

These are inexpensive and ramshackle lodgings on this pedestrian-only street leading from Plaza Nueva up to the Alhambra.

$$ Hotel Puerta de las Granadas has 16 rooms with a sterile business-class vibe, an inviting cafeteria courtyard, and a handy location (basic patio-view Db-€59-89, €5-10 more for street view, €15 more for cathedral view, €25 more for Alhambra view, ask for 5 percent Rick Steves discount in 2012 if you book direct, breakfast-€8 or included during slow times, air-con, free Internet access and Wi-Fi, free tea in cafeteria all day, Cuesta de Gomérez 14, tel. 958-216-230, fax 958-216-231, www.hotelpuertadelasgranadas .com, reservas@hotelpuertadelasgranadas.com).

$ Pensión Landazuri is run by friendly English-speaking Matilde Landazuri, her son Manolo, and daughters Margarita and Elisa. Their characteristic old house has 18 rooms—some are well-worn, while others are renovated. It boasts hardworking, helpful management and a great roof garden with an Alhambra view (S-€24, Sb-€36, D-€34, Db-€45, Tb-€60, Qb-€70, eggs-and-bacon breakfast-€3.50, parking-€10/day, Cuesta de Gomérez 24, tel. & fax 958-221-406, www.hostallandazuri.com, info@hostallandazuri.com). The Landazuris also run a good, cheap café.

$ Hostal Residencia Britz, overlooking Plaza Nueva, is simple and no-nonsense. All of its 22 basic rooms are streetside— bring earplugs (S-€25, D-€36, Db-€48, no breakfast, fans but no air-con, elevator, free Wi-Fi, Plaza Nueva y Gomérez 1, tel. & fax 958-223-652, www.lisboaweb.com, reservasbritz@hotmail.com).

$ Hostal Navarro Ramos is a little cash-only cheapie, renting seven rooms (five with private baths) facing an interior air-shaft (S-€20, D-€27, Db-€36, no breakfast, free Wi-Fi, Cuesta de Gomérez 21, tel. 958-250-555, www.pensionnavarroramos.com, Carmen).

$ Hostal Austria, run by English-speaking Austrian Irene (ee-RAY-nay), rents 16 basic but tidy backpacker-type rooms (Sb-€25-30, Db-€35-40, Tb-€50-60, Qb-€65-75, Quint/b-€80-90, family rooms, no breakfast, air-con, free Wi-Fi, Cuesta de

Gomérez 4, tel. & fax 958-227-075, www.pensionaustria.com, pensionaustria@pensionaustria.com).

Near the Cathedral

$$ Hotel Los Tilos offers 30 comfortable, business-like rooms (some with balconies) on the charming traffic-free Plaza de Bib-Rambla behind the cathedral. Guests are welcome to use the fourth-floor terrace with views of the cathedral and the Alhambra (Sb-€45-55, Db-€55-80, Tb-€77-100, prices may be cheaper if you reserve online, free breakfast when you book direct and show the 2012 edition of this book at check-in, air-con, free Wi-Fi, parking-€18/day, Plaza de Bib-Rambla 4, tel. 958-266-712, fax 958-266-801, www.hotellostilos.com, clientes@hotellostilos.com, friendly José María).

On or near Plaza de la Trinidad

The charming, park-like square called Plaza de la Trinidad is just a short walk west of the cathedral area (Pescadería and Bib-Rambla squares). It's also home to several good accommodations.

$$$ Hotel Reina Cristina has 55 quiet, elegant rooms a few steps off Plaza de la Trinidad. Check out the great Mudejar ceiling and the painting at the entrance of this house, where the famous Spanish poet Federico García Lorca hid until he was captured and executed by the Guardia Civil (Sb-€46-90, Db-€66-139, Tb-€81-169, skip breakfast to save €13 per person, air-con, elevator, pay Internet access, free Wi-Fi in lobby, parking-€18/day, near Plaza de la Trinidad at Tablas 4, tel. 958-253-211, fax 958-255-728, www .hotelreinacristina.com, clientes@hotelreinacristina.com).

$ Hostal Lima, run with class by Manolo, has 25 small but well-appointed rooms in two buildings a block off the square. The public areas are decorated with flamboyant medieval flair— colorful tiles, wood-carved life-sized figures, and so on (Sb-€33, Db-€42, Tb-€65, breakfast-€6, air-con, elevator in one building only, free Wi-Fi, parking-€12, Laurel de las Tablas 17, tel. 958-295-029, www.hostallimagranada.com).

$ Hostal Rodri, run by Manolo's brother José, has 10 similarly good rooms a few doors down that feel new and classy for their price range (Sb-€30, Db-€43, breakfast-€6, air-con, free cable Internet, parking-€12, Laurel de las Tablas 9, tel. 958-288-043, www.hostalrodri.com, info@hostalrodri.com).

$ Zurita Pensión, well-run by Francisco and Loli, faces Plaza de la Trinidad. Eight of the 14 rooms have small balconies, but even with their double-paned windows, they may come with night noise (S-€21, D-€34, Db-€42, Tb-€63, air-con, free Wi-Fi, parking-€12-15/day, Plaza de la Trinidad 7, tel. 958-275-020, www .pensionzurita.com, pensionzurita@gmail.com).

In the Albayzín

Note that some consider this area sketchy after dark (see sidebar on page 112.

$$ Hotel Santa Isabel la Real, an elegant medieval mansion, has 11 rooms ringing a noble courtyard. Each room is a bit different; basic rooms look to the patio, while various pricier rooms have better exterior views. Buried deep in the Albayzín and furnished in a way that gives you the old Moorish Granada ambience, it offers a warm welcome and rich memories (Db-€85-105 with breakfast, air-con, elevator, free Internet access and Wi-Fi, parking-€14/day, midway between San Nicolás viewpoint and Plaza San Miguel Bajo on Calle Santa Isabel la Real, immediately at a bus stop, tel. 958-294-658, fax 958-294-645, www.hotelsantaisabellareal.com, info@hotelsantaisabellareal.com).

$$ El Numero 8 "Casa de Rafa" is a traditional house in the heart of the Albayzín that's been converted into four small, funky kitchenette apartments with an eclectic, ever-evolving artistic feel. Chicago-raised, easygoing owner Rafa lives on-site. You'll share two tiny patios and a rooftop terrace with a spectacular, in-your-face view of the Alhambra. Contact Rafa in advance to set up a time to check in. He'll ease your arrival by meeting you at a taxi or bus drop-off point and walking you back to the apartment (Sb-€40-50, Db-€50-65, extra person-€10, 2-night minimum, fans but no air-con, free Wi-Fi, 5-minute walk from Plaza Nueva at tiny Plaza Virgen del Carmen, tel. 958-220-682, mobile 610-322-216, www.elnumero8.com, casaocho @gmail.com).

$$ 1001 Nights Granada, run by American Frederick and his Spanish wife, rents 15 renovated and fully furnished duplexes and apartments in traditional Moorish houses situated in the Albayzín district, many with grand Alhambra views (Db-€90 in March-May and Sept-Oct, €72 in July-Aug and Jan-Feb, prices vary with size—see photos and videos on website, 2-night minimum—longer during holidays, 20 percent deposit required to reserve online, pay the balance in cash after you arrive, electronic check-in so arrive when you like, no breakfast, air-con, free Wi-Fi, some units have private terraces and swimming pools, mobile 620-585-594, www.1001nights.es, info@1001nights.es).

$ Makuto Guesthouse, a hostel tucked deep in the Albayzín, feels like a hippie commune you can pay to join for a couple of days. With 40 beds in seven rooms clustered around a lush garden courtyard that feels made for hanging out—including several hammock-and-lounge-sofa "hang-out zones"—it exudes an easygoing Albayzín vibe (Db-€50-60, bunk in 4-to-6-bed room-€15-18, includes breakfast, free Internet access and Wi-Fi, dinners available most nights, Calle Tiña 18, tel. 958-805-876, www .makutoguesthouse.com).

In or near the Alhambra

If you want to stay on the Alhambra grounds, you have two popular options (famous, overpriced, and generally booked up long in advance) and one practical and economic place above the parking lot. All are a half-mile up the hill from Plaza Nueva.

$$$ Parador de Granada San Francisco offers 40 designer rooms in a former Moorish palace that was later transformed into a 15th-century Franciscan monastery. It's considered Spain's premier parador...and that's saying something (standard Db-€320, breakfast-€20, air-con, free Wi-Fi, free parking, Calle Real de la Alhambra, tel. 958-221-440, fax 958-222-264, www.parador.es, granada@parador.es). You must book months ahead to spend the night in this lavishly located, stodgy, and historic palace. Any peasant, however, can drop in for a coffee, drink, snack, or meal.

$$$ Hotel América is classy and cozy, with 17 rooms in an early-19th-century house next to the parador (Sb-€74, Db-€120, €25-40 more for a bigger room with a terrace, breakfast-€8, free Wi-Fi, parking-€14/day, closed Dec-Feb, Calle Real de la Alhambra 53, tel. 958-227-471, fax 958-227-470, www.hotelamerica granada.com, reservas@hotelamericagranada.com, friendly Isabel). Book well in advance.

$$ Hotel Guadalupe, big and modern with 57 sleek rooms, is quietly and conveniently located overlooking the Alhambra parking lot. While a 30-minute hike above the town, many (especially drivers) find this to be a practical option (Sb-€50-72, Db-€55-115, Tb-€80-135, bigger "superior" rooms with Jacuzzis and balconies aren't worth the extra cost, breakfast-€9, air-con, elevator, free Wi-Fi in lobby, parking in Alhambra lot-€14, Paseo de la Sabica 30, tel. 958-225-730, www.hotelguadalupe.es, info @hotelguadalupe.es).

Eating in Granada

Restaurants generally serve lunch from 13:00 to 16:00 and dinner from 20:00 until very late (Spaniards don't start dinner until about 21:00). Many of Granada's bars still serve a small tapas plate free with any beer or wine—a tradition that's dying out in most of Spain. Save on your food expenses by doing a tapas crawl (especially good along Calle Navas, right off Plaza del Carmen) and claim your "right" to a free tapa with every drink. For more budget-eating thrills, buy picnic supplies near Plaza Nueva, and sling them up to the Albayzín. This makes for a great cheap date at the San Nicolás viewpoint or on one of the scattered squares and lookout points.

In search of an edible memory? A local specialty, *tortilla Sacromonte,* is a spicy omelet with pig's brain and other organs. *Berenjenas fritas* (fried eggplant) and *habas con jamón* (small green fava beans cooked with cured ham) are worth seeking out. *Tinto de verano*—a red-wine spritzer with lemon and ice—is refreshing on a hot evening.

In the Albayzín

The most interesting meals hide out deep in the Albayzín (Moorish quarter). The easy way to get there is by taking minibus #31 from Plaza Nueva or #32 from Plaza Isabel La Católica. To find a particular square, ask any local, or follow my directions and the full-color Granada map at the front of this book. If dining late, take the minibus or a taxi back to your hotel; Albayzín back streets can be poorly lit, confusing to follow, and plagued by pickpockets.

Part of the charm of the quarter is the lazy ambience on its squares: **Plaza Larga** is extremely characteristic, with tapas bar tables spilling out onto the square, a morning market, and a much-loved pastry shop. But the next area is even more enticing...

Plaza San Miguel el Bajo: The farthest hike into the Albayzín, this neighborhood square boasts my favorite funky local scene—kids kicking soccer balls, old-timers warming benches, and women gossiping under the facade of a humble church. It's circled by inviting little bars and restaurants. **El Acebuche** promises "Andalusian flavor with a light dash of the Orient" (€11-16 meals, daily). **Rincón de la Aurora** has a €10 weekday fixed-price meal and €6-12 meals anytime, plus tapas (closed Wed and Sun afternoon). **El Ají** is a sit-down restaurant with a mod vibe and a bit of Argentinian flair (€10-14 starters, €12-20 main dishes, closed Tue). And just down the street (beyond El Ají) is a little hole-in-the-wall **take-away shop** selling empanadas and pizza by the slice to munch out on the square (closed Tue). This is a great spot to end your Albayzín visit, as there's a viewpoint overlooking the modern city a block away. Minibuses #31 and #32 rumble by every few minutes, ready to zip you back to Plaza Nueva.

Casa Torcuato is a hardworking eatery serving straightforward yet creative food in a smart upstairs dining room. They serve good fixed-price meals for lunch (€10) and dinner (€15). Plates of fresh fish run €8-12 and their tropical salad includes a Tahitian wonderland of fruits (closed Sun, 2 blocks beyond Plaza

Larga at Calle Aqua 20, second location on nearby Calle Pagés, tel. 958-202-039).

Restaurante El Ladrillo, with outdoor tables on a peaceful square, is *the* place for piles of fish. Their popular €12 *barco* ("boat-load" of mixed fried fish) is a fishy feast that stuffs two to the gills. The smaller €7.50 *canoa* ("canoe") fills one person adequately, or, when combined with a salad, can feed two (€5 salads, €9-12 fish dishes, daily 12:00-24:00, on Placeta de Fátima, just off Calle Pagés).

Near the San Nicolás Viewpoint

This area is thoroughly touristy, so don't expect any local hangouts here. But these two options are suitable for a good meal.

Restaurante Estrellas de San Nicolás, in the former home of a well-loved Albayzín bigwig, immediately next to the view terrace, features similar views from its two floors of indoor seating. Serving well-regarded food, this splurge has quickly acquired a loyal local following (€10-20 starters, €20-27 main dishes, €31 fixed-price diner, €20 or €27 fixed-price lunch, Atrazana Vieja 1, tel. 958-288-739).

Bar Kiki, a laid-back and popular bar-restaurant on an unpretentious square, serves simple tapas. Try their tasty fried eggplant (random hours, closed Wed, just behind viewpoint at Plaza de San Nicolás 9).

Paseo de los Tristes: This spot is like a stage set of outdoor bars on a terrace over the river gorge. While it lacks a serious restaurant and the food values are mediocre at best, the scene—cool along a stream under trees, with the floodlit Alhambra high above, and a happy crowd of locals enjoying a meal or drink out—is a winner. As this is at the base of the Albayzín, there's no issue of danger after dark here. It's a simple, level five-minute walk back to Plaza Nueva.

Carmens in the Albayzín

For a more memorable but expensive experience, consider fine dining with Alhambra views in a *carmen,* a typical Albayzín house with a garden (buzz to get in). After the Reconquista, the Albayzín became depopulated. Wealthy families took larger tracts of land and built fortified mansions with terraced gardens within their walls. Today, rather than growing produce, the gardens of many of these *carmens* host dining tables and pricey, romantic restaurants.

Carmen Mirador de Aixa, small and elegant, has the dreamiest Alhambra views among the *carmens.* You'll pay a little more, but the food is exquisitely presented and the view makes the splurge worthwhile (€10-20 starters, €20-27 main dishes; closed Sun dinner, all day Mon, and Tue lunch; next to Carmen de las

Tomasas at Carril de San Agustín 2, tel. 958-223-616).

Carmen de las Tomasas serves gourmet traditional Andalusian cuisine with killer views in a dressy/stuffy atmosphere (€9-17 starters, €20-26 main dishes, Wed-Sun 13:00-16:00 & 20:15-23:30, generally—but not always—closed Mon-Tue, reservations required, Carril de San Agustín, tel. 958-224-108, Cristina).

Carmen de Aben Humeya is the least expensive, least stuffy, and least romantic. Its outdoor-only seating lets you enjoy a meal or just a long cup of coffee while gazing at the Alhambra. This is a rare place enthusiastic about dinner salads (€10-18 starters and main dishes, daily 13:00-24:00, food served 13:30-15:30 & 20:30-23:30, closed Wed, also closed Tue evenings in winter, Cuesta de las Tomasas 12, tel. 958-226-665).

Near Plaza Nueva

For people-watching, consider the many restaurants on Plaza Nueva or Plaza de Bib-Rambla (south of cathedral). For a happening scene, check out the bars on and around Calle de Elvira. It's best to wander and see where the biggest crowds are.

Bodegas Castañeda is the best mix of lively, central, and cheap among the tapas bars I visited. Just a block off Plaza Nueva, it requires a bit of self-service: When crowded, you need to power your way to the bar to order; when quiet, you can order at the bar and grab a little table (same budget prices). Consider their *tablas combinadas*—variety plates of cheese, meat, and *ahumados* (four different varieties of smoked fish)—and tasty *croquetas* (breaded and fried mashed potatoes and ham). Order a glass of their gazpacho. The big kegs tempt you with different local sherries. Tapas can be ordered from an easy menu and cost €2-3 apiece (€6-11 half-*raciones*, €10-15 *raciones*, daily 11:30-16:30 & 19:00-1:00 in the morning, Calle Almireceros 1, tel. 958-215-464). Don't be confused by the neighboring, similar "Antigua Bodega Castañeda" restaurant nearby (run by a relative and not as good).

Restaurante Sevilla, with its tight and charming little dining room behind a high-energy tapas bar, has been a favorite of well-dressed natives for 75 years. Specialties include paella, other rice dishes, soups, and salads. You'll eat surrounded by old photos of local big shots who've dined here. On hot nights, tables pour out onto the little square facing the Royal Chapel. It's a local-feeling, elegant, urban scene. In the evenings, the bar displays a yummy spread of tapas—you get one free with any drink you buy, and can pay €0.50 for each additional one (€8-12 starters, €14-20 main dishes, daily 9:00-24:00 except closed Sun evenings in summer, may close for renovation in 2012; across from Royal Chapel at Calle Oficios 12, tel. 958-221-223).

La Cueva de 1900 is a fresh, family-friendly deli-like place on the main drag appreciated for its simple dishes and quality ingredients. It's proud of its homemade hams, sausages, and cheeses—sold in 100-gram lots and served with checkered-tablecloth style. Their fixed-price lunch is €10, but if you've had enough meat, try one of their good €5-7 salads (€3-4 *bocadillo* sandwiches, €8-16 meaty meals, daily 12:00-24:00, Calle Reyes Católicos 42, tel. 958-229-327).

At **Arrayanes,** a good Moroccan restaurant, Mostafa will help you choose among the many salads, the *briwat* (a chicken-and-cinnamon pastry appetizer), the *pastela* (a first-course version of *briwat*), the couscous, or *tajin* dishes. He treats his guests like old friends...especially the ladies (€4-10 starters, €10-14 main dishes, Wed-Mon 13:30-16:30 & 19:30-23:30, closed Tue, Cuesta Marañas 4, where Calles Calderería Nueva and Vieja meet, tel. 958-228-401, mobile 619-076-862).

Hippie Options on Calle Calderería Nueva: From Plaza Nueva, walk two long blocks down Calle de Elvira and turn right onto the wonderfully hip and Arabic-feeling Calle Calderería Nueva, which leads uphill into the Albayzín. The street is lined with trendy *teterías.* These small tea shops, open all day, are good places to linger, chat, and imagine you're in Morocco. Many also have the opportunity to rent a hookah (water pipe) to smoke some fruit-flavored tobacco with friends. Some are conservative and unmemorable, and others are achingly romantic, filled with incense, beaded cushions, live African music, and effervescent young hippies. They sell light meals such as crêpes, and a worldwide range of teas, all marinated in a candlelit snake-charmer ambience.

Dessert: **Los Italianos,** Italian-run and teeming with locals, is popular for its ice cream, *horchata* (*chufa*-nut drink), and shakes. When Michelle Obama visited Granada in 2010, this is where she got her ice-cream fix (mid-March-mid-Oct daily 8:00-24:00, closed off-season, across the street from cathedral and Royal Chapel at Gran Vía 4, tel. 958-224-034).

Markets: Though heavy on meat, **Mercado San Agustín** also sells fruits and veggies. Throughout the EU, locals lament the loss of the authentic old market halls as they are replaced with new hygienic versions. If nothing else, it's as refreshingly cool as a meat locker (Mon-Sat 9:00-15:00, closed Sun, very quiet on Mon, a block north of cathedral and a half-block off Gran Vía on Calle Cristo San Agustín). Tucked away in the back of the market is a very cheap and colorful little eatery: **Cafetería San Agustín.** They make their own *churros* and give a small tapa free with each drink (menu on wall). If waiting for the cathedral or Royal Chapel to open, kill time in the market. The stalls around the market and the **Pescadería** square, downhill from the actual market and a block from Plaza de Bib-Rambla, are actually more popular with locals looking to buy produce.

Granada Connections

From Granada by Train to: Barcelona (1/day Wed, Thu, and Sat only, 11.5 hours; also 1/night daily, 12.5 hours), **Madrid** (2/day on Altaria, 4.5 hours), **Toledo** (all service is via Madrid, nearly hourly AVE connections to Toledo), **Algeciras** (3/day, 4.25 hours), **Ronda** (3/day, 2.5 hours), **Sevilla** (4/day, 3 hours), **Córdoba** (2/day, 2.5 hours), **Málaga** (3/day, 2.5-3.25 hours on AVE, transfer in Bobadilla or Antequera). Train info: toll tel. 902-320-320, www.renfe.com. Many of these connections have a more frequent (and sometimes much faster) bus option—see below.

By Bus to: Nerja (7/day, 2-2.5 hours, more possible with transfer in Motril), **Sevilla** (to Plaza de Armas Station: 8/day, 3 hours *directo*, 4 hours *ruta*; to El Prado Station: 2/day, 3.25 hours), **Córdoba** (8/day, 2.5-3 hours), **Madrid** (roughly hourly, 5 hours, most to Estación Sur, a few to Intercambiador de Avenida de América, one direct to Barajas Airport), **Málaga** (hourly, 1.5-2 hours), **Algeciras** (4/day *directo*, 4 hours; 1/day *ruta*, 5.5 hours), **La Línea de la Concepción/Gibraltar** (2/week on Fri and Sun, 5.5 hours; otherwise change in Algeciras), **Jerez** (1/day, 4.75 hours), **Barcelona** (4/day, 12.75-15 hours, often at odd times, only one fully daytime connection departs Granada at 10:00 and arrives Barcelona at 24:15). To reach **Ronda,** change in Málaga or Antequera; to reach **Tarifa,** change in Algeciras or Málaga. All of these buses are run by Alsa (tel. 902-422-242, www.alsa.es). If there's a long line at the ticket windows, you can use the automated machines (press the flag for English)—but these only sell tickets for some major routes (such as Málaga), and sometimes eat credit cards like a Spaniard eats *jamón*.

By Car: To drive to **Nerja** (1.5 hours away), take the exit for the coastal town of Motril. You'll wind through 50 scenic miles south of Granada, then follow signs for Málaga. You can also hop a taxi to Nerja (€125 fixed rate).

CÓRDOBA

Straddling a sharp bend of the Guadalquivir River, Córdoba has a glorious Roman and Moorish past, once serving as a regional capital for both empires. It's home to Europe's best Islamic sight after Granada's Alhambra: the Mezquita, a splendid and remarkably well-preserved mosque that dates from A.D. 784. When you step inside the mosque, which is magical in its grandeur, you can imagine Córdoba as the center of a thriving and sophisticated culture. During the Dark Ages, when much of Europe was barbaric and illiterate, Córdoba was a haven of enlightened thought—famous for religious tolerance, artistic expression, and dedication to philosophy and the sciences.

Beyond the magnificent Mezquita, the city of Córdoba has two sides: The extremely touristy maze of streets immediately surrounding the giant main attraction, lined with trinket shops, hotels, and restaurants; and the workaday part of town (centered on Plaza de las Tendillas). While the over-commercialized vibe of the touristy area can be off-putting, a quick walk takes you to real-life Córdoba.

Planning Your Time

Ideally, Córdoba is worth two nights and a day. Don't rush the magnificent Mezquita, but also consider sticking around to experience the city's other pleasures: Wander the evocative Jewish Quarter, enjoy the tapas scene, and explore the modern part of town.

However, if you're tight on time, it's possible to do Córdoba more quickly—especially since it's conveniently located on the AVE bullet-train line (and because, frankly, Córdoba is less interesting than the other two big Andalusian cities, Sevilla and Granada). To see Córdoba as an efficient stopover between Madrid and Sevilla (or as a side-trip from Sevilla—frequent trains, 45-minute trip), focus on the Mezquita: Taxi from the station, spend two hours there, explore the old town for an hour...and then scram.

Orientation to Córdoba

Córdoba's big draw is the mosque-turned-cathedral called the Mezquita (for pronunciation ease, think female mosquito). Most of the town's major sights are nearby, including the Alcázar, a former royal castle. And though the town seems to ignore its marshy Guadalquivir River (a prime bird-watching area), the riverbank sports a Renaissance triumphal arch next to a stout "Roman Bridge." The bridge leads to the town's old fortified gate (which now houses a museum on Moorish culture, the Museum of Al-Andalus Life). The Mezquita is buried in the characteristic medieval town. Around that stretches the Jewish Quarter, then the modern city—which feels much like any other in Spain, but with some striking Art Deco buildings at Plaza de las Tendillas and lots of Art Nouveau lining Avenida del Gran Capitán.

Tourist Information

Córdoba has helpful TIs at the train station, Alcázar, and Plaza de las Tendillas (all open daily 9:30-14:00 & 17:00-19:30, tel. 902-201-774, www.turismodecordoba.org). Another TI, near the Mezquita, is run separately and covers all of Andalucía (Mon-Fri 9:30-19:30, Sat-Sun 9:30-15:00, Torrijos 10, tel. 957-355-179).

Arrival in Córdoba

By Train or Bus: Córdoba's train station is located on Avenida de América. Built in 1991 to accommodate the high-speed AVE train line, the slick train station has ATMs, restaurants, a variety of shops, a TI booth (on the concourse above the track), an information counter, and a small lounge for first-class AVE passengers. Taxis and local buses are just outside.

The bus station is across the street from the train station (on Avenida Vía Augusta, to the north). It's about a 25-minute walk from either station to the old town. There's no luggage storage at the train station, but the bus station has lockers (€3.50, look for *consigna* sign and buy token at machine).

To get to the old town, hop a **taxi** (€6 to the Mezquita) or catch **bus** #3 or #16 (buy €1.15 ticket on board, ask driver for *"mezquita,"* get off at Calle San Fernando, and take Calle del Portillo, following the twists and turns—and occasional signs—to the Mezquita).

CÓRDOBA

Córdoba

200 YARDS
200 METERS

BUS STN.

AUGUSTA

TRAIN STATION   ARFE

AV. DE LA LIBERTAD

AV. DE

AV. CERVANTES

AV. MOZARABES

JARDINES DE

AMERICA

AV. DE GRAN CRUZ

JOSÉ CRUZ

TEJARES

OSARIO

PLAZA COLÓN

STA. MARINA

PALACIO DE VIANA

ZARCO

LOSA

JUAN RUFO

SAN PABLO

AV. MEDINA AZAHARA

TO MADINAT AL-ZAHRA

ANT. MAURA

AV. REP. ARGENTINA

AV. DE LA VICTORIA

PASEO DE LA VICTORIA

CONC

CAPITÁN

ALF. XII

CLAUDIO

P. LOPEZ

PL. CORREDERA

P

V. LOPE HOCES

BARROSO

CONDE HEREDIA

PLAZA DE LAS TENDILLAS

J. VALERA

M. LUIS

TO

SAN FERNANDO

LUCANO

JEWISH QUARTER

CASA DE SEFARAD

JUDIOS

CARD. HERRERO

B

P. RIBERA

N

AV. AEROPUERTO

AV. CONDE VALL.

SYNAGOGUE

OLD WALL

MEZQUITA

AV. CUSTODIOS

SAN BASILIO

CAB.

ALCÁZAR

RONDA ISASA

GUADAL RIVER QUIVIR

ROMAN BRIDGE

M. PIDAL

CORR.

AV. ALCÁZAR

AV. DE FRA ALBINO

MUSEUM OF AL-ANDALUS LIFE

PATIOS AREA

TO MECCA

SEE CORDOBA CENTER DETAIL MAP

1 The Terrace Backpackers Hostel

2 To Bodegas Campos

3 Taverna Salinas

4 Taberna San Miguel

P PARKING

B BUS STOPS FROM STATION

DCH

To **walk** the 25 minutes from the train station to the Mezquita, turn left onto Avenida de América, then right on Avenida del Gran Capitán, which becomes a pedestrian zone. At the end, ask someone, "*¿Dónde está la Mezquita?*" You'll be directed downhill, through the whitewashed old Jewish Quarter.

Helpful Hints

Closed Days: The synagogue, Madinat Al-Zahra, and Palacio de Viana are closed on Monday. The Mezquita is open daily.

Festival: During the first half of May, Córdoba hosts the Concurso Popular de Patios Cordobeses—a patio contest.

Cheap Tricks: The Alcázar de los Reyes Cristianos and related Baths of the Caliphate Alcázar are free all day Wednesday.

Laundry: The helpful staff at **Sol y Mar** will wash, dry, and fold your laundry (€13.10/load, usually same-day service if you drop off in the morning, cheaper for self-service, Mon-Fri 9:30-13:30 & 17:00-20:30, Sat 9:30-13:30, closed Sun, Calle del Doctor Fleming 8, tel. 957-298-929).

Local Guides: Isabel Martinez Richter is a charming archaeologist who loves to make the city come to life for curious Americans (mobile 669-369-645, isabmr@terra.es). **Angel Lucena** is also a good teacher and a joy to be with (€100/3 hours, mobile 607-898-079, lucenaangel@hotmail.com).

Sights in Córdoba

▲▲▲The Mezquita

This massive former mosque—now with a 16th-century church rising up from the middle—was once the center of Western Islam and the heart of a cultural capital that rivaled Baghdad and Istanbul. A wonder of the medieval world, it's remarkably well-preserved, giving today's visitors a chance to soak up the ambience of Islamic Córdoba in its 10th-century prime.

Cost and Hours: €8, ticket kiosk inside the Patio de los Naranjos, Mon-Sat free entry until 10:00 (because they don't want to charge a fee to attend the 9:30 Mass), dry €3.50 audioguide; open March-Oct Mon-Sat 8:30-19:00, Sun 8:30-10:30 & 14:00-19:00; Nov-Feb Mon-Sat 10:00-18:00, Sun 8:30-10:30 & 14:00-18:00; last entry 30 minutes before closing, Christian altar accessible only after 10:30 unless you attend Mass, try to avoid midday crowds (11:00-15:00) by coming early or late; tel. 957-470-512, www .catedraldecordoba.es.

⊙ Self-Guided Tour: Before entering the patio, take in the exterior of the Mezquita. The mosque's massive footprint is clear when you survey its sprawling walls from outside. At 600 feet by 400 feet, it seems to dominate the higgledy-piggledy medieval

The Mezquita

CÓRDOBA

PUERTA DEL PERDÓN
ENTER

CALLE   HERRERO

50 YARDS
50 METERS

② Tickets Audioguides

PATIO DE LOS NARANJOS

① Fountain

③ EXIT ↑

CALLE DE TORRIJOS

CALLE

GONZÁLEZ FRANCES

④

⑫ ⑪

CATHEDRAL

⑦ ⑧

⑥ **MIHRAB**

WC ⑤

⑨ ⑩

CALLE CORR. LUIS DE LA CERDA

↓ TO RIVER ↓

DCH

① Patio de los Naranjos
② Bell Tower
③ Entrance
④ Visigothic Mosaic
⑤ Mihrab
⑥ Visigoth Ruins

⑦ Villaviciosa Chapel
⑧ Royal Chapel
⑨ Treasury
⑩ Stonemason Marks & Signatures
⑪ Cathedral
⑫ Choir

town that surrounds it.

Patio de los Naranjos: The Mezquita's big, welcoming courtyard is free to enter. When this was a mosque, the Muslim faithful would gather in this courtyard to perform ablution—ritual washing before prayer, as directed by Muslim law. Historians believe this was the first such courtyard with trees for shade. The trees (probably olive, palm, or orange) were planted in rows that line up with the colonnades inside the mosque, symbolically extending the place of worship through the courtyard. The courtyard walls display many of the mosque's carved ceiling panels and beams, which date from

the 10th century. Gaze up through the trees for views of the **bell tower** (c. 1600), built over the remains of the original Muslim minaret. For four centuries, five times a day, a cleric (called a muezzin) would climb the minaret that once stood here to call Muslims to face Mecca and pray.

• *Buy your ticket (and, if you wish, rent an audioguide at a separate kiosk to the right). Enter the building by passing through the keyhole gate at the far right corner (pick up an English map-brochure as you enter).*

Interior: Entering the former mosque from the patio, you pass from an orchard of orange trees into a forest of delicate columns dating from 786. The 850 red-and-blue columns are

topped with double arches—a round Romanesque arch above a Visigothic horseshoe arch—made from alternating red brick and white stone. The columns and capitals (built of marble, granite, and alabaster) were recycled from ancient Roman ruins and conquered Visigothic churches.

(Golden Age Arabs excelled at absorbing both the technology and the building materials of the people they conquered.) The columns seem to recede to infinity, as if reflecting the immensity and complexity of Allah's creation. Supporting such a tall ceiling with thin columns required extra bracing with the double arches you see—a beautiful solution to a practical problem.

Although it's a vast room, the low ceilings and dense columns create an intimate and worshipful atmosphere. The original mosque was brighter, before Christians renovated the place for their use and closed in the arched entrances from the patio and street. The

Islamic Córdoba (756-1236): Medieval Europe's Cultural Capital

After his family was slaughtered by political rivals (A.D. 750), 20-year-old Prince Abd Al-Rahman fled the royal palace at Damascus, headed west across North Africa, and went undercover among the Berber tribesmen of Morocco. For six years he avoided assassination while building a power base among his fellow Arab expatriates and the local Muslim Berbers. As an heir to the title of "caliph," or ruler of Islam, he sailed north and claimed Moorish Spain as his own, confirming his power by decapitating his enemies and sending their salted heads to the rival caliph in Baghdad. This split in Islam is somewhat like the papal schism of medieval Christian Europe, when the Church split into factions over who was the rightful pope.

Thus began an Islamic flowering in southern Spain under Abd Al-Rahman's family, the Umayyads. They dominated Sevilla and Granada, ruling the independent state of "Al-Andalus," with their capital at Córdoba.

By the year 950—when the rest of Europe was mired in poverty, ignorance, and superstition—Córdoba was Europe's greatest city, rivaling Constantinople and Baghdad. It had well over 100,000 people (Paris had a third that many), with hundreds of mosques, palaces, and public baths. The streets were paved and lighted at night with oil lamps, and running water was piped in from the outskirts of the city. Medieval visitors marveled at the size and luxury of the Mezquita mosque, a symbol that the Umayyads of Spain were the equal of the caliphs of Baghdad.

This Golden Age was marked by a remarkable spirit of tolerance and cooperation in this region among the three great monotheistic religions: Islam, Judaism, and Christianity. Giving that society a positive spin, my guide explained, "Umayyad

giant cathedral sits in the center of the mosque. For now, pretend it doesn't exist. We'll visit it after exploring the mosque.

The mosque sits on the site of an early-Christian church built during the Visigothic period (sixth century). Five columns in from the entrance, a wooden railing marks a hole where you can look down to see a Visigothic **mosaic** from that original church. This is important to the locals, proving there was a church here before the mosque, and making it defensible for this newer church to have "violated" the great mosque. When modern-day Muslims called to have the Mezquita become a mosque again, the local bishop responded by changing the tourist information to make it clear: This is a living church and will stay that way.

• *Walk to the center of the far wall (opposite the entrance), where you'll find the focal point of the mosque, the...*

Mihrab: The mosque equivalent of a church's high altar, this

Al-Andalus was not one country with three cultures. It was one culture with three religions...its people shared the same food, dress, art, music, and language. Different religious rituals within the community were practiced in private. But clearly, Muslims ruled. No church spire could be taller than a minaret, and while the call to prayer rang out five times daily, there was no ringing of church bells."

The university rang with voices in Arabic, Hebrew, and Latin, sharing their knowledge of *al-jibra* (algebra), medicine, law, and literature. The city fell under the enlightened spell of the ancient Greeks, and Córdoba's 70 libraries bulged with translated manuscripts of Plato and Aristotle, works that would later inspire medieval Christians.

Ruling over the Golden Age were two energetic leaders—Abd Al-Rahman III (912-961) and Al-Hakam II (961-976)—who conquered territory, expanded the Mezquita, and boldly proclaimed themselves caliphs.

Córdoba's Y1K crisis brought civil wars that toppled the caliph (1031), splintering Al-Andalus into several kingdoms. Córdoba came under the control of the Almoravids (Berbers from North Africa), who were less sophisticated than the Arab-based Umayyads. Then a wave of even stricter Islam swept through Spain, bringing the Almohads to power (1147) and driving Córdoba's best and brightest into exile. The city's glory days were over, and it was replaced by Sevilla and Granada as the centers of Spanish Islam. On June 29, 1236, Christians conquered the city. That morning Muslims said their last prayers in the great mosque. That afternoon, the Christians set up their portable road altar and celebrated the church's first Mass. Córdoba's days as a political and cultural superpower were over.

was the focus of the mosque and is the highlight of the Mezquita today. Picture the mosque at prayer time. Each floor stone is about the size of a prayer rug...more than 20,000 people could pray at once here. Imagine the multitude kneeling in prayer, facing the mihrab, rocking forward to touch their heads to the ground, and saying, *"Allahu Akbar, La illa a il Allah, Muhammad razul Allah"*—"Allah is great, there is no god but Allah, and Muhammad is his prophet."

The mihrab, a feature in all mosques, is a decorated "niche"—in this case, more like a small room with a golden-arch entrance. During a service, the imam (prayer leader) would stand here to read scripture and give sermons. He spoke loudly into the niche, his back to the assembled crowd, and the architecture worked to amplify his voice so all could hear. Built in the mid-10th century by Al-Hakam II, the exquisite room reflects the wealth of Córdoba in its prime. Three thousand pounds of multicolored glass-and-enamel cubes panel the walls and domes in mosaics designed by Byzantine craftsmen, depicting flowers and quotes from the Quran. Gape up. Overhead rises a colorful, starry dome with skylights and interlocking lobe-shaped arches.

• *In the far-right corner, you'll find...*

Visigoth Ruins: On display in the corner to the right of the mihrab are bits of carved stone from the Visigothic Christian church of San Vicente that stood here in the sixth century. (The Christian symbolism was scratched off so the stones could be reused by Muslims.) Abd Al-Rahman I bought the church from his Christian subjects before leveling it to build the mosque. From here pan 90 degrees to enjoy a view that reveals the vastness of the mosque. (Perhaps you might also appreciate a hidden WC and drinking fountain—in the corner.)

• *In front of the mihrab and a bit to the left is a roped-off open area that was the...*

Villaviciosa Chapel: In 1236, Saint-King Ferdinand III conquered the city and turned the mosque into a church. Still, the locals continued to call it "La Mezquita," and left the structure virtually unchanged (70 percent of the original mosque structure survives to this day). Sixteen columns were removed and replaced by Gothic arches to make this chapel. It feels as if the church architects appreciated the opportunity to incorporate the sublime architecture of the pre-existing mosque into their church. Notice how the floor was once almost entirely covered with the tombs of nobles and big shots eager to make this their final resting place.

• *Immediately to your right (as you face the main entrance of the Mezquita), you'll see the...*

Royal Chapel: The chapel—designed for the tombs of Christian kings—is completely closed off. While it was never open to the public, the tall, well-preserved Mudejar walls and dome are easily visible. The lavish Arabic-style decor dates from the 1370s, done by Muslim artisans after the Reconquista. The fact that a Christian king chose to be buried in a tomb so clearly Moorish in design indicates the mutual respect between the cultures (before the Inquisition changed all that).

• *Return to the mihrab, then go through the big door to your immediate left, which leads into the Baroque...*

Treasury (Tesoro): The treasury is filled with display cases of religious artifacts and the enormous monstrance that is paraded through the streets of Córdoba each Corpus Christi, 60 days after Easter (notice the handles). The monstrance was an attempt by 16th-century Christians to create something exquisite enough to merit being the holder of the Holy Communion wafer. As they believed the wafer actually was the body of Christ, this trumped any relics. The monstrance is designed like a seven-scoop ice-cream cone, held together by gravity. While the bottom is silver-plated 18th-century Baroque, the top is late Gothic—solid silver with gold plating courtesy of 16th-century conquistadors.

The big canvas nearest the entrance shows Saint-King Ferdinand III, who conquered Córdoba in 1236, accepting the keys to the city's fortified gate from the vanquished Muslims. The victory ended a six-month siege and resulted in a negotiated settlement: The losers' lives were spared, providing they evacuated. Most went to Granada, which remained Muslim for another 250 years. The same day, the Spaniards celebrated Mass in a makeshift chapel right here in the great mosque.

Among the other Catholic treasures, don't miss the ivory crucifix (next room, body carved from one tusk, arms carefully fitted on) from 1665. Get close to study Jesus' mouth—it's incredibly realistic. The artist? No one knows.

Just outside the treasury exit, a glass case shows off casts of the many **stonemason marks and signatures** found in this one building. Try to locate the actual ones on nearby columns. (I went five for six.) This part of the mosque has the best light for photography, thanks to skylights put in by 18th-century Christians.

The mosque grew over several centuries under a series of rulers. Remarkably, each ruler kept to the original vision—rows and rows of multicolored columns topped by double arches. Then came the Christians.

Cathedral: Rising up in the middle of the forest of columns is the bright and newly restored cathedral, oriented in the Christian tradition, with its altar at the east end. This doesn't jibe with the mihrab, which normally also faces east (but to Mecca, not Jerusalem), because this mihrab actually faces south—as mosques in Syria do in order to face Mecca. (Syria was the ancestral home of Córdoba's zealous Umayyad branch of Islam.) Gazing up at the rich decoration, it's easy to forget that you were in a former mosque just seconds ago. While the mosque is about 30 feet high, the cathedral's ceiling soars 130 feet up. Look at the glorious ceiling.

In 1523 Córdoba's bishop proposed building this grand church in the Mezquita's center. The town council opposed it, but King Charles V ordered it done. According to a false but believable legend, when the king saw the final product, he declared that they'd destroyed something unique to build something ordinary. For a more positive take on this, acknowledge that it would have been quicker and less expensive for the Christian builders to destroy the mosque, but they respected its beauty and built their church into it.

It's interesting to ponder the aesthetics and psychology of the Catholic Church versus Islam in the styles of these two great places of worship (horizontal versus vertical, intimate versus powerful, fear-inspiring versus loving, dark versus bright, simple versus elaborate, feeling close to God versus feeling small before God).

The basic structure is late-Gothic, with fancy Isabelline-style columns. The nave's towering Renaissance arches and dome emphasize the triumph of Christianity over Islam in Córdoba. The twin pulpits feature a marble bull, eagle, angel, and lion—symbols of the four evangelists. The cathedral's new Carrara marble throne *(cátedra)* is the seat of the bishop.

Choir: The Baroque-era choir stalls were added much later—made in 1750 of New World mahogany. While cluttering up a previously open Gothic space, the choir is considered one of the masterpieces of 18th-century Andalusian Baroque. Each of the 109 stalls (108 plus the throne of the bishop) features a scene from the Bible: Mary's life on one side facing Jesus' life on the other. The lower chairs feature carved reliefs of the 49 martyrs of Córdoba (from Roman, Visigothic, and Moorish times), each with a palm frond symbolizing martyrdom and the scene of their death in the background. The medieval church strayed from the inclusiveness taught by Jesus. Choirs (which seem to consume otherwise-spacious church interiors throughout Spain) were only for canons, priests, and the bishop. Those days are long gone. In fact, a public Mass is now held right here (Mon-Sat mornings at 9:30).

Near the Mezquita

All of these sights are within a few minutes' walk of the Mezquita.

On and near the River

Just downhill from the Mezquita is the Guadalquivir River (which flows on to Sevilla and eventually out to the Atlantic). While silted

Central Córdoba

200 YARDS
200 METERS

1. La Hospedería de El Churrasco & Rest. El Choto
2. Hotel Albucasis
3. Hotel González
4. Hotel Mezquita
5. Hostal Alcázar
6. Hotel Califa
7. Hotel Boston
8. Bodegas Mezquita (2)
9. Mesón San Basilio
10. Bodega Guzmán
11. Casa Mazal
12. Launderette
13. Calle de las Flores
14. Maimonides Statue
15. Puerta de Almodóvar Gate
16. Baths of the Caliphate Alcázar
17. Café La Gloria

CÓRDOBA

up today, it was once navigable from here. The town now seems to turn its back on the Guadalquivir, but the arch next to the Roman Bridge (with its ancient foundation surviving) and the fortified gate on the far bank (now housing a museum, described later) evoke a day when the river was key to the city's existence.

Triumphal Arch and Plague Monument—The unfinished Renaissance arch was designed to give King Philip II a royal welcome, but he arrived before its completion—so the job was canceled. The adjacent monument with the single column is an 18th-century plague monument dedicated to St. Raphael (he was in charge of protecting the population from the main scourges in this region at that time: plague, hunger, and floods).

Roman Bridge—The bridge sits on its first-century-A.D. foundations and retains its 16th-century arches, but was poorly restored in 2009. It feels like so much other modern work along this riverbank—done on the cheap. As it was the first bridge over this river, it established Córdoba as a strategic point. Walk across the bridge for a fine view of the city—especially the huge mosque with its cathedral busting through the center. You'll be steps away from the museum described next.

▲Museum of Al-Andalus Life—The Museo Vivo de Al-Andalus fills the fortified gate (built in the 14th century to protect the Christian city) at the far side of the Roman Bridge. It is a velvety, philosophical, almost evangelical attempt to humanize the Muslim Moorish culture, and is funded by a foundation started by Roger Garaudy, a former French politician and writer controversial for Holocaust revisionism. Don a headset and wander through simple displays as the clear, engrossing soundtrack lets you sit at the feet of the great poets and poke into Moorish living rooms. It's worth the climb up to the rooftop terrace for the best panoramic view of Córdoba. Garaudy's one-hour "Multivision" video is a flowery story taking you from prehistory to the formation of the great monotheistic religions...the greatest of which—in his opinion—is Islam.

Cost and Hours: €4.50, daily May-Sept 10:00-14:00 & 16:30-20:30, Oct-April 10:00-18:00; "Multivision" video is €1.20 extra, played in English, 5-6/day, generally at the top of the hour, or at :30 past the hour on summer mornings—ask about next showing as you enter; Torre de la Calahorra, tel. 957-293-929, www.torrecalahorra.com.

Jewish Córdoba

Córdoba's Jewish Quarter dates from the late Middle Ages, after Muslim rule and during the Christian era. Now little remains. For a sense of it in its thriving heyday, visit the synagogue and the cultural center located a few steps away (both described in this section). For a pretty picture, find **Calle de las Flores** (a.k.a. "Blossom Lane"). This narrow flower-bedecked street frames the cathedral's bell tower as it hovers in the distance (the view is a favorite for local guidebook covers).

Synagogue (Sinagoga)—The small yet beautifully preserved synagogue was built in 1315, under Christian rule, but the Islamic decoration has roots way back to Abd Al-Rahman I. During Muslim times, Córdoba's sizable Jewish community was welcomed, though they paid substantial taxes to the city—money that enlarged the Mezquita and generated goodwill. That goodwill came in handy when Córdoba's era of prosperity and mutual respect ended with the arrival of the intolerant Almohad Berbers. Christians and Jews were repressed, and brilliant minds—such as the rabbi and philosopher Maimonides—fled for their own safety.

The Christian Reconquista of Córdoba (1236) brought another brief period of religious tolerance. That's when this synagogue was built—the result of a joint effort by Christians, Jews, and Muslim (Mudejar) craftsmen. By the end of the 14th century, however, Spain's Jews were again persecuted. They were finally expelled or forced to convert in 1492; this is one of only three surviving synagogues in Spain built before that year.

Rich Mudejar decorations of intertwined flowers, arabesques, and Stars of David plaster the walls. What appear to be quotes from the Quran in Arabic are actually quotes from the Bible in Hebrew. On the east wall (the symbolic direction of Jerusalem), find the niche for the Ark, which held the scrolls of the Torah (the Jewish scriptures). The upstairs gallery was reserved for women. This synagogue, the only one that survives in Córdoba, was left undisturbed because it was used as a church until the 19th century—in fact, you can see a cross painted into a niche.

Cost and Hours: €0.30—but since it's free for EU residents, they rarely accept payment; Tue-Sun 9:30-14:00 & 15:30-17:30, closed Mon, Calle de los Judíos 20, tel. 957-202-928. To learn more about the synagogue and its community, head next to the Casa de Sefarad, just 10 steps uphill.

Córdoba's Jewish Quarter: A Ten-Point Scavenger Hunt

Whereas most of the area around the Mezquita is commercial and touristy, the neighborhood to the east seems somehow almost untouched by tourism and the modern world (as you leave the Mezquita, turn right and exit the orange-grove patio). To catch a whiff of Córdoba as it was before the onslaught of tourism and the affluence of the 21st century, explore this district. Just wander and observe. Here are a few characteristics to look for:

1. **Narrow streets.** Skinny streets make sense in hot climates, as they provide much-appreciated shade. Skinny streets were also a practical necessity, since the city's Jews had to make the most of the limited space in which they were allowed to live.

2. **Thick, whitewashed walls.** Both features serve as a kind of natural air-conditioning—and the chalk ingredient in the whitewash "bugs" bugs.

3. **Colorful doors and windows.** What little color there is in this famously white city helps counter the boring whitewash.

4. **Iron grilles.** Historically, these were more artistic, but modern ones are more practical. Their continued presence is a reminder of the persistent gap through the ages between rich and poor. The wooden latticework covering many windows is a holdover from days when women were extremely modest and wanted privacy.

5. **Stone bumpers on corners.** These protected buildings against reckless drivers. Scavenged secondhand ancient Roman pillars worked well.

6. **Scuff guards.** Made of harder materials, these guards sit at the base of the whitewashed walls—and, from the looks of it, are serving their purpose.

7. **Riverstone cobbles.** These stones were cheap and local, and provided drains down the middle of a lane. They were flanked by smooth stones that stayed dry for walking (and now aid the rolling suitcases of modern-day tourists).

8. **Pretty patios.** Córdobans are proud of their patios. Walk up to the inner iron gates of the wide-open front doors and peek in (see "Patios" sidebar, later).

9. **Remnants of old towers from minarets.** Muslim Córdoba peaked in the 10th century with an estimated 400,000 people, which meant lots of neighborhood mosques.

10. **A real neighborhood.** People really live here. There are no tacky shops, and just about the only tourist is...you.

Casa de Sefarad—Set inside a restored 14th-century home directly across from the synagogue, this interpretive museum brings to life Córdoba's rich Jewish past. Eight rooms around a central patio are themed to help you understand different aspects of daily life for Spain's former Jewish community. The rooms focus on themes such as contributions from women in the community, Jewish holidays, and musical traditions. Upstairs is an interpretive center for the synagogue, along with rooms dedicated to Maimonides, the Inquisition, and the synagogue. The Casa de Sefarad is a cultural center for Sephardic (the Hebrew word for "Spanish") Jewish heritage. Jaime and his staff stress that the center's purpose is not political or religious, but cultural. Along with running this small museum, they teach courses, offer a library, and promote an appreciation of Córdoba's Jewish heritage.

Cost and Hours: €6, includes audioguide, Mon-Sat 11:00-18:00, Sun 11:00-14:00, 30-minute guided tours in English available by request if a guide is available, next to the synagogue at the corner of Calle de los Judíos and Calle Averroes, tel. 957-421-404, www.casadesefarad.es. The Casa de Sefarad hosts weekly concerts—acoustic, Sephardic, Andalusian, and flamenco—on its patio (€15, most Saturdays in season at 20:00, reservations smart).

City Wall—Built upon the foundation of Roman Córdoba's wall, these fortifications date mostly from the 12th century. While the city stretched beyond the wall in Moorish times, this wall protected its political, religious, and commercial center. Of the seven original gates, the Puerta de Almodóvar (near the synagogue) is best preserved today. Just outside this gate, you'll find statues of Córdoba's great thinkers: Seneca (the Roman philosopher and adviser to Nero), Maimonides, and Averroes.

Statues of Maimonides and Averroes—Statues honor two of Córdoba's deepest-thinking homeboys—one Jewish, one Muslim, both driven out during the wave of Islamic intolerance after the fall of the Umayyad caliphate. (Maimonides is 30 yards downhill from the synagogue; Averroes is at the end of the old wall, where Cairuán and Doctor Fleming streets meet.)

Maimonides (1135-1204) was born in Córdoba and raised on both Jewish scripture and Aristotle's philosophy. Like many tolerant Córdobans, he saw no conflict between the two. Maimonides—sometimes called the "Jewish Aquinas"—wrote the *Guide of the Perplexed* (in Arabic), in which he asserted (as the Christian philosopher St. Thomas Aquinas later would) that secular knowledge and religious faith could go hand-in-hand.

Córdoba changed in 1147, when the fundamentalist Almohads assumed power. Maimonides was driven out, eventually finding work in Cairo as the sultan's doctor. Today tourists, Jewish scholars, and fans of Aquinas rub the statue's foot in the hope that some of Maimonides' genius and wisdom will rub off on them.

The story of **Averroes** (1126-1198) is a near match of Maimonides', except that Averroes was a Muslim lawyer, not a Jewish doctor. He became the medieval world's number-one authority on Aristotle, influencing Aquinas. Averroes' biting tract *The Incoherence of the Incoherence* attacked narrow-mindedness, asserting that secular philosophy (for the elite) and religious faith (for the masses) both led to truth. The Almohads banished him from the city and burned his books, ending four centuries of Córdoban enlightenment.

The Alcázar

Alcázar de los Reyes Cristianos—Tourists line up to visit Córdoba's overrated fortress, the "Castle of the Christian Monarchs," which sits strategically next to the Guadalquivir River. Upon entering, look to the right to see a big, beautiful garden rich with flowers and fountains. To the left is a modern-feeling, unimpressive fort. While it was built along the Roman walls in Visigothic times, constant reuse and recycling has left it sparse and barren (with the exception of a few interesting Roman mosaics on the walls). Crowds squeeze up and down the congested spiral staircases of "Las Torres" for meager views. Ferdinand and Isabel donated the castle to the Inquisition in 1482, and it became central in the church's effort to discover "false converts to Christianity"—mostly Jews who had decided not to flee Spain in 1492.

Cost and Hours: €4, free on Wed; open mid-June-mid-Sept Tue-Sat 8:30-14:30, Sun 9:30-14:30, closed Mon; off-season Tue-Fri 8:30-19:30, Sat 9:30-16:30, Sun 9:30-14:30, closed Mon; last entry 30 minutes before closing. On Fridays and Saturdays you're likely to see civil wedding parties here.

Baths of the Caliphate Alcázar (Baños Califales)—The scant but evocative remains of these 10th-century royal baths are all that's left from the caliph's palace complex. They date from a time when the city had hundreds of baths and a population of several hundred thousand. The exhibit teaches about Arabic baths in general and the caliph's in particular. A 10-minute video (normally in Spanish, English on request) tells the story well.

Cost and Hours: €2, free on Wed; open mid-June-mid-Sept Tue-Sat 8:30-14:30, Sun 9:30-14:30, closed Mon; off-season Tue-Fri 8:30-19:30, Sat 9:30-16:30, Sun 9:30-14:30, closed Mon; last entry 30 minutes before closing, just outside the wall near the Alcázar.

Away from the Mezquita

Plaza de las Tendillas—While most tourists leave Córdoba having seen only the Mezquita and the cute medieval quarter that surrounds it, the modern city offers a good peek at urban Andalucía. Perhaps the best way to sample this is to browse Plaza de las Tendillas and the surrounding streets. The square, with an Art Deco charm, acts like there is no tourism in Córdoba. On the hour, a clock here chimes the guitar chords of Juan Serrano—a Córdoban classic.

Characteristic cafés and shops abound. For example, **Café La Gloria** provides an earthy Art Nouveau experience. Located just down the street from Plaza de las Tendillas, it has an unassuming entrance, but a sumptuous interior. Carved floral designs wind around the bar, mixing with *feria* posters and bullfighting memories. Pop in for a quick beer or coffee (daily from 8:00 until late, quiet after lunch crowd clears out, Calle Claudio Marcelo 15, tel. 957-477-780).

Palacio de Viana—Decidedly off the beaten path, this former palatial estate is a 25-minute walk northeast from the cluster of sights near the Mezquita. A guided tour whisks you through each room of an exuberant 16th-century estate, while an English handout drudges through the dates and origin of each important piece. But the house is best enjoyed by ignoring the guide and gasping at the massive collection of—for lack of a better word—stuff. Decorative-art fans will have a field day. The sight is known as the "patio museum" for its 12 connecting patios, each with a different theme:

Cost and Hours: House-€6, patios only-€3; July-Aug Tue-Sun 9:00-15:00; Sept-June Tue-Fri 10:00-19:00, Sat-Sun 10:00-15:00; closed Mon year-round, last entry one hour before closing, no photos inside, Plaza Don Gome 2, tel. 957-496-741.

Near Córdoba

Madinat Al-Zahra (Medina Azahara)—Five miles northwest of Córdoba, these ruins of a once-fabulous palace of the caliph were completely forgotten until excavations began in the early 20th century. Built in A.D. 929 as a power center to replace Córdoba,

CÓRDOBA

Patios

In Córdoba, patios are taken very seriously, as shown by the fiercely fought contest that takes place the first half of every May to pick the city's most picturesque. Patios, a common feature of houses throughout Andalucía, have a long history here. The Romans used them to cool off, and the Moors added lush, decorative touches. The patio functioned as a quiet outdoor living room, an oasis from the heat. Inside elaborate iron-

work gates, roses, geraniums, and jasmine spill down white-washed walls, while fountains play and caged birds sing. Some patios are owned by individuals, some are communal courtyards for several homes, and some grace public buildings like museums or convents.

Today homeowners take pride in these mini-paradises, and have no problem sharing them with tourists. Keep an eye out for square metal signs that indicate historic homes. As you wander Córdoba's back streets, pop your head into any wooden door that's open. The proud owners (who keep inner gates locked) enjoy showing off their picture-perfect patios. A concentration of patio-contest award-winners runs along Calle de San Basilio and Calle Martín Roa, just across from the Alcázar gardens.

Madinat Al-Zahra was both a palace and an entirely new capital city—the "City of the Flower"—covering nearly half a square mile (only about 10 percent has been uncovered). Extensively planned

with an orderly design, Madinat Al-Zahra was meant to symbolize and project a new discipline on an increasingly unstable Moorish empire in Spain. It failed. Only 75 years later, the city was looted and destroyed.

The site is underwhelming—a jigsaw puzzle waiting to be reassembled by patient archaeologists. Upper terrace excavations have uncovered stables and servants' quarters. Farther downhill, the house of a high-ranking official has been partially reconstructed. At the lowest level, you'll come to the remains of the mosque—placed at a diagonal, facing true east. The highlight of the visit is an elaborate reconstruction of the caliph's throne room, capturing a moody world of horseshoe arches and delicate stucco.

Legendary accounts say the palace featured waterfall walls, lions in cages, and—in the center of the throne room—a basin filled with mercury, reflecting the colorful walls. The effect likely humbled anyone fortunate enough to see the caliph.

Cost and Hours: €1.50, Tue-Sat 10:00-18:30, Sun 10:00-14:00, closed Mon, tel. 957-352-860.

Getting There: Madinat Al-Zahra is located on a back road five miles from Córdoba. By **car,** head to Avenida de Medina Azahara (one block south of the train station), following signs for *A-431*; the site is well-signposted from the highway. Though the ruins aren't accessible by regular public transportation, the TI runs a **shuttle bus** that leaves each morning and returns two hours later (€7, buy ticket at any of the city TIs—train station, Alcázar, or Plaza de las Tendillas; runs year-round Tue-Fri and Sun at 9:30 and 10:15; Sat at 9:30, 10:15, and 15:00; informative English booklet provided). Catch the bus near the Cruz Roja Hospital at Paseo de la Victoria.

Sleeping in Córdoba

I've listed prices for the high season; most of these are cheaper outside peak times. If it's hot and you've got a lot of luggage, don't bother with the inconvenient city buses; just hop in a taxi.

Near the Mezquita

These are all within a five-minute stroll of the Mezquita.

$$$ La Hospedería de El Churrasco is a nine-room jewel box of an inn, featuring plush furniture, tasteful traditional decor, and hardwood floors. Quiet and romantic, it's tucked in the old quarter just far enough away from the tourist storm, yet still handy for sightseeing (Sb-€120, Db-€140, superior Db-€180, €20 more per room in April-May and Oct, website shows off each distinct room, no twin rooms, includes breakfast, air-con, free Internet access, free cable Internet in rooms, parking-€20, midway between Puerta de Almodóvar and the Mezquita at Calle Romero 38, tel. 957-294-808, fax 957-421-661, www.elchurrasco.com, hospederia @elchurrasco.com).

$$ Hotel Albucasis, at the edge of the tourist zone, features 15 basic, clean rooms, all of which face quiet interior patios. The friendly, accommodating staff and cozy setting make you feel right at home (Sb-€55, Db-€85, breakfast-€6, air-con, elevator, free

CÓRDOBA

Sleep Code

(€1 = about $1.40, country code: 34)
S = Single, **D** = Double/Twin, **T** = Triple, **Q** = Quad, **b** = bathroom, **s** = shower only. Unless otherwise noted, credit cards are accepted, English is spoken, and breakfast generally costs extra.

To help you easily sort through these listings, I've divided the accommodations into three categories, based on the price for a standard double room with bath during high season:

$$$ Higher Priced—Most rooms €100 or more.
 $$ Moderately Priced—Most rooms between €60-100.
  $ Lower Priced—Most rooms €60 or less.

Prices can change without notice; verify the hotel's current rates online or by email. For other updates, see www.ricksteves.com/update.

Wi-Fi in lobby, parking-€12 but free in off-season, Buen Pastor 11, tel. 957-478-625, www.hotelalbucasis.com, hotelalbucasis@hotmail.com).

$$ Hotel Mezquita, just across from the main entrance of the Mezquita, rents 31 modern and comfortable rooms. The grand entrance lobby elegantly recycles an upper-class mansion (Sb-€46, Db-€79, Tb-€117, breakfast-€4, air-con, elevator, free Wi-Fi in lobby, Plaza Santa Catalina 1, tel. 957-475-585, fax 957-476-219, www.hotelmezquita.com, hotelmezquita@wanadoo.es).

$$ Hotel González, with many of its 17 basic rooms facing its cool and peaceful patio, is sparse but sleepable. It's clean and well-run, with a good location and price (Sb-€42, Db-€75, Tb-€110, higher prices for busy times—especially weekends, breakfast-€4, air-con, elevator, free Wi-Fi in lobby, Manríquez 3, tel. 957-479-819, fax 957-486-187, www.hotel-gonzalez.com, hotelgonzalez@wanadoo.es).

$ Hostal Alcázar is your best cheapie. Run-down and budget-priced, without a real reception desk, this friendly place is just outside the old city wall on a quiet cobbled traffic-free street known for its prizewinning patios. Its 16 rooms are split between 2 homes on opposite sides of the lane, conveniently located 50 yards from a taxi and bus stop (Sb-€20, small Db-€36, bigger Db-€45, Tb-€60, 2-room apartment-€60 for 3 or €80 for 4, breakfast-€4, air-con, free Wi-Fi on patio, parking-€6, near Alcázar at Calle de San Basilio 2, tel. 957-202-561, www.hostalalcazar.com, hostalalcazar@hotmail.com, ladies' man Fernando and family, son Demitrio speaks English).

In the Modern City

While still within easy walking distance of the Mezquita, these places are outside of the main tourist zone—not buried in all that tangled medieval cuteness.

$$ Hotel Califa, a modern 65-room business-class hotel from the NH chain, sits on a quiet street a block off busy Paseo Victoria, on the edge of the jumbled old quarter. Still close enough to the sights, its slick modern rooms can be a great value if you get a deal (vast price range depending on demand but Db generally €80-90 during the week, €120 weekends, around €70 in heat of summer, Tb generally €20-25 more, air-con, elevator, free Internet access, pay Wi-Fi, parking-€15, Lope de Hoces 14, tel. 957-299-400, www.nh-hotels.com, nhcalifa@nh-hotels.com).

$$ Hotel Boston, with 39 rooms, is a decent budget bet if you want a reliable, basic hotel away from the touristy Mezquita zone. It's a taste of workaday Córdoba (Sb-€40-48, Db-€55-76, Tb-€75-90, breakfast-€5, air-con, elevator, pay Internet access, free Wi-Fi, parking-€12, Málaga 2, just off Plaza de las Tendillas, tel. 957-474-176, www.hotel-boston.com, info@hotel-boston.com).

$ The Terrace Backpackers Hostel rents dorm beds and simple doubles in a great neighborhood (dorm beds-€15-19, D-€40-50, air-con, free Wi-Fi, terrace, kitchen, self-service laundry, lots of hostel-type info and help, at Potro bus stop—take #3 from station—at Calle Lucano 12, tel. 957-492-966, theterracebackpackers hostel@yahoo.com).

Eating in Córdoba

Córdoba is a great dining town, with options ranging from obvious touristy bars in the old center to enticing, locals-only hangouts a few blocks away. Specialties include *salmorejo,* Córdoba's version of gazpacho. It's creamier, with more bread and olive oil and generally served with pieces of ham and hard-boiled egg. Most places serve white wines from the nearby Montilla-Moriles region; these *finos* are slightly less dry but more aromatic than the sherry produced in Jerez de la Frontera. For a good value and truly local scene, explore the little characteristic bars in the lanes around Plaza de la Corredera.

Near the Mezquita

There are plenty of touristy options around the Mezquita, designed for out-of-towners and tour groups. By walking a couple blocks away along Calle del Cardenal González, you get into a district of cheap, accessible little places offering a better value. Listed here, in order, are a bright and efficient diner about 50 yards from the mosque, a colorful neighborhood restaurant, a down-and-dirty wine bar, a Jewish restaurant, and a steak house.

Bodegas Mezquita is a good bet for a bright, air-conditioned place a block from the mosque. They have a good *menú del día*, or you can order from their menu of €3-4 tapas, €4-10 half-*raciones*, and €8-16 *raciones* (long hours daily, one block above the Mezquita garden at Céspedes 12, tel. 957-490-004). They have a second location below the Mezquita (Corregidor Luis de la Cerda 73, tel. 957-498-117).

Mesón San Basilio is the local hangout on Calle de San Basilio, just outside the wall. Although there's no seating outside, the restaurant still offers great "patio ambience"—with a view of the kitchen action. No tourists, no pretense...it's understandably the neighborhood favorite (classic €18.50 fixed-priced meal, €8 lunch special weekdays, lots of €9-15 fish and meat dishes, Mon-Sat 13:00-16:00 & 20:00-24:00, Sun 13:00-16:00 only, Calle de San Basilio 19, tel. 957-297-007). For something rougher—rustic meals, tapas, and crowds—go to the church and head a block left to **Bodega San Basilio** (Calle de Enmedio, tel. 957-297-832).

Bodega Guzmán, which proudly displays the heads of brave-but-unlucky bulls, serves cold, very basic tapas to locals who call the waiters by their first names and burst into song when they feel the flamenco groove. Arrive early to get a table. While it feels like a drinks-only place, they do have rustic €2 tapas and €6 *raciones* (ask for the list in English). Choose a table or belly up to the bar and try a local Montilla-Moriles white wine: dry *(blanco seco)* or sweet *(blanco dulce)* for €1 a glass. For grape juice, ask for *mosto* (closed Thu; if entering the old town from Puerta de Almodóvar take the first right—it's 100 yards from the gate at Calle de los Judíos 7).

Casa Mazal, run by the nearby Casa de Sefarad Jewish cultural center, serves updated, modern Jewish cuisine. Small dining rooms sprawl around the charming medieval courtyard of a former house. With a seasonal menu that includes several vegetarian options, it offers a welcome dose of variety from the typical Spanish standards (€7-9 starters, €10-15 main dishes, Wed-Mon 12:00-17:00 & 20:00-24:00, closed Tue, also closed Mon off-season, Tomás Conde 3, tel. 957-941-888).

Restaurante El Choto is bright, formal, and dressy, with a small leafy patio, buried deep in the Jewish Quarter. It's touristy yet intimate, serving well-presented international dishes with an emphasis on grilled meat. The favorite is kid goat with garlic—*choto al ajillo* (€23 house fixed-price meal, €36 tasting-menu fixed-price meal, €15-25 main dishes, closed Sun evening and all day Mon, Calle de Almanzor 10, tel. 957-760-115).

Just East of the Mezquita Zone

Bodegas Campos, my favorite place in town, is a historic and venerable house of eating, attracting so many locals it comes with its own garage. It's worth the 10-minute walk from the tourist zone. They have a stuffy and expensive formal restaurant upstairs (€12-20 starters, €17-27 main dishes), but I'd eat in the more relaxed and affordable tavern on the ground floor (€6-9 half-*raciones*). The service is great and the menu is inviting. In two visits I nearly ate my way through the offerings, a half-*ración* at a time, and enjoyed each dish. Experiment—you can't go wrong. House specialties are bull-tail stew (*rabo de toro*—rich, tasty, and a good splurge) and anything with *pisto,* the local ratatouille-like vegetable stew. Don't leave without exploring the sprawling complex, which fills 14 old houses that have been connected to create a network of dining rooms and patios, small and large. The place is a virtual town history museum: Look for the wine barrels signed by celebrities and VIPs, the old refectory from a convent, and a huge collection of classic, original *feria* posters and great photos (Mon-Sat 12:00-17:00 & 20:00-24:00, Sun 12:00-17:00 only; from river end of Mezquita walk east along Cardenal González, continue 10 minutes straight to Calle de Lineros 32; tel. 957-497-500).

In the Modern City

These are worth the 10-to-15-minute walk from the main tourist zone—walking here, you feel a world apart from the touristy scene. Combine a meal here with a paseo through the Plaza de las Tendillas area to get a good look at modern Córdoba.

Taverna Salinas seems like a movie set designed to give you the classic Córdoba scene. Though all the seating is indoors, it's still pleasantly patio-esque, and popular with locals for its traditional cuisine and exuberant bustle. The seating fills a big courtyard and sprawls through several smaller, semi-private rooms. The fun menu features a slew of enticing €6-7 plates (spinach with chickpeas is a house specialty). Study what locals are eating before ordering. There's no drinks menu—just basic beer or inexpensive wine. If there's a line (as there often is later in the evening), leave your name and throw yourself into the adjacent tapas-bar mosh pit for a drink (Mon-Sat 12:30-16:00 & 20:00-23:30, closed Sun and Aug; from Plaza de las Tendillas walk 3 blocks to the Roman temple, then go 1 more block and turn right to Tundidores 3; tel. 957-480-135).

Taberna San Miguel is nicknamed "Casa el Pisto" for its famous vegetable stew *(pisto).* Well-respected, it's packed with locals who appreciate regional cuisine, a good value, and a place with a long Córdoban history. Go to the bar to be seated (€2-3 tapas, €6-10 half-*raciones*, €7-14 *raciones*, 20 percent extra to sit in patio or outside, closed Sun-Mon and Aug, 2 blocks north of Plaza de las Tendillas at Plaza San Miguel 1, tel. 957-478-328).

Córdoba Connections

From Córdoba by Train: Córdoba is on the slick AVE train line (reservations required), making it an easy stopover between **Madrid** (2-3/hour, 1.75 hours, €69, railpass-holders pay €10.35 for required reservation) and **Sevilla** (2-3/hour, 45 minutes, €34, railpass-holders pay €10.35 for required reservation). The Avant train connects Córdoba to Sevilla just as fast for half the price (9/day, 45 minutes, €17, railpass-holders pay €6.50 for required reservation). The slow regional train to Sevilla takes nearly twice as long, but doesn't require a reservation and is even cheaper (8/day, 80 minutes, €11 one-way).

Other trains go to **Granada** (2/day on Altaria, 2.5 hours, €36—bus is more frequent, cheaper, and nearly as fast), **Ronda** (2/day direct on Altaria, 1.75 hours, €40; 1/day much cheaper but much longer with transfer in Bobadilla, 4 hours, €17), **Jerez** (to transfer to Arcos; 8/day, 2.5-3 hours, €24 on regional train, €30-40 on fast train), **Málaga** (fast and cheap Avant train, 6/day, 1 hour, €23; fast and expensive AVE train, 11/day, 1 hour, €44), and **Algeciras** (2/day, 3.5 hours). Train info: toll tel. 902-320-320.

By Bus to: Granada (5/day *directo*, 2.75 hours, €13; 2/day *ruta*, 4 hours, €17), **Sevilla** (6/day, 2 hours, €11), **Madrid** (6/day, 5 hours, €16), **Málaga** (4/day, 3-3.5 hours, €13), **Barcelona** (2/day, 10 hours). The efficient staff at the information desk prints bus schedules for you—or you can check all schedules at www.estacionautobuses cordoba.es. Bus info: tel. 957-404-040.

ANDALUCÍA'S WHITE HILL TOWNS

*Arcos de la Frontera • Ronda •
Zahara and Grazalema • Jerez*

Just as the American image of Germany is Bavaria, the Yankee dream of Spain is Andalucía. This is the home of bullfights, flamenco, gazpacho, pristine whitewashed hill towns, and glamorous Mediterranean resorts. The big cities of Andalucía (Granada, Sevilla, and Córdoba) and the South Coast (Costa del Sol) are covered in separate chapters. This chapter explores Andalucía's hill-town highlights.

The Route of the White Hill Towns (Ruta de los Pueblos Blancos), Andalucía's charm bracelet of cute towns perched in the sierras, gives you wonderfully untouched Spanish culture. Spend a night in the romantic queen of the white towns, Arcos de la Frontera. (Towns with "de la Frontera" in their names were established on the front line of the centuries-long fight to recapture Spain from the Muslims, who were slowly pushed back into Africa.) Farther east, the larger town of Ronda stuns visitors with its breathtaking setting—straddling a gorge that thrusts deep into the Andalusian bedrock. Ronda's venerable old bullring, smattering of enjoyable sights, and thriving tapas scene round out its charms. Smaller hill towns, such as Zahara and Grazalema, offer plenty of beauty. As a whole, the hill towns—no longer strategic, no longer on any frontier—are now just passing time peacefully. Join them.

Between Sevilla and the hill towns, the city of Jerez—teeming with traffic and lacking in charm—is worth a peek for its famous Horse Symphony and a glass of sherry on a sherry bodega tour.

To study ahead, visit www.andalucia.com for information on hotels, festivals, museums, nightlife, and sports in the region.

Planning Your Time

On a three-week vacation in Spain, the Andalucía region is worth two nights and up to two days sandwiched between visits to Sevilla and Tarifa. Arcos makes the best home base, as it's close to interesting smaller towns, near Jerez, and conveniently situated halfway between Sevilla and Tarifa. The towns can also be accessed from the Costa del Sol resorts via Ronda.

See Jerez on your way in or out, spend a day hopping from town to town in the more remote interior (including Grazalema and Zahara), and enjoy Arcos early and late in the day. For more details on exploring this region by car, see "Route Tips for Drivers" at the end of this chapter.

Without a car, keep things simple and focus only on Arcos and Jerez (both well-served by frequent-enough public buses from Sevilla). If you're more interested in Ronda, it's easy to visit, right on a train line.

Spring and fall are high season throughout this area. In summer you'll encounter intense heat, but empty hotels, lower prices, and no crowds.

Arcos de la Frontera

Arcos smothers its long, narrow hilltop and tumbles down the back of the ridge like the train of a wedding dress. It's larger than most other Andalusian hill towns, but equally atmospheric. Arcos consists of two towns: the fairy-tale old town on top of the hill and the fun-loving lower, or new, town. The old center is a labyrinthine wonderland, a photographer's feast. Viewpoint-hop through town. Feel the wind funnel through the narrow streets as cars inch around tight corners. Join the kids' soccer game on the churchyard patio. Enjoy the moonlit view from the main square.

Though it tries, Arcos doesn't have much to offer other than its basic whitewashed self. The locally produced English guidebook on Arcos waxes poetic and at length about very little. You can arrive late and leave early and still see it all.

Orientation to Arcos

Tourist Information

The TI, on the main road leading up into the old town, is helpful and loaded with information, including bus schedules (March-Nov daily 9:30-14:00 & 15:00-19:30, Sun from 10:00; Dec-Feb daily until 18:30; Cuesta de Belén 5, tel. 956-702-264, www.ayuntamientoarcos.org).

On the floors above the TI is a skippable local history museum called Centro de Interpretación Ciudad de Arcos (CICA), with few artifacts and sparse exhibits described only in Spanish.

The TI organizes a one-hour **walking tour,** which includes a tour of CICA and a walk through the old town, learning about Arcos' history, lifestyles, and Moorish influences. You also get a peek at some private courtyard patios (€6, Mon-Fri at 11:00 and 18:00, Sat only at 11:00, none on Sun, meet at TI, in Spanish and/or English; for private tours call TI).

Arrival in Arcos

By Bus: The bus station is on Calle Corregidores, at the foot of the hill. To get up to the old town, catch the shuttle bus marked *Centro* (€1, pay driver, 2/hour, runs roughly Mon-Fri 7:00-22:00, Sat 9:00-22:00, none on Sun), hop a taxi (€5 fixed rate; if there are no taxis waiting, call 956-704-640), or hike 20 uphill minutes (see map).

By Car: The old town is a tight squeeze with a one-way traffic flow from west to east (coming from the east, circle south under town). The TI and my recommended hotels are in the west. If you miss your target, you must drive out the other end, double back, and try again. Driving in Arcos is like threading needles (many drivers pull in their side-view mirrors to buy a few extra precious inches). Turns are tight, parking is frustrating, and congestion can lead to long jams.

Small cars can park in the main square of the old town at the top of the hill (Plaza del Cabildo). Get a €3.50 all-day pass from your hotel or buy a ticket from the machine (€0.70/hour, 2-hour maximum, only necessary Mon-Fri 9:00-14:00 & 17:00-21:00 and Sat 9:00-14:00—confirm times on machine). If staying overnight, tell the uniformed parking attendant the name of your hotel. If there's no spot, wait until one opens up (he'll help...for a little tip). Once you grab a spot, tell him you'll be back from your hotel with a ticket.

It's less stressful (and better exercise) to park in the modern underground pay lot at Plaza de España in the new town. From this lot, catch a taxi or the shuttle bus up to the old town (2/hour; as you're looking uphill, the bus stop is to the right of the traffic circle), or hike 15 minutes.

Getting Around Arcos

The old town is easily walkable, but it's fun and relaxing to take a circular **minibus** joyride. The little shuttle bus (also mentioned in "Arrival," above) constantly circles through the town's one-way system and around the valley (€1, 2/hour, runs roughly Mon-Fri 7:00-22:00, Sat 9:00-22:00, none on Sun). For a 30-minute tour, hop on. You can catch it just below the main church in the old town near the mystical stone circle (generally departs roughly at :20 and :50 past the hour). Sit in the front seat for the best view of the tight squeezes and the school kids hanging out in the plazas as you wind through the old town. After passing under a Moorish gate, you enter a modern residential neighborhood, circle under the eroding cliff, and return to the old town by way of the bus station and Plaza de España.

Arcos de la Frontera

Helpful Hints

Internet Access: Most hotels have Wi-Fi for guests, and some also have Internet terminals. There's no real Internet café in Arcos' old town, but the TI may have a terminal where you can pay to get online.

Post Office: It's at the lower end of the old town at Paseo de los Boliches 24, a few doors up from Hotel Los Olivos (Mon-Fri 8:30-14:30, Sat 9:30-13:00, closed Sun).

Viewpoint: For drivers, the best town overlook is from a tiny park just beyond the new bridge on the El Bosque road. In town, there are some fine viewpoints (for instance, from the main square), but the church

towers are no longer open to the public.

Self-Guided Walk

Welcome to Arcos' Old Town

This walk will introduce you to virtually everything worth seeing in Arcos.

• *Start at the top of the hill, in the main square dominated by the church.* *(Avoid this walk during the hot midday siesta.)*

Plaza del Cabildo: Stand at the viewpoint opposite the church on the town's main square. Survey the square, which in the old days doubled as a bullring. On your right is the parador, a former

Arcos de la Frontera's Old Town

NOT TO SCALE -
PLAZA CABILDO TO
MARKET IS ABOUT
A 3 MINUTE WALK

SANTA MARIA

TO ST. PETER

MAG. AMAYA

CORREDERA

BELÉN

GRADAS

NUEVA

BOTICAS

MARKET

MALDONADO

TO BOLICHES

PLAZA CABILDO

CASTLE (NOT OPEN)

BUS STN. & NEW TOWN

CLIFFS

CLIFFS

PARADOR

VIEWPOINT

N

VIEW
Ⓣ TAXI STAND

TO BUS STN. & NEW TOWN

AV. DUQUE DE ARCOS

RIO GUADALETE

TO RONDA

❶ Parador de Arcos de la Frontera
❷ Hotel El Convento
❸ La Casa Grande
❹ Rincón de las Nieves
❺ Hostal & Bar San Marcos
❻ Hostal Callejón de las Monjas
❼ Bar-Hostal Zindicato

❽ To Hotel Los Olivos
❾ To Hostal Málaga
❿ Bar La Carcel
⓫ Alcaraván Restaurante
⓬ Plaza Boticas, Mesón Don Fernando & Cloistered Nuns
⓭ Mama Ttina
⓮ Las Doce Campañas Bakery

palace of the governor. It flies three flags: green for Andalucía, red-and-yellow for Spain, and blue-and-yellow for the European Union. On your left are the City Hall and the TI, below the 11th-century Moorish castle where Ferdinand and Isabel held Reconquista strategy meetings (castle privately owned and closed to the public).

Now belly up to the railing and look down. The people of Arcos boast that only they see the backs of the birds as they fly. Ponder the parador's erosion concerns (it lost part of its lounge in the 1990s when it dropped right off), the orderly orange groves, and fine views toward Morocco. The city council considered building an underground parking lot to clear up the square, but nixed it because of the land's fragility. You're 330 feet above the Guadalete River. This is the town's suicide departure point for men (women jump from the other side).

• *Looming over the square is the…*

Church of Santa María: After Arcos was retaken from the Moors in the 13th century, this church was built atop a mosque.

Notice the church's fine but chopped-off bell tower. The old one fell in the earthquake of 1755 (famous for destroying Lisbon). The replacement was intended to be the tallest in Andalucía after Sevilla's—but money ran out. It looks like someone lives on an upper floor. Someone does—the church guardian resides there in a room strewn with bell-ringing ropes.

Buy a ticket (€2, Mon-Fri 10:00-13:00 & 16:00-19:00, Sat 10:00-14:00, closed Sun and Jan-Feb), and step into the center, where you can see the beautifully carved choir. The organ was built in 1789 with that many pipes. At the very front of the church, the nice Renaissance high altar—carved in wood—covers up a Muslim prayer niche that survived from the older mosque. The altar shows God with a globe in his hand (on top), and scenes from the life of Jesus (on the right) and Mary (left). Circle the church counterclockwise and notice the elaborate chapels. Although most of the architecture is Gothic, the chapels are decorated in Baroque and Rococo styles. The ornate statues are used in Holy Week processions. Sniff out the "incorruptible body" (miraculously never rotting) of St. Felix—a third-century martyr (directly across from the entry). Felix may be nicknamed "the incorruptible," but take a close look at his knee. He's no longer skin and bones...just bones and the fine silver mesh that once covered his skin. Rome sent his body here in 1764, after recognizing this church as the most important in Arcos. In the back of the church, under a huge fresco of St. Christopher (carrying his staff and Baby Jesus), is a gnarly Easter candle from 1767.

• *Back outside, examine the...*

Church Exterior: Circle clockwise around the church, down four steps, to find the third-century Roman votive altar with a carving of the palm tree of life. Though the Romans didn't build this high in the mountains, they did have a town and temple at the foot of Arcos. This carved stone was discovered in the foundation of the original Moorish mosque, which stood here before the first church was built.

Head down a few more steps and come to the main entrance (west portal) of the church (closed until restoration is complete). This is a good example of Plateresque Gothic—Spain's last and most ornate kind of Gothic.

In the pavement, notice the 15th-century magic circle with 12 red and 12 white stones—the white ones have various "constellations" marked (though they don't resemble any of today's star

HILL TOWNS

charts). When a child would come to the church to be baptized, the parents would stop here first for a good Christian exorcism. The exorcist would stand inside the protective circle and cleanse the baby of any evil spirits. While locals no longer do this (and a modern rain drain now marks the center), Sufis, members of a sect of Islam, still come here in a kind of pilgrimage every November. (Down a few more steps and 10 yards to the left, you can catch the public bus for a circular minibus joyride through Arcos; see "Getting Around Arcos," earlier.)

Continue around the back of the church. On your left, look for **Señor González Oca's tiny barbershop,** with some exciting posters of bulls running Pamplona-style through the streets of Arcos during Holy Week—an American from the nearby Navy base at Rota was killed here by a bull in 1994. (Señor González Oca is now semi-retired, but if he's in, he's happy to show off his posters; drop in and say, "Hola." Need a haircut, guys? €9.)

Continuing along under the **flying buttresses,** notice the scratches of innumerable car mirrors on each wall (and be glad you're walking). The buttresses were built to shore up the church when it was damaged by an earthquake in 1699. (Thanks to these supports, the church survived the bigger earthquake of 1755.) The security grille (over the window above) protected cloistered nuns when this building was a convent. Look at the arches that prop up the houses downhill on the left; all over town, arches support earthquake-damaged structures.

• *Now make your way...*

From the Church to the Market: Completing your circle around the church (huffing back uphill), turn left under more arches built to repair earthquake damage and walk east down the bright, white Calle Escribanos. From now to the end of this walk, you'll basically follow this lane until you come to the town's second big church (St. Peter's). After a block, you hit Plaza Boticas.

On your right is the last remaining **convent** in Arcos. Notice the no-nunsense, spiky window grilles high above, with tiny peepholes in the latticework for the cloistered nuns to see through. Step into the lobby under the fine portico to find their one-way mirror and a spinning cupboard that hides the nuns from view. Push the buzzer, and one of the eight sisters (several are from Kenya and speak English well) will spin out some boxes of excellent, freshly baked cookies—made from pine nuts, peanuts, almonds, and other nuts—for you to consider buying (€6-7, open daily but not reliably 8:30-14:30 & 17:00-19:00; be careful—if you stand big and tall to block out the light, you can actually see the sister through the glass). If you ask for *magdalenas,* bags of cupcakes will swing around (€1.50). These are traditional goodies made from natural ingredients. Buy some goodies to support their church work, and give them to kids as you complete your walk.

The **covered market** *(mercado)* at the bottom of the plaza (down from the convent) resides in an unfinished church. At the entry, notice what is half of a church wall. The church was being built for the Jesuits, but construction stopped in 1767 when King Charles III, tired of the Jesuit appetite for politics, expelled the order from Spain. The market is closed on Sunday and Monday—they rest on Sunday, so there's no produce, fish, or meat ready for Monday. Poke inside. It's tiny but has everything you need. Pop into the *servicio público* (public WC)—no gender bias here.

• *Continue straight down Calle Botica...*

From the Market to the Church of St. Peter: As you walk, peek discreetly into private patios. These wonderful, cool-tiled courtyards filled with plants, pools, furniture, and happy family activities are typical of Arcos. Except in the mansions, these patios are generally shared by several families. Originally, each courtyard served as a catchment system, funneling rainwater to a drain in the middle, which filled the well. You can still see tiny wells in wall niches with now-decorative pulleys for the bucket.

On the left (at #11), look for **Las Doce Campanas bakery,** where Juan Miguel or Encarni sells traditional and delicious sultana cookies (€1.20 each). These big, dry macaroons (named for the wives of sultans) go back to Moorish times. At the next corner, squint back above the bakery to the corner of the tiled rooftop. The tiny stone—where the corner hits the sky—is a very eroded mask, placed here to scare evil spirits from the house. This is Arcos' last surviving mask from a tradition that lasted until the mid-19th century.

Also notice the ancient columns on each corner. All over town, these columns—many actually Roman, appropriated from their original ancient settlement at the foot of the hill—were put up to protect buildings from reckless donkey carts and tourists in rental cars.

As you continue straight, notice that the walls are scooped out on either side of the windows. These are a reminder of the days when women stayed inside but wanted the best possible view of any people action in the streets. These "window ears" also enabled boys in a more modest age to lean inconspicuously against the wall to chat up eligible young ladies.

Across from the old facade ahead, find the **Association of San Miguel.** Duck right, past a bar, into the oldest courtyards in town—you can still see the graceful Neo-Gothic lines of this noble home from 1850. The bar is a club for retired men—always busy when a bullfight's on TV or during card games. The guys are friendly, and drinks are cheap. You're welcome to flip on the light and explore the old-town photos in the back room.

Just beyond, facing the elegant front door of that noble house, is Arcos' second church, **St. Peter's** (€1 donation, Mon-Fri 9:00-14:00 & 15:30-18:30, Sat 9:00-12:00, closed Sun). You know it's St. Peter's because St. Peter, mother of God, is the centerpiece of the facade. Let me explain. It really is the second church, having had an extended battle with Santa María for papal recognition as the leading church in Arcos. When the pope finally favored Santa María, St. Peter's parishioners changed their prayers. Rather than honoring "María," they wouldn't even say her name. They prayed "St. Peter, mother of God." Like Santa María, it's a Gothic structure, filled with Baroque decor, many Holy Week procession statues, humble English descriptions, and relic skeletons in glass caskets (two from the third century A.D.).

In the cool of the evening, the tiny square in front of the church—about the only flat piece of pavement around—serves as the old-town soccer field for neighborhood kids. Until a few years ago, this church also had a resident bellman—notice the cozy balcony halfway up. He was a basket-maker and a colorful character, famous for bringing a donkey into his quarters, which grew too big to get back out. Finally, he had no choice but to kill and eat the donkey.

Twenty yards beyond the church, step into the nice **Galería de Arte San Pedro,** featuring artisans in action and their reasonably priced paintings and pottery. Walk inside. Find the water drain and the well.

Across the street, a sign directs you to **Mirador**—a tiny square 100 yards downhill that affords a commanding view of Arcos. The reservoir you see to the east of town is used for water sports in the summertime, and forms part of a power plant that local residents protested—to no avail—based on environmental concerns.

From the Church of St. Peter, circle down and around back to the main square, wandering the tiny neighborhood lanes. Just below St. Peter's is a delightful little Andalusian garden (formal Arabic style, with aromatic plants such as jasmine, rose, and lavender, and water in the center). The lane called Higinio Capote, below Santa María, is particularly picturesque with its many geraniums. Peek into patios, kick a few soccer balls, and savor the views.

Nightlife in Arcos

Evening Action in the New Town—The newer part of Arcos has a modern charm. In the cool of the evening, all generations enjoy life out around Plaza de España (10-minute walk from the old town). Several good tapas bars border the square or are nearby.

The big park (Recinto Ferial) below Plaza de España is the late-night fun zone in the summer (June-Aug) when *carpas* (restaurant tents) fill with merrymakers, especially on weekends. The scene includes open-air tapas bars, disco music, and dancing. There are sometimes free evening events here in the summer—ask at the TI.

Sleeping in Arcos

Hotels in Arcos consider April, May, August, September, and October to be high season. Note that some hotels double their rates during the motorbike races in nearby Jerez (usually April or May, varies yearly, call TI or ask your hotel) and during Holy Week (the week leading up to Easter); these spikes are not reflected in the prices below.

In the Old Town

For all of these (except Zindicato), the nearest parking is at Plaza Cabildo, the main square in front of the church (buy €3.50 parking pass from your hotel).

$$$ Parador de Arcos de la Frontera is royally located, with 24 elegant, recently refurbished and reasonably priced rooms (8

have balconies). If you're going to experience a parador, this is a good one (Sb-€120-131, Db-€150-163, Db with terrace-€174-196, cheaper rates are for Nov-Feb, breakfast-€16, air-con, elevator, free Internet access, free parking, Plaza del Cabildo, tel. 956-700-500, fax 956-701-116, www.parador.es, arcos@parador.es).

$$ Hotel El Convento, deep in the old town just beyond the parador, is the best value in town. Run by a hardworking family and their wonderful staff, this cozy hotel offers 13 fine rooms—all with great views, most with balconies. In 1998 I enjoyed a big party with most of Arcos' big shots as they dedicated a fine room with a grand-view balcony to "Rick Steves, Periodista Turístico." Guess where I sleep when in Arcos... (Sb with balcony-€56, Sb with terrace-€69, Db with balcony-€71, Db with terrace-€86, extra person-€19; 10 percent discount in 2012 when you book direct, pay in cash, and show this book; usually closed Nov-Feb;

Sleep Code

(€1 = about $1.40, country code: 34)
S = Single, **D** = Double/Twin, **T** = Triple, **Q** = Quad, **b** = bathroom, **s** = shower only. Unless otherwise noted, you can assume credit cards are accepted, English is spoken, and the IVA tax is included in the price, but breakfast is not included.

To help you easily sort through these listings, I've divided the accommodations into three categories, based on the price for a standard double room with bath during high season:

$$$ Higher Priced—Most rooms €100 or more.
$$ Moderately Priced—Most rooms between €50-100.
$ Lower Priced—Most rooms €50 or less.

Prices can change without notice; verify the hotel's current rates online or by email. For other updates, see www.ricksteves.com/update.

Maldonado 2, tel. 956-702-333, fax 956-704-128, www.hotelel convento.es, reservas@hotelelconvento.es). Over an à la carte breakfast, bird-watch on their view terrace, with all of Andalucía spreading beyond your *café con leche.*

$$ La Casa Grande is a lovingly appointed *Better Homes and Moroccan Tiles* kind of place that rents eight rooms with big-view windows. Like in a lavish yet very authentic old-style B&B, you're free to enjoy its fine view terrace, homey library, and atrium-like patio, where you'll be served a traditional breakfast. They also offer guided visits and massage services (Db-€71-85; junior suites: Db-€82-119, Tb-€106-119, Qb-€123-140; breakfast-€9, air-con, free Internet access, Maldonado 10, tel. 956-703-930, fax 956-717-095, www.lacasagrande.net, info@lacasagrande.net, Elena).

$$ Rincón de las Nieves, with simple Andalusian style, has a cool inner courtyard surrounded by three rooms and a sprawling apartment which can accommodate up to seven people. Two of the rooms have their own outdoor terraces with obstructed views, and all have access to the rooftop terrace (Db-€50-65, higher for Holy Week and Aug, apartment-€20-24/person, air-con, Boticas 10, tel. 956-701-528, mobile 656-886-256, rincondelasnieves@gmail.com).

$ Hostal San Marcos, above a neat little bar in the heart of the old town, offers four air-conditioned rooms and a great sun terrace with views of the reservoir (Sb-€25, Db-€35, Tb-€45, air-con, Marqués de Torresoto 6, best to reserve by phone, tel. 956-700-721, mobile 615-375-077, www.hsanmarcos.es, info@hsanmarcos.es). Loli speaks no English.

$ Hostal Callejón de las Monjas (a.k.a. Hostal El Patio) offers the best cheap beds in the old town. With a tangled floor plan and nine simple rooms, it's on a sometimes-noisy street behind the Church of Santa María (Sb-€20, D-€27, Db-€33, Db with terrace-€39, Tb-€44, Qb apartment-€66, air-con, Calle Deán Espinosa 4, tel. & fax 956-702-302, mobile 605-839-995, www.mesonelpatio .com, padua@mesonelpatio.com, staff speak no English). There's a bar-restaurant with bullfighting posters in the cellar.

$ At Bar-Hostal Zindicato, the bar comes first, but they also rent four tidy, modern, air-conditioned rooms really cheap out back on the ground floor (Db-€30, Calle Corredera 2, tel. 956-701-841, mobile 657-911-851). It's in a less quaint zone at the bottom end of the old town.

In the New Town

$$ Hotel Los Olivos is a bright, cool, and airy place with 19 rooms, an impressive courtyard, roof garden, generous public spaces, bar, view, friendly folks, and easy parking. The seven view rooms can be a bit noisy in the afternoon, but—with double-paned windows— are usually fine at night (Sb-€43-48, Db-€65-80, Tb-€80-95, extra bed-€15, breakfast-€8.50; 10 percent discount when you book direct, pay in cash, and show this book; free Internet access and Wi-Fi, Paseo de los Boliches 30, tel. 956-700-811, fax 956-702-018, www.hotel-losolivos.es, reservas@hotel-losolivos.es, Raquel and Miguel Ángel).

$ Hostal Málaga is surprisingly nice, if for some reason you want to stay on the big, noisy road at the Jerez edge of town. Nestled on a quiet lane between truck stops on A-382, it offers 18 clean, attractive rooms and a breezy two-level roof garden (Sb-€20-25, Db-€35-38, Qb apartment-€50, air-con, Wi-Fi, easy parking, Ponce de León 5, tel. & fax 956-702-010, www.hostalmalaga.com, hostal malagaarcos@hotmail.com, Josefa speaks German if that helps).

Eating in Arcos

Restaurants generally serve lunch from 13:00 to 16:00 and dinner from 20:00 until very late (Spaniards don't start dinner until about 21:00).

Dining

The **Parador** (described earlier, under "Sleeping in Arcos") has an expensive restaurant with a cliff-edge setting. A costly drink on the million-dollar-view terrace can be worth the price (€13-14 starters, €16-19 main dishes, €24 lunch deal, €32 three-course fixed-price meal at lunch or dinner, daily 13:30-16:00 & 20:30-23:00, on main square).

Cheaper Eating in the Old Town

Several decent, rustic bar-restaurants are in the old town, within a block or two of the main square and church. Most serve tapas at the bar and *raciones* at their tables. Prices are fairly consistent (€2 tapas, €5 *media-raciones*, €8 *raciones*).

Bar La Carcel ("The Prison") is run by a hardworking family that brags about its exquisite tapas and small open-faced sandwiches. I agree. The menu is accessible; prices are the same at the bar or at the tables; and the place has a winning energy, giving the traveler a fun peek at this community (Tue-Sun 12:00-16:00 & 20:00-24:00, closed Mon; July-Aug it's open Mon and closed Sun; Calle Deán Espinosa 18, tel. 956-700-410).

Alcaraván tries to be a bit trendier yet *típico*, with a hibachi hard at work out front. A flamenco ambience fills its medieval vault in the castle's former dungeon. This place attracts French and German tourists who give it a cool vibe. Francisco and his wife cook from 13:00 and from 21:00 (closed Mon, Calle Nueva 1).

Bar San Marcos is a tiny, homey bar with five tables, an easy-to-understand menu offering hearty, simple home cooking, and cheap €5 plates and €7 fixed-price meals (kitchen open long hours daily, Marqués de Torresoto 6).

Mesón Don Fernando gives rustic a feminine twist with an inviting bar and both indoor and great outdoor seating on the square just across from the little market (Tue-Thu 13:30-16:00 & 20:15-23:00 for food, closed Wed, longer hours for drinks on the square, on Plaza Boticas).

Mama Ttina gives you an Italian break from Andalucía, with pizza and pastas to go along with the Italian pop music and international Italian/Andaluz/Moroccan/British staff (€7-12 pizzas and pastas, daily 14:00-16:00 & 20:00-24:00 except closed for lunch Tue-Wed, Deán Espinosa 10, tel. 956-703-937).

Tapas in the New Town

Plaza de España, in the lower new town, is lined with tapas bars and restaurants. There's even an Egyptian restaurant if you're in the mood for a change. For a great perch while enjoying the local family scene, consider the busy **Restaurante Bar Terraza** (€12 plates) at the end of Plaza de España.

Arcos Connections

By Bus

Leaving Arcos by bus can be frustrating (especially if you're going to Ronda)—buses generally leave late, the schedule information boards are often inaccurate, and the ticket window usually isn't open (luckily, you can buy your tickets on the bus). But local buses do give you a glimpse at *España profunda* ("deep Spain"), where everyone seems to know each other, no one's in a hurry, and despite any language barriers, people are quite helpful when approached.

Two bus companies (Los Amarillos and Comes) share the Arcos bus station. Call the Jerez offices for departure times, or ask your hotelier for help. If you want to find out about the Arcos–Jerez schedule, make it clear you're coming from Arcos (Los Amarillos tel. 902-210-317; Comes toll tel. 902-199-208, www.tgcomes .es). Also try the privately run www.movelia.es for bus schedules and routes.

From Arcos by Bus to: Jerez (hourly, 30 minutes), **Ronda** (2-3/ day, 2 hours, 4 hours with transfer in Villamartín—when transferring, confirm with driver what the final destination is—bus could be headed to Ronda or Sevilla, and dashboard destination signs are often inaccurate), **Cádiz** (4-5/day, 1.25 hours), **Sevilla** (2/day, 2 hours, more departures with transfer in Jerez). Buses run less frequently on weekends. The closest train station to Arcos is Jerez.

Route Tips for Drivers

The trip to **Sevilla** takes just over an hour if you pay €5 for the toll road. To reach **southern Portugal,** follow the freeway to Sevilla, skirt the city by turning west on C-30 in the direction of Huelva, and it's a straight shot from there.

For more driving tips for the region, see the end of this chapter.

Ronda

With nearly 40,000 people, Ronda is one of the largest white hill towns. It's also one of the most spectacular, thanks to its gorge-straddling setting. Approaching the town from the train or bus station, it seems flat...until you reach the New Bridge and realize that it's clinging to the walls of a canyon.

While day-trippers from the touristy Costa del Sol clog Ronda's streets during the day, locals retake the town in the early evening, making nights peaceful. If you liked Toledo at night, you'll love the local feeling of evenings in Ronda. Since it's served by train and bus, Ronda makes a relaxing break for non-drivers traveling between Granada, Sevilla, and Córdoba. Drivers can use

Ronda as a convenient base from which to explore many of the other *pueblos blancos*.

Ronda's main attractions are its gorge-spanning bridges, the oldest bullring in Spain, and an intriguing old town. The cliff-side setting, dramatic today, was practical back in its day. For the Moors, it provided a tough bastion, taken by the Spaniards only in 1485, seven years before Granada fell. Spaniards know Ronda as the cradle of modern bullfighting and the romantic home of 19th-century *bandoleros*. The real joy of Ronda these days lies in exploring its back streets and taking in its beautiful balconies, exuberant flowerpots, and panoramic views. Walking the streets, you feel a strong local pride and a community where everyone seems to know everyone.

Orientation to Ronda

Ronda's breathtaking ravine divides the town's labyrinthine Moorish quarter and its new, noisier, and more sprawling Mercadillo quarter. A massive-yet-graceful 18th-century bridge connects these two neighborhoods. Most things of touristic importance (TI, post office, hotels, bullring) are clustered within a few blocks of the bridge. The paseo (early evening stroll) happens in the new town, on Ronda's major pedestrian and shopping street, Carrera Espinel.

Tourist Information

Ronda has two competing TIs. The **city TI** is across the square from the bullring. It gives out a decent town map (free), sells the Bono Turístico city pass (described below), and organizes walking tours (Mon-Fri 10:00-19:00, until 18:00 late-Oct-late March; Sat-Sun 10:00-14:00 & 15:00-17:00; Paseo Blas Infante, tel. 952-187-119, www.turismoderonda.es). The **regional TI**—on the main square, Plaza de España, opposite the bridge—covers all of Andalucía (Mon-Fri 9:00-19:30, Sat-Sun 9:30-15:00, longer hours in summer, tel. 952-169-311). It hands out several free maps, including a better Ronda map, an excellent Andalusian road map, and maps of Granada, Sevilla, and the Route of the White Towns. Both TIs have listings of the latest museum hours.

If you're an avid sightseer, consider getting the **Bono Turístico** city pass. The €9 version gets you into five sights (including the Arab Baths, Museo Joaquín Peinado, and Mondragón Palace); the €14 version covers eight sights (adding the Lara Museum and others). Both are valid for one week and are sold only at the city TI and a few participating sights (such as the Arab Baths and Museo Joaquín Peinado).

Ronda

TO PILETA CAVE, ARCOS, SEVILLA & ❹

BUS STATION

TO TRAIN STATION & ❿

200 YARDS
200 METERS

Ⓣ TAXI STAND
View
Ⓟ PARKING

CALLE JEREZ
SAN JOSÉ
ANDALUCÍA
MADRID
MONTERO
LAURIA
MONTENDAS
CRUZ VERDE
POZO
SUBTRON
ALMENDRA
NARANJA
ESPINEL
VIRGEN DE LA PAZ
M. CABRERA
CORTES
CANTOS
PEÑAS
REAL
S. DOMINGO
ARMIÑAN
TENORIO
ARMIÑAN
ARMIÑAN
LOS REMEDIOS
VILLANUEVA
NUEVA

PLAZA MERCED

ALAMEDA DEL TAJO
WC

PLAZA DEL SOCORRO
POST

PLAZA DE ESPAÑA

PLAZA C. ABELA

MERCADILLO
QUARTER

BULLRING

PARADOR

GUADALEVÍN RIVER

NEW BRIDGE

TRAIL TO PUERTA DE LOS MOLINOS

OLD BRIDGE

ARAB BRIDGE

ARAB BATHS MUSEUM

PLAZA DE MARÍA AUXILIADORA

MOORISH QUARTER

CITY WALL

MONDRAGÓN PALACE

SANTA MARÍA LA MAYOR

CITY HALL

BANDOLERO MUSEUM

TO COSTA DEL SOL, ⓬ & ⓲

HILL TOWNS

❶ Hotel San Gabriel
❷ Hotel Ronda
❸ Hotel Alavera de los Baños
❹ To Hotel Reina Victoria
❺ Hotel Enfrente Arte Ronda
❻ Hotel Don Miguel
❼ Hotel El Tajo & Spar Market
❽ Hotel San Francisco
❾ Hotel Royal
❿ To Hostal Andalucía
⓫ Hostal Doña Carmen
⓬ To Hotel Bandolero
⓭ Confitería Daver

⓮ Tragatapas
⓯ Bar Lechuguita
⓰ Café & Bar Faustino
⓱ La Tradicional
⓲ To Almocábar Gate, Bar-Restaurante Almocábar, Casa Maria & Bodega San Francisco
⓳ Restaurante del Escudero
⓴ Restaurante Pedro Romero
㉑ Rest. Casa Santa Pola
㉒ Casa del Rey Moro Garden
㉓ Palacio del Marqués de Salvatierra
㉔ Lara Museum
㉕ Museo Joaquín Peinado

Arrival in Ronda

By Train: From the station, it's a 15-to-20-minute **walk** to the center: Turn right out of the station on Avenida de Andalucía, and go through the roundabout (you'll see the bus station on your right). Continue straight down the street (now called San José) until it dead-ends. Turn left and walk downhill past a church and the Alameda del Tajo park. Keep going down this street, passing the bullring, to get to the TI and the famous bridge. A **taxi** to the center costs about €6.50.

By Bus: To get to the center from the bus station, leave the station walking to the right of the roundabout, then follow the directions for train travelers (described above). To use the station's baggage lockers, buy a token *(ficha)* at the kiosk by the exit (€4).

By Car: Street parking away from the center is often free. The handiest place to park in the center of Ronda is the underground lot at Plaza del Socorro (one block from bullring, €18/24 hours).

Tours in Ronda

Walking Tours—The TI opposite the bullring offers two-hour guided walks of the city on Saturdays and Sundays, starting at 12:30. Reserve at the TI, then pay the guide (€10 includes Mondragón Palace, €15 adds the bullring, sometimes in two languages). Tours can be canceled if there aren't enough sign-ups.

Local Guide—Energetic and knowledgeable **Antonio Jesús Naranjo** will take you on a two-hour walking tour of the city's sights. He showed Michelle Obama around when she was in town (from €118 Mon-Fri, from €130 Sat-Sun and holidays, reserve early, tel. 952-870-614, mobile 639-073-763, www.guiaoficialderonda.com, guiajesus@yahoo.es). The TI has a list of other local guides.

Sights in Ronda

Ronda's New Town

▲▲▲**The Gorge and New Bridge (Puente Nuevo)**—The ravine, called El Tajo—360 feet down and 200 feet wide—divides Ronda into the whitewashed old Moorish town (La Ciudad) and the new town (El Mercadillo) that was built after the Christian reconquest in 1485. The New Bridge mightily spans the gorge. A different bridge was built here in 1735, but fell after six years. This one was built from 1751 to 1793. Look down...carefully.

You can see the foundations of the

HILL TOWNS

original bridge (and a super view of the New Bridge) from the Jardines de Cuenca park (daily in summer 9:30-21:30, winter 9:30-18:30): From Plaza de España, walk down Calle Rosario, turn right on Calle Los Remedios, and then take another right at the sign for the park. There are also good views from the parador, which overlooks the gorge and bridge from the new-town side.

From the new-town side of the bridge, on the right, you'll see the entrance to the **New Bridge Interpretive Center,** where you can pay to climb down and enter the structure of the bridge itself. Inside the mostly empty-feeling hall are modest audio-visual displays about the bridge's construction and famous visitors to Ronda. But the views of the bridge and gorge from the outside are far more thrilling than anything you'll find within (€2; Mon-Fri 10:00-19:00, late Oct-late March until 18:00; Sat-Sun 10:00-15:00 year-round; mobile 649-965-338).

▲▲▲**Bullring**—Ronda is the birthplace of modern bullfighting, and this was the first great Spanish bullring. Philip II initi-

ated bullfighting as war training for knights in the 16th century. Back then, there were two kinds of bullfighting: the type with noble knights on horseback, and the coarser, man-versus-beast entertainment for the commoners (with no rules...much like when the WWF wrestlers bring out the folding chairs). Ronda practically worships Francisco Romero, who melded the noble and chaotic kinds of bullfighting with rules to establish modern bullfighting right here in the early 1700s. He introduced the scarlet cape, held unfurled with a stick. His son Juan further developed the ritual (local aficionados would never call it a "sport"—you'll read newspaper coverage of fights not on the sports pages but in the culture section), and his grandson Pedro was one of the first great matadors (killing nearly 6,000 bulls in his career).

Ronda's bullring and museum are Spain's most interesting to tour (even better than Sevilla's). To tour the ring, stables, chapel, and museum, buy a ticket at the back of the bullring, the farthest point from the main drag.

Cost and Hours: €6, daily April-Sept 10:00-20:00, March and Oct 10:00-19:00, Nov-Feb 10:00-18:00, tel. 952-874-132. The excellent €2 audioguide describes everything and is essential to fully enjoy your visit.

Bullfights: Bullfights are scheduled only for the first weekend of September during the *feria* (fair) and occur rarely in the spring. Whereas every other *feria* in Andalucía celebrates a patron saint, the Ronda fair glorifies legendary bullfighter Pedro Romero. For September bullfights, tickets go on sale the preceding July. (As these sell out immediately, Sevilla and Madrid are more practical places for a tourist to see a bullfight.)

Visiting the Bullring: I'd visit in this order. Directly to the right as you enter is the bullfighters' **chapel.** Before going into the ring, every matador would stop here to pray to Mary for safety—and hope to see her again.

• Just beyond the chapel are the doors to the museum exhibits: horse gear and weapons on the left, and the story of bullfighting on the right, with some English translations.

The **horse gear and guns exhibit** makes the connection with bullfighting and the equestrian upper class. As through-

out Europe, "chivalry" began as a code among the sophisticated, horse-riding gentry. (In Spanish, the word for "gentleman" is the same as the word for "horseman" or "cowboy"—*caballero*.) And, of course, nobles are into hunting and dueling, hence the fancy guns. Don't miss the well-described dueling section with gun cases for two, as charming as a picnic basket with matching wine glasses.

Backtrack past the chapel to see Spain's best **bullfighting exhibit.** It's a shrine to bullfighting and the historic Romero family. First it traces the long history of bullfighting, going all the way back to the ancient Minoans on Crete. Historically, there were only two arenas built solely for bullfighting: in Ronda and Sevilla. Elsewhere, bullfights were held in town squares—you'll see a painting of Madrid's Plaza Mayor filled with spectators for a bullfight. (For this reason, to this day, even a purpose-built bullring is generally called *plaza de toros*—"square of bulls.") You'll also see stuffed bull heads, photos, "suits of light" worn by bullfighters, and capes (bulls are actually colorblind, but the traditional red cape was designed to disguise all the blood). One section explains some of the big "dynasties" of fighters. At the end of the hall are historic posters from Ronda's bullfights (all originals except the Picasso). Running along the left wall are various examples of artwork glorifying bullfighting, including original Goya engravings.

• From the museum, take advantage of the opportunity to walk in the actual arena.

Here's your chance to play *toro*, surrounded by 5,000 empty seats. The two-tiered arena was built in 1785—on the 300th anniversary of the defeat of the Moors in Ronda. Notice the 136 classy Tuscan columns, creating a kind of 18th-century Italian theater.

Lovers of the "art" of bullfighting will explain that the event is much more than the actual killing of the bull. It celebrates the noble heritage and the Andalusian horse culture. When you leave the museum and walk out on the sand, look across to see the ornamental columns and painted doorway where the dignitaries sit (over the gate where the bull enters). On the right is the place for the band (marked *música*), which in the case of a small town like Ronda, is most likely a high school band.

• *Just beyond the arena are more parts of the complex.*

From the arena, walk through the bulls' entry into the bullpen and the **stables.** There are six bulls per fight (and three matadors). The bulls are penned up here beforehand, and ropes and pulleys safely open the right door at the right time. Climb upstairs and find the indoor arena (Picadero) and see Spanish thoroughbred horses training from the **Equestrian School** of the Real Maestranza (Mon-Fri).

Alameda del Tajo—One block away from the bullring, the town's main park is a great place for people-watching, a snooze in the shade, or practicing your Spanish with seniors from the old folks' home.

Ronda's Old Town

▲ **Santa María la Mayor Collegiate Church**—This 15th-century church with a fine Mudejar bell tower shares a park-like square with orange trees and the City Hall. It was built on and around the remains of Moorish Ronda's main mosque (which was itself built on the site of a temple to Julius Caesar). With a pleasantly eclectic interior that features some art with unusually modern flair, and a good audioguide to explain it all, it's worth a visit.

Cost and Hours: €4, includes audioguide, daily April-Sept 10:00-20:00, March and Oct 10:00-19:00, Nov-Feb 10:00-18:00, closed Sun 12:30-14:00 for Mass, Plaza Duquesa de Parcent in the old town.

Visiting the Church: In the room where you purchase your ticket, look for the only surviving mosque prayer niche (that's a mirror; look back at the actual mihrab, which faces not Mecca, but Gibraltar—where you'd travel to get to Mecca). Partially destroyed by an earthquake, the reconstruction of the church resulted in the Moorish/Gothic/Renaissance/Baroque fusion (or confusion) you see today.

HILL TOWNS

The front of the church interior is dominated by a magnificent Baroque high altar with the standard statue of the *Immaculate Conception* in the center. The even more ornate chapel directly to the right is a good example of Churrigueresque architecture, a kind of Spanish Rococo in which decoration obliterates the architecture—notice that you can hardly make out the souped-up columns. This chapel's fancy decor provides a frame for an artistic highlight of the town, the "Virgin of the Ultimate Sorrow." The big fresco of St. Christopher with Baby Jesus on his shoulders (on the left, where you entered) shows the patron saint both of Ronda and of travelers.

Facing the altar is an elaborately carved choir with a wall of modern bronze reliefs depicting scenes from the life of the Virgin Mary. Similar to the Via Crucis (Way of the Cross), this is the Via Lucis (Way of the Light), with 14 stations (such as #13—the Immaculate Conception, and #14—Mary's assumption into heaven) that serve as a worship aid to devout Catholics. The centerpiece is Mary as the light of the world (with the moon, stars, and sun around her).

Head to the left around the choir, noticing the bright paintings along the wall by French artist Raymonde Pagegie, who gave sacred scenes a fresh twist—like the Last Supper attended by female servants, or the scene of Judgment Day, when the four horsemen of the apocalypse pause to adore the Lamb of God.

The treasury (at the far-right corner, with your back to the high altar) displays vestments that look curiously like matadors' brocaded outfits—appropriate for this bullfight-crazy town.

Mondragón Palace (Palacio de Mondragón)—This beautiful Moorish building was erected in the 14th century, possibly as the residence of Moorish kings, and was carefully restored in the 16th century. At the entrance (free to view without a ticket) is a topographic model of Ronda, which helps you envision the fortified old town apart from the grid-like new one. The rest of the building houses Ronda's Municipal Museum, focusing on prehistory and geology. Wander through its many rooms to find the kid-friendly prehistory section, with exhibits on Neolithic toolmaking and early metallurgy (described in English). If you plan to visit the Pileta Cave, find the panels that describe the cave's formation and shape. Even if you have no interest in your ancestors or speleology, the building's architecture is impressive; linger in the two small gardens, especially the shaded one.

Cost and Hours: €3; Mon-Fri 10:00-19:00, late Oct-late

March until 18:00; Sat-Sun 10:00-15:00, on Plaza Mondragón in old town, tel. 952-870-818.

Nearby: Leaving the palace, wander left a few short blocks to the nearby Plaza de María Auxiliadora for more views and a look at the two rare *pinsapos* (resembling extra-large Christmas trees) in the middle of the park; this part of Andalucía is the only region in Europe where these ancient trees still grow. For an intense workout but a picture-perfect view, find the *Puerta de los Molinos* sign and head down, down, down. (Just remember you have to walk back up, up, up.) Not for the faint of heart or in the heat of the afternoon sun, this pathway leads down to the viewpoint where windmills once stood. Photographers go crazy reproducing the most famous postcard view of Ronda—the entirety of the New Bridge. Wait until just before sunset for the best light and cooler temperatures.

Lara Museum—This discombobulated collection of Ronda's history in dusty glass cases displays everything from sewing machines to fans to old movie projectors to matador outfits (with decent English explanations). The highlight for many is the basement, with juvenile displays showing torture devices from the Inquisition and local witchcraft (€4, daily 11:00-20:00, mid-Oct-mid-March until 19:00, Calle Arminan 29, tel. 952-871-263, www.museolara .org).

Museo del Bandolero—This tiny museum, while not as intriguing as it sounds, is an interesting assembly of *bandolero* photos, guns, clothing, knickknacks, and old documents and newspaper clippings. The Jesse Jameses and Billy el Niños of Andalucía called this remote area home. One brand of romantic bandits fought Napoleon's army—often more effectively than the regular Spanish troops. The exhibits profile specific *bandoleros* and display books (from comics to pulp fiction) that helped romanticize these heroes of Spain's "Old West." The museum feels a bit like a tourist trap (with a well-stocked gift shop), but brief but helpful English descriptions make this a fun stop. Next door is a free 22-minute movie about *bandoleros*, but it's only in Spanish.

Cost and Hours: €3.50, daily May-Sept 10:30-20:00, Oct-April until 19:00, across main street below Church of Santa María la Mayor at Calle Armiñan 65, tel. 952-877-785, www.museo bandolero.com.

▲Museo Joaquín Peinado—Housed in an old palace, this fresh museum features an impressively large professional overview of the life's work of Joaquín Peinado (1898-1975), a Ronda native and pal of Picasso. Because Franco killed creativity in Spain for much of the last century, nearly all of Peinado's creative work was done in Paris. His style evolved through the big "isms" of the 20th century, ranging from Expressionist to Cubist, and even to erotic. While

HILL TOWNS

Peinado's works seem a bit derivative, perhaps that's understandable as he was friends with one of the art world's biggest talents. The nine-minute movie that kicks it off is only in Spanish, though there are good English explanations throughout the museum. You'll have an interesting modern-art experience here, without the crowds of Madrid's museums. It's fun to be exposed to a lesser-known but very talented artist in his hometown.

Cost and Hours: €4, Mon-Fri 10:00-18:00, Sat-Sun 10:00-15:00, Plaza del Gigante, tel. 952-871-585.

Walk Through Old Town to Bottom of Gorge—From the New Bridge you can descend down Cuesta de Santo Domingo (crossing the bridge from the new town into the old, take the first left at the former Dominican Church, once the headquarters of the Inquisition in Ronda) into a world of whitewashed houses, tiny grilled balconies, and winding lanes—the old town.

A couple of blocks steeply downhill (on the left), you'll see the **Casa del Rey Moro** (House of the Moorish King). It was never the home of any king; it was given its fictitious name by the grandson of President McKinley, who once lived here. It offers visitors entry to the fine "Moorish-Hispanic" belle époque garden, designed in 1912 by a French landscape architect (the house interior is not open to visitors). Follow signs to "the Mine," an exhausting series of 280 slick, dark, and narrow stairs (like climbing down and then up a 20-story building) leading to the floor of the gorge. The Moors cut this zigzag staircase into the wall of the gorge in the 14th century to access water when under siege, then used Spanish slaves to haul water up to the thirsty town (€4, generally daily 10:00-19:00, June-Aug until 20:00).

Fifty yards downhill from the garden is **Palacio del Marqués de Salvatierra** (closed to public). As part of the "distribution" following the Reconquista here in 1485, the Spanish king gave this grand house to the Salvatierra family (who live here to this day). The facade is rich in colonial symbolism from Spanish America—note the pre-Columbian-looking characters (four Peruvian Indians) flanking the balcony above the door and below the family coat of arms.

Just below the palace, stop to enjoy the view terrace. Look below. A series of square vats are all that remains of the old tanneries. There are two old bridges, with the Arab Baths just to the right, and at the edge of town is a rectangular horse-training area.

Twenty steps farther down, you'll pass through the Philip V

gate, for centuries the main gate to the fortified city of Ronda. Continuing downhill, you come to the **Old Bridge** (Puente Viejo),

rebuilt in 1616 upon the ruins of an Arabic bridge. Enjoy the views from the bridge (but don't cross it yet), then continue down the old stairs. From the base of the staircase, look back up to glimpse some of the surviving highly fortified Moorish city walls. You've now reached the oldest bridge in Ronda, the Arab Bridge (also called the San Miguel Bridge). Sometimes given the misnomer of Puente Romano (Roman Bridge), it was more likely built long after the Romans left. For centuries, this was the main gate to the fortified city. In Moorish times, you'd purify both your body and your soul here before entering the city, so just outside the gate was a little mosque (now the ruined chapel) and the Arab Baths.

The **Arab Baths**, worth ▲, are evocative ruins that warrant a quick look. They were located half underground to maintain the

temperature and served by a horse-powered water tower. You can still see the top of the shaft (30 yards beyond the bath rooftops, near a Cyprus tree, connected to the baths by an aqueduct). Water was hoisted from the river below to the aqueduct by ceramic containers that were attached to a belt powered by a horse walking in circles. Inside, two of the original eight columns scavenged from the Roman ruins still support brick vaulting. A delightful 10-minute video brings the entire complex to life—Spanish and English versions run alternately (€3, free on Mon; open Mon-Fri 10:00-19:00, Nov-April until 18:00; Sat-Sun 10:00-15:00 year-round; sometimes open later in summer, call ahead before making the trip, mobile 656-950-937).

From here, hike back to the new town along the other side of the gorge: Return to the bridge just uphill. Cross it and take the stairs immediately on the left, which lead scenically along the gorge up to the New Bridge.

Near Ronda: Pileta Cave

The Pileta Cave (Cueva de la Pileta) offers Spain's most intimate look at Neolithic and Paleolithic paintings that are up to 25,000 years old. Set in a dramatic, rocky limestone ridge at the eastern edge of Sierra de Grazalema Natural Park, Pileta Cave is 14 miles from Ronda, past the town of Benaoján, at the end of an access road. It's particularly handy if you're driving between Ronda and Grazalema.

Farmer José Bullón and his family live down the hill from the cave, and because they strictly limit the number of visitors, Pileta's rare paintings are among the best-preserved in the world. Señor Bullón and his son lead up to 25 people at a time through the cave, which was discovered by Bullón's grandfather in 1905. Call the night before to see if there's a tour and space available at the time you want. Note that if you simply show up for the 13:00 tour and it is full, it'll be another three hours before the next one starts. Bring a sweater and good shoes. You need a good sense of balance to take the tour. The 10-minute hike, from the parking lot up a trail with stone steps to the cave entrance, is moderately steep. Inside the cave, there are no handrails, and it can be difficult to keep your footing on the slippery, uneven floor while being led single-file, with only a lantern light illuminating the way.

Señor Bullón is a master at hurdling the language barrier. As you walk the cool half-mile, he'll spend an hour pointing out lots of black, ochre, and red drawings, which are five times as old as the Egyptian pyramids. Mostly it's just lines or patterns, but there are also horses, goats, cattle, and a rare giant fish, made from a mixture of clay and fat by finger-painting prehistoric *hombres*. The 200-foot main cavern is impressive, as are some weirdly recognizable natural formations such as the Michelin man and a Christmas tree.

Cost and Hours: €8, 60-minute tours generally on the hour but depends on the number of people, daily 10:00-13:00 & 16:00-18:00, Nov-mid-April until 17:00, closing times indicate last tour, €10 guidebook, no photos, tel. 952-167-343, www.cuevadelapileta .org.

Getting There: It's possible to get here without wheels, but I wouldn't bother (you'd have to take the Ronda–Benaoján bus—2/day, departs at 8:30 and 13:00, 30 minutes—and then it's a 2-hour, 3-mile uphill hike). You can get from Ronda to the cave by taxi—it's about a half-hour drive on twisty roads—and have the driver wait (€60 round-trip). If you're driving, it's easy: Leave Ronda through the new part of town, and take A-374. After a few miles, passing Cueva del Gato, exit left toward Benaoján on MA-555. Go through Benaoján and follow the numerous signs to the cave. Leave nothing of value in your car.

Eating near the Cave: Nearby Montejaque has several good restaurants clustered around the central square.

Sleeping near the Cave: A good base for visiting Ronda and

the Pileta Cave (as well as Grazalema) is **$$ Cortijo las Piletas.**
Nestled at the edge of Sierra de Grazalema Natural Park (just a
15-minute drive from Ronda, with easy access from the main high-
way), this spacious family-run country estate has nine rooms and
plenty of opportunities for swimming, hiking, bird-watching, and
exploring the surrounding area. They can also arrange for biking
and horseback riding (Sb-€68-74, Db-€84-90, extra bed-€15-18,
includes breakfast but not tax, dinner offered some days—book
in advance, mobile 605-080-295, www.cortijolaspiletas.com, info
@cortijolaspiletas.com, Pablo and Elisenda). Another countryside
option is **$$ Finca La Guzmana,** run by expat Brit Peter. Seven
beautifully appointed pastel rooms surround an open patio at this
renovated estate house. Bird-watching, swimming, and trekking
are possible (Db-€70-80, includes breakfast, mobile 600-006-305,
www.laguzmana.com, info@laguzmana.com).

Sleeping in Ronda

(€1 = about $1.40, country code: 34)
Ronda has plenty of reasonably priced, decent-value accommodations. It's crowded only during Holy Week (the week leading up
to Easter) and the first week of September (for bullfighting season). Most of my recommendations are in the new town, a short
stroll from the New Bridge and about a 10-minute walk from the
train station. In the cheaper places, ask for a room with a *ventana*
(window) to avoid the few interior rooms. Breakfast is usually not
included.

In the Old Town

Clearly the best options in town, these hotels are worth reserving
early. The first two are right in the heart of the Old Town, while
the Alavera de los Baños is a steep 15-to-20-minute hike below,
but still easily walkable to all the sights (if you're in good shape)
and in a bucolic setting.

$$ Hotel San Gabriel has 22 pleasant rooms, a kind staff,
public rooms filled with art and poetry books, a cozy wine cellar,
and a fine garden terrace. It's a large 1736 townhouse, once the
family's home, that's been converted to a characteristic hotel, mar-
inated in history. If you're a cinephile, kick back in the charming
TV room—with seats from Ronda's old theater and a collection of
DVD classics—then head to the breakfast room to check out pho-
tos of big movie stars (and, ahem, bespectacled travel writers) who
have stayed here (Sb-€66, Db-€85, bigger superior Db-€95, Db
junior suite-€109, lavish honeymoon suite-€150, breakfast-€6, air-
con, incognito elevator, free Internet access and Wi-Fi, double-park
in front and they'll direct you to a €9 parking spot, follow signs on

the main street of old town to Calle Marqués de Moctezuma 19, tel. 952-190-392, fax 952-190-117, www.hotelsangabriel.com, info @hotelsangabriel.com, family-run by José Manuel and Ana).

$$ Hotel Ronda provides an interesting mix of minimalist and traditional Spanish decor, with five rooms located in the old town. Although there are no views, the refurbished mansion is quiet and homey (Sb-€52, Db-€67, additional bed-€21, no breakfast, air-con, free Internet access and Wi-Fi, Ruedo Doña Elvira 12, tel. 952-872-232, www.hotelronda.net, laraln@telefonica.net, no English spoken).

$$ Alavera de los Baños, a delightful oasis located next to ancient Moorish baths at the bottom of the hill, has nine small rooms and big inviting public places, with appropriately Moorish decor. This hotel offers a swimming pool, a peaceful Arabic garden, and a restaurant open every day for a €15 tapas lunch and sporadically at dinner for guests who've made reservations. The artistic ambience urges, "Relax!" You're literally in the countryside, with sheep and horses outside near the garden (Sb-€60-70, Db-€80-95, Db with terrace-€90-105, includes breakfast, free Wi-Fi in some rooms, free and easy parking, closed Jan, steeply below the heart of town at Calle San Miguel, tel. & fax 952-879-143, www .alaveradelosbanos.com, alavera@telefonica.net, well-run by personable Christian and Inma).

In the New Town

More convenient than charming (except the Hotel Enfrente Arte Ronda—in a class all its own), these hotels put you in the thriving new town.

$$$ Hotel Reina Victoria, with 89 rooms, hangs royally over the gorge at the edge of town and has a marvelous view—Hemingway loved it. While it feels a bit past its prime, and the service is spotty, I'd choose this—with all its romantic Old World elegance—over the more central parador (Sb-€97-117, Db-€112-156, breakfast-€9, air-con, elevator, free Wi-Fi in lobby, pool, free parking, 10-minute walk from city center; easy to miss—look for intersection of Avenida Victoria and Calle Jerez, Jerez 25; tel. 952-871-240, fax 952-871-075, www.hotelreinavictoria.es, info@hotel reinavictoria.es).

$$ Hotel Enfrente Arte Ronda, on the edge of things a steep 10-to-15-minute walk below the heart of the new town, is relaxed, funky, and friendly. The 12 rooms are spacious and exotically decorated, but dimly lit. It features a sprawling maze of exuberantly decorated public spaces, including a peaceful bamboo garden, game and reading room, small swimming pool, sauna, and terraces with sweeping countryside views. Guests can enjoy themed dinners on certain nights (€15, confirm with reception in advance), and can help themselves to free drinks from the self-service bar. This one-of-a-kind place is in all the guidebooks, so reserve early (Db-€80-105, extra bed-€28, prices do not include tax, includes buffet breakfast, air-con, elevator, free Internet access and Wi-Fi in lobby, Real 40, tel. 952-879-088, fax 952-877-217, www.enfrentearte.com, reservations@enfrentearte.com).

$$ Hotel Don Miguel, facing the gorge just left of the bridge, has disinterested staff and all the charm of a tour-group hotel, but it couldn't be more central. Of its 30 sparse but comfortable rooms, 20 have balconies and/or gorgeous views at no extra cost. Street rooms come with a little noise (Sb-€55-65, Db-€85-100, Tb-€110-135, tax not included, includes buffet breakfast, air-con, elevator, free Wi-Fi in lobby, parking garage a block away-€9/day, Plaza de España 4, tel. 952-877-722, fax 952-878-377, www.dmiguel.com, reservas@dmiguel.com).

$$ Hotel El Tajo has 33 decent, quiet rooms—once you get past the tacky faux-stone Moorish decoration in the foyer (Sb-€43, Db-€65, breakfast-€6, air-con, elevator, free Wi-Fi in some rooms, parking-€10, Calle Cruz Verde 7, a half-block off the pedestrian street, tel. 952-874-040, fax 952-875-099, www.hoteleltajo.com, reservas@hoteleltajo.com).

$$ Hotel San Francisco offers 27 small, nicely decorated rooms a block off the main pedestrian street in the town center (Sb-€35-40, Db-€50-65, Tb-€70-80, breakfast-€4, air-con, elevator, parking-€8.50, María Cabrera 20, tel. 952-873-299, fax 952-874-688, hotelronda@terra.es).

$ Hotel Royal has a dreary reception and 29 clean, spacious, simple rooms—many on the main street that runs between the bullring and bridge. Thick glass keeps out most of the noise, while the tree-lined Alameda del Tajo park across the street is a treat. Some rooms and hallways are dimly lit (Sb-€38, Db-€45-50, Tb-€55-60, breakfast-€4, air-con, free Wi-Fi, parking-€13, Calle Virgen de la Paz 42, 3 blocks off Plaza de España, tel. 952-871-141, fax 952-878-132, www.ronda.net/usuar/hotelroyal, hroyal@ronda.net, some English spoken).

$ Hostal Andalucía has 11 clean, comfortable, and recently renovated rooms immediately across the street from the train station (Sb-€27, Db-€42, Tb-€53, breakfast-€2, air-con, free Wi-Fi, easy street parking, Martínez Astein 19, tel. 952-875-450, www.hostalandalucia.net, info@hostalandalucia.net).

$ Hostal Doña Carmen, a basic cheapie, rents 32 bare-bones rooms in two sections. The rooms sharing a shower down the hall, with no air-con or TV, are especially reasonable (S-€17, Sb-€25, D-€28, Db-€45, T-€40, Tb-€55, no breakfast, air-con and TV only in rooms with bath, free Wi-Fi in lobby, Calle Naranja 28, tel. 952-871-994).

HILL TOWNS

Near Ronda

$$ Hotel Bandolero, about 12 miles south of Ronda in the village of Júzcar, is for nature-lovers. Settle into the rustic rooms, go hiking and bird-watching, or take a dip in the pool (Sb-€40-45, standard Db-€58-96, superior Db-€68-106, Db suite-€79-117, higher prices are for half-board, restaurant, Avenida Havaral 43, tel. 952-183-660, www.hotelbandolero.com, reservas@hotelbandolero.com, David).

Eating in Ronda

Plaza del Socorro, a block in front of the bullring, is an energetic scene, bustling with tourists and local families enjoying the square and its restaurants. The pedestrian-only **Calle Nueva** is lined with hardworking eateries. To enjoy a drink or a light meal with the best view in town, consider the terraces of Hotel Don Miguel just under the bridge. For coffee and pastries, locals like the elegant little **Confiteria Daver** (café open daily 8:00-20:30, take-away until 21:00, Calle Los Remedios 6). Picnic shoppers find the **Spar** supermarket convenient, opposite Hotel El Tajo (Mon-Sat 9:00-21:00, closed Sun, Calle Cruz Verde 18). The Alameda del Tajo park (with WC) near the bullring is a good picnic spot.

Tapas in the City Center

Ronda has a fine tapas scene. You won't get a free tapa with your drink as in some other Spanish towns, but these bars have accessible tapas lists, and they serve bigger plates. Each of the following places could make a fine solo destination for a meal, but they're close enough that you can easily try more than one.

Tragatapas, the accessible little brother of the acclaimed gourmet Restaurante Tragabuches, serves super-creative and always-tasty tapas in a stainless-steel minimalist bar. There's just a handful of tall tiny tables and stools, and an enticing blackboard of the day's specials. If you want to sample Andalusian gourmet (e.g., a variety of €1.50-3 tapas such as asparagus on a stick sprinkled with manchego cheese grated coconut-style) without going broke, this is the place to do it (also €6-12 larger plates, daily 12:00-17:00 & 20:00-24:00, closed Sun evenings off-season, Calle Nueva 4, tel. 952-877-209).

Bar Lechuguita, a hit with older locals early and younger ones later, serves a long and tasty list of tapas for a good price. Rip off a tapas inventory sheet and mark which ones you want (most cost €0.75; €5 plates also available). Be adventurous and don't miss the bar's namesake, #15, *Lechuguita* (a wedge of lettuce with vinegar, garlic, and a secret ingredient). The order-form routine makes it easy to communicate and get exactly what you like, plus you know the exact price (Mon-Sat 13:00-15:15 & 20:15-23:30, closed Sun, no chairs or tables, just a bar and tiny stand-up ledges, Calle los Remedios 35).

Café & Bar Faustino is a place Brueghel would paint—a festival of eating with a fun and accessible menu that works both at the bar and at tables. The atmosphere makes you want to stay, and the selection makes you wish your appetite was even bigger (lots of €1 tapas, €3 sandwiches, €5-8 *raciones*, Tue-Sun 12:00-24:00, closed Mon, just off Plaza Carmen Abela at Santa Cecilia 4, tel. 952-190-307).

La Tradicional, run by Elias (from Casa María—described below), serves up €1.20 tapas and €4-11 *raciones* with an emphasis on meats (Thu-Tue 12:00-17:00 & 18:30-24:00, closed Wed, Las Tiendas 2, tel. 952-875-683).

Outside the Almocábar Gate

To entirely leave the quaint old town and bustling city center with all of its tourists and grand gorge views, hike 10 minutes out to the far end of the old town, past the Church of the Holy Ghost, to a big workaday square that goes about life as if the world didn't exist outside Andalucía. Among the numerous eateries here are two of special note: The tiny, quirky Casa María is the ultimate in an intimate home-cooking experience, and Bodega San Francisco is a cheap tapas bar and a more normal little restaurant.

Bar-Restaurante Almocábar is a favorite eatery for many Ronda locals. Its restaurant—a cozy eight-table room with Moorish tiles and a window to the kitchen—serves up tasty, creative, well-presented meals from a menu that's well-described in English (plus a handwritten list of the day's specials). Many opt for the good €8-15 salads—rare in Spain. At the busy bar up front, you can order anything from the dining room menu, or choose from the list of €1.50-2 tapas (€5-15 starters, €12-20 main dishes, closed Tue, Calle Ruedo Alameda 5, tel. 952-875-977).

Casa María is like eating in the home of Elias and Isabel and their daughter María. There's little English spoken and no menu, so this is the adventure—you trust Elias to cook up whatever's seasonal for a four-course rustic fiesta for €28 to €35, including drinks (Elias loves red meat). Show Elias this book and you'll get more than the standard glass of house wine, although wine-lovers will want to pay a bit more for a better bottle (Thu-Tue 12:30-16:30 & 19:30-24:00, closed Wed, facing Plaza Ruedo Alameda at #27, tel. 952-876-212).

Bodega San Francisco is a rustic bar with tables upstairs and a homey restaurant across the street. The bar is your budget option with an accessible list of €4-9 *raciones* and €1.50 tapas; the restaurant, while also rustic, comes with serious plates and big splittable portions (from the same menu). This place is understandably a neighborhood favorite (closed Thu, Ruedo de Alameda 32, tel. 952-878-162).

Dining in the City Center

Ronda is littered with upscale-seeming restaurants that toe the delicate line between a good dinner spot and a tourist trap. While (admittedly) none of the following could be called "untouristy," they each offer decent food with either a striking setting, a venerable ambience, or both. For a more authentic dining experience, do a tapas crawl through town, or head for the far more characteristic eateries just outside the Almocábar Gate (both described above).

Restaurante del Escudero serves lovingly presented Spanish food with a posh modern touch in a crystal- and cream-colored dining room or on a terrace overlooking the gorge (€12-18.50 fixed-price meals, €29 gourmet tasting meals, €7-13 starters, €16-20 main dishes, daily 12:00-22:30 except closed Sun eve in summer, behind bullring at Paseo Blas Infante 1, tel. 952-871-367).

Restaurante Pedro Romero, though touristy and overpriced, is a venerable institution in Ronda. Assuming a shrine to bullfighting draped in *el toro* memorabilia doesn't ruin your appetite, it gets good reviews. Rub elbows with the local bullfighters or dine with the likes (well, photographic likenesses) of Orson Welles, Ernest Hemingway, and Francisco Franco (€15-25 fixed-price meals, €7-12 starters, €16-20 main dishes, daily 12:00-16:00 & 19:30-23:00, air-con, across the street from bullring at Calle Virgen de la Paz 18, tel. 952-871-110).

Restaurante Casa Santa Pola offers gourmet versions of traditional food with friendly, professional service, with several small dining rooms and a delightful terrace perched on the side of the gorge—worth reserving ahead (€15-18 fixed-price meals, €7-12 starters, €14-24 main dishes; good oxtail stew, roasted lamb, and honey-tempura eggplant; daily 12:30-16:30 & 19:00-22:30; after crossing New Bridge from the bullring, take the first left downhill and you'll see the sign, Calle Santo Domingo 3; tel. 952-879-208).

Ronda Connections

Note that some destinations are linked with Ronda by both bus and train. Direct bus service to other hill towns can be sparse (as few as one per day), and train service usually involves a transfer in Bobadilla. It's worth spending a few minutes in the bus or train station on arrival to plan your departure. Your options improve from major transportation hubs such as Málaga.

From Ronda by Bus to: Algeciras (6/day, 2 hours, Comes), **La Línea/Gibraltar** (no direct bus, transfer in Algeciras; Algeciras to Gibraltar—2/hour, 45 minutes, can buy ticket on bus), **Arcos** (2-3/day, 2 hours, Comes), **Benaoján** (2/day, 30 minutes, Los Amarillos), **Jerez** (4/day, 2.5-3 hours, Comes), **Grazalema** (2/day, 45 minutes, Los Amarillos), **Zahara** (1/day, Mon-Fri only, 1 hour, Comes), **Sevilla** (8/day, 2-2.5 hours, fewer on weekends, Los Amarillos; also see trains below), **Málaga** (*directo* 10/day, less on weekends, 1.75 hours, Los Amarillos; *ruta* 2/day, 4 hours, Portillo; access other Costa del Sol points from Málaga), **Marbella** (5/day, 1.25 hours, Portillo), **Fuengirola** (5/day, 1.75 hours, Portillo), **Nerja** (4 hours, transfer in Málaga; can take train or bus from Ronda to Málaga). If traveling to **Córdoba,** it's easiest to take the train since there are no direct buses (see below). There's no efficient way to call "the bus company" because four share the same station: Los Amarillos (tel. 952-187-061, www.losamarillos.es), Portillo (tel. 902-450-550, www.ctsa-portillo.es), Comes (tel. 902-199-208, www.tgcomes.es), and GPP (tel. 952-875-435). It's best to just drop by and compare schedules (on Plaza Concepción García Redondo, several blocks from train station).

By Train to: Algeciras (3-4/day, 1.5-2 hours), **Bobadilla** (4/day, 1 hour), **Málaga** (2/day, 2-3 hours—morning train direct, evening train with transfer in Bobadilla), **Sevilla** (2/day, 4 hours, transfer in Bobadilla), **Granada** (3/day, 2.5 hours), **Córdoba** (2/day direct, 1.75 hours; more with transfer in Bobadilla, 3.5 hours), **Madrid** (2/day, 4 hours). Transfers are a snap and time-coordinated in Bobadilla; with four trains arriving and departing simultaneously, double-check that you're jumping on the right one. Train info: toll tel. 902-320-320, www.renfe.com.

More Hill Towns: Zahara and Grazalema

There are plenty of undiscovered and interesting hill towns to explore. About half of the towns I visited were memorable. Unfortunately, public transportation is frustrating, so I'd do these towns only by car. Useful information on the area is rare. Fortunately, a good map, the tourist brochure (pick it up in Sevilla or Ronda), and a spirit of adventure work fine.

Along with Arcos, Zahara and Grazalema are my favorite white villages.

Zahara

This tiny town in a tingly setting under a Moorish castle (worth the climb) has a spectacular view. While the big church facing the town square is considered one of the richest in the area, the smaller church has the most-loved statue. The Virgin of Dolores is Zahara's answer to Sevilla's Virgin of Macarena (and is similarly paraded through town during Holy Week). While Grazalema is a better overnight stop, Zahara is a delight for those who want to hear only the sounds of the wind, birds, and elderly footsteps on ancient cobbles.

Orientation to Zahara

Tourist Information

The TI is located in the main plaza (Mon-Fri 10:00-13:30, Sat-Sun 10:00-12:30, gift shop, Plaza del Rey 3, tel. 956-123-114). It has a single computer with Internet access (€1.50, one-hour limit). Upstairs from the TI are Spanish-only displays about the flora and fauna of nearby Sierra de Grazalema Natural Park.

Drivers can park for free in the main plaza, or continue up the hill to the parking lot at the base of the castle, just past the cliffside Hotel Arco de la Villa, the town's only real hotel (16 small modern rooms, Db-€60, breakfast-€3, tel. 956-123-230, www.tugasa.com).

Sights in Zahara

▲**Zahara Castle**—During Moorish times, Zahara lay within the fortified castle walls above today's town. It was considered the gateway to Granada and a strategic stronghold for the Moors by the Christian forces of the Reconquista. Locals tell of the Spanish conquest of the Moors' castle (in 1482) as if it happened yesterday: After the Spanish failed several times to seize the castle, a clever Spanish soldier noticed that the Moorish sentinel would check if any attackers were hiding behind a particular section of the wall by tossing

HILL TOWNS

Route of the White Hill Towns

TO
SEVILLA
& FREEWAY
A-371

TO SEVILLA
A-375

TO SEVILLA

N

PUERTO
SERRANO

ALGODONALES

OLVERA

TO
GRANADA
A-384

A-384

BORNOS
RESERVOIR

ZAHARA

ZAHARA
RESERVOIR

SETENIL

❶

A-374

RONDA

TO
JEREZ
A-382

ARCOS
RESERVOIR

❸

❷

MONTE-
JAQUE

A-372

BENA.

ARCOS
DE LA FRONTERA

EL
BOSQUE

PUERTO
BOYAR

GRAZALEMA

A-366

A-373

BENAOJÁN

A-369

TO
MEDINA
SIDONIA,
VEJER,
& TARIFA

UBRIQUE

A-374

PILETA
CAVE

TO
SAN
PEDRO
& MARBELLA

A-375

CORTES

TO GIBRALTAR
& TARIFA

10 MILES

6 KM

DCH

SIERRA DE GRAZALEMA
NATURAL PARK

❶ Garganta Verde Hike

VIEW

❷ El Torreón Hike

❸ Pinsapar Hike

HILL TOWNS

a rock and setting the pigeons in flight. If they flew, the sentinel figured there was no danger. One night a Spaniard hid there with a bag of pigeons and let them fly when the sentinel tossed his rock. Upon seeing the birds, the guard assumed he was clear to enjoy a snooze. The clever Spaniard then scaled the wall and opened the door to let in his troops, who conquered the castle. Ten years later Granada fell, the Muslims were back in Africa, and the Reconquista was complete.

It's a fun climb up to the remains of the castle. Start at the paved path across from the town's upper parking lot. It's a moderately easy 15-minute hike past some Roman ruins and along a cactus-rimmed ridge to the top, where you can enter the tower. Use your penlight or feel along the stairway to reach the roof, and enjoy spectacular views from this almost impossibly high perch far above the town. As you pretend you're defending the tower, realize that what you see is quite different from what the Moors saw: The huge lake dominating the valley is a reservoir—before 1991, the valley had only a tiny stream.

Cost and Hours: Free, tower always open.

Sierra de Grazalema Natural Park

Sierra de Grazalema Natural Park is unique for its rugged mountain landscape and its relatively rainy climate, which support a wide variety of animals and plant life. One-third of Spain's flowers bloom here, wild ibex (mountain goats) climb the steep slopes, and Europe's largest colony of griffon vultures soars high above. The park's plant poster child is the *pinsapo*, a type of fir tree left over from the last Ice Age (the park is one of the few places in Europe where these trees still grow). About a fifth of the 200-square-mile park is a special reserve area, where access is limited, largely to protect these rare trees from forest fires. Hikers need to get (free) permits for most trails in the reserve.

Zahara, Grazalema, and the Pileta Cave all fall within the park boundaries. Drivers will get an eyeful of scenery just passing through the park on their way to these sights.

If you want to more fully experience the park—by hiking, caving, canoeing, kayaking, or horseback riding—the easiest way is to take a tour from Zahara Catur (in Zahara, www.zahara catur.com) or Horizon (in Grazalema, www.horizonaventura .com). They also handle the permit procedure for you.

If you want to hike in the park on your own, you'll need a park map, a permit for most hikes within the reserve area (see permit procedure on next page), and a car to get to the trailhead. From July through September, you may have to go with a guided group anyway, if you want to hike in the reserve (about €13/per-

Grazalema

A beautiful postcard-pretty hill town, Grazalema offers a royal balcony for a memorable picnic, a square where you can watch old-timers playing cards, and plenty of quiet whitewashed streets and shops to explore. Situated within Sierra de Grazalema Natural Park, Grazalema is graced with lots of scenery and greenery. Driving here from Ronda on A-372, you pass through a beautiful park-like grove of cork trees. While the park is known as the rainiest place in Spain, the clouds seem to wring themselves

HILL TOWNS

son for a half-day hike, offered by Zahara Catur and Horizon).

Popular hikes in the reserve (all requiring permits) include:

Garganta Verde: Explore a canyon with a huge open cave near vulture breeding grounds (1.5 miles each way, initially gentle hike then very steep descent, allow 4-5 hours).

El Torreón: Climb the park's highest mountain, at 5,427 feet (1.75 miles each way, steep incline to summit, allow 4-5 hours).

Pinsapar: Hike on mountain slopes forested with *pinsapo* trees (8.5 miles each way, steep climb for first third of trail then downhill, allow 6 hours).

Information: The TIs in Grazalema and Zahara sell a Spanish-only park guide with descriptions and trail maps (€15).

Getting a Hiking Permit: A permit is free but required; a ranger will fine you if you don't have one. To get a permit, email, call, or visit the park office in the town of El Bosque, a gateway to the park. You can request a permit for a specific hike up to 30 days in advance. Pick up the permit in El Bosque, or have them fax it to the TI in Grazalema or Zahara (El Bosque park office hours generally Mon-Sat 10:00-14:00 & 17:00-19:00, Sun 9:00-14:00, Avenida de la Diputación, tel. 956-727-029, cv_elbosque @egmasa.es). Include the date, the number of people in your group, the hike you want to do, and your passport number (allow plenty of time for this process). If you're staying at the recommended La Mejorana Guest House in Grazalema, your host will help you with the paperwork.

Hikes from Grazalema (No Permit Required): If you'd rather not hassle with getting a permit, or if you don't have a car to reach the trailheads, try one of several hikes that start from the town of Grazalema. You'll find descriptions in pamphlets available at the Grazalema TI or Horizon (€1).

HILL TOWNS

out before they reach the town—I've only ever had blue skies. If you want to sleep in a small Andalusian hill town, this is a good choice.

The TI is located at the car park at the cliffside viewpoint, Plaza de los Asomaderos (tel. 956-132-052, www.centrode informaciongrazalema.info). Enjoy the view, then wander into the town. A tiny lane leads a block from the center rear of the plaza to Plaza de Andalucía (filled by the tables of a commotion of tapas bars). Shops sell the town's beautiful and famous handmade wool blankets and good-quality leather items from nearby Ubrique. A block farther uphill takes you to the main square with the church, Plaza de España. A coffee on the square here is a joy. Small lanes stretch from here into the rest of the town.

Popular with Spaniards, the town makes a good home base for exploring Sierra de Grazalema Natural Park—famous for its

HILL TOWNS

Grazalema

1 La Mejorana Guest House
2 Hotel Peñón Grande
3 Casa de Las Piedras
4 Plaza de Andalucía Eateries
5 El Torreón Restaurante
6 El Pinsapar Restaurante
7 Meson el Simancon Rest.
8 Horizon Adventure Tours

👓 VIEW
🅿 PARKING

100 YARDS
100 METERS

spectacularly rugged limestone landscape of cliffs, caves, and gorges (see sidebar). For outdoor gear and adventures, including hiking, caving, and canoeing, contact **Horizon** (summer Tue-Sat 9:00-14:00 & 17:00-20:00, rest of year Tue-Sat 9:00-14:00 & 16:00-19:00, closed Sun-Mon year-round, off Plaza de España at Corrales Terceros 29, tel. & fax 956-132-363, mobile 655-934-565, www.horizonaventura.com, grazalema@horizonaventura.com).

Sleeping in Grazalema

$$ La Mejorana Guest House is the best bet in town—if you can manage to get one of its six rooms. You won't want to leave this beautifully perched garden villa, with its royal public rooms overlooking the valley from the upper part of town. Helpful Ana and Andres will help you get a hiking permit in the park (Db-€58, includes breakfast, Wi-Fi, pool, located at top of town on tiny lane below Guardia Civil headquarters at Santa Clara 6, tel. 956-132-327, mobile 649-613-272, www.lamejorana.net, info@lamejorana.net).

$$ Hotel Peñón Grande, named for a nearby mountain, is just off the main square and rents 16 comfortable business-class rooms (Sb-€38, Db-€55, extra bed-€14, air-con, Plaza Pequeña 7, tel. 956-132-434, fax 956-132-435, www.hotelgrazalema.es, hotel@hotelgrazalema.es).

$ Casa de Las Piedras, just a block from the main square, has 16 comfortable rooms with private baths (Sb-€35, Db-€48); 2 other rooms that share 1 bathroom and have access to a kitchen and washing machine (D-€40); and 14 super-cheap basic rooms that share 5 bathrooms (D-€28, no access to kitchen or washing machine). The beds feature the town's locally made wool blankets (10 percent discount with this book and two-night minimum stay, buffet breakfast-€6, Calle Las Piedras 32, tel. & fax 956-132-014, www.casadelaspiedras.org, reservas@casadelaspiedras.net, Katy and Rafi).

Eating in Grazalema

Grazalema offers many restaurants and bars. Tiny Plaza de Andalucía has several good bars for tapas with umbrella-flecked tables spilling across the square, including **Zulema** (big salads, tel. 956-132-402) and **La Posadilla** (tel. 956-132-051).

El Torreón specializes in local lamb and game dishes, and also has many vegetarian options (closed Wed, Calle Agua 44, tel. 956-132-313).

El Pinsapar, up the hill from the main plaza, is appreciated for its good prices and local specialties, including fresh trout

HILL TOWNS

(closed Wed, air-con, Dr. Mateos Gago 22, tel. 956-132-202).

Meson el Simancon serves well-presented cuisine typical of the region in a romantic setting. While a bit more expensive, it's considered the best restaurant in town (closed Tue, facing Plaza de los Asomaderos and the car park, tel. 956-132-421).

Grazalema Connections

From Grazalema by Bus to: Ronda (2/day, 45 minutes), **El Bosque** (2/day, 45 minutes). Bus service is provided by Los Amarillos (www.losamarillos.es).

Jerez

With nearly 200,000 people, Jerez (*h*ay-RETH, with a guttural *h*) is your typical big-city mix of industry and dusty concrete suburbs, but it has a lively old center and two claims to touristic fame: horses and sherry. Jerez is ideal for a noontime visit on a weekday. See the famous horses, sip some sherry, wander through the old quarter, and swagger out.

Orientation to Jerez

There is no easy way to feel oriented in Jerez due to the complicated, medieval street plan, so ask for directions liberally.

Tourist Information

The helpful TI, on Plaza Alameda Cristina, gives out free maps and info on the sights (June-Sept Mon-Fri 9:00-15:00 & 17:00-19:00, Sat-Sun 9:30-14:30; Oct-May Mon-Fri 9:00-15:00 & 16:30-18:30, Sat-Sun 9:30-14:30; tel. 956-338-874, www.turismojerez.com).

Arrival in Jerez

By Bus or Train: Both the bus and train stations are by the enormous headless statue at Glorieta del Minotauro. Unfortunately, you can't store luggage at either one. However, you can stow bags for free in the Royal Andalusian School's *guardaropa* (coat room), if you attend their Horse Symphony show, described later under "Sights in Jerez."

The center of town and the TI are a 20-minute walk from both stations. When exiting either station, keep the large parking lot on your left. You'll soon be greeted by the gigantic Glorieta del Minotauro statue at a traffic circle. Take the crosswalk straight

Jerez

over to Calle Medina and follow it faithfully. At the confusing five-way intersection, angle right on Honda, continue past a small roundabout decorated with empty sherry barrels, and go straight until you reach Plaza Alameda Cristina—the TI is tucked away on your right.

By Car from Arcos: Driving in Jerez can be frustrating. The outskirts are filled with an almost endless series of roundabouts. Continuing straight through each one will eventually bring a rail bridge into sight. Continue to follow traffic and signs to *centro ciudad*. The route may seem circuitous (it is), but it will eventually take you past the main TI on Plaza Alameda Cristina.

If you're going straight to see the horses, follow the directions in the listing on page 197; otherwise it's best to park in one of the many underground garages and catch a cab or walk. Plaza Arenal (€1.30/hour) is the most centrally located lot, or there's the handy underground parking lot at Plaza Alameda Cristina. For street parking, blue-line zones require prepaid parking tickets on your dashboard (Mon-Fri 9:00-13:30 & 17:00-20:00, Sat 9:00-14:00, Sun and July-Aug afternoons free).

Sights in Jerez

▲▲Royal Andalusian School of Equestrian Art (Fundación Real Escuela Andaluza del Arte Ecuestre)—If you're into horses, this is a must. Even if you're not, this is art like you've never seen. The school does its Horse Symphony show Tuesday and Thursday at 12:00 during most of the year (also on Fri in Aug, Nov-Feb Thu only; €19 general seating, €25 "preference" seating, 1.5 hours with 15-minute intermission; no photos in show, stables, or museum; tel. 956-318-008, fax 956-318-015, tickets available online at www.realescuela .org). General seating is fine; some "preference" seats are too close for good overall views. The show explanations are in Spanish.

This is an equestrian ballet with choreography, purely Spanish music, and costumes from the 19th century. The stern riders and their talented, obedient steeds prance, jump, hop on their hind legs, and do-si-do in time to the music, all to the delight of an arena filled with mostly tourists and local horse aficionados.

The riders, trained in dressage (dreh-SAZH), cue the horses with the slightest of commands, whether verbal or with body movements. You'll see both purebred Spanish horses (of various colors, with long tails, calm personalities, and good jumping ability) and the larger mixed breeds (with short tails and a walking—not prancing—gait). The horses must be three years old before their three-year training begins, and most performing horses are male (stallions or geldings), since mixing the sexes brings problems.

The equestrian school is a university, open to all students in the EU, and with all coursework in Spanish. Although still a male-dominated activity, there have recently been a few female graduates. Tight-fitted mushroom hats are decorated with different stripes to show each rider's level. Professors often team with students and evaluate their performance during the show.

Training sessions on non-performance days offer the public a sneak preview (€10; Mon, Wed, and Fri—except no Fri in Aug, also on Tue in Nov-Feb; arrive anytime between 11:00-13:00). Big tour groups crowd in at 11:00 and schedules may vary, so it's wise to call ahead. Sessions can be exciting or dull, depending on what the trainers are working on. After the training session, you can take a 1.5-hour guided tour of the stables, horses, multimedia and carriage museums, tack room, gardens, and horse health center. Sip sherry in the arena's bar to complete this Jerez experience.

Getting There: After passing the TI on Plaza Alameda Cristina, follow pink signs with arrows pointing to the *Real Escuela de Arte Ecuestre.* Parking is located behind the horse school, and one-way streets mean there is only one way to arrive. Expect to make at least one wrong turn, so allow a little extra time.

From the bus or train stations to the horses, it's about a €5 taxi ride or a 40-minute walk.

▲▲**Sherry Bodega Tours**—Spain produces more than 10 million gallons per year of this fortified wine. The name "sherry" comes from English attempts to pronounce Jerez. Although traditionally the drink of England's aristocracy, today it's more popular with Germans. Your tourist map of Jerez is speckled with *venencia* symbols, each representing a sherry bodega that offers tours and tasting. *Venencias* are specially designed ladles for dipping inside the sherry barrel, breaking through the yeast layer, and getting to the good stuff.

Sandeman: Just around the corner from the horse school is the venerable Sandeman winery, founded in 1790 and the longtime

choice of English royalty. This tour is the aficionado's choice for its knowledgeable guides and their quality explanations of the process. Each stage is explained in detail, with visual examples of *flor* (the yeast crust) in backlit barrels, graphs of how different blends are made, and a quick walk-through of the bottling plant. The finale is a chance to taste three varieties (€7 for regular sherries, up to €21 for rare sherries, €7.50 adds tapas to the tasting, tour/tasting lasts 60-90 minutes; English tours Mon, Wed, and Fri at 11:30, 12:30, and 13:30 plus April-Oct also at 14:30; Tue and Thu at 10:30, 12:00, 13:00, and 14:00 plus April-Oct also at 15:00; closed Sun; tour times adjust with the horse show, call to confirm, reservations not required, tel. 956-151-710, www.sandeman.eu). For efficiency, first see the Horse Symphony, which ends at 13:30, then walk to Sandeman's for the

Sherry

Spanish sherry is not the sweet dessert wine sold in the States as sherry. In Spain, sherry is (most commonly) a chilled very dry fortified white wine, often served with appetizers such as tapas, seafood, and cured meats.

British traders invented the sherry-making process as a way of transporting wines so they wouldn't go bad on a long sea voyage. Some of the most popular brands (such as Sandeman and Osbourne) were begun by Brits, and for years it was a foreigners' drink. But today, sherry is typically Spanish.

Sherry is made by blending wines from different grapes and vintages, all aged together. Start with a strong, acidic wine (from grapes that grow well in the hot, chalky soil around Jerez). Mature it in large vats until a yeast crust *(flor)* forms on the surface, protecting the wine from the air. Then fortify it with distilled alcohol.

Next comes sherry-making's distinct *solera* process. Pour the young fortified wine into the top barrel of a unique contraption—a stack of oak barrels called a *criadera*. Every year, one-third of the oldest sherry (in the barrels on the ground level) is bottled. To replace it, one-third of the sherry in the barrel above is poured in, and so on. This continues until the top barrel is one-third empty, waiting to be filled with the new year's vintage.

Fino is the most popular type of sherry (and the most different from Americans' expectations)—white, dry, and chilled. The best-selling commercial brand of *fino* is Tío Pepe; *manzanilla* is a regional variation of *fino,* as is *montilla* from Córdoba. Darker-colored and sometimes sweeter varieties of sherry include *amontillado* and *oloroso.* And yes, Spain also produces the thick, sweet cream sherries served as dessert wines. A good raisin-y, syrupy-sweet variety is Pedro Ximénez, made from sun-dried grapes of the same name.

next English tour. Or do the 10:30 Sandeman's tour before the Horse Symphony.

González Byass: The makers of the famous Tío Pepe offer a tourist-friendly tour, with more pretense and less actual sherry-making on display (that's done in a new, enormous plant outside of town). The tourist train through fake vineyards and a video presentation are forgettable, but the grand circle of sherry casks signed by a *Who's Who* of sherry-drinkers is worthwhile. Taste two sherries at the end of the 1.5-hour tour (€11, light tapas lunch with tour-€16;

tours run Mon-Sat at 12:00, 13:00, 14:00, 17:00, and 18:30; Sun at 12:00, 13:00, and 14:00; Manuel María González 12, tel. 902-440-077, www.bodegastiopepe.com).

Others: You'll come across many other sherry bodegas in town, including **Fundador Pedro Domecq,** located near the cathedral (Calle San Ildefonso 3, tel. 956-346-000, www.bodegas fundadorpedrodomecq.com).

Alcázar—This gutted castle looks tempting, but don't bother. The €3 entry fee doesn't even include the Camera Obscura (€5.40 combo-ticket covers both, Mon-Fri 10:00-18:00—or until 20:00 in mid-July-mid-Sept, Sat-Sun 10:00-15:00). Its underground parking is convenient for those touring González Byass (€1.30/hour).

Jerez Connections

Jerez's bus station is shared by six bus companies, each with its own schedule. Some specialize in certain destinations, while others share popular destinations such as Sevilla and Algeciras. The big ones serving most southern Spain destinations are Los Amarillos (toll tel. 902-210-317, www.losamarillos.es), Comes (toll tel. 902-199-208, www.tgcomes.es), and Linesur (tel. 956-341-063, www .linesur.com). Shop around for the best departure time and most direct route. While here, clarify routes for any further bus travel you may be doing in Andalucía—especially if you're going through Arcos de la Frontera, where the ticket office is often closed. Also try the privately run www.movelia.es for bus schedules and routes.

From Jerez by Bus to: Tarifa (1/day on Algeciras route with Comes, 2 hours, more frequent with transfer in Cádiz), **Algeciras** (1/day with Comes, 8/day with Linesur, fewer on weekends 1.5 hours), **Arcos** (hourly, 30 minutes), **Ronda** (4/day, 2.5-3 hours), **La Línea/Gibraltar** (1/day, 3 hours), **Sevilla** (7-10/ day, 1.5 hours), **Málaga** (2/day Mon-Sat, 1/day Sun, 4.5 hours), **Granada** (1/day, 4.75 hours), **Madrid** (3/day, more service on weekends, 7 hours).

By Train to: Sevilla (nearly hourly, 1.25 hours), **Madrid** (2/ day, 4.5 hours), **Barcelona** (1/day, 7 hours). Train info: toll tel. 902-320-320, www.renfe.com.

By Car: It's a zippy 30 minutes from Jerez to Arcos.

HILL TOWNS

Near the Hill Towns

If you're driving between Arcos and Tarifa, here are several sights to explore.

Yeguada de la Cartuja

This breeding farm, which raises Hispanic Arab horses according to traditions dating back to the 15th century, offers shows on Saturday at 11:00 (€19 for best seats in *tribuna* section, €14 for seats in the stands, Finca Fuente del Suero, Carretera Medina–El Portal, km 6.5, Jerez de la Frontera, tel. 956-162-809, www.yeguada cartuja.com). From Jerez, take the road to Medina Sidonia, then turn right in the direction of El Portal—you'll see a cement factory on your right. Drive for five minutes until you see the farm. A taxi from Jerez will cost about €14 one-way.

Medina Sidonia

This town is as whitewashed as can be, surrounding its church and hill, which is topped with castle ruins. I never drive through here without a coffee break and a quick stroll. Signs to *centro urbano* route you through the middle to Plaza de España (lazy cafés, bakery, plenty of free parking just beyond the square out the gate). If it's lunchtime, consider buying a picnic, as all the necessary shops are nearby and the plaza benches afford a solid workaday view of a perfectly untouristy Andalusian town. According to its own TI, the town is "much appreciated for its vast gastronomy." Small lanes lead from the main square up to Plaza Iglesia Mayor (church and TI open daily 10:30-14:00 & 16:30-18:30, tel. 956-412-404, www .medinasidonia.com). At the church, a man will show you around for a tip. Even without giving a tip, you can climb yet another belfry for yet another vast Andalusian view. The castle ruins just aren't worth the trouble.

Vejer de la Frontera

Vejer, south of Jerez and just 30 miles north of Tarifa, will lure all but the very jaded off the highway. Vejer's strong Moorish roots give it a distinct Moroccan (or Greek Island) flavor—you know, black-clad women whitewashing their homes, and lanes that can't decide if they're roads or stairways. Only a generation ago, women here wore veils. The town has no real sights—other than its women's faces—and very little tourism, making it a pleasant stop. The TI is at Remedios 2 (tel. 956-451-736, www.turismovejer.es).

The coast near Vejer has a lonely feel, but its pretty, windswept beaches are popular with windsurfers and sand flies. The Battle of Trafalgar was fought just off Cabo de Trafalgar (a nondescript lighthouse today). I drove the circle so you don't have to.

Sleeping in Vejer: A newcomer on Andalucía's tourist map, the old town of Vejer has just a few hotels.

$$ Hotel Convento San Francisco is a poor man's parador in a refurbished convent with pristine, spacious rooms and elegant public lounges (Sb-€51, Db-€72, breakfast-€3.35, air-con, free Wi-Fi in lobby, La Plazuela, tel. 956-451-001, fax 956-451-004, www.tugasa.com, convento-san-francisco@tugasa.com).

$ Hostal La Posada's 10 clean and charming rooms, in a modern apartment flat, are cheap and funky. This family-run place has no reception (S-€20-25, Db-€35-50, higher prices are for mid-July-Aug, Los Remedios 21, tel. & fax 956-450-258, www.hostal -laposada.com, no English spoken).

Route Tips for Drivers

Sevilla to Arcos (55 miles): The remote hill towns of Andalucía are a joy to tour by car with Michelin map 578 or any other good map. Drivers can zip south on N-IV from Sevilla along the river, following signs to *Cádiz.* Take the fast toll expressway (blue signs, E-5, A-4); the toll-free N-IV is curvy and dangerous. About half-way to Jerez, at Las Cabezas, take CA-403 to Villamartín. From there, circle scenically (and clockwise) through the thick of the Pueblos Blancos—Zahara and Grazalema—to Arcos.

It's about two hours from Sevilla to Zahara. You'll find decent but winding roads and sparse traffic. It gets worse (but very scenic) if you take the tortuous series of switchbacks over the 4,500-foot summit of Puerto de Las Palomas (Pass of the Pigeons, climb to the viewpoint) on the direct but difficult road from Zahara to Grazalema (you'll see several hiking trailheads into Sierra de Grazalema Natural Park, though most require free permits.

Another scenic option through the park from Grazalema to Arcos is the road that goes up over Puerto del Boyar (Pass of the Boyar), past the pretty little valley town of Benamahoma, and down to El Bosque. The road from Ronda to El Gastor, Setenil (cave houses and great olive oil), and Olvera is another picturesque alternative.

Arcos to Tarifa (80 miles): You can drive from Arcos to Jerez in 30 minutes. If you're going to Tarifa, take the tiny C-343 road at the Jerez edge of Arcos toward Paterna and Vejer. Later, you'll pick up signs to *Medina Sidonia,* and then to *Vejer* and *Tarifa.*

Costa del Sol to Ronda and Beyond: Drivers coming up from the coast catch A-397 at San Pedro de Alcántara and climb about 20 miles into the mountains. A-369 offers a much longer, wind-ing, but scenic alternative that takes you through a series of white-washed villages.

HILL TOWNS

Beware if you have old maps. The road-numbering system from the coast into Sevilla was changed a couple of years ago: From Marbella to Ronda, take A-397 (formerly A-376). From Ronda to Jerez, start on A-374 (formerly A-376) then get on A-384 (which at Arcos may still be labeled with its old number, A-382). To head to Sevilla, branch off from A-384 onto A-375.

SPAIN'S SOUTH COAST

Nerja • Gibraltar • Tarifa

Spain's famous Costa del Sol is so bad, it's interesting. To northern Europeans, the sun is a drug, and this is their needle. Anything resembling a quaint fishing village has been bikini-strangled and Nivea-creamed. Oblivious to the concrete, pollution, ridiculous prices, and traffic jams, tourists lie on the beach like game hens on skewers—cooking, rolling, and sweating under the sun.

Where Europe's most popular beach isn't crowded by highrise hotels, most of it's in a freeway choke hold. Wonderfully undeveloped beaches between Tarifa and Cádiz, and east of Almería, are ignored, while human lemmings make the scene where the coastal waters are so polluted that hotels are required to provide swimming pools. It's a fascinating study in human nature. The Costa del Sol has suffered through the recent economic crisis: Real estate, construction, and tourism had powered the economy, and the effects of its decline are still apparent. Crime and racial tension have risen, as many once-busy individuals are now without work.

Particularly in the resorts west of Málaga, most of the foreign visitors are British—you'll find beans on your breakfast plate and Tom Jones for Muzak. Spanish visitors complain that some restaurants have only English menus, and indeed, the typical expats here actually try *not* to integrate. I've heard locals say of the British, "If they could, they'd take the sun back home with them—but they can't, so they stay here." They enjoy English TV and radio, and many barely learn a word of Spanish. (Special school buses take British children to private English-language schools that connect with Britain's higher-education system.) For an insight into this British community, read the free local expat magazines.

Costa del Sol

☺ DELIGHTFUL
☺ TOLERABLE
☹ AWFUL

50 MILES
50 KM

SPAIN

TO SEVILLA
GRANADA
LANJARÓN
PUEBLOS BLANCOS
ARCOS
RONDA ☺
FRIGILIANA
CAVES
ALM. ☺ MOTRIL
S. PEDRO
MÁLAGA
NERJA ☺
SALO-BREÑA
CÁDIZ
VEJER D.L.F. ☺
TORREMOLINOS ☹
FUENGIROLA ☹
MARBELLA ☹
ESTEPONA ☹
COSTA DE LA LUZ
ALGE-CIRAS
LA LÍNEA ☹
GIBRALTAR ☹ (U.K.)
COSTA DEL SOL
TARIFA ☺
CEUTA (SP.)
ATLANTIC OCEAN
TANGIER MED
MEDITERRANEAN SEA
TANGIER ☺
MOROCCO

DCH

Laugh with Ronald McDonald at the car-jammed resorts. But if you want a place to stay and play in the sun, unroll your beach towel at Nerja, the most appealing beach-resort town on the coast. And don't forget that you're surprisingly close to jolly olde England: The land of tea and scones, fish-and-chips, pubs and bobbies awaits you—in Gibraltar. Although a British territory, Gibraltar has a unique cultural mix that makes it far more interesting than the

anonymous resorts that line the coast. Beyond "The Rock," the whitewashed port of Tarifa—the least-developed piece of Spain's generally overdeveloped southern coast—is a workaday town with a historic center, broad beaches, and good hotels and restaurants. Most importantly, Tarifa is the perfect springboard for a quick trip to Morocco (see next chapter). These three places alone—Nerja, Gibraltar, and Tarifa—make the Costa del Sol worth a trip.

Planning Your Time

My negative opinions on the "Costa del Turismo" are valid for peak season (mid-July-mid-Sept). If you're there during a quieter time and you like the ambience of a beach resort, it can be a pleasant stop. Off-season it can be neutron-bomb quiet.

The whole 150 miles of coastline takes six hours by bus or three hours to drive with no traffic jams. You can resort-hop by bus

SPAIN'S SOUTH COAST

across the entire Costa del Sol and reach Nerja for dinner. If you want to party on the beach, it can take as much time as Mazatlán.

To day-trip to Tangier, Morocco, head for Tarifa.

Nerja

While cashing in on the fun-in-the-sun culture, Nerja (NEHR-*h*ah, with a guttural *h*) has actually kept much of its quiet Old

World charm. It has good beaches, a fun evening paseo (strolling scene) that culminates in the proud Balcony of Europe terrace, enough pastry shops and nightlife, and locals who get more excited about their many festivals than the tourists do.

Although Nerja's population swells from about 22,000 in winter to about 90,000 in the summer, it's more of a year-round destination and a real town than many other resorts. Thanks to cheap airfares and the completion of the expressway, real estate boomed here in the last decade (property values doubled in six years). The bubble collapsed to some extent with the recent financial crisis, but Nerja has remained hardier than other parts of the Costa del Sol. New restaurants and hotels are still opening here all the time.

Nerja is more diverse than many of the rival resorts—in addition to British accents, you'll overhear French, German, Dutch, and Scandinavian being spoken on the beaches. There's also a long tradition of Spanish people retiring and vacationing here. Pensioners from northern Spain move here—enjoying long life spans, thanks in part to the low blood pressure that comes from a diet of fish and wine. While they could afford to travel elsewhere, an inertia remains from Franco's day, when people generally vacationed within the country. In summer, to escape the brutal heat of inland Spain and the exhaustion that comes with having kids home from school all day, many Spanish moms take the kids to condos on the south coast, while dads stay home to work. This is a time when many husbands get to "be Rodriguez" (i.e., anonymous and free), and enjoy (at a minimum) a break from the rigors of family life.

Nerja

SPAIN'S SOUTH COAST

1. Hotel Balcón de Europa
2. Hotel Plaza Cavana
3. Hotel Carabeo & Restaurant 34
4. Hostal Marissal & Cochran's Terrace
5. Hostal Don Peque
6. Hostal Miguel
7. Pensión Mena
8. Hostal Lorca
9. Papagayo Beach Rest.
10. Casa Luque Restaurante
11. Pepe Rico & El Pulguilla Restaurante
12. Pinocchio Restaurante
13. Haveli Restaurante
14. El Chispa/Bar Dolores
15. La Puntilla Bar Restaurante
16. Los Cuñaos
17. La Taberna de Pepe
18. To Ayo's Café
19. Bar El Molino
20. El Burro Blanco
21. Bodega Los Bilbainos
22. Black and White Bar
23. El Valenciano Helados Ice Cream
24. Mercadona Supermarket
25. To Internet Café

* NOT TO SCALE —
BUS INFO KIOSK TO
BALCONY OF EUROPE
IS A 10 MIN. WALK

Ⓑ BUS STOP
 VIEW
🅿 PARKING

SPAIN'S SOUTH COAST

Orientation to Nerja

The tourist center of Nerja is right along the water and crowds close to its famous bluff, the "Balcony of Europe" (Balcón de Europa). Fine strings of beaches flank the bluff, stretching in either direction. The old town is just inland from the Balcony, while the more modern section slopes up and away from the water.

Tourist Information

The helpful English-speaking TI has bus schedules, tips on beaches and side-trips, and brochures for nearby destinations, such as the Caves of Nerja, Frigiliana, Málaga, and Ronda (July-Aug Mon-Sat 10:00-14:00 & 18:00-22:00, Sun 18:00-22:00; April-June and Sept-Oct Mon-Sat 10:00-14:00 & 17:00-20:00, Sun 10:00-14:00; Nov-March daily 10:00-14:00; 100 yards from the Balcony of Europe and half a block inland from the big church, tel. 952-521-531, www.nerja.org). Ask for a free city map and the *Leisure Guide,* which has a comprehensive listing of activities. Their *Hiking the Sierra of Nerja and Cliffs of Maro* booklet describes good local walks.

Arrival in Nerja

By Bus: The Nerja bus station is actually just a bus stop with an info kiosk on Avenida de Pescia (Mon-Tue and Fri 6:00-20:15, Wed-Thu and Sat-Sun 7:00-12:00 & 14:45-19:15, schedules posted, tel. 952-521-504). To travel from Nerja, buy tickets at the kiosk—don't assume they're available on the bus. Because many buses leave at the same times, arrive at least 15 minutes before departure to avoid having to elbow other tourists.

By Car: For the most central parking, follow *Balcón de Europa* signs, and then pull into the big underground parking lot (which deposits you 200 yards from the Balcony of Europe; €1.80/hour, €18.30/24 hours). Other relatively central parking lots (including the enormous Municipal Parking Carabeo, just east of the Balcony) cost nearly as much. The handiest free parking is about a 10-minute walk farther out, next to the bridge over the dry riverbed (near the town bus stop, just off N-340). Street parking in Nerja is free and unlimited, but it's very tight. If you do find a space, avoid parking next to yellow lines, and read signs carefully—on certain days of the month you're required to move your car.

Helpful Hints

Internet Access: Nerja's scenically situated Internet café, **Europ@ Web,** is on a square overlooking Playa la Torrecilla, where Calle de Castilla Pérez meets Calle Málaga (daily 10:00-22:00, until 24:00 in summer, 24 computers, tel. 952-526-147).

Radio: For a taste of the British expat scene, pick up the monthly *Street Wise* magazine or tune in to Coastline Radio at 97.6 FM.

Local Guide: Carmen Fernandez is good, with knowledge of the entire region (standard rate €125/5-hour day, mobile 610-038-437, mfeyus@yahoo.es).

Massage: Tiny yet muscular Marie, who moved here from France, runs a massage parlor out of her apartment. She does an excellent one-hour massage for €40 (€10 more on weekends)—just give her a call (**Amarilys Masaje,** Calle de Castilla Perez 10, mobile 667-825-828).

Getting Around Nerja

You can easily **walk** anywhere you need to go.

Nerja's **taxis** are pricey—the in-town minimum is €6, even for a short trip. They don't use meters—instead, most journeys have a set fee (e.g., €7 to Burriana Beach, €12 to Frigiliana, tel. 952-524-519 or 952-520-537).

To clip-clop in a **horse and buggy** through town, it's €35 for about 25 minutes (you'll usually find these at the Plaza de los Cangrejos above Playa la Torrecilla).

Sights in Nerja

▲▲**Balcony of Europe (Balcón de Europa)**—The bluff, jutting happily into the sea, was completely pedestrianized in 2010. It's the center of Nerja's paseo and a magnet for street per-formers. The mimes, music, and puppets can draw big-ger crowds than the Balcony itself, which overlooks the Mediterranean, miles of coastline, and little coves and caves below. A castle, and later a fort, occupied this spot from the ninth century until the earthquake of 1884. Now it's a people-friendly view terrace.

Built in the early 1800s to defend against Napoleon, the English-Spanish fort here protected the harbor with the help of seven cannons. When the 1884 earthquake destroyed the castle and fort, it sent the cannons into the sea. A century later, two were salvaged, cleaned up, and placed here. Study the beautifully aged metal work.

The cute statue of King Alfonso XII reminds locals of how this popular sovereign (the great-grandfather of today's King Juan Carlos) came here after the devastating earthquake (a huge

SPAIN'S SOUTH COAST

Costa del Sol History

Many Costa del Sol towns come in pairs: the famous beach town with little history, and its smaller yet much more historic partner established a few miles inland—safely out of reach of the Barbary pirate raids that plagued this coastline for centuries. Nerja is a good example of this pattern. Whereas it has almost no history and was just an insignificant fishing village until tourism hit, its more historic sister, Frigiliana, hides out in the nearby hills. The Barbary pirate raids were a constant threat. In fact, the Spanish slang for "the coast is clear" is *"no hay moros en la costa"* (there are no Moors on the coast).

Nerja was overlooked by the tourism scene until about 1980, when the phenomenal Spanish TV show *Verano Azul (Blue Summer)* was set here. This post-Franco program featured the until-then off-limits topics of sexual intimacy, marital problems, adolescence, and so on in a beach-town scene (imagine combining *All in the Family, Baywatch,* and *The Hills*). To this day, when Spaniards hear the word "Nerja," they think of this TV hit.

Despite the fame, development didn't really hit until about 2000, when the expressway finally and conveniently connected Nerja with the rest of Spain. Thankfully, a building code prohibits any new buildings higher than three stories in the old town.

number of locals had died). He mobilized the local rich to dig out the community and put things back together. Standing on this promontory amid the ruins of the earthquake-devastated castle, he marveled at the view and coined its now-famous name, "Balcón de Europa."

The Nerja castle was part of a 16th-century lookout system. After the Christian Reconquista in 1492 drove Muslim Moors into exile, pirate action from Muslim countries in North Africa picked up. Lookout towers were stationed within sight of one another all along the coast. Warnings were sent whenever pirates threatened (smoke by day, flames by night). Look to the east—you can see three towers crowning bluffs in the distance.

Also to the east you can just see the tip of Burriana Beach. Spaniards love their *chiringuitos,* as local beach restaurants are called. The *chiringuito* immediately below you, Papagayo, is understandably popular.

Scan the horizon. Until recently this was a favored land-ing spot (just beyond the tighter security zone near Gibraltar) for illegal immigrants and drug runners coming in from Africa. Many Moroccan teens try to sneak into Europe here, as local laws prohibit turning away undocumented children (the police use DNA tests to determine the age of recent arrivals—if they're under 18, they stay). Laws also grant automatic EU citizenship to anyone born in Europe, so many pregnant women try to slip in (once the baby's born, the mother's legal, too). However, illegal immigration is down: With the help of a new high-tech satellite-scanning system, the Guardia Civil can now detect floating objects as small as makeshift rafts and intercept them before they reach land.

Walk beneath the Balcony for views of the scant remains (bricks and stones) of the ninth-century Moorish castle. Locals claim an underground passage connected the Moorish fortress with the mosque that stood where the San Sebastián church stands today.

Church of San Salvador—Just a block inland from the Balcony, this church was likely built upon the ruins of a mosque (c. 1600). Its wooden ceiling is Mudejar—made by Moorish artisans working in Christian times. The woodworking technique is similar to that featured in the Alhambra in Granada. The modern fresco of the *Annunciation* (in the rear of the nave) is by Paco Hernandez, the top local artist of this generation. In front, on the right, is a niche featuring Jesus with San Isidoro (as a little boy). Isidoro is the patron saint of Madrid, Nerja, and farmers (sugar-cane farming was the leading industry here before tourism hit). From the porch of the church, look inland to see City Hall, marked by four flags (Andalucía's is green for olive trees and white for the color of the houses in this part of Spain).

Town Strolls—Nerja was essentially destroyed after the 1884 earthquake—and at the time there was little more here beyond the castle anyway—so there's not much to see in the town itself. However, a few of its main streets are worth a quick look. From the Balcony of Europe head inland. Consider first grabbing some ice cream at El Valenciano Helados, a local favorite run by a Valencia family. Try the refreshing *chufa*-nut Valencian specialty called *horchata*.

A block farther inland, the old town's three main streets come together. The oldest street, Calle Carabeo, heads off to your right (notice how buildings around here are wired on the outside). On the left, Calle Pintada heads inland. Its name means "the painted street," as it was spiffed up in 1885 for the king's visit. Today it's the town's best shopping street. And between those streets runs Calle Almirante Ferrandiz, Nerja's restaurant row, which is particularly lively in the evenings.

Beaches (Playas)

The single best thing to do on a sunny day in Nerja is to hit the beach: swim, sunbathe, sip a drink, go for a hearty hike along the rocky coves...or all of the above.

Nerja's many beaches are well-equipped, with bars and restaurants, free showers, and rentable lounge chairs and umbrellas (about €4/person for chair and umbrella, same cost for 10 minutes or all day). Nearby restaurants rent umbrellas, and you're welcome to take drinks and snacks out to your spot. Spanish law requires that all beaches are open to the public (except the one in Rota, which is reserved for American soldiers). While there are some nudist beaches, keep in mind that in Europe, any beach can be topless. During the summer, Spanish sun-worshippers pack the beach from about 11:00 until around 13:30, when they move into the beach restaurants for relief from the brutal sun. Watch out for red flags on the beach, which indicate when the seas are too rough for safe swimming (blue = safe, orange = caution, red = swimming prohibited). Don't take valuables to the beach, as thieves have fast fingers.

Beaches lie east and west of the Balcony of Europe. For each area, I've listed beaches from nearest to farthest. Even if you're not swimming or sunbathing, walking along these beaches (and the trails that connect them, if open) is a delightful pastime.

East of the Balcony of Europe

Paseo de los Carabineros—One of Nerja's most appealing draws has been the walkway called the Paseo de los Carabineros, which scampers up and down cliffs, just above the pebbles and sand, to connect the enticing beaches east of the Balcony. Unfortunately, due to erosion concerns and a lack of funds (and municipal motivation), the path has been closed for the past few years. For now, only the first little bit, to Calahonda Beach (described next), is completely open. To reach the other beaches east of the Balcony of Europe, you'll have to walk through the modern town above the beaches...less fun.

To discourage people from using the Paseo de los Carabineros, city officials have erected concrete barriers in a few places along the walkway, removed guardrails (so in some cases you're walking precariously along the cliffs), and allowed the path to become overgrown with plants. While it's possible to follow this pathway at your own risk, it's quite treacherous—in a couple of places you have to actually scale a wall. (Because the path closure is well-advertised at both ends, you're completely liable if anything happens.) Gung-ho travelers still make this walk (I did...carefully), and in summer and at low tide, you can likely walk along the sand and pebbles around the giant rocks (slow going)—but it's not recommended if a pleasant stroll is what you want. The good news is that plans are afoot to restore and reopen the Paseo de los Carabineros. Ask locally, but don't be disappointed if this often-delayed project fails to materialize.

Calahonda Beach (Playa Calahonda)—Directly beneath the Balcony of Europe (to the left as you face the sea) is one of Nerja's most characteristic little patches of sun. This pebbly beach is full of fun pathways, crags, and crannies, and its humble Papagayo restaurant is open all day. Antonio can be seen each morning working with his nets and sorting through his fish. His little pre-tourism beach hut—a stuccoed-and-whitewashed marshmallow bulge with blue trim burrowed into the cliff—is wonderfully photogenic. To get here from the Balcony, simply head down through the arch across from the El Valenciano Helados ice-cream stand...you'll be on the beach in seconds.

Carabeo Beach (Playa Carabeo)—Less developed than the others listed here, Carabeo is wedged into a cove between the bustling Calahonda and Burriana beaches. For many, its lack of big restaurants is a plus. If the Paseo de los Carabineros is closed, you can reach the beach by walking along Calle Carabeo and taking the stairs down from the viewpoint at the park.

Burriana Beach (Playa de Burriana)—Nerja's leading beach is a 20-minute walk east from the Balcony of Europe. Big, bustling, crowded, and fun, it's understandably a top attraction.

Burriana is fun for families, with paddleboats, playgrounds, volleyball courts, and other entertainment options. The beach is also lined with a wide range of cafés and restaurants—but the best is clearly Ayo's, whose paella feast is a destination in itself.

Getting There: Assuming Paseo de los Carabineros is closed, from Nerja's main intersection (with the triple fork), follow the right fork and walk along Calle Carabeo. You'll pass the viewpoint park with the stairs leading down to Carabeo Beach; keep going until you're forced to jog left (up Cómpeta) into a dull modern part of town. You'll see the boxy parador on your right; circle around behind it, following the low-profile signs for *Playa Burriana* (near the parador entrance) to the right. Curl around to the right, then twist down the switchback road to the beach. It's a €7 taxi ride.

Cantarriján Beach—The only beach listed here not within easy walking distance of Nerja, this is the place if you're craving a more desolate beach (and have a car). Drive about 4.5 miles (15 minutes) east (toward Herradura) to the Cerro Gordo exit, and follow *Playa Cantarriján* signs (paved road, just before the tunnel). Park at the viewpoint and hike 30 minutes down to the beach (or, in mid-June-Sept, ride the shuttle bus down). Down below, rocks and two restaurants separate two pristine beaches—one for people with bathing suits (or not); the other, more secluded, more strictly for nudists. As this beach is in a natural park and requires a long hike, it provides a fine—and rare—chance to experience the Costa del Sol in some isolation.

West of the Balcony of Europe

Unlike the walkways east of the Balcony, the promenades to the west are open for business—making this a delightful place to stroll.

Del Salón Beach (Playa del Salón)—The sandiest—and most crowded—beach in Nerja is down the walkway to the right of Cafetería Marissal, just west of the Balcony of Europe (to the right as you look out to sea). For great drinks with a view, stop by the recommended Cochran's Terrace or Casa Luque on the way down. Continuing farther west, you'll reach another sandy beach, **Playa la Torrecilla,** at the end of Calle Málaga.

El Playazo ("Big Beach")—A short hike on a promenade west of Playa la Torrecilla, this beach is preferred by locals, as it's less developed than the more central ones, offering a couple of miles of wide-open spaces that allow for fine walks and a chance to "breathe in the beach."

Near Nerja

▲**Caves of Nerja (Cuevas de Nerja)**—These caves (2.5 miles east of Nerja, exit 295), with an impressive array of stalactites and stalagmites, are a classic roadside attraction. The huge caverns are filled with backlit formations and a big hit with cruise-ship groups and Spanish families. The visit involves a 30-minute unguided ramble deep into the mountain, up and down 400 dark stairs. At the end you reach the Hall of the Cataclysm, where you'll circle the world's largest stalactite column (certified by *Guinness Book of World Records*). Someone figured out that it took one trillion drops to make the column.

The free exhibit in the Centro de Interpretación explains the cave's history and geology (in house next to bus parking; exhibit in Spanish, but includes free English brochure).

Cost and Hours: €8.50, daily 10:00-14:00 & 16:00-18:30, July-Aug until 19:30, easy parking-€1, tel. 952-529-520.

Concerts: During the festival held here the third week of July, the caves provide a cool venue for hot flamenco and classical concerts (tickets sold out long in advance).

Services: The restaurant offers a view and three-course fixed-price meals for €8, and the picnic spot (behind the ticket office) offers pine trees, benches, and a kids' play area.

Getting There: To reach the caves, catch a bus from Nerja's main bus stop (€1, 13/day, 10 minutes).

Frigiliana—The picturesque whitewashed village of Frigiliana (free-*h*ee-lee-AH-nah, with a guttural *h*), only four miles inland from Nerja, is easily reached by bus (€1, 9/day, none on Sun, 15 minutes) or taxi (€12 one-way). While it doesn't match up to the striking White Towns listed in the preceding chapter, its proximity to Nerja makes it an enticing side-trip if this is the nearest you'll get to hill towns on your trip.

The bus stop is in the middle of town, on Plaza del Ingenio. This is also the point that separates the new town from the old town (the steep old Moorish quarter climbing the hill up ahead). The **TI** is a 100-yard walk uphill, in the new town (Mon-Fri 10:00-17:00, Sat-Sun 10:00-14:00 & 16:00-19:30, tel. 952-534-261, www.frigiliana.com). Pick up a map and the translations of the tile you'll see displayed around town. The TI shares a building with the local archaeological museum, with artifacts unearthed near Frigiliana; their prized piece is the fifth-century B.C. skull of a 10-year-old child (free, same hours as TI).

Focus your visit on the old town. Begin by climbing up to the terrace in front of the factory *(ingenio)*—the blocky, unwhitewashed, double-smokestack building that dominates the town. Dating from the 16th century, this still produces sugarcane honey. From the end of the terrace, hike up the steep street, bearing right at the fork up Calle Hernando el Darra. At #10 (on the right), notice the tile in the wall—the first in a series of a dozen around town that describe, in poetic Spanish, the story of the 1568 Battle of Peñón. At the next fork, bear right (uphill) on Calle Amargura and walk steeply uphill, enjoying the flowerpot-lined lane. Notice the distinctive traditional door-knockers, shaped like a woman's hand. More common in Morocco, these are the "hand of Fatima"—the daughter of the Prophet Muhammad—and are intended to ward off evil.

After turning the corner, take the left/downhill road at the next fork, than head right up Calle Sta. Teresa de Ávila. Then head left down the steep, stepped Calle del Garral. You'll pop out just below the main church. Before going there, detour a few steps to the right, then head left to Plaza de la Fuente Vieja—home of a 17th-century fountain that's one of the town's trademarks. Then head back up the way you came to find your way to the inviting café-lined plaza in front of the Church of San Antonio of Padua (with a stark interior). From here, you can follow the main drag back to where you entered town, or enjoy exploring Frigiliana's back lanes.

Hiking—Europeans visiting the region for a longer stay generally use Nerja as a base from which to hike. The TI can describe a variety of hikes. One of the most popular includes a refreshing two-to-three-hour walk up a river (at first through a dry riverbed, and later up to your shins in water; 7.5 miles one-way). Another, more demanding hike takes you to the 5,000-foot summit of El Cielo for the best memorable king-of-the-mountain feeling this region offers.

Nightlife in Nerja

Bar El Molino offers live Spanish folk singing nightly in a rustic cavern that's actually an old mill—the musicians perform where the mule once tread. It's touristy but fun (starts at 22:00 but pretty dead before 23:00, no cover—just buy a drink, Calle San José 4). The local sweet white wine, *vino del terreno*—made up the hill in Frigiliana—is popular here (€3/glass).

El Burro Blanco is a touristy flamenco bar with shows nightly from 22:30. Keeping expectations pretty low, they advertise "The Best One in Nerja" (no cover—just buy a drink, on corner of Calle Pintada and Calle de la Gloria).

Bodega Los Bilbainos is a classic dreary old dive—a favorite with local men and communists (tapas and drinks, Calle Alejandro Bueno 8).

For more trendy and noisy nightlife, check out the **Black and White Bar** karaoke bar on Pintada (karaoke nightly, near El Burro Blanco at Calle Pintada 35) and the bars and dance clubs on Antonio Millón and Plaza Tutti Frutti.

Sleeping in Nerja

The entire Costa del Sol is crowded during August and Holy Week (the week leading up to Easter), when prices are at their highest. Reserve in advance for peak season—basically mid-July through mid-September—which is prime time for Spanish workers to hit the beaches. Any other time of year, you'll find that Nerja has

Sleep Code

(€1 = about $1.40, country code: 34)
S = Single, **D** = Double/Twin, **T** = Triple, **Q** = Quad, **b** = bathroom,
s = shower only. Unless otherwise noted, credit cards are
accepted and English is spoken, but breakfast is not included.

To help you easily sort through these listings, I've divided
the accommodations into three categories, based on the price
for a standard double room with bath during high season:

$$$ **Higher Priced**—Most rooms €100 or more.
$$ **Moderately Priced**—Most rooms between €50-100.
$ **Lower Priced**—Most rooms €50 or less.

Prices can change without notice; verify the hotel's
current rates online or by email. For other updates, see www
.ricksteves.com/update.

plenty of comfy, easygoing low-rise resort-type hotels and rooms.
Room rates are generally three-tiered: low season (Nov-March),
middle season (April-June and Oct), and high season (July-Sept).

Compared to the pricier hotels, the better *hostales* are an excellent value. Hostal Don Peque, Hostal Miguel, and Pensión Mena
are all within a few blocks of the Balcony of Europe.

Breakfast: Some hotels here overcharge for breakfast. Don't
hesitate to go elsewhere, as many places serve breakfast for more
reasonable prices. For a cheap breakfast with a front-row view of
the promenade action on the Balcony of Europe, head to **Cafetería
Marissal** (in the *hostal* of the same name) and grab a wicker seat
under the palm trees (€3-5.50 options include English breakfasts,
daily from 9:00). **Papagayo** serves breakfast on the beach, just
below the Balcony of Europe, to those who don't mind a little sand
in their coffee (from 10:00). If you're up for a short hike before
breakfast, consider the recommended **Ayo's** on Burriana Beach
(daily from 9:00).

Close to the Balcony of Europe

$$$ **Hotel Balcón de Europa** is the most central place in town.
It's right on the water and the square, with the prestigious address
Balcón de Europa 1. It has 110 rooms, recently renovated with
modern style, plus all the comforts—including a pool and an ele-
vator down to the beach. It's popular with groups. All the suites
have seaview balconies, and most regular rooms also come with
views (Sb-€72/83/109, standard Db-€100/117/142, about €30 extra
for sea view and balcony, prices don't include tax, breakfast-€12,
air-con, elevator, pay Internet access, free Wi-Fi, parking-€11,

tel. 952-520-800, fax 952-524-490, www.hotelbalconeuropa.com, reservas@hotelbalconeuropa.com).

$$$ Hotel Plaza Cavana, with 39 rooms, overlooks a plaza lily-padded with cafés. It feels a bit institutional, but if you'd like a central location, marble floors, modern furnishings, an elevator, and a small unheated rooftop swimming pool, dive in (Sb-€39-119, Db-€49-129, bigger superior Db-€10 more, Tb-20 percent more, Qb-30 percent more; 10 percent discount for my readers for 1-to-2-night stays, 15 percent for stays of 3 nights or more, and free breakfast for those booking direct with this guidebook in 2012; some view rooms, air-con, elevator, pay Internet access, free Wi-Fi in lobby, second small unheated pool in basement, parking-€10-15, 2 blocks from Balcony of Europe at Plaza de Cavana 10, tel. 952-524-000, fax 952-524-008, www.hotelplazacavana.com, info @hotelplazacavana.com).

$$$ Hotel Carabeo, a boutique-hotel splurge, has seven classy rooms on the cliff east of downtown—less than a 10-minute walk away, but removed from the bustle of the Balcony of Europe (non-view Db-€75-85/80-90/85-100; seaview Db-€100-155/130-175/145-195, price range depends on type of room, prices don't include tax, air-con, free Wi-Fi in lobby, Calle Carabeo 34, tel. 952-525-444, www.hotelcarabeo.com, info@hotelcarabeo.com). This is also home to the recommended Restaurant 34.

$$ Hostal Marissal has an unbeatable location next door to the fancy Balcón de Europa hotel, and 23 modern, spacious rooms with old-fashioned furniture and clever gadgets on the doors to prevent them from slamming. Some rooms have small view balconies overlooking the Balcony of Europe action. Their cafeteria and bar, run by helpful staff, make the Marissal even more welcoming (Sb-€30/35/45-50, Db-€40/50/60-70, apartment for up to 4 people-€80-155, breakfast-€3-5.50, double-paned windows, air-con, elevator, free Wi-Fi, Balcón de Europa 3, reception at Marissal café, tel. 952-520-199, fax 952-526-654, www.hostal marissal.com, reserva@hostalmarissal.com, Carlos and María).

$$ Hostal Don Peque sits in a dull urban zone an easy couple of blocks' walk from the Balcony of Europe—but it compensates with 10 bright, colorful, and cheery rooms (eight with balconies—a few with sea views). Owners Roberto and Clara moved here from France and have infused the place with their personality. They rent beach equipment at reasonable prices, but their bar-terrace with rooftops-and-sea views may be more enticing (Sb-€35/48/55, Db-€40/55/70, Tb-€55/70/90, bunk-bed family room for up to 4-€15 more than Tb, rates decrease for extended stays and increase for holidays, prices include basic breakfast—or pay €6 extra for a much fancier one, air-con, thin walls, free Wi-Fi, Diputación 13,

tel. 952-521-318, www.hostaldonpeque.com, info@hostaldonpeque
.com).

$ Hostal Miguel offers nine sunny and airy rooms in the heart of "Restaurant Row" (so expect some street noise). Top-floor rooms have mountain views, and breakfast is served on the pretty green terrace. The owners—British expats Ian, Jane, and Hannah—are long-time Nerja devotees (Sb-€29-40, Db-€36-54, book direct for these prices, 4 percent more if paying with credit card, breakfast-€5, family suite, no air-con but fans and fridges, free Wi-Fi in most rooms, laundry service-€5, beach equipment available on request, Almirante Ferrándiz 31, tel. 952-521-523, mobile 696-799-218, www.hostalmiguel.com, hostalmiguel@gmail.com).

$ Pensión Mena rents 11 nice rooms—four with seaview terraces (€5 extra and worth it)—and offers a quiet, breezy garden (Sb-€18-28, Db-€27-43, no breakfast, some street noise, free Wi-Fi in lobby, El Barrio 15, tel. & fax 952-520-541, www.hostal mena.es, info@hostalmena.es, María). The reception has limited hours (daily 9:30-13:30 & 17:00-20:30); if they're closed when you arrive to check in, report to their sister hotel, Hotel Mena Plaza, a few blocks away at Plaza de España 2.

In a Residential Neighborhood

$ Hostal Lorca is located in a quiet residential area five minutes from the center, three blocks from the bus stop, and close to a small, handy grocery store. Run by a friendly young Dutch couple, Femma and Rick, this *hostal* has nine modern, comfortable rooms and an inviting compact backyard with a terrace, a palm tree, and a small pool. You can use the microwave and take drinks (on the honor system) from the well-stocked fridge. This quiet, homey place is a winner (Sb-€25-33, Db-€29-52, extra bed-€12, cash only, no air-con but fans, free Wi-Fi, look for yellow house at Mendez Nuñez 20, tel. 952-523-426, www.hostallorca.com, info@hostal lorca.com).

Eating in Nerja

There are three Nerjas: the private domain of the giant beachside hotels; the central zone, packed with fun-loving (and often tipsy) expats and tourists eating and drinking from trilingual menus; and the back streets, where local life goes on as if there were no tourists. The whole old town (around the Balcony of Europe) is busy with lively restaurants. Wander around and see who's eating best.

To pick up picnic supplies, head to the **Mercadona** supermarket (Mon-Sat 9:15-21:15, closed Sun, inland from Plaza Ermita on Calle San Miguel).

Near the Balcony of Europe

Papagayo, a classic *chiringuito* (beach restaurant), lounges in the sand a few steps below the Balcony of Europe. You may be paying for the location, but it's quite a location. They serve drinks and snacks to those enjoying their beach umbrellas (€2-8 breakfasts, €4-12 snacks and meals, open with demand, daily breakfast from 10:00, lunch 12:00-17:00, tel. 952-523-816, "moon beach parties" on summer evenings).

Cochran's Terrace serves mediocre meals in a wonderful seaview setting, overlooking Del Salón Beach (€7-12 main dishes, daily all day for drinks, 12:00-15:00 & 19:00-23:00 for meals, just behind Hostal Marissal).

Casa Luque, between the Church of San Salvador and the cliffside, is a worthwhile splurge, featuring a terrace in back with wicker furniture, sea views, a stiffly formal vibe, and enough ambience to justify the price. Its dining room, despite its lack of view, is the most high-end and romantic I've seen in town (€6-12 small plates, €22 for 7-tapas tasting meal, wines can be purchased by the glass, Thu-Sat and Mon-Tue 12:30-15:30 & 19:30-23:30, Sun 19:30-23:30 only, closed Wed, tel. 952-521-004).

Restaurant 34, in Hotel Carabeo, manages white-tablecloth elegance in a relaxed atmosphere that successfully mixes eclectic antiques with modern accents. More tables sprawl outside, along the swimming pool and toward sweeping sea views (call ahead to reserve a seaview table). The staff is friendly, and the cuisine features seasonal local produce (€9-15 starters, €17-24 main dishes, €25 three-course fixed-price meal, Tue-Sun from 19:00, closed Mon, Calle Carabeo 34, tel. 952-525-444).

Along Restaurant Row

Strolling up Calle Almirante Ferrándiz (which changes its name farther uphill to "Cristo"), you'll find a good variety of eateries, albeit filled with tourists. On the upside, the presence of expats means you'll find places serving food earlier in the evening than the Spanish norm. Here are my choices in four categories: Romantic, Italian, Indian, and Spanish seafood and tapas.

Pepe Rico is the most romantic (in a schlocky adult-contemporary way) along this street, with a big terrace and a cozy dining room (€6-12 starters, €16-20 main dishes, €28 four-course meals, Mon-Sat 12:30-15:00 & 19:00-23:00, closed Sun, Calle Almirante Ferrándiz 28, tel. 952-520-247).

Pinocchio seems to be the local favorite for Italian (€7-9 pizzas and pastas, daily, Calle Almirante Ferrándiz 51, tel. 952-527-248).

Haveli, run by Amit and his Swedish wife, Eva, serves good Indian food in a nondescript atmosphere. For more than two decades, it's been a hit with Brits, who know their Indian food (€10-12 plates, daily 19:00-24:00 in summer, closed Mon off-season, Cristo 42, tel. 952-524-297).

El Pulguilla is a great, high-energy place for Spanish cuisine, fish, and tapas. Its two distinct zones (tapas bar up front and more formal restaurant out back) are both jammed with enthusiastic locals and tourists. The lively no-nonsense stainless-steel tapas bar doubles as a local pick-up joint later in the evening. Drinks come with a free small plate of clams, mussels, shrimp, chorizo sausage, or seafood salad. For a sit-down meal, head back to the gigantic terrace. Though not listed on the menu, half-portions *(media-raciones)* are available for many items, allowing you to easily sample different dishes (€10-15 dinners, closed Mon, Almirante Ferrándiz 26, tel. 952-521-384).

Tapas Bars near Herrera Oria

A 10-minute gently uphill hike from the water takes you into the residential thick of things, where the sea views come thumbtacked to the walls, prices are lower, and locals fill the tables. The first three are tapas bars within a block of one another. Each is a colorful local hangout with different energy levels on different nights. Survey all three before choosing one, or have a drink and tapa at each. These places are generally open all day for tapas and drinks, and serve table-service meals during normal dining hours. If you prefer a restaurant setting to a bar, try the last listing, La Taberna de Pepe.

Remember that in Nerja, tapas are snack-size portions, generally not for sale but free with each drink. To turn them into more of a meal, ask for the menu and order a full-size *ración*, or half-size *media-ración*. The half-portions are generally bigger than you'd expect.

El Chispa (a.k.a. Bar Dolores) is big on seafood, which locals enjoy on an informal terrace. Their *tomate ajo* (garlic tomato) is tasty, and their *berenjenas* (fried and salted eggplant) comes piping hot and is also worth considering. They'll want you to try the molasses-like sugar-cane syrup on the eggplant. They serve huge portions—*media-raciones* are enough for two (€5-12 *raciones*, daily, San Pedro 12, tel. 952-523-697).

La Puntilla Bar Restaurante is a boisterous little place, with its rickety plastic furniture spilling out onto the cobbles on hot summer nights (generous €4-6 splittable salads, €4-7 half-*raciones*, €7-13 *raciones*, daily 12:00-24:00, a block in front of Los Cuñaos at Calle Bolivia 1, tel. 952-528-951).

Los Cuñaos hangs the banners of the entire soccer league on the walls. Local women hang out to chat, and kids wander around like it's home. Although it has the least interesting menu, it has

SPAIN'S SOUTH COAST

the most interesting business card (€7.50 meals, €16-17 two-person meals, closed Sat, Herrera Oria 19, tel. 650-359-226).

La Taberna de Pepe is more of a sit-down restaurant, though it does have a small bar with tapas. The tight, cozy (almost cluttered) eight-table interior is decorated with old farm tools and crammed with happy eaters choosing from a short menu of well-executed seafood. It feels classier than the rough-and-tumble tapas bars listed above, but isn't pretentious (€6-12 dishes, Fri-Wed 12:15-16:00 & 19:00-24:00, closed Thu, Herrera Oria 30, tel. 952-522-195).

Paella Feast on Burriana Beach

Ayo's is famous for its character of an owner and its €6 beachside all-you-can-eat paella feast at lunchtime. For 30 years, Ayo—a lovable ponytailed bohemian who promises to be here until he dies—has been feeding locals. Ayo is a very big personality—one of the five kids who discovered the Caves of Nerja, formerly a well-known athlete, and now someone who makes it a point to hire hard-to-employ people as a community service. The paella fires get stoked up at about noon and continue through mid-afternoon. Grab one of a hundred tables under the canopy next to the rustic open-fire cooking zone, and enjoy the beach setting in the shade with a jug of sangria. For €6, you can fill your plate as many times as you like. It's a 20-minute walk from the Balcony of Europe, at the east end of Burriana Beach—look for Ayo's rooftop pyramid (daily "sun to sun," for breakfast—see below, paella served only at lunch, Playa de Burriana, tel. 952-522-289).

Breakfast at Ayo's: Consider arriving at Ayo's at 9:00. Locals order the *tostada con aceite de oliva* (toast with olive oil and salt—€0.50). Ayo also serves toasted ham-and-cheese sandwiches and good coffee.

Nerja Connections

While there are some handy direct bus connections from Nerja to major destinations, many others require a transfer in the town of **Málaga**. The closest train station to Nerja is in Málaga. Fortunately, connections between Nerja and Málaga are easy, and the train and bus stations in Málaga are right next to each other.

Nerja
From Nerja by Bus to: Málaga (1-2/hour, 1 hour *directo*, 1.5 hours *ruta*), **Caves of Nerja** (13/day, 10 minutes), **Frigiliana** (9/day, 20 minutes), **Granada** (6/day, 2-2.5 hours, more with transfer in Motril—but check the departure time from Motril to Granada to make sure you're really saving time; Nerja to Motril, 1 hour, Motril

to Granada, 1.25 hours), **Córdoba** (2/day, 4.5 hours), **Sevilla** (2/day, 4.75 hours), **Algeciras** (with connections to La Línea de la Concepción/Gibraltar and Tarifa; 1/day direct, 3.5 hours, more with transfer in Málaga; there are also connections to La Línea de la Concepción/Gibraltar and Tarifa via Málaga). To reach **Ronda,** you'll transfer in Málaga. Remember to double-check the codes on bus schedules—for example, 12:00*S* means 12:00 daily except Saturday. Almost all buses from Nerja are operated by Alsa (toll tel. 902-422-242, www.alsa.es), except the local bus to Frigiliana (Autocares Nerja, tel. 952-520-984).

To Málaga Airport (about 40 miles west): Catch the bus to Málaga (€4, 18/day, 1.25-1.5 hours), then take a local bus (€2, buy ticket on board, about 2/hour, 30 minutes) to the airport (airport tel. 952-048-804). If you'd rather take a taxi from Nerja to the airport, figure on paying about €65, or ask your Nerja hotelier about airport shuttle transfers (operated by various companies in town, generally less expensive than a taxi).

Málaga

This seaside city's busy airport is the gateway to the Costa del Sol. Málaga's bus and train stations—a block apart at the western edge of Málaga's town center—both have pickpockets and lockers (the train station's lockers are more modern).

Málaga's big, airy U-shaped **bus station,** on Paseo de los Tilos, has long rows of counters for the various bus companies. In the center of the building is a helpful info desk that can print out schedules for any destination and point you to the right ticket window (daily 7:00-10:00 & 10:30-19:00 & 19:30-22:00, tel. 952-350-061, www.estabus.emtsam.es). Flanking the information desk on either side are old-fashioned lockers (buy a €3.20 token, or *ficha*, from the automated machine). The station also has several basic eateries, newsstands, WCs, and so on. The train station is just a five-minute walk away: As you stand near the bus stalls, facing the building (with the buses behind you), the train station is over your right shoulder (exit at the far corner of the station, cross the street, and enter the big shopping mall labeled *Estación María Zambrano*—walk a few minutes through the mall to the train station). If you have time to kill near the bus station, explore the train station mall, or visit the mall across from the bus-station roundabout.

The **train station** (called Estación María Zambrano) is slick and modern, inside a big shopping mall (with a food court upstairs). Modern lockers are by the entrance to tracks 10-11 (€3-5 depending on size, security checkpoint), and car-rental offices are by the entrance to tracks 1-9 (Hertz, Avis, Europcar, and National/Atesa). A TI kiosk is in the main hall, just before the shopping mall. To reach the bus station, enter the mall by the TI kiosk and follow signs to *estación de autobuses*—it's across the street, a five-minute walk away.

From Málaga by Bus to: Nerja (1-2/hour, 1 hour *directo*, 1.5 hours *ruta*), **Ronda** (*directo* buses by Los Amarillos: 10/day Mon-Fri, 6/day Sat-Sun, 1.75 hours; avoid the *ruta* buses by Portillo: 2/day, 4 hours), **Algeciras** (4/day *directo*, 1.75 hours; 7/day *semi-directo*, 2.5 hours; 9/day *ruta*, 3 hours; all Portillo), **La Línea de Concepción/Gibraltar** (6/day, 3 hours, *ruta* only, Portillo), **Tarifa** (2/day direct, 3.5 hours, Portillo, many more possible with transfer in Algeciras), **Sevilla** (6/day, 2.5-3.5 hours, Alsa), **Jerez** (2/day Mon-Sat, 1/day Sun, 4.5 hours, Los Amarillos), **Granada** (hourly, 1.5-2 hours, Alsa), **Córdoba** (4/day, 3-3.5 hours *directo*, Alsa), **Madrid** (5/day, 6 hours, run by Daibus, tel. 902-277-999, www.daibus.es), **Barcelona** (4/day, 17 hours, Alsa), **Marbella** (at least hourly, 55 minutes *directo*, 1.25 hours *ruta*). Most buses are operated by Alsa (tel. 902-422-242, www.alsa.es), Portillo (tel. 902-450-550, www.ctsa-portillo.es), or Los Amarillos (tel. 952-363-024, www.losamarillos.es).

From Málaga by Train to: Ronda (1/day direct in evening, 2 hours; 2/day with transfer in Bobadilla, 2-3 hours), **Algeciras** (2/day, 4 hours, transfer in Bobadilla—same as Ronda train, above), **Madrid** (12/day, 2.5-3 hours on AVE), **Córdoba** (best option: 6/day on AVANT, 1 hour, €23; also possible for double the price but no faster on AVE: 11/day, 1 hour, €46), **Granada** (4/day, 3.25-5 hours, requires transfer in Bobadilla, Pedrera, or Osuna—bus is better), **Sevilla** (6/day on fast AVANT, 2 hours, €39; or 5/day on slower regional trains, 2.5 hours, €19), **Jerez** (4-5/day, 4.5 hours, transfer in Dos Hermanas), **Barcelona** (2/day on AVE, 5.5 hours, €145, trains leave at 8:20 and 16:50; or 1/day on slow Arco, 13.5 hours, €66). Train info: toll tel. 902-320-320, www.renfe.com.

Between Nerja and Gibraltar

Buses take five hours to make the Nerja–Gibraltar trip, including a transfer in Málaga, where you may have to change bus companies (they leave nearly hourly from Nerja to Málaga). Along the way, buses stop at each of the following towns.

Fuengirola and Torremolinos—The most built-up part of the region, where those most determined to be envied settle down, is a bizarre world of Scandinavian package tours, flashing lights, pink flamenco, multilingual menus, and all-night happiness. Fuengirola is like a Spanish Mazatlán with a few older, less-pretentious budget hotels between the main drag and the beach. The water here is clean and the nightlife fun and easy. James Michener's idyllic Torremolinos has been strip-malled and parking-metered.

Marbella—This is the most polished and posh town on the Costa del Sol. High-priced boutiques, immaculate streets set with intricate pebble designs, and beautifully landscaped squares testify to Marbella's arrival on the world-class-resort scene. Have a *café con leche* on the beautiful Plaza de Naranjos in the old city's pedestrian section. Wander down to new Marbella and the high-rise beachfront apartment buildings to walk along the wide promenade lined with restaurants. Check out the beach scene. Marbella is an easy stop on the Algeciras–Málaga bus route (as you exit the bus station, take a left to reach the center of town). You can also catch a handy direct bus here from the Málaga airport (20/day, fewer off-season, 45 minutes, www.ctsa-portillo.com).

San Pedro de Alcántara—This town's relatively undeveloped sandy beach is popular with young travelers. San Pedro's neighbor, Puerto Banús, is "where the world casts anchor." This luxurious, Monaco-esque jet-set port, complete with casino, is a strange mix of Rolls-Royces, yuppies, boutiques, rich Arabs, and budget browsers.

Gibraltar

One of the last bits of the empire upon which the sun never set, Gibraltar is a quirky mix of Anglican propriety, "God Save the Queen" tattoos, English bookstores, military memories, and tour-

ist shops. It's understandably famous for its dramatic Rock of Gibraltar, which rockets improbably into the air from an otherwise flat terrain, dwarfing everything around it. If the Rock didn't exist, some clever military tactician would have tried to build it to keep an eye on the Strait of Gibraltar.

Britain has controlled this highly strategic spit of land since they took it by force in 1704, in the War of Spanish Succession. In 1779, while Britain was preoccupied with its troublesome overseas colonies, Spain (later allied with France) declared war and tried to retake Gibraltar; a series of 14 sieges became a way of life, and the already imposing natural features of the Rock were used for defensive purposes. During World War II, the Rock was further fortified and dug through with more and more strategic tunnels.

Gibraltar

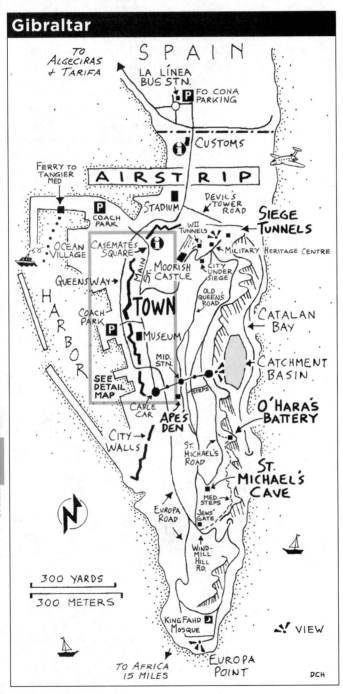

SPAIN

TO ALGECIRAS & TARIFA

LA LÍNEA BUS STN.

FO CONA PARKING

CUSTOMS

AIRSTRIP

FERRY TO TANGIER MED

STADIUM

DEVIL'S TOWER ROAD

WII TUNNELS

SIEGE TUNNELS

Military Heritage Centre

COACH PARK

OCEAN VILLAGE

CASEMATES SQUARE

CITY UNDER SIEGE

MOORISH CASTLE

QUEENSWAY

MAIN ST.

OLD QUEENS ROAD

TOWN

CATALAN BAY

COACH PARK

MUSEUM

CATCHMENT BASIN

HARBOR

MID. STN.

SEE DETAIL MAP

STEPS

O'HARA'S BATTERY

CABLE CAR

APE'S DEN

CITY WALLS

ST. MICHAEL'S ROAD

ST. MICHAEL'S CAVE

N

EUROPA ROAD

MED. STEPS

JEWS' GATE

WIND-MILL HILL RD.

300 YARDS

300 METERS

KING FAHD MOSQUE

VIEW

TO AFRICA 15 MILES

EUROPA POINT

DCH

SPAIN'S SOUTH COAST

As recently as the mid- to late 20th century, during the Franco period, tensions ran high—and Britain's grasp on the Rock was tenuous.

Strolling Gibraltar, you can see that it was designed as a modern military town (which means it's not particularly charming). But over the last 20 years the economy has gone from one dominated by the military to one based on tourism (as, it seems, happens to many empires). On summer days and weekends, the tiny colony is inundated by holiday-goers, primarily the Spanish (who come here for tax-free cigarettes and booze) and British (who want a change in weather but not in culture). As more and more glitzy high-rise resorts squeeze between the stout fortresses and ramparts—as if trying to create a mini-Monaco—there's a sense that this is a town in transition.

Though it may be hard to imagine a community of 30,000 that feels like its own nation, real Gibraltarians, as you'll learn when you visit, are a proud bunch. They were evacuated during World War II, and it's said that after their return, a national spirit was forged. If you doubt that, be here on Gibraltar's national holiday— September 10—when everyone's decked out in red and white, the national colors.

Gibraltarians have a mixed and interesting heritage. Spaniards call them Llanitos (yah-NEE-tohs), meaning "flat" in Spanish, though the residents live on a rock. The locals—a fun-loving and tolerant mix of British, Spanish, and Moroccan, virtually all of whom speak the Queen's English—call their place "Gib."

From a traveler's perspective, Gibraltar—with its quirky combination of Brits, monkeys, and that breathtaking Rock—is an offbeat detour that adds some variety to a Spanish itinerary. If you're heading to Gibraltar from Spain (as you almost certainly are), be aware most Spaniards still aren't thrilled with this enclave of the Commonwealth on their sunny shores. They basically ignore the place—so, for example, if you're inquiring about bus schedules, don't ask how to get to Gibraltar, but rather to La Línea de la Concepción, the neighboring Spanish town. A passport is required to cross the border (you'll only get a stamp if you need a visa— otherwise, you'll just get a wave-through).

Planning Your Time

Make Gibraltar a day trip (or just one overnight); rooms are expensive compared to Spain.

For the best day trip to Gibraltar, consider this plan: Walk across the border, catch bus #3, and ride it to the end, following my self-guided tour. Ride bus #3 back to the cable-car station, then catch the cable car to the peak for Gibraltar's ultimate top-of-the-rock view. From there, either walk down or take the cable car back into town. From the cable-car station, follow my self-guided town walk all the way to Casemates Square. Spend your remaining free time in town before returning to Spain. Note that, with all the old walls and fortresses, Gibraltar can be tricky to navigate. Ask for directions: Locals speak English.

Tourists who stay overnight find Gibraltar a peaceful place in the evening, when the town can just be itself. No one's in a hurry. Families stroll, kids play, seniors window-shop, and everyone chats...but the food is still pretty bad.

There's no reason to take a ferry from Gibraltar to visit Morocco—for many reasons, it's a better side-trip from Tarifa.

Orientation to Gibraltar

(tel. code: 350-200)

Gibraltar is a narrow peninsula (three miles by one mile) jutting into the Mediterranean. Virtually the entire peninsula is dominated by the steep-faced Rock itself. The locals live down below in the long, skinny town at the western base of the mountain (much of it on reclaimed land).

For information on all the little differences between Gibraltar and Spain—from area codes to electricity—see "Helpful Hints," later.

Tourist Information

Gibraltar's helpful TI is at Casemates Square, the grand square at the Spain end of town. Pick up a free map and—if it's windy—confirm that the cable car is running (Mon-Fri 9:00-17:30, Sat 10:00-15:00, Sun 10:00-13:00, tel. 74982, www.visitgibraltar.gi). There's also a TI window at the border in the customs building (Mon-Fri 9:00-16:30, closed Sat-Sun).

Arrival in Gibraltar

No matter how you arrive, you'll need your passport to cross the border. These directions will get you as far as the border; from there, see "Getting from the Border into Town," later.

By Bus: Spain's La Línea de la Concepción bus station is a five-minute walk from the Gibraltar border (baggage storage-€3/day; buy a token, or *ficha* from the security guard—if you can't find him, ask around; station closed, and lockers inaccessible, 22:00-6:00). To reach the border, exit the station and bear left toward the Rock (you can't miss it).

By Car: Customs checks at the border create a bit of a bottle-

Spain vs. Gibraltar

Spain has been annoyed about Gibraltar ever since Great Britain nabbed this prime 2.5-square-mile territory in 1704 (during the War of Spanish Succession) and was granted it through the Treaty of Utrecht in 1713. Although Spain long ago abandoned efforts to reassert its sovereignty by force, it still tries to make Gibraltarians see the error of their British ways. Over the years Spain has limited Gibraltar's air and sea connections, choked traffic at the three-quarter-mile border, and even messed with the local phone system in efforts to convince Britain to give back the Rock. Still, given the choice—which they got in referenda in 1967 and 2002—Gibraltar's residents steadfastly remain Queen Elizabeth's loyal subjects, voting overwhelmingly (99 percent in the last election) to continue as a self-governing British dependency. Gibraltar's governor is popular for dealing forcefully and effectively with Spain on these issues.

neck for drivers. But at worst there's a 15-minute wait during the morning rush hour into Gibraltar and the evening rush hour back out. Parking in town is free and easy except for weekday working hours, when it's tight and frustrating. It's simpler to park in La Línea (explained below) and just walk across the border.

Freeway signs in Spain say *Algeciras* and *La Línea*, pretending that Gibraltar doesn't exist until you're very close. After taking the La Línea–Gibraltar exit off the main Costa del Sol road, continue as the road curves left (with the Rock to your right). Enter the left-hand lane at the traffic circle before the border and you'll end up in La Línea. The Fo Cona underground parking lot is handy (€1/hour, €6/day, on "20th of April" street). You'll also find blue-lined parking spots in this area (€1/hour from meter, 6-hour limit 9:00-20:00, free before and after that, bring coins, leave ticket on dashboard). From La Línea, it's a five-minute stroll to the border, where you can catch a bus or taxi into town (see "Getting from the Border into Town," below).

If driving into Gibraltar, drive along the sea side of the ramparts (on Queensway—but you'll see no street name). There are big parking lots here and at the cable-car terminal. Parking is generally free—if you can find a spot. By the way, while you'll still find English-style roundabouts, cars here stopped driving on the British side of the road in the 1920s.

Getting from the Border into Town

The "frontier" (as the border is called) is a chaotic hubbub of travel agencies, confused tourists, crafty pickpockets, and duty-free shops (you may see people standing in long lines, waiting to buy cheap cigarettes). The guards barely even look up as you flash your passport. Before exiting the customs building, pick up a map at the TI window on your left (Mon-Fri 9:00-16:30, closed Sat-Sun).

To reach downtown, you can walk (30 minutes), catch a bus (€0.80/£0.60 one-way, runs every 15 minutes), or take a taxi (pricey at €9/£6 to the cable-car station).

To get into town by **foot,** walk straight across the runway (look left, right, and up), then head down Winston Churchill Avenue, angling right at the Shell station on Smith Dorrien Avenue.

Catch either the blue **bus #3** to Cathedral Square (you can stay on to cable-car station or to continue my self-guided tour) or the London-style double-decker bus #10 to Casemates Square (with the TI).

If you plan to join a **taxi tour** up to the Rock, note that you can book one right at the border.

Helpful Hints

Gibraltar Isn't Spain: Gibraltar, a British colony, uses different coins, currency (see below), stamps, and phone cards than those used in Spain. Note that British holidays such as the Queen's (official) Birthday (June 11 in 2012) and Bank Holidays (May 7, June 4, and Aug 27 in 2012) are observed, along with local holidays such as Gibraltar's National Day (Sept 10).

Use Pounds, not Euros: Gibraltar uses the British pound sterling (£1 = about $1.60). A pound is broken into 100 pence (abbreviated p). Like other parts of the UK (such as Scotland, Wales, and Northern Ireland), Gibraltar mints its own Gibraltar-specific banknotes and coins featuring local landmarks, people, and historical events—offering a colorful history lesson. Gibraltar's pounds are interchangeable with other British pounds.

Merchants in Gibraltar also accept euros...but at about a 20 percent extra cost to you. Gibraltar is expensive even at fair exchange rates. You'll save money by hitting up an ATM and taking out what you'll need. But before you leave, stop at an exchange desk and change back what you don't spend (at about a 5 percent loss), since Gibraltar currency is hard to change in Spain. (If you'll be making only a few purchases, you can try to avoid this problem by skipping the ATM and buying things with your credit card.) Be aware that if you pay for anything in euros, you may get pounds back in change.

Hours: This may be the United Kingdom, but Gibraltar follows a siesta schedule, with some businesses closing from 13:00 to 15:00 on weekdays, and shutting down at 14:00 on Saturdays until Monday morning.

Electricity: If you have electrical gadgets, note that Gibraltar uses the British three-pronged plugs (not the European two-pronged ones). Your hotel may be able to loan you an adapter.

Telephone: To telephone Gibraltar from anywhere in Europe, dial 00-350-200 and the five-digit local number. To call Gibraltar from the US or Canada, dial 011-350-200-local number.

Internet Access: The **King's Bastion Leisure Centre** has free Wi-Fi, but no terminals (see later). **Café Cyberworld** has several terminals with pricey Internet access (£0.10/minute, £2.50/30 minutes, £4.50/hour, daily 12:00-24:00, Queensway 14, in Ocean Heights Gallery, an arcade 100 yards toward the water from Casemates Square, tel. 51416). There's also Internet access at the cultural center, listed next.

John Mackintosh Cultural Centre: This is your classic British effort to provide a cozy community center. Without a hint of tourism, the upstairs library welcomes drop-ins to enjoy local newspapers and publications, and to check their email (Mon-Fri 9:30-19:30, closed Sat-Sun).

Activities: The recently opened **King's Bastion Leisure Centre** fills an old fortification (the namesake bastion) with a modern entertainment complex. On the ground floor is a huge bowling alley; upstairs are an ice-skating rink and a three-screen cinema (www.leisurecinemas.com). Rounding out the complex are bars, restaurants, discos, and lounges. Many of the activities are geared for families, especially tweens and teens. It's easy to find, just outside Cathedral Square (daily 10:00-24:00, air-con, free Wi-Fi).

Side-Trip to Tangier, Morocco: While a very sporadic ferry does run from Gibraltar directly to Tangier, it's designed for Moroccan workers (returning home to Tangier for the weekend) and doesn't work for a same-day round-trip. Instead, either go via Tarifa (best choice, with direct connections to downtown Tangier) or via Algeciras (closer to Gibraltar, but ferries drop you at a port farther from downtown Tangier). Various travel agencies in town sell package tours that include a bus transfer to the boat in Algeciras.

Self-Guided Bus Tour

Gibraltar Town Bus #3 Orientation Tour

Leaving the "frontier," walk straight ahead for 200 yards to the bus stop on the right. Catch bus #3 and enjoy this three-mile orientation ride that takes you from one end of the colony to the other (Mon-Fri 4/hour, Sat-Sun 2-3/hour, buy ticket from driver, ride 20 minutes to the end of the line: Europa Point). Your ticket options: one-way (£0.60/€0.80), round-trip (£0.90/€1.20—get this one if you're riding all the way out to Europa Point, then back into town), or all day (£1.50/€1.90).

This tour will zip you through town, including the touristy areas and some parts of workaday Gibraltar. It goes quickly. Read fast...

Airstrip: You enter Gibraltar by crossing an airstrip. Three or four times a day, the entry road into Gibraltar is closed to allow planes to land or take off. Originally a horse-racing stadium, this area was later filled in with stones excavated from the 30 miles of military tunnels carved into the Rock. This airstrip was a vital lifeline in the days when Spain and Britain were quarreling over Gibraltar (especially 1970-1985) and the border was closed. If you look at the face of the Rock, you can see the tiny windows that were once perches from where big cannons could fire. Behind them lie siege tunnels, open as a tourist attraction (described later in this chapter).

Moorish Castle: Just after the airstrip, at the first round-about, the bus passes a road leading left (which heads clockwise around the Rock to the town of Catalan Bay, peaceful beaches, and the huge mountainside rainwater-catchment wall). The Moorish Castle above dates back over a thousand years. On the right is land reclaimed in 1989, filled mostly with government-subsidized apartments.

Ramparts: You'll cross the bridge and drive onto the ram-parts. Water once came all the way up to the ramparts—50 percent of the city is on reclaimed land. Gibraltar's heritage shows in the architecture: tiles (Portuguese), shutters (Genoese Italian), and wrought iron (Georgian English).

On the right after the next stop you'll see World War memorials. The first is the American War Memorial (the building-like structure with a gold plaque and arch), built in 1932 to commemorate American sailors based here in World War I. Farther along you'll see 18th-century cannons and a memorial to Gibraltarians who died in World War II.

Downtown: The following sights come up quickly: Passing the NatWest House office tower on the left, you'll immediately see a **synagogue** (only the top peeks out above a wall; the wooden doors in the wall bear the Star of David). In the 19th century, half of Gibraltar was Jewish. The Jewish community now numbers 600. Just after the synagogue is little **Cathedral Square,** with a playground, TI, and the Moorish-looking Anglican cathedral (behind the playground). Gibraltar is the European headquarters of the

Anglican Church. Now you'll pass a long wall; most of it is the back of the Governor's Residence (a.k.a. The Convent).

Charles V Wall: The next bus stop is at the old Charles V wall, built in response to a 1552 raid in which the pirate Barbarossa captured 70 Gibraltarians into slavery. Notice the classic red telephone box near the bus stop. Immediately after you pass under the wall you'll see a green park on your left that contains the **Trafalgar cemetery.** Buried here are some British sailors who died defeating the French off the coast of Spain's Cape Trafalgar in 1805.

Cable-Car Lift and Botanical Gardens: The next stop is at the big parking lot for the cable car to the top of the Rock, as well as for the botanical gardens (free, daily 8:00-sunset), located at the base of the lift. You can get off to do this now—or finish the tour and come back here later, on the way back into town.

Out of Town: Heading uphill out of town, your best views are on the right. It's believed that the body of Admiral Nelson was pickled in a barrel of spirits in a harbor just below you after his victorious (yet fatal) Battle of Trafalgar. After riding through nondescript residential neighborhoods for several minutes, you'll go by the big former naval hospital and barracks. Reaching the end of the Rock, you'll pass modern apartments and the mosque.

King Fahd Mosque: This $20 million gift from the Saudi sultan was completed in 1997, and Gibraltar's 900 Muslims worship here each Friday. Five times a day—as across the strait in Morocco—an imam sings the call to prayer.

Europa Point: The lighthouse marks windy Europa Point—the end of the line. Buses retrace the route you just traveled, departing about every 15 minutes (every 20-30 minutes on weekends). This whole area is slated for a huge beautification project, so you may see lots of construction. Europa Point, up the mound from the bus stop and tourist shop (on right), is an observation post. A plaque here identifies the mountains of Morocco 15 miles across the strait.

The glow of the lighthouse (150 feet tall, from 1841, closed to visitors) can be seen from Morocco. The playground is a favorite for local kids.

Your tour is finished. Enjoy the views before catching a bus back into town (departs from where you got off). Hop off at the cable-car station to ride to the top of the Rock, tour the botanical gardens, or begin the town walk described next.

Self-Guided Walk

Welcome to Gibraltar

Gibraltar town is long and skinny, with one main street (called Main Street). Stroll the length of it from the cable-car station to Casemates Square, following this little tour. A good British pub and a room-temperature pint of beer await you at the end.

From the cable-car terminal, turn right (as you face the sea) and head into town. Soon you'll come to the **Trafalgar cemetery,** a reminder of the colony's English military heritage. Next you come to the **Charles V wall**—a reminder of its Spanish military heritage—built in 1552 by the Spanish to defend against marauding pirates. Gibraltar was controlled by Moors (711-1462), Spain (1462-1704), and then the British (since 1704). Passing through the Southport Gates, you'll see one of the many red history plaques posted about town.

Heading into town, you pass the tax office, then the **John Mackintosh Cultural Centre,** which has Internet access and a copy of today's *Gibraltar Chronicle* upstairs in its library. The *Chronicle* comes out Monday through Friday and has covered the local news since 1801. The Methodist church sponsors the cheap and cheery **Carpenter's Arms** tearoom just above one of several fish-and-chips joints (rare in Iberia).

The pedestrian portion of Main Street begins near the **Governor's Residence.** The British governor of Gibraltar took over a Franciscan convent, hence the name of the local white house: The Convent. The **Convent Guard Room,** facing the Governor's Residence, is good for photos.

Gibraltar's courthouse stands behind a **small tropical garden,** where John and Yoko got married back in 1969 (as the ballad goes, they "got married in Gibraltar near Spain"). Sean Connery did, too. Actually, many Brits like to get married here because weddings are cheap, fast (only 48 hours' notice required), and legally recognized as British.

Main Street now becomes a **shopping drag.** You'll notice lots of colorful price tags advertising tax-free booze, cigarettes, and sugar (highly taxed in Spain). Lladró porcelain, while made in Valencia, is popular here (because it's sold without the hefty Spanish VAT—Value-Added Tax). The Catholic cathedral retains a whiff of Arabia (as it was built upon the remains of a mosque), while the big **Marks & Spencer department store** helps vacationing Brits feel at home.

Continue several more blocks through

Gibraltar Town

1. O'Callaghan Eliott Hotel
2. Bristol Hotel
3. Cannon Hotel
4. Emile Hostel
5. The Clipper Pub
6. The Star Bar
7. Carpenter's Arms
8. Gaucho's Steakhouse
9. To Ocean Village
10. Queensway Quay Marina & Eateries
11. All's Well Pub
12. Market Place & Produce Market
13. Marks & Spencer; Bon Bon Cash & Carry

14. Cathedral Square
15. John Mackintosh Cultural Centre
16. Governor's Residence
17. Convent Guard Room
18. John & Yoko's Wedding Site
19. Café Cyberworld
20. King's Bastion Leisure Centre

TO TANGIER MED FERRY

TO AIRSTRIP & BORDER

CASEMATES SQUARE

TO MOORISH CASTLE & SIEGE TUNNELS

SMITH DORRIEN AVENUE

MKT. RD.

FISH MKT. ROAD

QUEENSWAY

RECLAMATION ROAD

LINE WALL ROAD

COOP.

PARL.

ENGINEER LANE

CORNWALL

BELL LANE

TUCKEY'S LANE

IRISH TOWN

MAIN STREET

CASTLE RD.

WILLIS'S RD.

COLL.

KING STREET

CANNON LANE

SYNAGOGUE

MUSEUM

LIB.

GEO.

ST.

GOV.

PRINCE EDWARD'S ROAD

FLAT BASTION RD.

P PARKING

50 YARDS

50 METERS

TOWN RANGE

CHARLES V WALL

QUEENSWAY QUAY & MARINA

SOUTHPORT GATES

TRAFALGAR CEMETERY

EUROPA RD.

DCH

ROSIA

BOYD

BOTANICAL GARDENS

CABLE-CAR STATION

TO TOP OF THE ROCK

TO ST. MICHAEL'S CAVE

the bustling heart of Gibraltar. If you enjoy British products, this is your chance to stock up on Cadbury chocolates, digestive biscuits, wine gums, and Weetabix—but you'll pay a premium, since it's all "imported" from the UK.

The town (and this walk) ends at **Casemates Square.** While a lowbrow food circus today, it originated as a barracks and place for ammunition storage. When Franco closed the border with Spain in 1969, Gibraltar suffered a labor shortage, as Spanish guest workers could no longer commute into Gibraltar. The colony countered by inviting Moroccan workers to take their place—ending a nearly 500-year Moroccan absence, which began when the Moors fled in 1462. As a result, today's Moroccan community dates only from the 1970s. Whereas the previous Spanish labor force simply commuted into work, the Moroccans needed apartments, so Gibraltar converted the Casemates barracks for that purpose. Cheap Spanish labor has crept back in, causing many locals to resent store clerks who can't speak proper English.

At the far end of Casemates Square is a crystal shop that makes its own crystal right there (you can watch). They claim it's the only thing actually "made in Gibraltar." But just upstairs, on the upper floor of the barracks, you'll find a string of local crafts shops.

If you go through the triple arches at the end of the square (behind the TI), you'll reach the covered **produce market** and food stalls. Across the busy road a few minutes' walk farther is the well-marked entrance to the **Ocean Village** boardwalk and entertainment complex (described later, under "Eating in Gibraltar.")

Sights in Gibraltar

In Gibraltar Town

▲Gibraltar Museum—Built atop a Moorish bath, this museum tells the story of a chunk of land that has been fought over for centuries. Start with the fine 15-minute video overview of the story of the Rock—a worthwhile prep for the artifacts (such as ancient Roman anchors made of lead) you'll see in the museum. Then wander through the scant remains of the 14th-century Moorish baths. Upstairs you'll see military memorabilia, a 15-foot-long model of the Rock, wonderful century-old photos of old Gibraltar, paintings by local artists, and, in a cave-like room off the art gallery, a collection of prehistoric remains and artifacts. The famous skull of a Neanderthal woman found in Forbes' Quarry is a copy (the original is in the British Museum in London). Found in Gibraltar in 1848, this was the first Neanderthal skull ever discovered. No one realized its significance until a similar skull found years later in Germany's Neanderthal Valley was correctly identified—stealing the name, claim, and fame from Gibraltar (£2, Mon-Fri 10:00-18:00, Sat 10:00-14:00, last entry 30 minutes before closing, closed Sun, no photos, on Bomb House Lane near the cathedral).

Up on the Rock

The actual Rock of Gibraltar is the colony's best sight. Its attractions: the stupendous view from the very top, quirky apes, a hokey cave (St. Michael's), and the impressive Siege Tunnels drilled through the rock face for military purposes. Frankly, the sights that charge admission aren't that exciting; the Rock's best attractions—enjoying views from the top and seeing the monkeys—are free. Hikers can ride the lift up and take a long, steep, scenic walk down, connecting the various sights by strolling along paved military lanes.

Cost: There's a £0.50 fee to enter the grounds of the Rock, technically called the "Upper Rock Nature Reserve"—that's just to walk around and enjoy the views and the monkeys. A £10 ticket is required to visit any or all of these major sights within the reserve: St. Michael's Cave, Siege Tunnels, Moorish Castle, Military Heritage Centre, and City Under Siege exhibit (includes the £0.50 nature-reserve entrance fee). If you take a taxi tour, entry to the nature reserve and sights is included; if you ride the cable car, the nature-reserve entry fee is included, but you'll have to buy the £10 ticket to go in the sights. (Both options are explained below).

Hours: Daily 9:30-19:15, until 18:15 late Oct-late March, last entry 30 minutes before closing.

Additional Sights at the Rock: Two sights at the Rock are not part of the official reserve ticket, and have their own separate tickets and hours: O'Hara's Battery and the World War II Tunnels (both described later).

Visiting the Rock: You have two options for touring the Rock: Take a 1.5-hour taxi tour (£22/person) or ride the cable car (£9 round-trip; or £7.50 one-way plus £10 to see the sights as you hike back down).

The **taxi tour** includes entry to St. Michael's Cave and the Siege Tunnels, a couple of extra stops, and the running commentary of your licensed cabbie/guide. Because the cable car doesn't get you very close to the cave and tunnels (and doesn't cover cave and tunnel admission), take the taxi tour if you'll be visiting these sights and don't want to walk. On the other hand, the **cable car** takes you to the very top of the Rock (which the taxi tours don't). You can still see the sights, but you'll have to pay £10 and connect them by foot (not a bad thing—it's a pleasant walk down).

There's certainly no reason to take a big-bus tour (advertised and sold all over town) considering how fun and easy the taxi tours are. Private cars are not allowed high on the Rock.

Here are more details on each option:

Taxi Tours: Minibuses driven by cabbies trained and licensed to lead these little trips are standing by at the border and at various points in town (including Cathedral Square, John Mackintosh Square, Casemates Square, and Trafalgar Cemetery near the cable-car station). They charge £22/person (4-person minimum, or £65 for only 2 people in one taxi, includes £10 reserve sights ticket, tel. 70027). Taxi tours and big buses do the same 1.5-hour loop tour with four stops: a Mediterranean viewpoint (called the Pillar of Hercules), St. Michael's Cave (15-minute visit), a viewpoint near the top of the Rock where you can get up close to the monkeys, and the Siege Tunnels (20-minute visit). Buddy up with other travelers and share the cost.

Cable Car to the Summit: A dizzying array of colorfully named combo-tickets are offered for the cable car and its partner attractions. The only ones worth considering are the "Skyline Supreme" (just a ticket for the cable car: £7.50 one-way, £9 round-trip) and the "SkyWalk Combo" (combining the cable car and the £10 reserve sights ticket—this doesn't save any money over buying the tickets separately, and only makes sense one-way—£17.50). The cable car runs every 10-15 minutes (daily from 9:30, last ascent at 19:15, last descent at 19:45), or continuously in busy times. Lines can be long if a cruise ship is in town. The cable car won't run if it's windy or rainy; if the weather is questionable, ask at the TI before heading to the station. The cable-car ride includes a hand-held audio/videoguide that explains what you're seeing from the spectacular viewpoints (pick it up at the well-marked booth when you disembark at the top, must leave ID as a deposit). In the winter (Oct-March), the cable car stops halfway down for those who want to get out, gawk at the monkeys, and take a later car down—but you'll probably see monkeys at the top anyway.

To take in all of the sights, you'll need to **hike down,** rather than taking the cable car back (be sure to specify you want a one-way ticket up). Simply hiking down without visiting the sights is enjoyable, too. Approximate hiking times: from the top of the cable car to St. Michael's Cave—25 minutes; from the cave to the Apes' Den—20 minutes; from the Apes' Den to the Siege Tunnels—30 minutes; from the tunnels back into town, passing the Moorish Castle—20 minutes. Total from top to bottom: about 1.5 hours (on paved roads with almost no traffic), not including sightseeing. For hikers, I've connected the dots with directions below.

▲▲▲**The Summit of the Rock**—The cable car takes you to the real highlight of Gibraltar: the summit of the spectacular Rock itself. (Taxi tours don't go here; they stop on a ridge below the summit, where you enjoy a commanding view—but one that's nowhere near as good.) The limestone massif, or large rock mass, is nearly a mile long, rising 1,400 feet high with very sheer faces. According to legend, this was one of the Pillars of Hercules (paired with

Djebel Musa, another mountain across the strait in Morocco), marking the edge of the known world in ancient times. Local guides say that these pillars are the only places on the planet where you can see two seas and two continents at the same time.

In A.D. 711, the Muslim chieftain Tarik ibn Ziyad crossed over from Africa and landed on the Rock, beginning the Moorish conquest of Spain and naming the Rock after himself—Djebel-Tarik ("Rock of Tarik"), which became "Gibraltar."

At the top of the Rock (the cable-car terminal) there's a view terrace and a restaurant. From here you can explore old ramparts and drool at the 360-degree view of Morocco (including the Rif Mountains and Djebel Musa), the Strait of Gibraltar, the bay stretching west toward Algeciras, and the twinkling Costa del Sol arcing eastward. The views are especially crisp on brisk off-season days. Below you (to the east) stretches the giant catchment system that the British built to collect rainwater in the not-so-distant past, when Spain allowed neither water nor tourists to cross its disputed border. Broad sheets catch the rain, sending it through channels to reservoirs located inside the rock.

• *Up at the summit, you'll likely see some of the famed...*

▲▲**Apes of Gibraltar**—The Rock is home to about 200 "apes" (actually, tailless Barbary macaques—a type of monkey). Taxi tours come with great monkey fun, but if you're on your own, you'll probably see them at the top and at various points on the walk back down (basically, the monkeys congregate anywhere that tourists do—hoping to get food). The males are bigger, females have beards, and newborns are black. They live about 15-20 years. Legend has it that as long as the monkeys remain here, so will the Brits. (According to a plausible local legend, when word came a few decades back that the ape population was waning, Winston Churchill made a point to import reinforcements.) Keep your distance from the monkeys. (Guides say that for safety reasons, "They can touch you, but you can't touch them." And while guides feed them, you shouldn't—it disrupts their diet.) Beware of the monkeys' kleptomaniac tendencies; they'll ignore the peanut in your hand and claw after the full bag in your pocket. Because the monkeys associate plastic bags with food, keep your bag close to your body: Tourists who wander by absent-mindedly, loosely clutching a bag, are apt to have it stolen by a purse-snatching simian. If there's no ape action, wait for a banana-toting taxi tour to stop by and stir some up. Guides love to get the monkeys to actually climb onto the backs and shoulders of their tour members—always a crowd-pleaser.

• *If you're hiking down, you'll find that your options are clearly marked at most forks. I'll narrate the longest route down, which passes all of the sights en route.*

From the top cable-car station, exit and head downhill on the well-paved path (toward Africa). You'll pass the viewpoint for taxi tours (with monkeys hanging around, waiting for tour groups to come feed them), pass under a ruined observation tower, and eventually reach a wide part of the road. Most will want to continue to St. Michael's Cave (skip down to that section), but you also have an opportunity to hike (or ride a shuttle bus) steeply up to...

O'Hara's Battery—At 1,400 feet, this is the actual highest point on the Rock. A massive 9.2-inch gun sits on the summit, where a Moorish lookout post once stood. The battery was built after World War I, and the last test shot was fired in 1974. Locals are glad it's been mothballed—during test firings, they had to open their windows, which might otherwise have shattered from the pressurized air blasted from this gun. The battery was recently opened to the public; you can go inside to see not only the gun, but also the powerful engines underneath that were used to move and aim it. The iron rings you see every 30 yards or so along the military lanes around the Rock once anchored pulleys used to haul up guns like the huge one at O'Hara's Battery (£3.50, not covered by reserve sights ticket, shuttle runs up when open, Mon-Fri 10:30-17:00, closed Sat-Sun).

• *From the crossroads below O'Hara's Battery, taking the right (downhill) fork leads you down to a restaurant and shop, then the entrance to...*

▲**St. Michael's Cave**—Studded with stalagmites and stalactites, eerily lit, and echoing with classical music, this cave is dramatic, corny, and slippery when wet. Considered a one-star sight since Neolithic times, these caves were alluded to in ancient Greek legends—when the caves were believed to be the Gates of Hades (or the entrance of a tunnel to Africa). All taxi tours stop here (entry included in cost of taxi tour). This sight requires a long walk for cable-car riders (who must have the £10 reserve sights ticket to enter; same hours as other reserve sights). Walking through takes about 15 minutes; you'll pop out at the gift shop.

• *From here, most will head down to the Apes' Den (see next paragraph), but serious hikers have the opportunity to curl around to Jews' Gate at the tip of the Rock, then circle around the back of the Rock on the strenuous* **Mediterranean Steps** *(leading back up to O'Hara's Battery). To do this, turn sharply left after St. Michael's Cave and head for Jews' Gate. Since it's on the opposite side from the town, it's the closest thing in Gibraltar to "wilderness." If this challenging 1.5-to-2-hour hike sounds enjoyable, ask for details at the TI.*

The more standard route is to continue downhill. At the three-way fork, you can take either the middle fork (more level) or the left fork (hillier, but you'll see monkeys at the Apes' Den) to the Siege Tunnels. The **Apes' Den**, *at the middle station for the cable car, is a scenic terrace where monkeys tend to gather, and where taxi tours stop to do some monkeying around.*

Continue on either fork (they converge), following signs for Siege Tunnels, *for about 30 more minutes. Eventually you'll reach a terrace with three flags (from highest to lowest: United Kingdom, Gibraltar, EU) and a fantastic view of Gibraltar's airport, "frontier" with Spain, and the Spanish city of La Línea de la Concepción. From here, the Military Heritage Centre is beneath your feet (described later), and it's a short but steep hike up to the...*

▲**Siege Tunnels**—Also called the Upper Galleries, these chilly tunnels were blasted out of the rock by the Brits during the Great Siege by Spanish and French forces (1779-1783). The clever British, safe inside the Rock, wanted to chip and dig to a highly strategic outcrop called "The Notch," ideal for mounting a big gun. After blasting out some ventilation holes for the miners, they had an even better idea: Use gunpowder to carve out a whole network of

tunnels with shafts that would be ideal for aiming artillery. Eventually they excavated "St. George's Hall," a huge cavern that housed seven guns. These were the first tunnels inside the Rock; more than a century and a half later, during World War II, 30 more miles of tunnels were

blasted out. Hokey but fun dioramas help recapture a time when Brits were known more for conquests than for crumpets. All taxi tours stop here (entry included in cost of taxi tour); hikers must have or buy the £10 reserve sights ticket to enter (same hours as other reserve sights).

• Hiding out in the bunker below the three flags (go down the stairs and open the heavy metal door—it's unlocked) is the...

Military Heritage Centre—This small one-room collection features old military photographs from Gibraltar. The second room features a poignant memorial to the people who "have made the supreme sacrifice in defence of Gibraltar" (covered by £10 reserve sights ticket—but tickets rarely checked, same hours as other reserve sights).

• From here, the road switchbacks down into town. At each bend in the road you'll find one of the next three sights.

City Under Siege—This hokey exhibit is worth a quick walk-through if you've been fascinated by all this Gibraltar military history. Displayed in some of the first British structures built on Gibraltar soil, it re-creates the days of the Great Siege, which lasted for more than three and a half years (1779-1783)—one of 14 sieges that attempted but failed to drive the Brits off the Rock. With evocative descriptions, some original "graffiti" scratched into the wall by besieged Gibraltarians, and some borderline-hokey dioramas, the exhibit explains what it was like to live on the Rock, cut off from the outside world, during those challenging times (covered by £10 reserve sights ticket—but tickets rarely checked, same hours as other reserve sights).

World War II Tunnels—This privately run operation takes you through some of the tunnels carved out of the Rock during a much later conflict than the others described here. You'll emerge back up at the Military Heritage Centre (£8, not covered by reserve sights ticket, Mon-Sat 10:00-17:00, closed Sun).

Moorish Castle—Actually more a tower than a castle, this recently restored building is basically an empty shell. (In the interest of political correctness, the tourist board recently tried to change the name to "Medieval Castle"...but it *is* Moorish, so the name didn't stick.) It was constructed on top of the original castle built in A.D. 711 by the Moor Tarik ibn Ziyad, who gave his name to Gibraltar.

• The tower marks the end of the Upper Rock Nature Reserve. Heading downhill, you begin to enter the upper part of modern Gibraltar. While you could keep on twisting down the road, keep an eye out for staircase shortcuts into town (most direct are the well-marked Castle Steps).

Nightlife in Gibraltar

If you're coming from the late-night bustle of Spain, where you'll see young parents out strolling with their toddlers at midnight, you'll find Gibraltar extremely quiet after-hours. Main Street is completely dead (with the exception of a few lively pubs, mostly a block or two off the main drag). Head instead to the Ocean Village complex, a five-minute walk from Casemates Square, where the boardwalk is lined with bars, restaurants, and a casino. Another waterfront locale—a bit more sedate—is the Queensway Quay Marina. (Both areas are described later, under "Eating in Gibraltar.") Kids love the King's Bastion Leisure Centre (described earlier, under "Helpful Hints").

Some pubs, lounges, and discos—especially on Casemates Square—offer live music (look around for signs, or ask at the TI). O'Callaghan Eliott Hotel hosts free live jazz on Thursday evenings.

Sleeping in Gibraltar

Gibraltar is not a good value for accommodations. There are only a handful of hotels and (disappointingly) no British-style B&Bs. As a general rule, the beds are either bad or overpriced. Remember, you'll pay a 20 percent premium if paying with euros—pay with local cash or your credit card.

$$$ O'Callaghan Eliott Hotel, with four stars, boasts a roof-top pool with a view, a fine restaurant, bar, terrace, inviting sit-a-bit public spaces, and 121 modern, mildly stylish business-class rooms—all with balconies (sky-high rack rates of Db-£240-270, but often around Db-£100 with Web booking for non-peak days, breakfast-£14, non-smoking, air-con, elevator, pay Wi-Fi, free parking, centrally located at Governor's Parade 2, up Library Street from main drag, tel. 70500, fax 70243, www.ocallaghan hotels.com, eliott@ocallaghanhotels.com).

Sleep Code

(£1 = about $1.60, tel. code: 350-200)
S = Single, **D** = Double/Twin, **T** = Triple, **Q** = Quad, **b** = bathroom, **s** = shower only. All of these places accept credit cards, and their staffs speak English.

To help you easily sort through these listings, I've divided the accommodations into three categories, based on the price for a standard double room with bath during high season:

  $$$ Higher Priced—Most rooms £75 or more.
   $$ Moderately Priced—Most rooms between £35-75.
    $ Lower Priced—Go back to Spain.

Prices can change without notice; verify the hotel's current rates online or by email. For other updates, see www .ricksteves.com/update.

$$$ Bristol Hotel offers 60 basic, slightly worn English rooms in the heart of Gibraltar (Sb-£63-68, Db-£81-87, Tb-£93-99, higher prices for exterior rooms, breakfast-£5, air-con, elevator, free Wi-Fi in lobby, swimming pool, limited free parking—first come, first served, Cathedral Square 10, tel. 76800, fax 77613, www.bristolhotel.gi, reservations@bristolhotel.gi).

$$ Cannon Hotel is a run-down dive. But it's also well-located and friendly and has the only cheap hotel rooms in town. Its 18 rooms (most with wobbly cots and no private bathrooms) look treacherously down on a little patio (S-£30, D-£42, Db-£53, T-£52.50, Tb-£60, includes full English breakfast, free Wi-Fi, behind cathedral at Cannon Lane 9, tel. 51711, fax 51789, www .cannonhotel.gi, cannon@sapphirenet.gi).

$ Emile Hostel, simple and the cheapest place in town, welcomes people of any age (42 beds, bunk in 6-bed dorm-£17, S-£25, D-£40, à la carte breakfast—full English is £3.50, cash only, free Wi-Fi, on Montagu Bastion diagonally across the street from Shell station, ramped entrance on Line Wall Road, tel. & fax 51106, www.emilehostel.net, emilehostel@yahoo.co.uk).

Eating in Gibraltar

Take a break from *jamón* and sample some English pub grub: fish-and-chips, meat pies, jacket potatoes (baked potatoes with fillings), or a good old greasy English breakfast. English-style beers include chilled lagers and room-temperature ales, bitters, and stouts. In general, the farther you venture away from Main Street, the cheaper and more local the places become. Since budget-priced English food isn't exactly high cuisine, the best plan may be to stroll the streets and look for the pub with the ambience you like best (various options: lots of chatting, sports fans riveted to a football match, noisy casino machines, or whatever). I've listed a few of my favorites below. Or venture to one of Gibraltar's more upscale recent developments at either end of the old town: Ocean Village or Queensway Quay.

If you're bothered by smoke, be aware that Gibraltar (unlike Britain and Spain) has not imposed a smoking ban—so many places can still be smoky.

Downtown, Near Main Street

The Clipper, my favorite pub for dinner, offers filling £7 meals and Murphy's stout on tap (English breakfast-£5, Mon-Sat 9:30-22:00, Sun 13:00-22:00, on Irish Town Lane, tel. 79791).

The Star Bar, which brags that it's "Gibraltar's Oldest Bar," is on a quiet street with a pubby interior and good £6-9 plates (daily 7:00-24:00, food served till 22:00, on Parliament Lane off Main Street, across from Corner House Restaurant, tel. 75924).

Carpenter's Arms is a fast, cheap-and-cheery café run by the Methodist church, serving £3 meals with a missionary's smile. It's upstairs in the Methodist church on Main Street (Mon-Fri 9:00-14:00, closed Sat-Sun and Aug, volunteer-run, 100 yards past the Governor's Residence at 297 Main Street).

Gaucho's is a classy, atmospheric steakhouse actually inside the casemates, just outside Casemates Square (£5 salads, £5-6 starters, £16-22 steaks, daily 12:00-15:00 & 19:00-23:00, Waterport Casemates, tel. 59700).

Casemates Square Food Circus: The big square at the entrance of Gibraltar contains a variety of restaurants, ranging from fast food (fish-and-chips joint, Burger King, and Pizza Hut) to inviting pubs spilling out onto the square. The **All's Well** pub serves £8-10 meals (Moroccan *tajine,* salads, burgers, fish-and-chips, and more) and offers pleasant tables with umbrellas under leafy trees (daily 10:00-19:00). Fruit stands and cheap take-out food stalls bustle just outside the entry to the square at the **Market Place** (Mon-Sat 9:00-15:00, closed Sun).

Groceries: The **Bon Bon Cash & Carry** minimarket is on the main drag, off Cathedral Square (daily 9:30-19:00, Main Street 239). Nearby, **Marks & Spencer** has a small food market on the ground floor, with pre-made meals and fresh-baked cookies (Mon-Thu 9:00-19:00, Fri 11:00-18:00, Sat 9:30-17:00, closed Sun).

Ocean Village

This brand-new development is the best place to get a look at the bold new face of Gibraltar. Formerly a dumpy port, it's been turned into a swanky marina fronted by glassy high-rise condo buildings. The boardwalk arcing around the marina is packed with shops, restaurants, and bars—Indian, Mexican, sports bar, pizza parlor, Irish pub, fast food, wine bar, and more. Anchoring the development is Gibraltar's casino. While the whole thing can feel a bit corporate, it offers an enjoyable 21st-century contrast to the "English village"

vibe of Main Street (which can be extremely sleepy after-hours).

Queensway Quay Marina

To dine in yacht-club ambience, stroll the marina and choose from a string of restaurants serving the boat-owning crowd. When the sun sets, the quay-side tables at each of these places are prime dining real estate. **Waterfront Restaurant** has a lounge-lizard interior and great marina-side tables outside (£5-7 starters, £10-16 main dishes, daily specials, Indian, and classic British; daily 9:00-24:00, last orders 22:45, tel. 45666). Other options include Indian, Italian, trendy lounges, and (oh, yeah) Spanish.

Gibraltar Connections

By Bus
Bus travelers walk five minutes from Gibraltar's border into Spain to reach La Línea de la Concepción, the nearest bus station (tel. 902-199-208 or 956-172-396). The nearest train station is at Algeciras, which is the region's main transportation hub.

From La Línea de la Concepción by Bus to: Algeciras (2/hour, less on weekends, 45 minutes, can buy €2.10 ticket on bus), **Tarifa** (6/day direct, 1 hour; more possible with change in Algeciras, 1.5 hours), **Málaga** (5/day, 3 hours), **Ronda** (no direct bus, transfer in Algeciras; Algeciras to Ronda: 3-4/day, 2 hours), **Granada** (1/day, 5.25 hours), **Sevilla** (4/day, 4-4.5 hours), **Jerez** (1/day, 3 hours), **Córdoba** (1/day, 5.25 hours), **Madrid** (1/day, 8 hours).

By Plane
From Gibraltar, you can fly to various points in Britain: British Airways flies to London Heathrow (www.ba.com); easyJet connects to London Gatwick and Liverpool (www.easyjet.com); and Monarch Airlines goes to London Luton and Manchester (www.flymonarch.com). The airport is easy to reach; after all, you can't enter town without crossing its runway, one way or another.

Tarifa

Mainland Europe's southernmost town is whitewashed and Arab-feeling, with a lovely beach, an old castle, restaurants swimming

in fresh seafood, inexpensive places to sleep, enough windsurfers to sink a ship, and, best of all, hassle-free boats to Morocco.

As I stood on Tarifa's town promenade under the castle, looking out at almost-touchable Morocco across the Strait of Gibraltar, my only regret was that I didn't have this book to steer me clear of gritty Algeciras on earlier trips. Tarifa, with hourly 35-minute boat transfers to Tangier, is the best jumping-off point for a Moroccan side-trip, as its ferry route goes directly to Tangier's city-center Medina Port—for details, see the Tangier chapter. The other routes, from Algeciras and Gibraltar, take you to the Tangier MED Port, 25 miles east of Tangier city. (It's possible that in the future Tarifa boats may also be steered to the MED Port—but even if this happens, Tarifa is still a much more appealing home base than Algeciras.)

Tarifa has no blockbuster sights (and can be quiet off-season), but it's a town where you just feel good to be on vacation. Don't expect a snazzy Riviera-style beach resort, à la Nerja. Tarifa is a functional, dreary-in-parts port city with an atmospheric old town and a long, broad stretch of relatively undeveloped but wildly popular sandy beach. The town is a hip and breezy mecca among windsurfers, drawn here by the strong winds created by the bottleneck at the Strait of Gibraltar. Tarifa is mobbed with young German and French adventure-seekers in July and August. This crowd from all over Europe (and beyond) makes Tarifa one of Spain's trendiest-feeling towns. It has far more artsy boutique hotels than most Spanish towns its size, and its restaurant offerings are atypically eclectic for normally same-Jane Spain—you'll see vegetarian and organic, Italian and Indian, gourmet burgers and tea houses, and on each corner, it seems, there's a stylish bar-lounge with techno music, mood lighting, and youthful Europeans just hanging out.

Orientation to Tarifa

The old town, surrounded by a wall, slopes gently up from the water's edge (and the port to Tangier). The modern section stretches farther inland from Tarifa's fortified gate.

Tourist Information

The TI is on Paseo de la Alameda (Mon-Fri 9:30-13:30 & 16:00-18:00, Sat-Sun 9:30-13:30; hours may be slightly longer in summer, or slightly shorter on slow or bad-weather days, tel. 956-680-993, www.aytotarifa.com, turismo@aytotarifa.com).

Experiencia Tarifa: This organization, run by can-do Quino of the recommended Hostal Alborada, produces a good free magazine and town map featuring hotels, restaurants, and a wide array of activities (also online at www.experienciatarifa.com).

Arrival in Tarifa

By Bus: The bus station (actually a couple of portable buildings with an outdoor sitting area) is on Batalla del Salado, about a five-minute walk from the old town. (The more central TI also has bus schedules.) Buy tickets directly from the driver if the ticket booth is closed (Mon-Fri 7:30-9:30 & 10:00-11:00 & 14:30-18:30, Sat-Sun 15:00-19:30, hours vary slightly depending on season, tel. 956-684-038, toll tel. 902-199-208). To reach the old town, walk away from the wind turbines perched on the mountain ridge.

By Car: If you're staying in the center of town, follow signs for *Alameda* or *Puerto,* and continue along Avenida de Andalucía. Follow signs to make an obligatory loop to the port entrance, then swing right and park for free in the lot at the far end of Calle Juan Núñez (on the harbor, at the base of the castle). During the busiest summer months (July-Aug), this parking lot can fill up, in which case you'll need to use one of the pay lots on either side of the old-town wall (to the west, just off of Avenida de la Constitución on Calle Joaquín Tena Artigas; or to the east, off of Camino del Olivar). Or you can try finding street parking, which is most abundant in the new town just north of the old-town walls. Blue lines indicate paid parking, and yellow lines are no-parking areas.

Helpful Hints

Internet Access: Pandor@, in the heart of the old town, has 16 computers across from Café Central, near the church (€2.50/1 hour, generally daily in summer 10:00-23:00, in winter 10:00-14:30 & 16:30-21:30, tel. 956-680-816).

Ferry Tickets: You can buy Morocco ferry tickets right at the port, but if you want to avoid that short walk, FRS (the more established of the two ferry companies) also has an office just outside the old-town wall, at the corner of Avenida de Andalucía and Avenida de la Constitución. You can buy tickets or book a seat on one of their tours here (Mon-Fri 8:00-21:00, Sat 8:00-15:00, closed Sun, tel. 956-684-847,

Side-Tripping to Morocco

Tangier, worth ▲▲, is the main reason to go to Tarifa. The ride on fast, modern catamarans (huge car ferries that zip

over every hour all year long) takes less than an hour and drops you off in the city center (unlike boats from Algeciras and Gibraltar that dock at the Tangier MED Port, about 25 miles from downtown Tangier). You walk from the Tangier port into a remarkable city—the fifth-largest in Morocco—which is no longer the Tijuana of Africa, but a booming town enjoying the enthusiastic support and can-do vision of a new and activist king.

Most tourists do the mindless belly-dancing-and-shopping excursion (which costs about €60 including the ferry ride—actually cheaper than the round-trip ferry ride sans tour). They're met by a guide, taken on a bus tour and a walk through the old-town market, offered a couple of crass Kodak moments with snake charmers and desert dancers, and given lunch with live music and belly-dancing. Then they visit a big shop and are hustled back down to their boat where—five hours after they landed—they return to the First World thankful they don't have diarrhea.

The alternative is to simply take the ferry on your own and leave the tourist track. Things are cheap and relatively safe. Since more than 90 percent of visitors choose the comfort of a tour, independent adventurers rarely see another tourist and avoid all the kitsch. You can catch a morning boat and spend the entire day, returning that evening; extend with an overnight in Tangier; or even head deeper into Morocco.

Whether you're planning a day trip or an overnight stay, see the Tangier chapter for all the details. If you're going to stay longer in Morocco, you'll need the help of another guidebook.

www.frs.es). For specifics on side-tripping to Morocco, see the Tangier chapter.

Excursions: Girasol Adventure offers a variety of outdoor excursions, including mountain-bike rentals (€18/day with helmet), guided bike tours, hikes in the national park, rock-climbing classes, tennis lessons, and, when you're all done...a massage (€50/hour). The various activities generally last a half-day and cost around €25-35. Ask Sabine or Chris for details (Mon-Fri 10:15-14:00 & 18:30-20:30, Sat 11:00-14:00, closed Sun, Calle Colón 12, tel. 956-627-037, www.girasol-adventure.com).

Tarifa

ATLANTIC OCEAN

BEACH

1. Hostal Alborada
2. Hotel La Mirada
3. La Sacristía
4. Casa Blan+co
5. Hotel Misiana
6. La Casa Amarilla
7. Hostal La Calzada
8. Hostal Alameda
9. Hostal Africa
10. Pensión Correo
11. Hostal/Rest. Villanueva
12. Restaurante Morilla
13. To El Puerto Restaurante
14. La Oca da Sergio
15. Ristorante La Trattoria
16. To Restaurante Souk & Surfing Sushi
17. Bar El Francés
18. Café Bar Los Melli & Bar El Pasillo
19. El Otro Melli
20. La Posada
21. Café Central & FIRMM
22. Casino Tarifeno
23. Confitería La Tarifeña
24. Churrería La Palmera
25. Supermarket
26. Mercado (Farmers Market)
27. Internet Café
28. Girasol Adventure
29. Whale Watch Tarifa & Baelo Tour
30. FRS Ferry Office
31. Tarifa Travel
32. Travelsur

TO BEACH

BULLRING

BERING

CASTILLE JOS

ALMADRABA

31

AVENIDA DE

AV. FUERZAS ARMADAS

PADRE FONT

HUERTA DEL REY

J.T. ARTIGAS

CRUZ ROJA

CALLE ALCALDE JUAN NÚÑEZ

DOUBLE ARCH

TO 13, BEACH FREE P & ISLA DE LAS PALOMAS

BOAT TO TANGIER (MOROCCO)

HARBOR

SPAIN'S SOUTH COAST

Sights in Tarifa

Church of St. Matthew (Iglesia de San Mateo)—Tarifa's most important church, facing its main drag, is richly decorated for being in such a small town. Most nights, it seems life squirts from the church out the front door and into the fun-loving Calle El Bravo. Wander inside.

Cost and Hours: Free, daily 9:00-13:00 & 17:30-20:30; there may be English-language leaflets inside on the right.

Visiting the Church: Find the fragment of an **ancient tombstone**—a tiny square (eye-level, about the size of this book) in the wall just before the transept on the right side. Probably the most important historical item in town, this stone fragment proves there was a functioning church here during Visigothic times, before the Moorish conquest. The tombstone reads, in a kind of Latin Spanish (try reading it), "Flaviano lived as a Christian for 50 years, a little more or less. In death he received forgiveness as a servant of God on March 30, 674. May he rest in peace." If that gets you in the mood to light a candle, switch on an electric "candle" by dropping in a coin. (It works.) A bit closer to the main entrance, you'll see a sign offering you the chance to light a digital candle by sending a text message (for a pricey €1.50).

Step into the side chapel around the corner, in the right transept. The centerpiece of the **altar** is a boy Jesus. By Andalusian tradition, he used to be naked, but these days he's clothed with outfits that vary with the Church calendar. Underneath the dome, cherubs dance around on the pink-and-purple interior above an exquisite chandelier.

Head back out into the main nave, and face the high altar. A statue of **St. James the Moor-Slayer** (missing his sword) is on the right wall of the main central altar. Since the days of the Reconquista, James has been Spain's patron saint.

The left side of the nave harbors several **statues**—showing typically over-the-top Baroque emotion—that are paraded through town during Holy Week. The **Captive Christ** (with hands bound) evokes a time when Christians were held captive by Moors. The door on the left side of the nave is the **"door of pardons."** For a long time Tarifa was a dangerous place—on the edge of the Reconquista. To encourage people to live here, the Church offered a second helping of forgiveness to anyone who lived in Tarifa for a year. One year and one day after moving to Tarifa, they would have the privilege of passing through this special "door of pardons," and a Mass of thanksgiving would be held in that person's honor.

Castle of Guzmán el Bueno—This castle, recently reopened after a long restoration, is a concrete hulk in a vacant lot, interesting

only for the harbor views from its ramparts. It was named after a 13th-century Christian general who gained fame in a sad show of courage while fighting the Moors. Holding Guzmán's son hostage, the Moors demanded he surrender the castle or they'd kill the boy. Guzmán refused, even throwing his own knife down from the ramparts. It was used on his son's throat. Ultimately, the Moors withdrew to Africa, and Guzmán was a hero. *Bueno.*

Cost and Hours: €2; Tue-Sat 11:00-14:00 & 18:00-20:00, Oct-April evening hours shift from 17:00-19:00 to 16:00-18:00; Sun 11:00-14:00 year-round, closed Mon).

Nearby: If you skip the castle, you'll get equally good views from the plaza just left of the town hall. Follow *ayto* signs to the ceramic frog fountain in front of the Casa Consistorial and continue left.

Bullfighting—Tarifa has a third-rate bullring where novices botch fights on occasional Saturdays through the summer. Professional bullfights take place the first week of September. The ring is a short walk from town. You'll see posters everywhere.

▲Whale-Watching—Several companies in Tarifa offer daily whale- and dolphin-watching excursions. Over the past four decades, people in this area went from eating whales to protecting them and sharing them with 20,000 visitors a year. Talks are under way between Morocco and Spain to protect the Strait of Gibraltar by declaring it a national park.

For any of the tours, it's wise (but not always necessary) to reserve one to three days in advance. You'll get a multilingual tour and a two-hour boat trip. Sightings occur on nearly every trip: Dolphins and pilot whales frolic here any time of year (they like the food), sperm whales visit from March through July, and orcas pass through in July and August. In bad weather, trips may be canceled or boats may leave instead from Algeciras (in which case, drivers follow in a convoy, people without cars usually get rides from staff, and you'll stand a lesser chance of seeing whales).

The best company is the Swiss nonprofit **FIRMM** (Foundation for Information and Research on Marine Mammals), which gives a 30-minute educational talk before departure. To reserve it's best to call ahead or stop by one of their two offices (€30/person, 1-5

SPAIN'S SOUTH COAST

trips/day April-Oct, sometimes also Nov, also offers intensive week-long courses that include boat trips, one office around the corner from Café Central—one door inland at Pedro Cortés 4, second office inside the ferry port, tel. 956-627-008, mobile 619-459-441, www.firmm.org, mail@firmm.org). If you don't see any whales or dolphins on your tour, you can join another trip for free.

Whale Watch Tarifa is another good option. In addition to a two-hour whale-watching trip (€30), they offer a three-hour orca trip in July and August (€45, Avenida de la Constitución 6, tel. 956-627-013, mobile 639-476-544, www.whalewatchtarifa .net, whalewatchtarifa@whalewatchtarifa.net, run by Lourdes and Ana).

Isla de las Palomas—Extending out between Tarifa's port and beaches, this island connected by a spit is the actual "southernmost point in mainland Europe." Walk along the causeway, with beaches stretching to your right and a bustling port to your left, to the tip, which was fortified in the 19th century to balance the military might of Britain's nearby Rock of Gibraltar. The actual tip, still owned by the Ministry of Defense, is closed to the public, but a sign at the gate still gives you that giddy "edge of the world" feeling.

▲▲**Beach Scene**—Tarifa's vast, sandy beach stretches west for

about five miles. You can walk the beach from Tarifa, while those with a car can explore farther (following Cádiz Road). On windy summer days, the sea is littered with sprinting windsurfers, while kitesurfers flutter in the sky. "Paddleboarding" (standing on a surfboard while maneuvering with a long, kayak-like paddle) is also becoming popular. It's a fascinating scene: A long string of funky beach resorts is packed with vans and fun-mobiles from northern Europe under mountain ridges lined with modern energy-generating windmills. The various resorts each have a sandy access road, parking, a cabana-type hamlet with rental gear, beachwear shops, a bar, and a hip, healthy restaurant. I like Valdevaqueros beach (five miles from Tarifa), with a wonderful thatched restaurant serving hearty salads, paella, and burgers. Camping Torre de la Peña also has some fun beach eateries.

In July and August, inexpensive buses do a circuit of nearby campgrounds, all on the waterfront (€2, departures about every 1-2 hours, confirm times with TI). Trying to get a parking spot in August can take the joy out of this experience.

Nightlife in Tarifa

You'll find plenty of enjoyable nightspots—the entire town seems designed to cater to a young, international crowd of windsurfers and other adventure travelers. Just stroll the streets of the old town and dip into whichever trendy lounge catches your eye. For something more sedate, the evening paseo fills the park-like boulevard called Paseo Alameda (just outside the old-town wall); the Almedina bar hosts flamenco shows every Thursday (at the south end of town, just below Plaza de Santa María); and the new theater next to the TI sometimes has musical performances (ask at the TI or look for posters).

Sleeping in Tarifa

Room rates vary with the season. For many hotels, I've listed the three seasonal tiers (highest prices—mid-June-Sept; medium prices—spring and fall; and lowest prices—winter).

Outside the City Wall

These hotels are about five blocks from the old town, right off the main drag, Batalla del Salado, in the plain, modern part of town. While in a drab area, both are well-run oases that are close to the beach and the bus station, with free and easy street parking.

$$ Hostal Alborada is a squeaky-clean, family-run 37-room place with two attractive courtyards and modern conveniences. Father Rafael, sons Quino (who speaks English and is generous

Sleep Code

(€1 = about $1.40, country code: 34)
S = Single, **D** = Double/Twin, **T** = Triple, **Q** = Quad, **b** = bathroom, **s** = shower only. Unless otherwise noted, credit cards are accepted and English is spoken. Breakfast is not included (unless noted).

To help you easily sort through these listings, I've divided the accommodations into three categories, based on the price for a standard double room with bath during high season:

$$$ Higher Priced—Most rooms €100 or more.
$$ Moderately Priced—Most rooms between €50-100.
$ Lower Priced—Most rooms €50 or less.

Prices can change without notice; verify the hotel's current rates online or by email. For other updates, see www.ricksteves.com/update.

with travel tips) and Carlos, and their family are happy to help make your Morocco tour or ferry reservation, or arrange any other activities you're interested in. If they're not too busy, they'll even give you a free lift to the port (Sb-€40/55/65, Db-€50/70/85, Tb-€80/90/110, pay for first night when reserving, upon arrival show this book for a 10 percent discount in 2012—not valid July-Sept, strict 15-day cancellation policy, basic breakfast-€2.50, breakfast with delicious tomato bread-€5, air-con, pay Internet access, free Wi-Fi, laundry-€14, Calle San José 40, tel. 956-681-140, fax 956-681-935, www.hotelalborada.com, info@hotel alborada.com).

$$ Hotel La Mirada, which feels sleek and stark, has 25 mod and renovated rooms—most with sea views at no extra cost. While the place lacks personality, it's well-priced and comfortable (Sb-€45/55/60, Db-€65/75/90, breakfast-€5, elevator, free Wi-Fi, expansive sea views from large roof terrace with inviting lounge chairs, Calle San Sebastián 41, tel. 956-684-427, fax 956-681-162, www.hotel-lamirada.com, reservas@hotel-lamirada.com, Antonio and Salvador).

Inside or next to the City Wall

The first three listings are funky, stylish boutique hotels in the heart of town—*muy* trendy and a bit full of themselves.

$$$ La Sacristía, formerly a Moorish stable, now houses travelers who want stylish surroundings. It offers 10 fine and uniquely decorated rooms, mingling eclectic elements of chic Spanish and Asian style. They offer spa treatments, custom tours of the area, and occasional special events—join the party since you won't sleep (Db-€117, superior Db-€137, extra bed-€35, can be cheaper off-season, includes breakfast, some superior rooms have air-con but most rooms have fans, massage room, sauna, roof terrace, TV on request, very central at San Donato 8, tel. 956-681-759, fax 956-685-182, www.lasacristia.net, tarifa@lasacristia.net, helpful Teresa). They also rent 10 apartments at a separate location.

$$$ Casa Blan+co, where minimalist meets Moroccan, is the newest reasonably priced designer hotel on the block. Each of its seven rooms (with double beds only—no twins) is decorated (and priced) differently. The place is decked out with practical amenities (mini-fridge and stovetop) as well as romantic touches—loft beds, walk-in showers, and subtle lighting (high-season Db-€92-133, low-season Db-€52-69, includes breakfast, small roof terrace, free Wi-Fi in lobby, off main square at Calle Nuestra Señora de la Luz 2, tel. 956-681-515, fax 956-681-990, www.casablan-co.com, info @casablan-co.com).

$$$ Hotel Misiana has 13 comfortable, newly remodeled, spacious rooms above a bar-lounge. Their designer gave the place a mod pastel boutique-ish ambience. To avoid noise from the lounge below (open until 3:00 in the morning), request a room on a higher floor (Sb-€50/60/115, Db-€70/85/135, fancy top-floor Db suite-€110/140/250, low- and mid-season rates are €10-20 more on weekends, includes breakfast, double-paned windows, elevator, free Wi-Fi in bar, 100 yards directly in front of the church at Calle Sancho IV El Bravo 16, tel. 956-627-083, fax 956-627-055, www.misiana.com, reservas@misiana.com).

$$ La Casa Amarilla ("The Yellow House") offers 10 posh apartments with tiny kitchens, plus three smaller studios with modern decor (studio Db-€57/78/114, apartment Db-€76/91/130, reserve with credit card, no breakfast, free Wi-Fi, across street from Café Central, Calle Sancho IV El Bravo 9, tel. 956-681-993, fax 956-684-029, www.lacasaamarilla.net, info@lacasaamarilla.net).

$$ Hostal La Calzada has eight airy, well-appointed rooms right in the lively old-town thick of things, though the management is rarely around (Db-€50-75, extra bed-€10, higher in Aug, closed Dec-March, air-con, free Wi-Fi in lobby, 20 yards from church at Calle Justino Pertinez 7, tel. 956-681-492, fax 956-680-366, www.hostallacalzada.com, info@hostallacalzada.com).

$$ Hostal Alameda, overlooking a square where the local children play, glistens with pristine marble floors and dark red decor. The main building has 11 bright rooms and the annex has 16 more-modern rooms; both face the same delightful square (Db-€60/70/90, extra bed-€20-30, à la carte breakfast, air-con, free Wi-Fi, Paseo de la Alameda 4, tel. 956-681-181, fax 956-680-264, www.hostalalameda.com, reservas@hostalalameda.com, Antonio).

$$ Hostal Africa, with 13 bright rooms and an inviting roof terrace, is buried on a very quiet street in the center of town. Its dreamy blue-and-white color scheme and stripped-down feel give it a Moorish ambience (S-€20/25/35, Sb-€25/35/50, D-€30/40/50, Db-€35/50/65, Tb-€50/75/100, no breakfast, laundry-€10—or €20 in high season, free Wi-Fi in public spaces, storage for boards and bikes, Calle María Antonia Toledo 12, tel. 956-680-220, mobile 606-914-294, www.hostalafrica.com, hostal_africa@hotmail.com, Miguel and Eva keep the reception desk open only 9:00-24:00).

$$ Pensión Correo rents nine simple rooms (three sharing a bathroom) at a fair value—especially Room 8, with its private roof terrace (S-€20-35, D-€35-60, Db-€45-80, Tb-€50-90, Qb-€60-110, extra bed-€15-20, reservations more than 24 hours in advance require first night prepaid by credit card—refundable up to 48 hours in advance, no breakfast, roof garden, free Wi-Fi in some rooms, Coronel Moscardo 8, tel. 956-680-206, www.pensioncorreo.com, welcome@pensioncorreo.com, María José and Luca).

$ **Hostal Villanueva** offers 12 remodeled rooms at budget prices over a good restaurant. It's simple, clean, and friendly. It lacks indoor public areas, but has an inviting terrace overlooking the old town. On a busy street, it's dominated by its restaurant. Pepe (who speaks a smidgen of English) asks that you reconfirm your reservation by phone the day before you arrive (Sb-€25-30, Db-€35-55, cash only, no breakfast, just west of the old-town gate at Avenida de Andalucía 11, access from outside the wall, tel. & fax 956-684-149, hostalvillanueva@hotmail.com).

Eating in Tarifa

I've grouped my recommendations below into two categories: Sit down to a real restaurant meal, or enjoy a couple of the many characteristic tapas bars in the old town.

Dining
Seafood
Restaurante Morilla, facing the church and on the town's prime piece of people-watching real estate, serves tasty local-style fish—grilled or baked. This is a real restaurant (€1.50 tapas sold only at the stand-up bar and sometimes at a few tables), with good indoor and outdoor seating. The waiter will tell you about today's fish; it's sold by weight, so confirm the price carefully (€4-11 starters, €10-16 main dishes, daily 9:00-24:00, Calle Sancho IV El Bravo, tel. 956-681-757).

El Puerto, in a dreary and untouristy area between the port and the beach (near the causeway out to Isla de las Palomas), has a great reputation for its pricey but very fresh seafood. Locals swear that it's a notch or two above the seafood places in town (€8-14 starters, €10-20 seafood dishes and some meats, Thu-Mon 12:00-16:00 & 20:00-24:00, Tue-Wed 12:00-16:00 only, Avenida Fuerzas Armadas 13, tel. 956-681-914).

Restaurante Villanueva is a homey-feeling, affordable seafood option, with a sprawling interior and outdoor tables on a busy street just outside the old-town wall (€7.50 lunch, €4-7 starters, €9-15 main dishes, Tue-Sun 13:00-16:00 & 19:45-23:00, closed Mon, Avenida de Andalucía 11, tel. 956-684-149).

Italian
La Oca da Sergio, cozy and fun, is one of the numerous pizza-and-pasta joints supported by the large expat Italian community. Sergio prides himself on importing actual Italian ingredients (€7-11 starters, €9-14 pastas, €7-10 pizzas, €14-16 meat and fish dishes, indoor and outdoor seating, daily 13:00-16:00 & 20:00-24:00 except closed Tue in winter; around the left side of the church

and straight back, just before the Moorish-style old-folks' home at Calle General Copons 6; tel. 956-681-249, mobile 615-686-571).

Ristorante La Trattoria, on the Alameda, is another good Italian option, with cloth-napkin class, friendly staff, and ingredients from Italy. Sit inside, near the wood-fired oven, or out along the main strolling street (€9-15 starters and pastas, €6-12 pizzas, €16-20 meat dishes; Thu-Tue 19:30-24:00, closed Wed; July-Aug open daily plus Sat-Sun 13:00-16:00; Paseo de la Alameda, tel. 956-682-225).

In the New Town

These two restaurants are in a residential area just above the beach, about a 15-minute walk (or easy car or taxi ride) from the old town. They're worth a detour for their great food, and for the chance to see an area away from the main tourist zone (though the sushi bar is on the beach and is no stranger to tourists). To get to either, begin by heading up Calle San Sebastián, which turns into Calle Pintor Pérez Villalta. When you see a big staircase on your right, head up the stairs to reach Restaurante Souk, or turn left toward the beach to find Surfing Sushi.

Restaurante Souk serves a tasty fusion of Moroccan, Indian, and Thai cuisine in a dark, exotic, romantic, purely Moroccan ambience. The ground floor (where you enter) is a bar and atmospheric tea house, while the dining room is downstairs (€6-9 starters, €12-17 main dishes; July-Sept daily 20:00-3:00 in the morning; Oct-June Wed-Mon 20:00-1:00, closed Tue; good wine list, Mar Tirreno 46, tel. 956-627-065, friendly Claudia).

Surfing Sushi, part of a cool surfer bar called Surla, serves up wonderfully executed sushi using only the freshest of ingredients. Situated just a few steps above the beachfront walkway, it's at the center of a sprawling zone of après-surf hangouts. They also offer delivery (€16-21 shareable sushi platters, mid-June-mid-Sept daily 20:00-24:00, closed Wed off-season, possible to order delivery sushi by phone at other times, Calle Pintor Pérez Villalta 1, tel. 956-685-175, www.surfingsushi.com).

Tapas

Bar El Francés is a thriving hole-in-the-wall where "Frenchies" (as the bar's name implies) Marcial and Alexandra serve tasty little plates of tapas. From Café Central, follow the cars 100 yards to the first corner on the left to reach this simple, untouristy standing-and-stools-only eatery. This spot is popular for its fine *raciones* (€6-10) and tapas (€1.30-1.50)—especially oxtail *(rabo del toro)*, pork with tomato sauce *(carne con tomate)*, pork with spice *(chicharrones)*, and garlic-grilled tuna *(atún a la plancha)*. The outdoor terrace with restaurant-type tables (no tapas served here) is an understandably popular spot to enjoy a casual meal. Show this book and Marcial will be happy to bring you a free glass of sherry (Mon-Sat open long hours, especially April-Sept, closed Sun; daily June-Aug; closed Dec-Feb; Calle Sancho IV El Bravo 21A, mobile 685-867-005).

Café Bar Los Melli is a local favorite for feasts on rickety tables set on cobbles. This family-friendly place, run by José, offers a good chorizo sandwich and *patatas bravas*—potatoes with a hot tomato sauce served on a wooden board (€5 half-*raciones*, €8 *raciones*, Thu-Tue 20:00-24:00, Sat-Sun also 13:00-16:00, closed Wed; from Bar El Francés, cross parking lot and take Calle del Legionario Ríos Moya up one block; mobile 605-866-444). **Bar El Pasillo,** next to Los Melli, also serves tapas (closed Mon-Tue). **El Otro Melli,** run by José's brother Ramón, is a few blocks away on Plaza de San Martín.

La Posada, a local-feeling place a block beyond the main tourist zone (and just up the street from Los Melli), takes prides in its fresh ingredients. There's a small dining room, a nondescript bar with a giant stone beer tap that's a replica of the city's first communal faucet, and tables out front near the real thing (€1.50 *montaditos*, €3 *tostadas*, €4-6 half-*raciones*, €7-11 *raciones;* July-Aug daily 13:00-16:30 & 20:00-24:00; Sept-June Mon and Wed-Fri 20:00-24:00, Sat-Sun 13:00-16:30 & 20:00-24:00, closed Tue; Calle Guzman el Bueno 3A, mobile 636-929-449).

Café Central is *the* happening place nearly any time of day—it's the perch for all the cool tourists. Less authentically Spanish than the others I've listed, it has a hip, international vibe. The bustling ambience and appealing setting in front of the church are better than the food (€1.30 tapas, €5 half-*raciones*), but they do have breakfast with eggs (€2-4), good €6 salads (study the menu), and impressively therapeutic healthy fruit drinks (daily 8:30-24:00, off Plaza San Mateo, near church, tel. 956-682-877).

Casino Tarifeno is just to the sea side of the church. It's an old-boys' social club "for members only," but it offers a musty Andalusian welcome to visiting tourists, including women. Wander through. There's a low-key bar with tapas, a TV room, a card room, and a lounge. There's no menu, but prices are standard. Just point and say the size you want: tapa (€1.20), *media-ración* (€4), or *ración* (€7). A far cry from some of the trendy options around town, this is a local institution (daily 12:00-24:00).

Pastries, Beach Bars, and Picnics

Breakfast or Dessert: **Confitería La Tarifeña** serves super pastries and flan-like *tocino de cielo* (daily 9:00-21:00, at the top of Calle Nuestra Señora de la Luz, near the main old-town gate).

Churrería La Palmera serves breakfast before most hotels and cafés have even turned on the lights—early enough for you to get your coffee fix, and/or bulk up on *churros* and chocolate, before hopping the first ferry to Tangier (Sanchez IV El Bravo 34).

Windsurfer Bars: If you have a car, head to the string of beaches. Many have bars and fun-loving thatched restaurants that keep the wet-suited gang fed and watered.

Picnics: Stop by the **mercado municipal** (farmers' market, Mon-Sat 8:00-14:00, closed Sun, in old town, inside gate nearest TI), any grocery, or the **superSol supermarket** (Mon-Sat 9:30-21:30, closed Sun, has simple cafeteria, near the hotels in the new town at Callao and San José).

Tarifa Connections

Tarifa

From Tarifa by Bus to: La Línea de la Concepción/Gibraltar (6/day direct, 1 hour, starting around 12:00; more possible with transfer in Algeciras, 1.5 hours), **Algeciras** (10/day, 30 minutes, first departure from Tarifa weekdays at 6:30, on Sat 8:15, on Sun 10:00; return from Algeciras as late as 21:00), **Jerez** (1/day, 2 hours, more frequent with transfer in Cádiz), **Sevilla** (4/day, 2.5-3.25 hours), and **Málaga** (3/day, 3.5 hours). All bus service from Tarifa is by Comes (tel. 956-684-038, www.tgcomes.es).

Algeciras

Algeciras (ahl-*h*eh-THEE-rahs, with a guttural *h*) is only worth leaving. It's useful to the traveler mainly as a transportation hub, with trains and buses to destinations in southern and central Spain (it also has a ferry to Tangier, but it takes you to the Tangier MED port about 25 miles from Tangier city—going from Tarifa is much better). If you're headed for Gibraltar or Tarifa by public transport, you'll almost certainly change in Algeciras at some point.

Everything of interest is on Juan de la Cierva, which heads inland from the port. The **TI** is about a block in (Mon-Fri 9:00-19:30, Sat-Sun 9:30-15:00, tel. 956-784-131), followed by the side-by-side **train station** (opposite Hotel Octavio) and **bus station** three more blocks later.

Trains: If arriving at the train station, head out the front door: The bus station (called San Bernardo Estación de Autobuses) is ahead and on the right; the TI is another three blocks ahead (the road becomes Juan de la Cierva when the road jogs), also on the right; and the port is just beyond.

From Algeciras by Train to: Madrid (2/day, 5.5 hours, arrives at Atocha), **Ronda** (3-4/day, 1.5-2 hours), **Granada** (3/day, 4.25-5 hours), **Sevilla** (3/day, 5 hours, transfer at Bobadilla; bus is better), **Córdoba** (2/day direct on Altaria, 3.5 hours; plus 1/day with transfer in Bobadilla, 5.25 hours), **Málaga** (2/day, 4 hours, transfer in Bobadilla; bus is faster). With the exception of the route to Madrid, these are particularly scenic trips; the best (though slow) is the mountainous journey to Málaga via Bobadilla.

Buses: Algeciras is served by three different bus companies (Comes, Portillo, and Linesur), all located in the same terminal (called San Bernardo Estación de Autobuses) next to Hotel Octavio and directly across from the train station. The companies generally serve different destinations, but there is some overlap. Compare schedules and rates to find the most convenient bus for you. By the ticket counter you'll find an easy red letter board that lists departures. Lockers are near the platforms—purchase a token at the machines.

From Algeciras by Bus: Comes (tel. 902-199-208, www.tgcomes.es) runs buses to **La Línea/Gibraltar** (2/hour, less on weekends, 45 minutes, 7:00-22:30), **Tarifa** (11/day, less on weekends, 30 minutes), **Ronda** (3-4/day, 2 hours), **Sevilla** (4/day, 3.5 hours), **Jerez** (1/day, 2.5 hours), and **Madrid** (3/day, 8 hours).

Portillo (tel. 956-654-304, www.ctsa-portillo.com) offers buses to **Málaga** (17/day, 1.75 hours *directo*, 3 hours *ruta*) and **Granada** (4/day, 4-5 hours).

Linesur (tel. 956-667-649, www.linesur.com) runs the most frequent direct buses to **Sevilla** (8/day, fewer on weekends, 2.75-3 hours) and **Jerez** (8/day, fewer on weekends, 1.5 hours).

Ferries from Algeciras to Tangier, Morocco: Although it's possible to sail from Algeciras to Tangier, the ferry takes you to the Tangier MED Port, which is 25 miles east of Tangier city and a hassle. You're better off taking a ferry from Tarifa: They sail direct to the port in Tangier. If you must sail from Algeciras, buy your ticket at the port (skip the divey-looking travel agencies littering the town). Official offices of the seven boat companies are inside the main port building, directly behind the helpful little English-speaking info kiosk (8-22 ferries/day, port open daily 6:45-21:45, tel. 956-585-463).

Route Tips for Drivers

Tarifa to Gibraltar (45 minutes): This short drive takes you past a silvery-white forest of windmills, from peaceful Tarifa past Algeciras to La Línea (the Spanish town bordering Gibraltar). Passing Algeciras, continue in the direction of Estepona. At San Roque, take the La Línea–Gibraltar exit.

Gibraltar to Nerja (130 miles): Barring traffic problems, the trip along the Costa del Sol is smooth and easy by car—much of it on a new highway. Just follow the coastal highway east. After Málaga, follow signs to *Almería* and *Motril*.

Nerja to Granada (80 miles, 1.5 hours, 100 views): Drive along the coast to Motril, catching N-323 north for about 40 miles to Granada. While scenic side-trips may beckon, don't arrive late in Granada without a confirmed hotel reservation.

MOROCCO

MOROCCO

Al-Maghreb

A young country with an old history, Morocco is a photographer's delight and a budget traveler's dream. It's cheap, exotic, and easier and more appealing than ever. Along with a rich culture, Morocco offers plenty of contrast—from beach resorts to bustling desert markets, from jagged mountains to sleepy, mud-brick oasis towns. And there's a distinct new energy as its popular activist king asserts his vision.

Morocco (*Marruecos* in Spanish; *Al-Maghreb* in Arabic) also provides a good dose of culture shock—both bad and good. It makes Spain seem meek and mild. You'll encounter oppressive friendliness, brutal heat, the Arabic language, the Islamic faith, ancient cities, and aggressive beggars.

While Morocco is clearly a place apart from Mediterranean Europe, it doesn't really seem like Africa either. It's a mix, reflecting its strategic position between the two continents. Situated on the Strait of Gibraltar, Morocco has been flooded by waves

of invasions over the centuries. The Berbers, the native population, have had to contend with the Phoenicians, Carthaginians, Romans, Vandals, and more.

The Arabs brought Islam to Morocco in the seventh century A.D. and stuck around, battling the Berbers in various civil wars. A series of Berber and Arab dynasties rose and fell; the Berbers won out and still run the country today.

From the 15th century on, European countries carved up much of Africa. By the early 20th century, most of Morocco was under French control, and strategic Tangier was jointly ruled by multiple European powers. The country wasn't granted independence until 1956. In the late 1970s, Morocco itself became an invading country, grabbing Spain's Western Sahara territory and causing the relatively few inhabitants to clamor for independence. Western Sahara's claim still has not been settled by the United Nations.

Unfortunately, most of the English-speaking Moroccans the typical tourist meets are hustlers. Many visitors develop some intestinal problems by the end of their visit. Most women are harassed on the streets by horny but generally harmless men. And in terms of efficiency, Morocco makes Spain look like Sweden.

When you cruise south across the Strait of Gibraltar, leave your busy itineraries and split-second timing behind. Morocco must be taken on its own terms. In Morocco things go smoothly only *"Inshallah"*—if God so wills.

Helpful Hints

Politics: Americans pondering a visit understandably wonder how they'll be received in this Muslim nation. Al Jazeera blares from televisions in all the bars, but I've seen no angry graffiti or posters and felt no animosity toward American individuals there (even on my last visit, literally days after US forces killed Osama bin Laden). Western visitors feel a warm welcome in post-9/11 Morocco. And it's culturally enriching for Westerners to experience Morocco—a Muslim monarchy with women still in traditional dress and roles,

MOROCCO

Islam 101

Islam has more than a billion adherents worldwide, and traveling in an Islamic country is an opportunity to better understand the religion. This admittedly basic and simplistic outline (written by a non-Muslim) is meant to help travelers from the Christian West understand a very rich but often misunderstood culture.

Muslims, like Christians and Jews, are monotheistic. They call God "Allah." The most important person in the Islamic faith is the prophet Muhammad, who lived in the sixth and seventh centuries A.D. The holy book of Islam is the Quran, believed by Muslims to be the word of Allah as revealed to Muhammad.

The "five pillars" of Islam are the core tenets of the faith. Followers of Islam should:

1. Say and believe, "There is only one God, and Muhammad is his prophet."

2. Pray five times a day, facing Mecca. Modern Muslims explain that it's important for this ritual to include washing, exercising, stretching, and thinking of God.

3. Give to the poor (one-fortieth of your wealth, if you are not in debt).

4. Fast during daylight hours through the month of Ramadan. Fasting is a great social equalizer and helps everyone to feel the hunger of the poor.

5. Make a pilgrimage to Mecca. Muslims who can afford it, and who are physically able, are required to travel to the sacred sites in Mecca and Medina at least once in their lifetimes.

Just as it helps to know about spires, feudalism, and the saints to comprehend European sightseeing, a few basics on Islam help make your sightseeing in Morocco more meaningful.

succeeding on its own terms without embracing modern Western "norms."

Hustler Alert: Moroccans may be some of Africa's wealthiest people, but you are still incredibly rich to them. This imbalance causes predictable problems. Wear your money belt. Assume con artists are more clever than you. Haggle when appropriate; prices skyrocket for tourists. You'll attract hustlers like flies at every famous tourist sight or whenever you pull out your guidebook or a map. In the worst-case scenario, they'll lie to you, get you lost, blackmail you, and pester the heck out of you. Never leave your car or baggage where you can't get back to it without someone else's "help." Anything you buy in a guide's company gets him a 20 percent commission. Normally locals, shopkeepers, and police will come to your rescue if the hustlers' heat becomes unbearable. Consider hiring a guide, since it's helpful to have a translator, and once you're "taken," the rest seem to leave you alone.

Marijuana Alert: In Morocco, marijuana *(kif)* is as illegal as it is popular, a fact that many Westerners in local jails would love to remind you of. As a general rule, just walk right by those hand-carved pipes in the marketplace. Some dealers who sell it cheap make their profit after you get arrested. Cars and buses are stopped and checked by police routinely throughout Morocco—especially in the north and in the Chefchaouen region, which is Morocco's *kif* capital.

Health: Morocco is much more hazardous to your health than Spain. Eat in clean—not cheap—places. Peel fruit, eat only cooked vegetables, and drink reliably bottled water (Sidi Ali or Sidi Harazem). When you do get diarrhea—and you should plan on it—adjust your diet (small and bland meals, no milk or grease) or fast for a day, but make sure you replenish lost fluids. Relax: Most diarrhea is not serious, just an adjustment that will run its course.

Closed Days: Friday is the Muslim day of rest, when most of the country (except Tangier) closes down.

Ramadan: During this major month-long religious holiday (July 20-Aug 18 in 2012), Muslims focus on prayer and reflection. Following Islamic doctrine, they refrain during daylight hours from eating, drinking (including water), smoking, and having sex. On the final day of Ramadan, Muslims celebrate *Eid* (an all-day feast and gift-giving party, similar to Christmas), and travelers may find some less-touristy stores and restaurants closed.

Money: Euros work here (as do dollars and pounds). If you're on a five-hour tour, bring along lots of €1 and €0.50 coins for tips, small purchases, and camel rides. But if you plan to do anything independently, change some money into Moroccan dirhams upon arrival (8 dh = about $1). Banks and ATMs have uniform rates. If you use an exchange desk, just be sure you can see the buying and selling rates; they should be within 10 percent of one another with no extra fees. Don't leave the

MOROCCO

country with Moroccan money unless you want a souvenir, since few places in Spain are willing to change dirhams to euros or dollars.

Information: Travel information, English or otherwise, is rare here. For an extended trip, bring guidebooks from home or Spain—Lonely Planet and Rough Guide both publish good ones. Buy the best map you can find locally—names are always changing, and if you need to ask someone, it's helpful to have towns, roads, and place names written in Arabic.

Language: With its unique history of having been controlled by so many different foreign and domestic rulers, Tangier is a babel of languages. Most locals speak Arabic first and French second (all Moroccans must learn it in schools); sensing that you're a foreigner, they'll most likely address you in French. Spanish ranks third, and English a distant fourth. The Arabic squiggle-script, its many difficult sounds, and the fact that French is Morocco's second language combine to make communication tricky for English-speaking travelers. A little French goes a long way, but learn a few words in Arabic. Have your first local friend help you with the pronunciation:

English	Arabic	Pronounced
Hello. ("Peace be with you")	*Salaam alaikum.*	sah-LAHM ah-LAY-koom
Hello. (response: "Peace also be with you")	*Wa alaikum salaam.*	wah ah-LAY-koom sah-LAHM
Please.	*Min fadlik.*	meen FAHD-leek
Thank you.	*Shokran.*	SHOH-kron (like "sugar on")
Excuse me.	*Ismahli.*	ees-SMAH-lee
Yes.	*Yeh.*	EE-yeh
No.	*Lah.*	lah
Give me five. (kids enjoy this...not above but straight ahead)	*Ham sah.*	hahm sah
OK.	*Wah hah.*	wah hah
Very good.	*Miz yen biz ef.*	meez EE-yehn beez ehf
Goodbye.	*Maa salama.*	mah sah-LEM-ah

Moroccans are more touchy-feely than their Spanish neighbors. Expect lots of hugs if you make an effort to communicate. When greeting someone, a handshake is customary, followed by placing your right hand over your heart. Listen carefully and write new words phonetically. Bring an Arabic phrase book. In markets, I sing, "la la la la la" to my

MOROCCO

opponents. *Lah shokran* means "No, thank you."

Getting Around Morocco: Moroccan trains are quite good. Second class is cheap and comfortable. Buses connect all smaller towns very well. By car, Morocco is easy, but drive defensively and never rely on the oncoming driver's skill. Night driving is dangerous. Pay a guard to watch your car overnight.

Keeping Your Bearings: Navigate the labyrinthine *medinas* (old towns) by altitude, gates, and famous mosques or buildings. Write down what gate you came in, so you can enjoy being lost—temporarily. *Souk* is Arabic for a particular market (such as leather, yarn, or metalwork). A *kasbah* is loosely defined as a fortress (or a town within old fortress walls).

TANGIER

Tanja

Go to Africa. As you step off the boat, you realize that the crossing (less than an hour) has taken you further culturally than did the trip from the US to Spain. Morocco needs no museums; its sights are living in the streets. For decades its once-grand coastal city of Tangier deserved its reputation as the "Tijuana of Africa." But that has changed. The current king is enthusiastic about Tangier, and there's a fresh can-do spirit in the air. The town is as Moroccan as ever...yet more enjoyable and less stressful.

Morocco in a Day?

Though Morocco certainly deserves more than a day, many visitors touring Spain see it in a quick side-trip. And, though such a short sprint through Tangier is only a tease, it's far more interesting than another day in Spain. A day in Tangier gives you a good introduction to Morocco, a legitimate taste of North Africa, and a nonthreatening slice of Islam. All you need is a passport (no visa or shots required) and €67 for the round-trip ferry crossing. Your big decisions: where to sail from; whether to go on your own or buy a ferry/guided tour day-trip package; and whether to make it a day trip or spend the night. Of these, the biggest decision is:

With a Tour or On My Own?: Because the ferry company expects you to do a lot of shopping (providing them with kickbacks), it's actually a bit cheaper to join a one-day tour than to buy a round-trip ferry ticket. The question is: Do you want the safety and comfort of having Morocco handed to you on a user-friendly platter; or do you want the independence to see what you want to see, with a more authentic experience, fewer cultural clichés, and less forced shopping? There are pros and cons to each approach, depending on your travel style. My preferred approach is sort of a hybrid: Go to Morocco "on your own," but arrange in advance to meet up with a local guide to ease your culture shock and accompany you to your choice of sights (I've listed several guides on page 284, or you can book a tour with the ferry company and pay for the "VIP" option). While this costs a bit more than joining a package tour, ultimately the cost difference (roughly €10-20 more per person) is pretty negligible, considering the dramatically increased cultural intimacy. Doing it entirely on your own (no guide at all) can be a great adventure, but potentially more stressful.

Time Difference: Morocco is on Greenwich Mean Time (like Great Britain)—that means one hour behind Spain. It typically observes Daylight Saving Time, but "springs forward" and "falls back" at different times than Europe. In general, Moroccans change their clocks in early April (a week after Spain), then again just before Ramadan (in 2011, that date was July 31—nearly three months before Spain). Therefore, during the summer months, Morocco is either one hour (if they've changed) or two hours (if they haven't changed, or have already changed back) behind Spain. In general, ferry and other schedules use the local time (if your boat leaves Tangier "at 17:00," that means 5:00 p.m. Moroccan time—not Spanish time)...be sure to change your watch when you get off the boat.

Terminology: Note that the Spanish refer to Morocco as "Marruecos" (mar-WAY-kohs) and Tangier as "Tánger" (TAHN-*h*air, with a guttural *h*).

Going on Your Own, by Ferry from Tarifa

While the trip to Tangier can be made from various ports, only the ferry from Tarifa takes you to Tangier's city-center port, called the Tangier Medina Port (Spaniards call it the *Puerto Viejo*, "Old Port"). Boats from Algeciras or Gibraltar dock instead at the Tangier MED Port (Spaniards call it the *Puerto Nuevo*, "New Port"), about 25 miles east of the city center. (Note: Confusingly, because the city-center port is being remodeled, some Moroccans call it the "new port"—exactly the opposite of the Spaniards.) Tangier's city-center port has been closed to cargo shipping, and is in the midst of a massive renovation and beautification project, which will extend the pier to accommodate large cruise ships and create a marina for yachts. Most sources indicate that ferries from Tarifa will continue to use the city-center port, though it's possible (temporarily—due to construction at the port) that Tarifa ships could be sent to the MED port. I'll describe the trip assuming you're sailing from Tarifa to Tangier's city-center Medina Port—the most logical route for the typical traveler.

Ferry Crossing: Two different companies make essentially

TANGIER

the same 35-minute crossing from Tarifa to Tangier, on alternating hours: **FRS** (tel. 956-684-847, www.frs.es) and **Comarit** (tel. 956-657-462, www.comarit.es). Prices are about the same

with either company (€37 one-way, €67 round-trip). Between them, boats leave Tarifa at the top of every hour from about 8:00 to 22:00—so go with the boat that best suits your schedule. For the return trip from Tangier to Tarifa, boats run from about 7:00 to 21:00.

Tickets are very easy to get: You can buy one at the port, through your hotel in Tarifa, from a local travel agency, or at FRS's ticket office in town. You can almost always just buy a ticket and walk on, though in the busiest summer months (July-Aug), the popular 9:00 departure could be booked up with tours. Boats are most crowded in July (when Moroccans in Spain go home for Ramadan) and in August (when the Costa del Sol groups come en masse). A few crossings a year are canceled because of storms or wind, mostly in winter.

Procedure: The ferry from Tarifa is a fast Nordic hydrofoil that theoretically takes 35 minutes to cross. It often leaves late.

You'll go through Spanish customs at the port and Moroccan customs on the ferry. Whether taking a tour or traveling on your own, you *must* get a stamp (available on board) from the Moroccan immigration officer. After you leave Spain, find the customs desk on the boat, line up, and get your passport and entry paper stamped. If you're coming back the same day and know your return time, the immigration official may also give you an exit stamp (for your return from Morocco), which prevents delays at the port at departure time. The ferry is equipped with WCs, a shop, and a snack bar. Tarifa's modern little terminal has a cafeteria and WCs.

Hiring a Guide: Even if you're visiting Morocco independently, I recommend hiring a local guide to show you around Tangier (for a list of recommended guides, see "Guides," on page 284).

Tangier MED Port: Ferries from Algeciras and Gibraltar (and, potentially but unlikely, ferries from Tarifa) arrive at the Tangier MED Port, 25 miles from downtown. While this wastes time (it's about an hour each way from the boat to downtown Tangier), the connection is simple: A free shuttle bus picks up passengers at the Tangier MED Port terminal and brings them right to the entrance of the Tangier Medina Port, in the city center. Remember that if you're coming from Tarifa, your ship will most likely dock at the Tangier Medina Port.

Returning to Tarifa: It's smart to return to the port about 20 minutes before your ferry departs. If you didn't get your passport's exit stamp on the way over, you must wait in line to get it stamped at the Tangier ferry terminal before you board the boat.

Taking a Tour

Taking a tour is easier but less rewarding than doing it on your own or with a private guide. A typical day-trip tour includes a round-trip crossing and a guide who meets your big group at a prearranged point in Tangier, then hustles you through the hustlers and onto your tour bus. Several guides await the arrival of each ferry in Tangier and assemble their groups. (Tourists wear stickers identifying which tour they're with.) All offer essentially the same five-hour Tangier experience: a city bus tour, a drive through the ritzy palace neighborhood, a walk through the

Medina (old town), and an overly thorough look at a sales-starved carpet shop (where prices include a 20 percent commission for your guide and tour company; some carpet shops are actually owned by the ferry companies). Longer tours may include a trip to the desolate Atlantic Coast for some rugged African scenery, and the famous ride-a-camel stop (five-minute camel ride for a couple of euros). Any tour wraps up with lunch in a palatial Moroccan setting with live music (and non-Moroccan belly dancing), topped off by a final walk back to your boat through

a gauntlet of desperate merchants.

Sound cheesy? It is. But no amount of packaging can gloss over this exotic and different culture. This kind of cultural voyeurism is almost embarrassing, but it's nonstop action.

The day trip is so tightly organized that tourists have hardly any time alone in Tangier. For many people, that's just fine. But frankly, seeing a line of day-trippers clutching their bags nervously like paranoid kangaroos reminded me of a self-imposed hostage crisis. It was pathetic.

You rarely need to book a tour more than a day in advance, even during peak season. Tours generally cost about €60 (less than a round-trip ferry ticket alone—they make their money off commissions if you shop, and get a group rate on the ferry tickets). Prices are roughly the same no matter where you buy. While some agencies run their own tours, others simply sell tickets on excursions operated by the two big ferry companies, FRS and Comarit. If you're choosing between these two companies, the more-established FRS has a better reputation for tours than the cheaper, newer Comarit. But ultimately, it's the luck of the draw as to which guide you're assigned. Don't worry about which tour company you select. (They're all equally bad.)

Tours leave Tarifa on a variable schedule: For example, one tour may depart at 9:00 and return at 15:00, the next could run 11:00-19:00 (offering a longer experience), and the next 13:00-19:00. If you're an independent type on a one-day tour, you could stay with your group until you return to the ferry dock, and then just slip back into town on your own, thinking, "Freedom!" You're welcome to use your return ferry ticket on any later boat run by the same company (FRS or Comarit; each has departures every two hours).

You can pay extra for various add-ons. For an extra €15 per person beyond the cost of a standard tour, they will arrange a **"VIP tour"** for up to four people—you'll get a private guide and vehicle, plus lunch. This is actually quite economical, especially if you're traveling as a foursome and would prefer a more personalized experience.

If you want a longer visit, it's cheap to book a package through the ferry company that includes staying in a Tangier hotel for one night (only €30-35 more than the regular tour, €10 extra in peak season, includes guiding and 2 lunches and 1 dinner). If you stay overnight, the first day is the same as the one-day tour, but rather than catching the boat that afternoon, you take the same boat—on your own—24 hours later. There's also a two-day option that includes no guiding or meals (€25-30 more than regular tour, €12 extra in peak season).

Booking a Tour: If you're taking one of these tours, you may as well book direct with the **ferry company** (see contact information earlier, under "Ferry Crossing," or visit their offices at the port in Tarifa), or through your **hotel** (you'll pay the same, but the hotel gets a commission; if you know you want to visit Morocco with a tour, ask your hotel to book it when you reserve). There's not much reason to book with a **travel agency,** but offices all over southern Spain and in Tarifa sell ferry tickets and seats on tours. In Tarifa, Luís and Antonio at Baelo Tour offer my readers a 10 percent discount (daily in summer 7:40-21:00, across from TI at Avenida de la Constitución 5, tel. 956-681-242); other Tarifa-based agencies are Tarifa Travel and Travelsur (both on Avenida de Andalucía, above the old-town walls).

TANGIER

Tangier

Artists, writers, and musicians have always loved Tangier. Delacroix and Matisse were drawn by its evocative light. The Beat generation, led by William S. Burroughs and Jack Kerouac, sought the city's multicultural, otherworldly feel. Paul Bowles found his sheltering sky here. From the 1920s through the 1950s, Tangier was an "international city," too strategic to give to any one nation, and jointly governed by as many as nine different powers, including France, Spain, Britain, Italy, Belgium, the Netherlands...and Morocco. The city was a tax-free zone (since there was no single authority to collect taxes), which created a booming free-for-all atmosphere, attracting playboy millionaires, bon vivants, globe-trotting scoundrels, con artists, and expat romantics. Tangier enjoyed a cosmopolitan golden age that, in many ways, shaped the city visitors see today.

Tangier is always defying expectations. Ruled by Spain in the 19th century and France in the 20th, it's a rare place where signs are in three languages...and English doesn't make the cut. In this Muslim city, you'll find a synagogue, Catholic and Anglican churches, and the town's largest mosque in close proximity.

Because of its "international zone" status, Morocco's previous king effectively disowned the city, denying it national funds for improvements. Over time, neglected Tangier became the arm-

pit of Morocco. But when the new king—Mohammed VI—was crowned in 1999, the first city he visited was Tangier. His vision is to restore Tangier to its former glory. Prodding his countrymen with the slogan "Morocco is moving," he's nudging the country into the future.

Thanks to King Mohammed VI, Tangier (with a population of 700,000 and growing quickly) is experiencing a rebirth. While the city has a long way to go, restorations are taking place on a grand scale: The beach has been painstakingly cleaned, pedestrian promenades are popping up, and gardens bloom with lush new greenery. A brand-new futuristic soccer stadium opened in 2011, and the city-center port is being converted into a huge, slick leisure-craft complex that will handle cruise megaships, yachts, and ferries from Tarifa.

I'm uplifted by the new Tangier—it's affluent and modern without having abandoned its roots and embraced Western values. Many visitors are impressed by the warmth of the Moroccan people. Notice how they touch their right hand to their heart after shaking hands or saying, "thank you"—a kind gesture meant to emphasize sincerity. (In Islam, the right hand is holy, while the left hand is evil. Moroccans who eat with their hands—as many civilized people do in this part of the world—always eat with their right hand; the left hand is for washing.)

A visit to Morocco—so close to Europe, yet embracing the Arabic language and script and Muslim faith—lets a Westerner marinated in anti-Muslim propaganda see what Islam aspires to be and can be...and realize it is not a threat.

Planning Your Time

If you're not on a package tour, pre-arrange for a guide to meet you at the ferry dock (see "Guides," later), hire a guide upon arrival, or head on your own to the big square called the Grand Socco to get oriented (you can walk or catch a Petit Taxi from the port to the Grand Socco). Get your bearings with my Grand Socco spin-tour, then delve into the old town (the lower Medina, with the Petit Socco, market, and American Legation Museum; and the upper Medina's Kasbah, with its museum and residential lanes). With more time, take a taxi to sightsee along the beach and then along Avenue Mohammed VI, through the urban new town, and back to the port. You'll rarely see other tourists outside the tour-group circuit.

After Dark: Nighttime is great in Tangier. If you're spending the night, don't relax in a fancy hotel restaurant. Get out and about in the old town after dark. It's an entirely different experience and a highlight of any visit. (But remember, this isn't night-owl Spain—things die down by around 22:00.)

Orientation to Tangier

Like almost every city in Morocco, Tangier is split in two: old and new. From the ferry dock you'll see the old town (Medina)—encircled by its medieval wall—on your right, behind Hotel Continental. The old town has the markets, the Kasbah (with its palace and the mosque of the Kasbah—marked by the higher of the two minarets you see), cheap hotels, characteristic guest houses, homes both decrepit and recently renovated, and 2,000 wannabe guides. The twisty, hilly streets of the old town are caged within a wall accessible by keyhole gates. The larger minaret (on the left) belongs to the modern Mohammed

Tangier

STRAIT OF GIBRALTAR

BOATS TO SPAIN

TO CAPE SPARTEL

GUIDES, HUSTLERS & WAITING TOUR BUSES

PETIT & GRAND TAXIS

FERRY TERMINAL & CUSTOMS

KASBAH

OLD TOWN

TANGIER MEDINA PORT

PETIT SOCCO

RUE DE LA KASBAH

RUE D'ITALIE

AVE HASSAN I

JEMAA KABIR

RUE AS-SIAGHIN

PORT DE TANGER GATEWAY

GRAND SOCCO

RUE BOUARRAQUIA

AVE D'ESPAGNE

SEE OLD TOWN DETAIL MAP

RUE SIDI BOUABIB

TO MOHAMMAD V MOSQUE

MARKET

RUE DE PORTUGAL

FACTORY AREA

❼

RUE D'ANGLETERRE

RUE DE LA PLAGE

❺

RUE DE LA LIBERTE

NEW CITY

❻

STAIRS

KING MOHAMMAD VI

BEACH "PLAGE DE CORNICHE"

PLACE DE FRANCE

❽

ℹ️

BLVD PASTEUR

R. MARCO POLO

❷

❸

❶

TO TRAIN STN. & TANGIER MED PORT

RUE DE MEXIQUE

R. PRINCE

BLVD MOH BEN ABDELLAH

RUE AL-ANTAKI

100 YARDS

100 METERS

RUE MOULAN ABDALLAH

ALLAL

❹

👁 VIEW

❶ Rif & Spa Hotel
❷ Hotel Rembrandt
❸ Hotel El Djenina
❹ Hotel Andalucía
❺ Le Saveur du Poisson
❻ El Minzah Hotel & Rest.
❼ Le Fabrique Restaurant
❽ Place de Faro Viewpoint

V mosque—the biggest one in town.

The new town, with the TI and modern international-style hotels, sprawls past the industrial port zone to your left. The big square, Grand Socco, is the hinge between the old and new parts of town.

Note that while tourists (and this guidebook) refer to the twisty old town as "the Medina," locals consider both the old and new parts of the city center to be medinas.

Tangier is the fifth-largest city in Morocco, and many visitors assume they'll get lost here. While the city could use more street signs, it's laid out simply—although once you enter the mazelike Medina, all bets are off. Nothing listed under "Sights in Tangier" is more than a 20-minute walk from the port. Petit Taxis (described later, under "Getting Around Tangier") are a remarkably cheap godsend for the hot and tired tourist. Use them liberally.

Because so many different colonial powers have had a finger in this city, it goes by many names: In English, it's Tangier (or Tangiers); in French, Tanger (tahn-zhay); in Arabic, it's Tanja (TAHN-zhah); in Spanish, Tánger (TAHN-*h*air, with a guttural *h*); and so on. Unless you speak Arabic, French is the handiest second language, followed by Spanish and (finally) English.

Tourist Information

The TI, about a 15-minute gradual uphill walk from the Grand Socco, is not particularly helpful (English is in short supply, but a little French goes a long way). But at least you can pick up a free town brochure—in French only—with a town map (Mon-Fri 8:30-16:30, closed Sat-Sun, in new town at Boulevard Pasteur 29, tel. 0539-94-80-50). There's also a TI desk at the Tangier MED Port, and there may be one at the city-center Tangier Medina Port in the future.

The urban area around the Tangier TI has a few interesting features. The yellow building across the small street from the TI (toward the Grand Socco) is a synagogue. A block farther is the beautiful Place de Faro terrace, with its cannons and views back to Spain. (Nicknamed "Terrace of the Lazy Ones," this momentum-killing spot is usually lined with men relaxing and enjoying the views.) Beyond that, Rue de la Liberté leads directly into the Grand Socco square, the hub of old Tangier.

Arrival in Tangier

By Ferry

If you're taking a tour, just follow the leader. If you're on your own, you'll want to head for the Grand Socco to get oriented. You can either take a taxi (cheap) or walk (about 10 gently uphill minutes through the colorful but confusing lanes of the Medina). Note that the entire port area is slated for an extensive reconstruction in the coming years, so you may find some changes from the way things are described here.

A small blue **Petit Taxi** is your easiest way to get from the port into town (described later, under "Getting Around Tangier");

unfortunately, prices are not regulated from the port. An honest cabbie will charge you 10 dh (about $1.25) for a ride from the ferry into town; less scrupulous drivers will try to charge closer to 100 dh. Set your price before hopping in.

To **walk** into town, head out through the port entrance checkpoint (by the mosque) and bear left at the stubby wall, passing the big bus parking lot and the white Hotel Continental on your right-hand side. After a few minutes, at the end of the bus lot, look for a mosque's white minaret with green tile high on the hill, and head toward it by going up the street just beyond the long, high white wall (behind the buses). Go through the yellow gateway (Bab Dar Dbagh) marked *1921* and *1339*. Bear right/uphill at the T-intersection, then turn left/uphill on Rue de la Marine. You'll pass a school on the right, then the mosque with the green minaret on your left. Continue straight up to the café-lined Petit Socco square, then continue to the top of the street and turn left before the white gate to enter the Grand Socco. Leave mental breadcrumbs as you walk, so you can find your way back to your boat.

By Plane

The Tangier Airport (Aeroport Ibn Battouta) is very new-feeling, slick, and well-organized, with ATMs, cafés, and other amenities. Iberia, Royal Air Maroc, easyJet, and Ryanair fly from here to Madrid (easyJet also has a route to Paris). Jet4you, another low-cost airline, is based in Casablanca, but offers flights from Tangier to Barcelona and Brussels (www.jet4you.com). To get into downtown Tangier, taxis should run you about 150 dh and take 30-45 minutes.

Getting Around Tangier

There are two types of taxis: Avoid the big, beige Mercedes "Grand Taxis," which are the most aggressive and don't use their meters (they're designed for longer trips outside of the city center, but have been known to take tourists for a ride in town...in more ways than one). Look instead for Petit Taxis—blue with a yellow stripe (they fit up to three people). These generally use their meters, are very cheap, and only circulate within the city. However, at the port, Petit Taxis are allowed to charge whatever you'll pay without using the meter, so it's essential to agree on a price up front (see "Arrival in Tangier," earlier).

Be aware that Tangier taxis "double up"—if you're headed somewhere, the driver may pick up someone else who's going in the same direction. However, in this case you don't get to split the fare—each of you pays full price (even though sometimes the other passenger's route takes you a bit out of your way).

Helpful Hints

Money: The exchange rate is 8 dh = about $1; 11 dh = about €1. While most businesses happily take euros or dollars, it's classier to use the local currency—and you'll save money. If you're on a tour, they'll rip you off anyway, so just stick with euros. If you're on your own, it's fun to get a pocket full of dirhams.

A few ATMs are around the Grand Socco (look for one just to the left of the archway entrance into the Medina); more are opposite the TI along Boulevard Pasteur. ATMs work as you expect them to. Exchange desks are quick, easy, and fair. (Just understand the buy-and-sell rates—there should be no other fee. If you change €50 into dirhams and immediately change the dirhams back, you should have about €45.) Look for the official *Bureaux de Change* offices, where you'll get better rates than at the banks. There are some on Rue Pasteur, and a handful between the Grand and Petit Soccos. The official change offices all offer the same rates, so there's no need to shop around.

Convert your dirhams back to euros before catching the ferry—it's cheap and easy to do here (change desks at the port keep long hours), but very difficult once you're back in Spain.

Telephone: To call Tangier from Spain, dial 00 (Europe's international access code), 212 (Morocco's country code), then the local number (dropping the initial zero). To dial Tangier from elsewhere in Morocco, dial the local number in full (keeping the initial zero).

Navigation: Tangier's maps and street signs are frustrating. I ask in French for the landmark: *Où est...?* ("Where is...?," pronounced oo ay, as in *"oo ay Medina?"* or *"oo ay Kasbah?"*). It can be fun to meet people this way. However, most people who offer to help you (especially those who approach you) are angling for a tip—young and old, locals see dollar signs when a traveler approaches. To avoid getting unwanted company, ask for directions only from people who can't leave what they're doing (such as the only clerk in a shop) or from women who aren't near men. There are fewer hustlers in the new (but less interesting) part of town. Be aware that most people don't know the names of the smaller streets (which don't usually have signs), and tend to navigate by landmarks. In case you get the wrong directions, ask three times and go with the consensus. If there's no consensus, it's time to hop into a Petit Taxi.

Mosques: Tangier's mosques (and virtually all of Morocco's) are closed to non-Muslim visitors.

Women in Morocco

Most visitors to Tangier expect to see the women completely covered head-to-toe by their kaftan. In fact, only about one-

quarter of Moroccan women still adhere strictly to this religious code. Some just cover their head (allowing their face to be seen), while others eliminate the head scarf altogether. Some women wear only Western-style clothing. This change in dress visibly reflects deeper, more fundamental shifts in Moroccan attitudes about women's rights.

Morocco happens to be one of the most progressive Muslim countries around. As in any border country, contact with other cultures fosters the growth of new ideas. Bombarded with Spanish television and visitors like you, change is inevitable. Another proponent of change is King Mohammed VI, who was only 35 years old when he rose to the throne in 1999. For the first time in the country's history, the king personally selected a female adviser to demonstrate his commitment to change. The king also married a commoner for...get this...*love*. And even more shocking, she's seen in public. (It's a first—locals don't even know what King Mohammed VI's mother looks like, as she is never in the public view.)

Recent times have brought even more sweeping transformations to Moroccan society. In order to raise literacy levels and understanding between the sexes, schools are now co-ed—something taken for granted in the West for decades. In 2004, the Mudawana, or judiciary family code, was shockingly overhauled. The legal age for women to marry is now 18 (just like men) instead of 15. Other changes make it more difficult to have a second wife. Verbal divorce and abandonment are no longer legal—disgruntled husbands must now take their complaints to court before divorce is granted. And for the first time, women can divorce their husbands. If children are involved, whoever takes care of the kids gets the house. Of course, not everyone has been happy with the changes, and Islamic fundamentalists were blamed for a series of bombings in Casablanca in 2003. But the reforms became law, and Morocco became a trendsetter for women's equality in the Islamic world.

Guides

If you're on your own, you'll be to street guides what a horse's tail is to flies...all day long. Seriously—it can be exhausting to constantly deflect come-ons from anyone who sees you open a guidebook. In order to have your own translator, and a shield from less scrupulous touts who hit up tourists constantly throughout the old town, I recommend hiring a guide. Stress your interest in the people and culture rather than shopping. Guides, hoping

to get a huge commission from your purchases, can cleverly turn your Tangier day into the Moroccan equivalent of the Shopping Channel. Truth be told, some of these guides would work for free, considering all the money they make on commissions when you buy stuff.

I've worked with a variety of guides who speak great English, are easy to get along with, will meet you at the ferry dock, and charge fixed rates. They've promised me they won't make you do any more shopping than you want to—so be very clear about your interests. If one of these guides is busy (or takes a long time responding to your email), try the others. Any of these guides will make your Tangier experience more enjoyable for a negligible cost. They can also book your ferry tickets for the same cost as booking direct: They'll give you a reference number to give at the ticket office in Tarifa, then you'll pay them for the tickets when you meet in Tangier. While each has their own specific itineraries, the two basic options are more or less the same: a half-day walking tour around the Medina and Kasbah (generally 3-5 hours); or a full-day "grand tour" that includes the walk around town as well as a mini-bus ride to outlying viewpoints—the Caves of Hercules and Cape Spartel (7-8 hours, generally also includes lunch at your expense in a restaurant the guide suggests). Prices are fairly standard from guide to guide. If you're very pleased with your guide, he'll appreciate a tip.

Aziz Begdouri, who enjoys teaching about Moroccan society and culture, has been a big help to me with my guidebook-writing and TV production in Tangier (half-day walking tour-€15/person, groups limited to 4-5 people; 8-hour grand tour-€35/person; mobile 06-6163-9332, from Spain dial 00-212-6-6163-9332, aziz tour@hotmail.com).

Ahmed Taoumi, who has been guiding for more than 30 years, is a great teacher—almost professorial—but also a good storyteller and fun to be around. He takes pride in tailoring his tours to his customers' interest (half-day walking tour–€18/person, full-day grand tour with minibus–€35/person, also offers minibus side-trips to nearby destinations and discounted ferry tickets, mobile 06-6166-5429, from Spain dial 00-212-6-6166-5429, www .visitangier.com, taoumitour@hotmail.com,).

If Aziz Begdouri and Ahmed are both busy, consider one of the following youthful go-getters who are a bit lighter on information, but enjoyable to spend time with and dedicated to making visitors comfortable: **Aziz Benami** (half-day walking tour–€15/person; all-day minibus and walking tour–€79/person, price includes ferry tickets from Spain; mobile 06-6126-3335, from Spain dial 00-212-6-6126-3335, www.tangierprivateguide.com, info@tangier privateguide.com) and **Abdellatif ("Latif") Chebaa** (half-day walking tour–€15/person, grand tour–€35/person, mobile 06-6107-2014, from Spain dial 00-212-6-6107-2014, visittangier@gmail .com).

Other Options: If you don't want to plan too far ahead, and any guide will do, you can book a **"VIP" tour** through the ferry companies in Tarifa for approximately the same prices listed above. I've also had good luck with the **private guides who meet the boat.** If you're a decent judge of character, try interviewing guides when you get off the ferry to find one you click with, then negotiate a good price. These hardworking, English-speaking, and licensed guides offer their services for the day for €15.

Sights in Tangier

▲▲The Grand Socco

This big, bustling square is a transportation hub, market, popular meeting point, and the fulcrum between the new town and the old town (Medina). Five years ago, it was a pedestrian nightmare and a perpetual traffic jam. But now, like much of Tangier, it's on the rise. Many of the sights mentioned in this spin-tour are described in more detail later in this chapter.

❷ Self-Guided Spin Tour: The Grand Socco is a good place to get oriented to the heart of Tangier. Stand on the square between the fountain and the mosque (the long building with arches and the tall tower). We'll do a slow clockwise spin.

Start by facing the **mosque**—newly remodeled with a long arcade of keyhole arches, and with a colorfully tiled minaret. Morocco is a decidedly Muslim nation, though its take on Islam

Tangier's Old Town

NOTE:
TANGIER'S OLD TOWN (MEDINA) IS A MAZE OF TINY STREETS. ONLY MAJOR STREETS ARE SHOWN.

TO CAPE SPARTEL

KASBAH GATE

PLACE DU TABOR

RUE TABOR

RUE DE LA KASBAH

R. RIAD

TOWN SULTAN

Museum

WALLS

STRAIT OF GIBRALTAR

100 YARDS
100 METERS

N

View

KASBAH

PLACE DE LA KASBAH

TO PORT

R. JEN. CAPTAN RAISOULI

OLD

RUE D'ITALIE

RUE AL MANZOR

GERMAN GRAVES

MENDOUBIA GARDENS

Gate

R. BOUARRAQUIA

SIDI BOUABIB
Mosque

D'ANGLETERRE

RUE DE LA LIBERTE

DCH

GRAND SOCCO

RUE AS-SIAGHIN

RUE TOUAHINE

PETIT SOCCO

TOWN

RUE DE LA PLAGE

ALMOHADES

TORRES

DAR EL BAROUD

BAB EL-MARSA (GATE)

JEMAA EL-KEBIR
Mosque

MOKHTAR AHARDANI

PORT DE TANGER GATEWAY

RUE DE PORTUGAL

JEWISH CEMETERY

TO BEACH PROMENADE & TANGIER MED PORT

N E W   T O W N

❶ Dar Chams Tanja	❾ Le Nabab Restaurant
❷ La Maison Blanche	❿ Hamadi Restaurant
❸ La Tangerina	⓫ Marhaba Palace Restaurant
❹ Dar Nour	⓬ Mamounia Palace Rest.
❺ Dar Sultan	⓭ Tangier American Legation Mus.
❻ Hotel Continental	⓮ Cinema Rif
❼ Maison Communitaire des Femmes (Café)	⓯ Anglican Church
❽ Le Salon Bleu Restaurant	⓰ Market
	⓱ Bureau de Change

TANGIER

is progressive, likely owing to the country's crossroads history. For example, women are relatively free to dress as they like. Five times a day, you'll hear the call to prayer echo across the rooftops of Tangier, from minarets like this one. Unlike many Muslim countries, Morocco doesn't allow non-Muslims to enter its mosques (with the exception of its biggest and most famous one, in Casablanca). This custom may have originated decades ago, when occupying French foreign legion troops spent the night in a mosque, entertaining themselves with wine and women. Following this embarrassing desecration, it was the French government—not the Moroccans—who instituted the ban that persists today.

Locals say that in this very cosmopolitan city, anytime you see a mosque, you'll find a church nearby. Sure enough, peeking up behind the mosque, you can barely make out the white, crenellated top of the **Anglican Church**'s tower (or at least the English flag above it—a red cross on a white field). A fascinating architectural hybrid of Muslim and Christian architecture, this house of worship is well worth a visit.

Also behind the mosque, you can see parts of a sprawling **market.** (This features mostly modern goods; the far more colorful produce, meat, and fish market is across the square.) Those market stalls used to fill the square you're standing in; traditionally the Grand Socco was Tangier's hub for visiting merchants. The gates of town would be locked each evening, and vendors who did not arrive in time spent the night in this area. (Nearby were many caravanserai, old-fashioned inns.) But a few years ago, this square was dramatically renovated by the visionary king, Mohammed VI, and given a new name: "April 9th Square," commemorating the date in 1947 when an earlier king, Mohammed V, appealed to his French overlords to grant his country its independence. (France eventually complied, peacefully, in 1956.) In just the last few years, Mohammed VI tamed the traffic, added the fountain you're standing next to (there was never a fountain here before), and turned this into a delightfully people-friendly space.

Spin a few more degrees to the right, where you'll see the crenellated gateway marked *Tribunal de Commerce*—the entrance to the **Mendoubia Garden,** a pleasant park with a gigantic tree and a quirky history that reflects the epic story of Tangier (particularly from the 1920s to the 1950s, when multiple foreign powers shared control of this city). At the top of the garden gateway, notice the Moroccan flag: a green five-pointed star on a red field.

The five points of the star represent the five pillars of Islam; green is the color of peace; and red represents the struggles of hard-fought Moroccan history.

Spinning farther right, you'll see the **keyhole arch** marking the entrance to the Medina. (If you need cash, notice the exchange booths and ATM just to the left of this gateway.) To reach the heart of the Medina—the Petit Socco (the café-lined little brother of the square you're on now)—go through this arch and take the first right.

In front of the arch, you'll likely see **day laborers** looking for work. Each one stands next to a symbol of the kind of work he specializes in: a bucket of paintbrushes for a painter, a coil of wiring for an electrician, and a loop of hose for a plumber.

Speaking of people looking for work, how many locals have offered to show you around ("Hey! What you looking for? I help you!") since you've been standing here, holding this guidebook? Get used to it. While irritating, it's understandable. To these very poor people, you're impossibly rich—your pocket change is at least a good day's wage. If someone pesters you, you can simply ignore them, or say *"Lah shokran"* (No, thank you). But be warned: The moment you engage them, you've just prolonged the sales pitch.

Back to our spin-tour: To the right of the main arch, and just before the row of green rooftops, is the low-profile entrance to the **market** *(souk)*. A barrage on all the senses, this is a fascinating place to explore. The row of green rooftops leads toward Rue de la Plage, with more market action.

Continue spinning another quarter-turn to the tall, white building at the top of the square labeled **Cinema Rif.** This historic movie house still plays films (in Arabic and French). The street to the left of the cinema takes you to Rue de la Liberté, which eventually leads through the modern town to the TI (about a 15-minute walk). Just to the right of the cinema, notice the yellow terrace, which offers the best view over the Grand Socco (just go up the staircase). It's also part of a café, where you can order a Moroccan tea (green tea, fresh mint, and lots of sugar), enjoy the view over the square, and plot your next move.

Near the Grand Socco

These sights are near the Grand Socco, but still outside the Medina (old town).

▲**Anglican Church**—St. Andrew's Anglican Church, tucked behind a showpiece mosque, embodies Tangier's mingling of Muslim and Christian tradition. The land on which the church sits was a gift from the sultan to the British community in 1881, during Queen Victoria's era. Shortly thereafter, this church was built. Although fully Christian, the church is designed in the style of a Muslim mosque. The Lord's Prayer rings the arch in Arabic, as verses of the Quran would in a mosque. Knock on the door—Ali or his son Yassin will greet you and give you a "thank you very much" tour (a

tip of about 20 dh is appreciated; daily 9:00-18:00 except closed during Sunday services). The garden surrounding the church is a tranquil, parklike cemetery.

Mendoubia Garden—This pleasant park, through the castle-like archway off of the Grand Socco, is a favorite place for locals to

hang out, but also has a surprising history. Walk through the gateway to see the trunk of a gigantic banyan tree, which, according to local legend, dates from the 12th century. Notice how the extra supportive roots have grown from the branches down to the ground. The large building to the left—today the business courthouse (*Tribunal de Commerce*)—was built to house the representative of the Moroccan king, back in the early 20th century when Tangier was ruled as a protectorate of various European powers and needed an ambassador of sorts to keep an eye out for Moroccan interests. The smaller house on the right (behind the giant tree) is currently the marriage courthouse (used exclusively for getting married or divorced), but it was once the headquarters of the German delegation in Tangier. France originally kept Germany out of the protectorate arrangement by giving them the Congo. But in 1941, when Germany was on the rise in Europe and allied with Spain's Franco, it joined the mix of ruling powers in Tangier. Although Germans were only here for a short time (until mid-1942), they had a small cemetery in what's now the big park in front of you. If you go up the stairs and around the blocky Arabic monument, at the bases of the trees beyond it you'll find headstones of German graves...an odd footnote in the very complex history of this intriguing city.

The Medina (Old Town)

Tangier's Medina is its convoluted old town—a twisty mess of narrow stepped lanes, dead-end alleys, and lots of local life spilling out into the streets. It's divided roughly into two parts: the lower Medina, with the Petit Socco, market, American Legation, and bustling street life; and, at the top, the more tranquil Kasbah.

The Lower Medina and Petit Socco

A maze of winding lanes and tiny alleys weave through the old-town market area.

Petit Socco—This little square, also called Souk Dahel ("Inner Market"), is the center of the lower Medina. Lined with tea shops and cafés, it has a romantic quality that has long made it a people magnet. In the 1920s, it was the meeting point for Tangier's wealthy and influential elite; by the 1950s and '60s, it drew Jack Kerouac and his counterculture buddies. Nursing a coffee or a mint tea here, it's easy to pretend you're a Beat Generation rebel, dropping out from Western society and delving deeply into an exotic, faraway culture. More recently, filmmakers have been drawn here. Scenes from both *The Bourne Ultimatum* and *Inception* were filmed on the streets between the Grand and Petit Soccos.

The Petit Socco is ideal for some casual people-watching over a drink. You can go to one of the more traditional cafés, but Café Central—with the modern awning—is the most accessible, and therefore the most commercialized and touristy (7-12-dh coffee drinks, 20-45-dh meals, daily 6:00-24:00).

▲▲Market (Souk)—The Medina's market, just off the Grand Socco, is a highlight. Wander past piles of fruit, veggies, and olives, countless varieties of bread, and fresh goat cheese wrapped in palm leaves. Phew! You'll find everything but pork.

Entering the market through the door from the Grand Socco, turn right to find butchers, a cornucopia of produce (almost all of it from Morocco), more butchers, piles of olives, and yet more butchers. The chickens are plucked and hung to show they have been killed according to Islamic guidelines (Halal): Animals are slaughtered with a sharp knife in the name of Allah, head to Mecca, and drained of their blood. The far aisle (parallel and to the left of where you're walking) has more innards and is a little harder to stomach.

You'll see women vendors wearing straw hats decorated with ribbons, and often also striped skirts, scattered around the mar-

Bargaining Basics

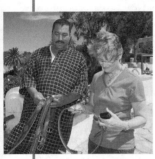

No matter what kind of merchandise you buy in Tangier, the shopping is...Moroccan. Bargain hard! The first price you're offered is simply a starting point, and it's expected that you'll try to talk the price way down. Bargaining can become an enjoyable game if you follow a few basic rules:

Determine what the item is worth to you. Before you even ask a price, decide what the item's value is to you. Consider the hassles involved in packing it or shipping it home.

Determine the merchant's lowest price. Many merchants will settle for a nickel profit rather than lose the sale entirely. Work the cost down to rock bottom, and when it seems to have fallen to a record low, walk away. That last price the seller hollers out as you turn the corner is often the best price you'll get. If the price is right, go back and buy.

Look indifferent. As soon as the merchant perceives the "I gotta have that!" in you, you'll never get the best price.

Employ a third person. Use your friend who is worried about the ever-dwindling budget or who doesn't like the price or who is bored and wants to return to the hotel. This trick can work to bring the price down faster.

Show the merchant your money. Physically hold out your money and offer him "all you have" to pay for whatever you are bickering over. He'll be tempted to just grab your money and say, "Oh, OK."

If the price is too much, leave. Never worry about having taken too much of the merchant's time. They are experts at making the tourist feel guilty for not buying. It's all part of the game.

ket; these are Berbers from the nearby Rif mountains. (Before taking photos of these women, or any people you see here, it's polite to ask permission.)

Eventually you'll emerge into the large white market of fish-sellers; with the day's catch from both the Mediterranean and the Atlantic, this is like a textbook of marine life. The door at the far end of the fish market pops you out on the Rue Salah El-dine Al Ayoubi; a right turn takes you back to the Grand Socco, but a left turn leads to the (figurative and literal) low end of the market—a world of very rustic market stalls under a corrugated plastic roof. While just a block from the main market, this is a world apart, and not to everyone's taste. Here you'll find cheap produce, junk shops, electronics (such as recordable CDs and old remote controls), old ladies sorting bundles of herbs from crinkled plastic bags, and far less sanitary-looking butchers than the ones inside the main market hall (if that's possible). Peer down the alley filled with a twitching poultry market, which encourages vegetarianism.

The upper part of the market (toward the Medina and Petit Socco) has a few food stands, but more non-perishable items, such as clothing, cleaning supplies, toiletries, and prepared foods. Scattered around this part of the market are spice and herb stalls (usually marked *hérboriste*), offering a fragrant antidote to the meat stalls. In addition to cooking spices, these sell homegrown Berber cures for ailments. Pots hold a dark-green gelatinous goo—a kind of natural soap.

If you're looking for souvenirs, you won't have to find them... they'll find you, in the form of aggressive salesmen who approach you on the street and push their conga drums, T-shirts, and other trinkets in your face. Most of the market itself is more focused on locals, but the Medina streets just above the market are loaded with souvenir shops. Aside from the predictable trinkets, the big-ticket items here are tilework (such as vases) and carpets. You'll notice many shops have tiles and other, smaller souvenirs on the ground floor, and carpet salesrooms upstairs.

▲▲▲**Exploring the Medina**—Appealing as the market is, one of the most evocative Tangier experiences is to simply lose yourself in the lanes of the Medina. A first-time visitor cannot stay oriented—so don't even try. I just wander, knowing that uphill will eventually get me to the Kasbah and downhill will eventually lead me to the port. Expect to get a little lost...going around in circles is part of the fun. Pop in to see artisans working in their shops: mosaic

tile-makers, thread spinners, tailors. While shops are on the ground level, the family usually lives upstairs.

Many people can't afford private ovens, phones, or running water, so there are economical communal options: phone desks (called *telebou-tiques*), baths, and bakeries. If you smell the aroma of baking bread, look for a hole-in-the-wall bakery, where locals drop off their ready-to-cook dough (as well as meat, fish, or nuts to roast). You'll also stumble upon communal taps, with water provided by the government, where people come to wash. Cubby-hole rooms are filled with kids playing video games on old TVs—they can't afford their own at home, so they come here instead.

Go on a photo safari for ornate "keyhole" doors, many of which lead to neighborhood mosques. Green doors are the color of Islam and symbolize peace. The ring-shaped door knockers double as a place to hitch a donkey.

As you explore, notice that some parts of the Medina seem starkly different, with fancy wrought-iron balconies. This is the approximately 20 percent of the town that was built and controlled by Spaniards and Portuguese living here (with the rest being Arabic and Berber). The two populations were separated by a wall, the remains of which you can still trace running through the Medina. It may seem at first glance that these European zones are fancier and "nicer" compared to the poorer-seeming Arabic/Berber zones. But the Arabs and Berbers take more care with the inside of their homes—if you went behind these hum-

ble walls, you'd be surprised how pleasant the interiors are. While European cultures externalize resources, Arab and Berber cultures internalize them.

Tangier American Legation Museum—Located at the bottom end of the Medina (just above the port), this unexpected museum

is worth a visit. Morocco was one of the first countries to recognize the newly formed United States as an independent country (in 1777). The original building, given to the United States by the sultan of Morocco, became the fledgling government's first foreign acquisition. This was the US embassy (or consulate) in Morocco from 1821 to 1961, and it's still American property—our only National Historic Landmark overseas. Today this nonprofit museum and research center, housed in a 19th-century mansion, is a strangely peaceful oasis within Tangier's intense old town. It offers a warm welcome and lots of interesting artifacts—all well-described in English in an evocative building. The ground floor is filled with an art gallery. In the stairwell, you'll see photos of kings with presidents, and a letter with the news of Lincoln's assassination. Upstairs are more paintings, as well as model soldiers playing out two battle scenes from Moroccan history. These belonged to American industrialist Malcolm Forbes, who had a home in Tangier (his son donated these dioramas to the museum). Rounding out the upper floor are more paintings, and evocative old maps of Tangier and Morocco. A visit here is a fun reminder of how long the US and Morocco have had good relations (free entry but donations appreciated, Mon-Thu 10:00-13:00 & 15:00-17:00, Fri 10:00-12:00 & 15:00-17:00, during Ramadan holiday 10:00-15:00, closed Sat-Sun, ring bell, Rue d'Amérique 8, tel. 0539-935-317, www.legation.org).

• *When you've soaked in enough old-town atmosphere, make your way to the Kasbah (see map). Within the Medina, head uphill, or exit the Medina gate and go right on Rue de la Kasbah, which follows the old wall uphill to Bab Kasbah (a.k.a. Porte de la Kasbah), a gateway into the Kasbah.*

Kasbah

Loosely translated as "fortress," a *kasbah* is an enclosed, protected residential area near a castle that you'll find in hundreds of Moroccan towns. Originally this was a place where a king or other leader could protect his tribe. Tangier's Kasbah comprises the upper quarter of the old town. A residential area with twisty lanes and some nice guest houses, this area is a bit more sedate and less claustrophobic than parts of the Medina near the market below.

▲**Kasbah Museum**—On Place de la Kasbah, you'll find the Dar el-Makhzen, a former sultan's palace that now houses a history

museum with a few historical artifacts. While there's not a word of English, some of the exhibits are still easy to appreciate, and the building itself is beautiful. Most of the exhibits surround the central, open-air courtyard; rooms proceed roughly chronologically as you move counter-clockwise, from early hunters and farmers to prehistoric civilizations, Roman times, the region's conversion to Islam, and the influence of European powers. The two-story space at the far end of the courtyard focuses on a second-century mosaic floor depicting the journey of Venus. The big 12th-century wall-size map (in Arabic) shows the Moorish view of the world: with Africa on top (Spain is at the far right). Nearby is an explanation of terra-cotta production (a local industry), and upstairs is an exhibit on funerary rituals. Near the entrance, look for signs to *jardin* and climb the stairs to reach a chirpy (if slightly overgrown) garden courtyard. While the building features some striking tilework, you just can't shake the feeling that the best Moorish sights are back in Spain.

Cost and Hours: 10 dh, Wed-Mon 9:00-16:00, closed for prayer Fri 12:30-14:30, closed all day Tue, tel. 0539-932-097.

Place de la Kasbah—Because the Kasbah Museum (while modest) is the city's main museum, the square in front of the palace

attracts more than its share of tourists. That means it's also a vivid gauntlet of amusements waiting to ambush parading tour groups: snake charmers, squawky dance troupes, and colorful water vendors. These colorful Kodak-moment hustlers make their living off the many tour groups passing by daily. (As you're cajoled, remember that the daily minimum wage here for

men as skilled as these beggars is $10. That's what the gardeners you'll pass in your walk earn each day. In other words, a €1 tip is an hour's wage for these people.) If you draft behind a tour group, you won't be the focus of the hustlers. But if you take a photo, you must pay.

Before descending out of the Kasbah, don't miss the ocean viewpoint—as you stand in the square and face the palace, look to the right to find the hole carved through the thick city wall (Bab Dhar, "Sea Gate"). This leads out to a large natural terrace with fine views over the port, the Mediterranean, and Spain.

The lower gate of the Kasbah (as you stand in Place de la Kasbah facing the palace, it's on your left) leads to a charming little alcove, between the gates, where you can see a particularly fine tile fountain: The top part is carved cedarwood, below that is carved plaster, and the bottom half is

hand-laid tiles. In this area, poke down the tiny lane to the left of the little shop—you'll find that it leads to a surprisingly large courtyard ringed by fine homes.

Matisse Route—The artist Matisse, who traveled to Tangier in 1912, was inspired by his wanderings through this area, picking up themes that show up in much of his art. The diamond-shaped stones embedded in the street (you'll see them on the narrow lane leading up along the left side of the palace) mark a "Matisse

Route" through the Kasbah, from the lower gate to the upper; those familiar with his works will recognize several scenes along this stretch.

Tangier Beach
(Plage de Corniche, a.k.a. Playa)

Lined with lots of fishy eateries and entertaining nightclubs, this fine, wide, white-sand crescent beach stretches eastward from the port. The locals call it by the Spanish word *playa*. It's packed with locals doing what people around the world do at the beach—with a few variations. Traditionally clad moms let their kids run wild. Along with lazy camels, you'll see people—young and old—covered in hot sand to combat rheumatism. Early, late,

and off-season, the beach becomes a popular venue for soccer teams. The palm-lined pedestrian street along the waterfront was renamed for King Mohammed VI, in appreciation for recent restorations. While the beach is cleaner than it once was, it still has more than its share of litter—great for a stroll, but maybe not for sunbathing or swimming. If you have a beach break in mind, do it on Spain's Costa del Sol.

Just past the beach on the port side (between here and the Medina) is a zone of nondescript factories. Here local women sew clothing for big, mostly European companies that pay about $8 a day. Each morning and evening rush hour, the street is filled with these women commuters...on foot.

Nightlife in Tangier

Most important: Be out in the **Medina** around 21:00. In the cool of the evening, the atmospheric squares and lanes become even more evocative. Then at about 22:00 things get dark, lonely, and foreboding.

El Minzah Hotel hosts **traditional music** most nights for those having dinner there (see "Eating in Tangier," later; 85 Rue de la Liberté, tel. 0539-935-885).

The **Rif Cinema,** the landmark theater at the top of the Grand Socco, shows movies in French—which the younger generation must learn—and Arabic. The cinema is worth popping into, if only to see the Art Deco interior. As movies cost only 20 dh, consider dropping by to see a bit of whatever's on...in Arabic (closed Mon, tel. 0539-934-683).

Sleeping in Tangier

I've recommended two vastly different types of accommodations in Tangier: cozy Moroccan-style (but mostly French-run) guest houses in the maze of lanes of the Kasbah neighborhood, at the top of the Medina (old town); and big, modern international-style hotels in the urban-feeling new town, a 10-to-20-minute walk from the central sights.

Remember, if you want to call Tangier from Europe, dial 00 (Europe's international access code), 212 (Morocco's country code), then the local number (dropping the initial zero). June through mid-September is high season, when rooms may be a bit more expensive and reservations are wise. Most hotels charge an extra tax of 15-25 dh per person per night (typically not included in the prices I've listed here).

Moroccan-Style Guest Houses in the Kasbah

In Arabic, *dar* means "guest house." You'll find these in the Medina, or atmospheric old quarter. While the lower part of the Medina is dominated by market stalls and tourist traps, and can feel a bit seedy after dark, the upper part (called the Kasbah, for the castle that dominates this area) is more tranquil and feels very residential. All of these are buried in a labyrinth of lanes that can be very difficult to navigate; the map on page 286 gives you a vague sense of where to go, but it's essential to ask for very clear directions when you reserve. If you're hiring a guide in Tangier, ask them to help you find your *dar*. (If you're on your own, you can try asking directions when you arrive—but many local residents

---

Sleep Code

(8 dh = about $1, country code: 212, area code: 539)
S = Single, **D** = Double/Twin, **T** = Triple, **Q** = Quad, **b** = bathroom, **s** = shower only. Unless otherwise noted, credit cards are accepted, English is spoken, and breakfast is included.

To help you easily sort through these listings, I've divided the accommodations into three categories, based on the price for a standard double room with bath (during high season):

  $$$ **Higher Priced**—Most rooms 1,000 dh or more.
    $$ **Moderately Priced**—Most rooms between 500-1,000 dh.
      $ **Lower Priced**—Most rooms 500 dh or less.

Prices can change without notice; verify the hotel's current rates online or by email. For other updates, see www.ricksteves.com/update.

take that as an invitation to tag along and hound you for tips.) All of these are in traditional old houses, with rooms surrounding a courtyard atrium, and all have rooftop terraces where you can relax and enjoy sweeping views over Tangier. There are rarely stand-alone showers; instead, in Moroccan style, you'll find a handheld shower in a corner of the bathroom.

$$$ Dar Chams Tanja, just below the Kasbah gate, has seven elegant, new-feeling rooms with all the comforts surrounding a clean-white inner courtyard with lots of keyhole windows. While pricey, it's impeccably decorated, calm, and stylish (five big Db-1,580 dh, two small Db-1,240 dh, sometimes discounts in slow times—check website, air-con, free Wi-Fi, hammam—Turkish-style bath, massage service, Rue Jnan Kabtan 2, tel. 0539-332-323, www.darchamstanja.com, darchamstanja@gmail.com).

$$$ La Maison Blanche ("The White House"), run by tour guide Aziz Begdouri, has nine rooms in a traditional Moroccan house with modern amenities in the Kasbah (Sb-1,000 dh, Db-1,100 dh, all with bathtubs, air-con, free Wi-Fi, just inside the upper gate of the Kasbah at Rue Ahmed Ben Ajiba 2, tel. 0539-373-545, www.lamaisonblanchetanger.com, info@ lamaison blanchetanger.com).

$$ La Tangerina, run by Jürgen (who's German) and his Moroccan wife Farida, has 10 comfortable rooms that look down into a shared atrium. At the top is a gorgeous rooftop seaview balcony (Db-600-935 dh in April and June-mid-Sept, otherwise Db-500-770; suite-1,520-1,650 dh in April and June-mid-Sept, otherwise 1,100-1,320 dh; prices depend on size and include tax, cash only, free Wi-Fi, wood-fired hammam, Riad Sultan 19, tel. 0539-947-731, www.lantangerina.com, info@latangerina.com).

$$ Dar Nour, run with funky French style by Philippe, Jean-Olivier, and Catherine, has an "Escher-esque" floor plan that sprawls through five interconnected houses (it's "labyrinthine like the Medina," says Philippe). The 10 homey rooms feel very tradi-tional, with lots of books and lounging areas spread throughout (Db-735 dh, junior suite Db-970 dh, suite Db-1,330 dh, cash only, free Wi-Fi in lobby, Rue Gourna 20, mobile 06-6211-2724, www .darnour.com, contactdarnour@yahoo.fr).

$$ Dar Sultan rents six romantically decorated rooms on a pleasant street in the heart of the Kasbah (Db-990 dh, larger Db-1,210 dh, Db with terrace-1,320 dh, free Wi-Fi in lobby and cable Internet in rooms, Rue Touila 49, tel. 0539-336-061, www .darsultan.com, dar-sultan@menara.ma).

Modern Hotels in the Modern City

These hotels are centrally located, near the TI, and within walking distance of the Grand Socco, Medina, and market. The first two are three-star hotels and take credit cards; the others are cash-only.

$$$ Rif & Spa Hotel, recently restored to its 1970s glamour, is a worthy splurge. Offering 127 plush, modern rooms, sprawling public spaces, a garden, a pool, and grand views, it feels like an oversized boutique hotel. The great Arabic lounge—named for Winston Churchill—with a harbor view compels you to relax (Sb-1,200 dh, Db-1,400 dh, 200-dh more July-Aug, 200-dh extra for sea view, see website for specials, breakfast-100 dh, air-con, elevator, free Wi-Fi in lobby, 3 restaurants, spa and sauna, Avenue Mohammed VI 152, tel. 0539-349-300, fax 0539-944-569, www.hotelsatlas.com, riftanger@menara.ma).

$$ Hotel Rembrandt feels just like the 1940s, with a restaurant, a bar, and a swimming pool surrounded by a great grassy garden. Its 70 rooms are outdated and simple, but clean and comfortable, and some come with views (Sb-450-550 dh, Db-600-710 dh, higher prices are for June-Aug, sea view-100 dh extra, includes tax, breakfast often included, otherwise-80 dh, air-con, elevator, free Wi-Fi, a 5-minute walk above the beach in a busy urban zone at Boulevard Mohammed VI 1, tel. 0539-937-870, fax 0539-930-443, www.hotel-rembrandt.com, hotelrembrandt@menara.ma).

$$ Hotel Continental—actually in the Medina (at the bottom of the old town, facing the port)—is the Humphrey Bogart option, a grand old place sprawling along the old town. It has lavish, atmospheric, and recently renovated public spaces, a chandeliered breakfast room, and 70 spacious bedrooms with rough hardwood floors and new bathrooms. Jimmy, who's always around and runs the shop adjacent to the lobby, says he offers everything but Viagra. When I said, "I'm from Seattle," he said, "206." Test him—he knows your area code (Sb-495 dh, Db-635 dh, about 100 dh more July-Sept, includes tax and breakfast, free Wi-Fi, Dar Baroud 36, tel. 0539-931-024, fax 0539-931-143, hcontinental@iam.net.ma). This hotel's terrace aches with nostalgia. Back during the city's glory days, a ferry connected Tangier and New York. American novelists would sit out on the terrace of Hotel Continental, never quite sure when their friends' boat would arrive from across the sea...

$ Hotel El Djenina is a local-style business-class hotel—extremely plain, reliable, safe, and well-located. Its 40 rooms are a block off the harbor, midway between the port and the TI. Request a room on the back side to escape the street noise (Sb-319-357 dh, Db-382-463 dh, higher prices are for mid-May-Sept, cash only, no breakfast, no air-con, elevator, free Wi-Fi, tel. 0539-942-244, fax 0539-942-246, Rue al-Antaki 8, eldjenina@menara.ma).

$ Hotel Residencia Andalucía is solid, clean, and minimal. It's buried in a totally non-touristy area in the new town, about a 20-minute walk from the Grand Socco. It has 19 rooms, a small reception, and a peaceful lobby (Sb-200-230 dh, Db-230-260 dh, higher prices are for mid-June-mid-Sept, cash only, Rue Omar Ben Abdelaziz 14, tel. 0539-941-334, Azdeen speaks a little English). Don't confuse it with the similarly named but very exclusive Hotel Andalucía Golf across town.

Eating in Tangier

Moroccan food is a joy to sample. First priority is a glass of the refreshing "Moroccan tea"—green tea that's boiled and steeped once, then combined with fresh mint leaves to boil and steep some more, before being loaded up with sugar. Tourist-oriented restaurants have a predictable menu. For starters, you'll find Moroccan vegetable soup *(harira)* or Moroccan salad (a combination of fresh and stewed vegetables). Main dishes include couscous (usually with chicken, potatoes, carrots, and other vegetables and spices); *tangine* (stewed meat served in a fancy dish with a cone-shaped top); and *briouates* (small savory pies). Everything comes with Morocco's distinctive round, flat bread. For dessert, it's pastries—typically, almond cookies.

I've mostly listed places in or near the Medina. (If you'd prefer the local equivalent of a yacht-club restaurant, survey the places along the beach.) Moroccan waiters expect about a 10 percent tip.

Le Saveur du Poisson is an excellent bet for the more adventurous, featuring one room cluttered with paintings adjoining a busy kitchen. There are no choices here. Just sit down and let owner Muhammad or his son, Hassan, take care of the rest. You get a rough hand-carved spoon and fork. Surrounded by lots of locals and unforgettable food, you'll be treated to a multicourse menu. Savor the delicious fish dishes—Tangier is one of the few spots in Morocco where seafood is a major part of the diet. The fruit punch—a mix of seasonal fruits brewed overnight in a vat—simmers in the back room. Ask for an explanation, or even a look. The desserts are full of nuts and honey. The big sink in the room is for locals who prefer to eat with their fingers (150-dh fixed-price meal, Sat-Thu 13:00-17:00 & 20:00-23:00, closed Fri and during Ramadan; walk down Rue de la Liberté roughly a block toward the Grand Socco from El Minzah Hotel, look for the stairs leading down to the market stalls and go down until you see fish on the grill; Escalier Waller 2, tel. 0539-336-326).

Maison Communitaire des Femmes, a community center for women, hides an inexpensive, hearty lunch spot that's open to everyone. A tasty three-course lunch is only 60 dh. Profits support the work of the center (Mon-Sat 12:00-16:00, last order at 15:30, also open 8:00-11:00 & 15:30-18:00 for cakes and tea, closed Sun, pleasant terrace out back, near slipper market just outside Grand

Socco, Place du 9 Avril).

El Minzah Hotel offers a fancier yet still authentic experience. The atmosphere is classy but low-stress. It's where unadventurous tourists and local elites dine. Dress up and choose between two dining zones: The white-tablecloth continental (French) dining area, called El Erz, is stuffy (80-150-dh starters, 120-240-dh main dishes); while in the Moroccan lounge, El Korsan, you'll be serenaded by live traditional music (music nightly 20:00-23:30, belly-dance show at 20:30 and 22:30, no extra charge for music; 70-120-dh starters, 170-260-dh main dishes). There's also a cozy wine bar here—a rarity in a Muslim country (50-120-dh starters, 120-190-dh main dishes, decorated with photos of visiting celebrities). At lunch, light meals and salads are served poolside (all dining areas open daily 13:00-16:00 & 20:00-22:30, Rue de la Liberté 85, tel. 0539-935-885, www.elminzah.com).

Le Salon Bleu has decent Moroccan food and some of the most spectacular seating in town: perched on a whitewashed terrace overlooking the square in front of the Kasbah Museum, with 360-degree views over the rooftops. Hike up the very tight spiral staircase to the top level, with the best views and lounge-a-while sofa seating. French-run (by the owners of Dar Nour guest house), it offers a simple menu of Moroccan fare—the 80-dh appetizer plate is a good sampler for lunch or to share for an afternoon snack. While there is some indoor seating, I'd skip this place if the weather's not ideal for lingering on the terrace (30-40-dh starters, 80-120-dh main dishes, Place de la Kasbah, mobile 06-5432-7618). You'll see it from the square in front of the Kasbah; to reach it, go through the gate to the left (as you face it), then look right for the stairs up.

Le Fabrique has nothing to do with old Morocco. But if you want a break from couscous and keyhole arches, this industrial-mod brasserie with concrete floors and exposed brick has a menu of purely French classics—a good reminder that in the 20th century, Tangier was nearly as much a French city as a Moroccan one (70-140-dh starters, 130-230-dh main dishes, Tue-Sat 12:00-14:30 & 20:00-23:00, closed Sun-Mon, Rue d'Angleterre 7, tel. 0539-374-057). It's a steep 10-minute walk up from the Grand Socco: Head up Rue d'Angleterre (left of Cinema Rif) and hike up the hill until the road levels out—it's on your left.

Le Nabab is geared for tourists, but offers more style and less crass commercialism than the tourist traps listed below. Squirreled away in a mostly residential neighborhood just below the lower Kasbah gate (near the top of the Medina), it has a menu of predictable Moroccan favorites in a sleek concrete-and-white-tablecloths dining room with a few echoes of traditional Moroccan decor (170-dh three-course meal is a good deal to sample several items,

40-55-dh starters, 100-150-dh main dishes, Mon-Sat 12:00-15:30 & 19:30-23:30, closed Sun; below the lower Kasbah gate—bear left down the stairs, then right, and look for signs; Rue Al Kadiria 4, mobile 06-6144-2220).

Tourist Traps

Tangier seems to specialize in very touristy Moroccan restaurants that are designed to feed and entertain dozens or even hundreds of tour-group members with overpriced and predictable menus of Moroccan classics, and often live music and belly-dancing. The only locals you'll see here are the waiters. For day-trippers who just want a safe, comfortable break in the heart of town, these restaurants' predictability and Moroccan clichés are just perfect. For other travelers, these places are tour-group hell and make you thankful to be free. Each local guide has their own favorite, but these are the best-known.

Hamadi is as luxurious a restaurant as a tourist can find in Morocco, with good food at reasonable prices (25-40-dh starters, 60-80-dh main dishes, long hours daily, Rue Kasbah 2, tel. 0539-934-514).

Marhaba Palace has the most impressive interior, with huge keyhole arches ringing a grand upstairs hall slathered in colorful tilework. It also has the highest prices—hardly a good value. It's near the upper gate to the Kasbah, so it's convenient for a meal just before heading downhill through town to the Medina and market (170-240-dh fixed-price meals, daily 10:00-23:00, Rue Kasbah, tel. 0539-937-927).

Mamounia Palace, considered by most the bottom of the barrel, is right on the Petit Socco and more in the middle of the action. At least it has a Hollywood connection: The Moroccan tea-house scenes from the movie *Inception* were filmed on its upstairs balcony. A meal here will cost you about 100 dh for four courses (no à la carte, daily 11:00-22:00, tel. 0539-935-099).

Tangier Connections

In Tangier, all train traffic comes and goes from the suburban Gare Tanger Ville train station, one mile from the city center and a short Petit Taxi ride away (10-20 dh). If you're traveling inland, check the information booth at the entrance of the train station for schedules (www.oncf.ma).

From Tangier by Train to: Rabat (5/day, 5 hours), **Casablanca** (station also called **Casa Voyageurs,** 6/day, 5 hours; a new train line will cut the trip to about 2 hours by 2014), **Marrakech** (4/day, 12 hours), **Fès** (4/day, 4.5 hours).

From Tangier by Bus to: Ceuta and **Tétouan** (hourly, 1 hour).

From **Fès** to: **Casablanca** (9/day, 4.5 hours), **Marrakech** (7/day, 7 hours), **Rabat** (9/day, 4 hours), **Meknès** (10/day, 45 minutes), **Tangier** (5/day, 5.5 hours).

From **Rabat** to: **Casablanca** (2/hour, 45 minutes), **Fès** (9/day, 3.5 hours), **Tétouan** (2 buses/day, 4.5 hours, 3 trains/day, 6 hours).

From **Casablanca** to: **Marrakech** (9/day, 3.5 hours).

From **Marrakech** to: **Meknès** (7/day, 7 hours), **Ouarzazate** (4/day, 4 hours).

By Plane: Flights within Morocco are convenient and reasonable (about $180 one-way from Tangier to Casablanca).

Extended Tour of Morocco

Morocco gets much better as you go deeper into the interior. The country is incredibly rich in cultural thrills, though you'll pay a

price in hassles and headaches—it's a package deal. But if adventure is your business, Morocco is a great option. Invest in a good Morocco guidebook to make this trip. Here are a few tips and insights to get you started.

To get a fair look at Morocco, you must get past the hustlers and con artists of the north coast (Tangier, Tétouan). It takes a minimum of four or five days to make a worthwhile visit—ideally seven or eight. Plan at least two nights in either Fès or Marrakech. A trip over the Atlas Mountains gives you an exciting look at Saharan Morocco. If you need a vacation from your vacation, check into one of the idyllic Atlantic beach resorts on the south coast. Above all, get past the northern day-trip-from-Spain, take-a-snapshot-on-a-camel fringe. (Oops, that's us. Oh well.)

If you're relying on public transportation for your extended tour, sail to Tangier, blast your way through customs, ignore any hustler who tells you there's no way out until tomorrow, and hop in a Petit Taxi for the Tanger Ville train station one mile away. From there set your sights on Rabat, a dignified European-type town with fewer hustlers, and make it your get-acquainted stop in Morocco. Trains go farther south from Rabat.

If you're driving a car, crossing the border can be a bit unnerving, since you'll be forced to jump through several bureaucratic hoops. You'll go through customs at both borders, buy Moroccan insurance for your car (cheap and easy), and feel at the mercy of a bristly bunch of shady-looking people you'd rather not be at the mercy of. Don't pay anyone on the Spanish side. Consider tipping a guy on the Moroccan side if you feel he'll shepherd you through. Relax and let him grease those customs wheels. He's worth it. As soon as possible, hit the road and drive to Chefchaouen, the best first stop for those with their own wheels.

Moroccan Towns

▲▲Chefchaouen—Just two hours by bus or car from Tétouan, this is the first pleasant town beyond the north coast. Monday and Thursday are colorful market days. Stay in the classy old Hotel Chaouen on Place el-Makhzen. The Hotel Parador (historic inn, but not the same as the Spanish government-run chain) faces the old town and offers good meals and a refuge from hustlers. Wander deep into the whitewashed old town from here.

▲▲Rabat—Morocco's capital and most European city, Rabat is the most comfortable and least stressful place to start your North African trip. You'll find a colorful market (in the old neighboring town of Salé), bits of Islamic architecture (Mausoleum of Mohammed V), the king's palace, mellow hustlers, and fine hotels.

▲▲▲Fès—More than just a funny hat that tipsy Shriners wear, Fès is Morocco's religious and artistic center, bustling with craftspeople, pilgrims, shoppers, and shops. Like most large Moroccan cities, it has a distinct new town from the French colonial period, as well as an exotic (and stressful) old walled Arabic town (the Medina), where you'll find the market.

For 12 centuries traders have gathered in Fès, founded on a river at the crossroads of two trade routes. Soon there was an irrigation system; a university; resident craftsmen from Spain; and a diverse population of Muslims, Christians, and Jews. When France claimed Morocco in 1912, they made their capital in Rabat, and Fès fizzled. But the Fès marketplace is still Morocco's best.

▲▲▲Marrakech—Morocco's gateway to the south, Marrakech is where the desert, mountain, and coastal regions merge. This market city is a constant folk festival, bustling with Berber tribespeople and a colorful center. The new city has the train station, and the main boulevard (Mohammed V) is lined with banks, airline offices, a post office, a tourist office, and comfortable hotels. The old city features the maze-like market and the huge Djemaa el-Fna, a square seething with people—a 43-ring Moroccan circus.

▲▲▲**Over the Atlas Mountains**—Extend your Moroccan trip several days by heading south over the Atlas Mountains. Take a bus from Marrakech to Ouarzazate (short stop), and then to Tinerhir (great oasis town, comfy hotel, overnight stop). The next day go to Er Rachidia and take the overnight bus to Fès.

By car, drive from Fès south, staying in the small mountain town of Ifrane, and then continue deep into the desert country past Er Rachidia and on to Rissani (market days: Sun, Tue, and Thu). Explore nearby mud-brick towns still living in the Middle Ages. Hire a guide to drive you past where the road stops, and head cross-country to an oasis village (Merzouga), where you can climb a sand dune and watch the sun rise over the vastness of Africa. Only a sea of sand separates you from Timbuktu.

PRACTICALITIES

This section covers just the basics on traveling in Spain (for much more information, see *Rick Steves' Spain*). You can find free advice on specific topics at www.ricksteves.com/tips.

Money

Spain uses the euro currency: 1 euro (€) = about $1.40. To convert prices in euros to dollars, add about 40 percent: €20 = about $28, €50 = about $70. (Check www.oanda.com for the latest exchange rates.)

The standard way for travelers to get euros is to withdraw money from a cash machine (called a *cajero automático*) using a debit or credit card, ideally with a Visa or MasterCard logo. Before departing, call your bank or credit-card company: Confirm that your card will work overseas, ask about international transaction fees, and alert them that you'll be making withdrawals in Europe.

Your US credit card might not work at some stores or at automated machines (e.g., train and subway ticket machines, luggage lockers, toll booths, parking garages, and self-serve gas pumps), because they're designed to accept European credit cards with a PIN code. If your card doesn't work, you have several options: Pay with euros, try your PIN code (ask your credit-card company in advance or use a debit card), or find a nearby cashier who should be able to process the transaction.

To keep your valuables safe, wear a money belt. But if you do lose your credit or debit card, report the loss immediately to the respective global customer-assistance centers. Call these 24-hour US numbers collect: Visa (410/581-9994), MasterCard (636/722-7111), and American Express (623/492-8427).

Phoning

Smart travelers use the telephone to reserve or reconfirm rooms, reserve restaurants, get directions, research transportation connections, confirm tour times, phone home, and lots more.

To call Spain from the US or Canada: Dial 011-34 and then the nine-digit number. (The 011 is our international access code, and 34 is Spain's country code.)

To call Spain from a European country: Dial 00-34 followed by the nine-digit number. (The 00 is Europe's international access code.)

To call within Spain: Just dial the local nine-digit number.

To call from Spain to another country: Dial 00 followed by the country code (for example, 1 for the US or Canada), then the area code and number. If calling European countries whose phone numbers begin with 0, you'll usually have to omit that 0 when you dial.

Tips on Phoning: To make calls in Spain, you can buy two different types of phone cards—international or insertable—sold locally at newsstands. Cheap international phone cards, which work with a scratch-to-reveal PIN code at any phone, allow you to call home to the US for pennies a minute, and also work for domestic calls within Spain. Insertable phone cards, which must be inserted into public pay phones, are reasonable for calls within Spain (and work for international calls as well, but not as cheaply as the international phone cards). Calling from your hotel-room phone is usually expensive, unless you use an international phone card. A mobile phone—whether an American one that works in Spain, or a European one you buy when you arrive—is handy, but can be pricey. For more on phoning, see www.ricksteves.com/phoning.

Emergency Telephone Numbers in Spain: For **police** help, dial 091. To summon an **ambulance**, call 112. For passport problems, call the **US Embassy** (in Madrid, tel. 915-872-240, after-hours emergency tel. 915-872-200) or the **Canadian Embassy** (in Madrid, tel. 913-828-400). For other concerns, get advice from your hotel.

Making Hotel Reservations

To ensure the best value, I recommend reserving rooms in advance, particularly during peak season. Email the hotelier with the following key pieces of information: number and type of rooms; number of nights; date of arrival; date of departure; and any special requests. (For a sample form, see www.ricksteves.com/reservation.) Use the European style for writing dates: day/month/year. For example, for a two-night stay in July, you could request:

"1 double room for 2 nights, arrive 16/07/12, depart 18/07/12." Hoteliers typically ask for your credit-card number as a deposit.

In general, hotel prices can soften if you do any of the following: offer to pay cash, stay at least three nights, or travel off-season. You can also try asking for a cheaper room (for example, with a bathroom down the hall), or offer to skip breakfast.

Eating

By our standards, Spaniards eat late, having lunch—their biggest meal of the day—around 13:00-16:00, and dinner starting about 21:00. At restaurants, you can dine with tourists at 20:00, or with Spaniards if you wait until later.

For a fun early dinner at a bar, build a light meal out of tapas—small appetizer-sized portions of seafood, salads, meat-filled pastries, deep-fried tasties, and so on. Many of these are displayed behind glass, and you can point to what you want. Tapas typically cost about €2 apiece, but can run up to €10 for seafood. While the smaller "tapa" size (which comes on a saucer-size plate) is handiest for maximum tasting opportunities, many bars sell only larger sizes: the *ración* (full portion, on a dinner plate) and *media-ración* (half-size portion). *Jamón* (hah-MOHN), an air-dried ham similar to prosciutto, is a Spanish staple. Other key terms include *bocadillo* (baguette sandwich), *frito* (fried), *a la plancha* (grilled), *queso* (cheese), *tortilla* (omelet), and *surtido* (assortment).

Many bars have three price tiers, which should be clearly posted: It's cheapest to eat or drink while standing at the bar *(barra),* slightly more to sit at a table inside *(mesa* or *salón),* and most expensive to sit outside *(terraza).* Wherever you are, be assertive or you'll never be served. *Por favor* (please) grabs the attention of the server or bartender. If you're having tapas, don't worry about paying as you go (the bartender keeps track). When you're ready to leave, ask for the bill: *"¿La cuenta?"* To tip for a few tapas, round up to the nearest euro; for a full meal, tip about 5 to 10 percent for good service.

Transportation

By Train and Bus: For train schedules, check www.renfe.es. Since trains can sell out, it's smart to buy your tickets a day in advance at a travel agency (easiest), at the train station (can be crowded; be sure you're in the right line), or online (at www.renfe.es; when asked for your Spanish national ID number, enter your passport number). Futuristic, high-speed trains (such as AVE) can be priced differently according to their time of departure. To see if a railpass could save you money, check www.ricksteves.com/rail.

Buses pick up where the trains don't go, reaching even small villages. But because routes are operated by various competing companies, it can be tricky to pin down schedules (inquire at local bus stations or TIs).

By Plane: Consider covering long distances on a budget flight, which can be cheaper than a train or bus ride. For flights within Spain, check out www.vueling.com, www.iberia.com, or www.spanair.com; to other European cites, try www.easyjet.com and www.ryanair.com; and to compare several airlines, see www.skyscanner.net.

By Car: It's cheaper to arrange most car rentals from the US. For tips on your insurance options, see www.ricksteves.com/cdw. Bring your driver's license. You're also technically required to have an International Driving Permit—a translation of your driver's license (sold at your local AAA office for $15 plus the cost of two passport-type photos; see www.aaa.com). For route planning, try www.viamichelin.com. Freeways come with tolls (about $4/hour), but save lots of time. A car is a worthless headache in cities—park it safely (get tips from your hotel). As break-ins are common, be sure all of your valuables are out of sight and locked in the trunk, or even better, with you or in your hotel room.

Helpful Hints

Theft Alert: Spain has particularly hardworking pickpockets. Assume beggars are pickpockets and any scuffle is simply a distraction by a team of thieves. If you stop for any commotion or show, put your hands in your pockets before someone else does. Better yet, wear a money belt.

Time: Spain uses the 24-hour clock. It's the same through 12:00 noon, then keep going: 13:00, 14:00, and so on. Spain, like most of continental Europe, is six/nine hours ahead of the East/West Coasts of the US.

Siesta and Paseo: Many Spaniards (especially in rural areas) still follow the traditional siesta schedule: From around 13:00 to 16:00, many businesses close as people go home for a big lunch with their family. Then they head back to work (and shops re-open) from about 16:00 to 20:00. (Many bigger stores stay open all day long, especially in cities.) Then, after a late dinner, whole families pour out of their apartments to enjoy the cool of the evening, stroll through the streets, and greet their neighbors—a custom called the paseo. Tourists are welcome to join this people-parade.

Sights: Major attractions can be swamped with visitors; carefully read and follow this book's crowd-beating tips (visit at quieter times of day, or—where possible—reserve ahead). At many churches, a modest dress code is encouraged and sometimes required (no bare shoulders, miniskirts, or shorts).

Holidays and Festivals: Spain celebrates many holidays, which can close sights and attract crowds (book hotel rooms ahead). For more on holidays and festivals, check Spain's website: www.spain.info. For a simple list showing major—though not all—events, see www.ricksteves.com/festivals.

Numbers and Stumblers: What Americans call the second floor of a building is the first floor in Europe. Europeans write dates as day/month/year, so Christmas is 25/12/12. Commas are decimal points and vice versa—a dollar and a half is 1,50, and there are 5.280 feet in a mile. Spain uses the metric system: A kilogram is 2.2 pounds; a liter is about a quart; and a kilometer is six-tenths of a mile.

Resources from Rick Steves

This Snapshot guide is excerpted from the latest edition of *Rick Steves' Spain*, which is one of more than 30 titles in my series of guidebooks on European travel. I also produce a public television series, *Rick Steves' Europe,* and a public radio show, *Travel with Rick Steves.* My website, www.ricksteves.com, offers free travel information, a Graffiti Wall for travelers' comments, guidebook updates, my travel blog, an online travel store, and information on European railpasses and our tours of Europe. If you're bringing a mobile device on your trip, you can download free information from Rick Steves Audio Europe, featuring podcasts of my radio shows, free audio tours of major sights in Europe, and travel interviews and other audio content about Spain (via www.ricksteves.com/audioeurope, iTunes, or the Rick Steves Audio Europe free smartphone app).

Additional Resources

Tourist Information: www.spain.info
Passports and Red Tape: www.travel.state.gov
Packing List: www.ricksteves.com/packlist
Cheap Flights: www.skyscanner.net
Airplane Carry-on Restrictions: www.tsa.gov/travelers
Updates for This Book: www.ricksteves.com/update.

How Was Your Trip?

If you'd like to share your tips, concerns, and discoveries after using this book, please fill out the survey at www.ricksteves.com/feedback. Thanks in advance—it helps a lot.

Spanish Survival Phrases

Spanish has a guttural sound similar to the J in Baja California. In the phonetics, the symbol for this clearing-your-throat sound is the italicized *h*.

Good day.	**Buenos días.**	**bway**-nohs **dee**-ahs
Do you speak English?	**¿Habla Usted inglés?**	**ah**-blah oo-**stehd** een-**glays**
Yes. / No.	**Sí. / No.**	see / noh
I (don't) understand.	**(No) comprendo.**	(noh) kohm-**prehn**-doh
Please.	**Por favor.**	por fah-**bor**
Thank you.	**Gracias.**	**grah**-thee-ahs
I'm sorry.	**Lo siento.**	loh see-**ehn**-toh
Excuse me.	**Perdóneme.**	pehr-**doh**-nay-may
(No) problem.	**(No) problema.**	(noh) proh-**blay**-mah
Good.	**Bueno.**	**bway**-noh
Goodbye.	**Adiós.**	ah-dee-**ohs**
one / two	**uno / dos**	**oo**-noh / dohs
three / four	**tres / cuatro**	trays / **kwah**-troh
five / six	**cinco / seis**	**theen**-koh / says
seven / eight	**siete / ocho**	see-**eh**-tay / **oh**-choh
nine / ten	**nueve / diez**	**nway**-bay / dee-**ayth**
How much is it?	**¿Cuánto cuesta?**	**kwahn**-toh **kway**-stah
Write it?	**¿Me lo escribe?**	may loh ay-**skree**-bay
Is it free?	**¿Es gratis?**	ays **grah**-tees
Is it included?	**¿Está incluido?**	ay-**stah** een-kloo-**ee**-doh
Where can I buy / find...?	**¿Dónde puedo comprar / encontrar...?**	**dohn**-day **pway**-doh kohm-**prar** / ayn-kohn-**trar**
I'd like / We'd like...	**Quiero / Queremos...**	kee-**ehr**-oh / kehr-**ay**-mohs
...a room.	**...una habitación.**	**oo**-nah ah-bee-tah-thee-**ohn**
...a ticket to ___.	**...un billete para ___.**	oon bee-**yeh**-tay **pah**-rah
Is it possible?	**¿Es posible?**	ays poh-**see**-blay
Where is...?	**¿Dónde está...?**	**dohn**-day ay-**stah**
...the train station	**...la estación de trenes**	lah ay-stah-thee-**ohn** day **tray**-nays
...the bus station	**...la estación de autobuses**	lah ay-stah-thee-**ohn** day ow-toh-**boo**-says
...the tourist information office	**...la oficina de turismo**	lah oh-fee-**thee**-nah day too-**rees**-moh
Where are the toilets?	**¿Dónde están los servicios?**	**dohn**-day ay-**stahn** lohs sehr-**bee**-thee-ohs
men	**hombres, caballeros**	**ohm**-brays, kah-bah-**yay**-rohs
women	**mujeres, damas**	moo-**heh**-rays, **dah**-mahs
left / right	**izquierda / derecha**	eeth-kee-**ehr**-dah / day-**ray**-chah
straight	**derecho**	day-**ray**-choh
When do you open / close?	**¿A qué hora abren / cierran?**	ah kay **oh**-rah **ah**-brehn / thee-**ay**-rahn
At what time?	**¿A qué hora?**	ah kay **oh**-rah
Just a moment.	**Un momento.**	oon moh-**mehn**-toh
now / soon / later	**ahora / pronto / más tarde**	ah-**oh**-rah / **prohn**-toh / mahs **tar**-day
today / tomorrow	**hoy / mañana**	oy / mahn-**yah**-nah

PRACTICALITIES

In a Spanish Restaurant

I'd like / We'd like...	Quiero / Queremos...	kee-**ehr**-oh / kehr-**ay**-mohs
...to reserve...	...reservar...	ray-sehr-**bar**
...a table for one / two.	...una mesa para uno / dos.	oo-nah **may**-sah **pah**-rah oo-noh / dohs
Non-smoking.	No fumador.	noh foo-mah-**dohr**
Is this table free?	¿Está esta mesa libre?	ay-**stah** ay-stah **may**-sah lee-bray
The menu (in English), please.	La carta (en inglés), por favor.	lah **kar**-tah (ayn een-**glays**) por fah-**bor**
service (not) included	servicio (no) incluido	sehr-**bee**-thee-oh (noh) een-kloo-**ee**-doh
cover charge	precio de entrada	**pray**-thee-oh day ayn-**trah**-dah
to go	para llevar	**pah**-rah yay-**bar**
with / without	con / sin	kohn / seen
and / or	y / o	ee / oh
menu (of the day)	menú (del dia)	may-**noo** (dayl **dee**-ah)
specialty of the house	especialidad de la casa	ay-spay-thee-ah-lee-**dahd** day lah **kah**-sah
tourist menu	menú turístico	meh-**noo** too-**ree**-stee-koh
combination plate	plato combinado	**plah**-toh kohm-bee-**nah**-doh
appetizers	tapas	**tah**-pahs
bread	pan	pahn
cheese	queso	**kay**-soh
sandwich	bocadillo	boh-kah-**dee**-yoh
soup	sopa	**soh**-pah
salad	ensalada	ayn-sah-**lah**-dah
meat	carne	**kar**-nay
poultry	aves	**ah**-bays
fish	pescado	pay-**skah**-doh
seafood	marisco	mah-**ree**-skoh
fruit	fruta	**froo**-tah
vegetables	verduras	behr-**doo**-rahs
dessert	postres	**poh**-strays
tap water	agua del grifo	**ah**-gwah dayl **gree**-foh
mineral water	agua mineral	**ah**-gwah mee-nay-**rahl**
milk	leche	**lay**-chay
(orange) juice	zumo (de naranja)	**thoo**-moh (day nah-**rahn**-hah)
coffee	café	kah-**feh**
tea	té	tay
wine	vino	**bee**-noh
red / white	tinto / blanco	**teen**-toh / **blahn**-koh
glass / bottle	vaso / botella	**bah**-soh / boh-**tay**-yah
beer	cerveza	thehr-**bay**-thah
Cheers!	¡Salud!	sah-**lood**
More. / Another.	Más. / Otro.	mahs / **oh**-troh
The same.	El mismo.	ehl **mees**-moh
The bill, please.	La cuenta, por favor.	lah **kwayn**-tah por fah-**bor**
tip	propina	proh-**pee**-nah
Delicious!	¡Delicioso!	day-lee-thee-**oh**-soh

For hundreds more pages of survival phrases for your trip to Spain, check out *Rick Steves' Spanish Phrase Book*.

INDEX

INDEX

Audio Europe

Rick's free app and podcasts

The FREE **Rick Steves Audio Europe**™ app for iPhone, iPad and iPod Touch gives you 29 self-guided audio tours of Europe's top museums, sights and historic walks—plus more than 200 tracks filled with cultural insights and sightseeing tips from Rick's radio interviews—all organized into geographic-specific playlists.

Let **Rick Steves Audio Europe**™ amplify your guidebook.

With Rick whispering in your ear, Europe gets even better.

Thanks Facebook fans for submitting photos while on location! From top: John Kuijper in Florence, Brenda Mamer with her mother in Rome, Angel Capobianco in London, and Alyssa Passey with her friend in Paris.

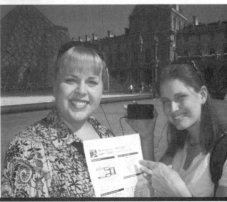

Find out more at ricksteves.com

Join a Rick Steves tour

Enjoy Europe's warmest welcome... with the flexibility and friendship of a small group getting to know Rick's favorite places and people. It all starts with our free tour catalog and DVD.

Great guides, small groups, no grumps.

Start your trip at

Free information and great gear to

▸ Plan Your Trip

Browse thousands of articles and a wealth of money-saving tips for planning your dream trip. You'll find up-to-date information on Europe's best destinations, packing smart, getting around, finding rooms, staying healthy, avoiding scams and more.

▸ Eurail Passes

Find out, step-by-step, if a railpass makes sense for your trip—and how to avoid buying more than you need. Get free shipping on online orders

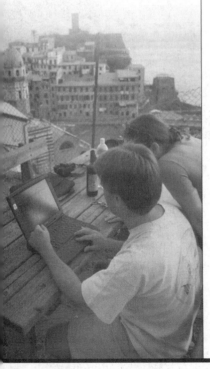

▸ Graffiti Wall & Travelers Helpline

Learn, ask, share—our online community of savvy travelers is a great resource for first-time travelers to Europe, as well as seasoned pros.

Rick Steves' Europe Through the Back Door, Inc.

Rick Steves

www.ricksteves.com

EUROPE GUIDES

Best of Europe
Eastern Europe
Europe Through the Back Door
Mediterranean Cruise Ports

COUNTRY GUIDES

Croatia & Slovenia
England
France
Germany
Great Britain
Ireland
Italy
Portugal
Scandinavia
Spain
Switzerland

CITY & REGIONAL GUIDES

Amsterdam, Bruges & Brussels
Budapest
Florence & Tuscany
Greece: Athens & the Peloponnese
Istanbul
London
Paris
Prague & the Czech Republic
Provence & the French Riviera
Rome
Venice
Vienna, Salzburg & Tirol

SNAPSHOT GUIDES

Barcelona
Berlin
Bruges & Brussels
Copenhagen & the Best of
    Denmark
Dublin
Dubrovnik
Hill Towns of Central Italy
Italy's Cinque Terre
Krakow, Warsaw & Gdansk
Lisbon
Madrid & Toledo
Munich, Bavaria & Salzburg
Naples & the Amalfi Coast
Northern Ireland
Norway
Scotland
Sevilla, Granada & Southern Spain
Stockholm

POCKET GUIDES

London
Paris
Rome

TRAVEL CULTURE

Europe 101
European Christmas
Postcards from Europe
Travel as a Political Act

Rick Steves guidebooks are published by Avalon Travel,
a member of the Perseus Books Group.

NOW AVAILABLE:
eBOOKS, APPS & BLU-RAY

eBOOKS

Most guides are available as eBooks from Amazon, Barnes & Noble, Borders, Apple, and Sony. Free apps for eBook reading are available in the Apple App Store and Android Market, and eBook readers such as Kindle, Nook, and Kobo all have free apps that work on smartphones.

RICK STEVES' EUROPE DVDs

10 New Shows 2011–2012
Austria & the Alps
Eastern Europe
England & Wales
European Christmas
European Travel Skills & Specials
France
Germany, BeNeLux & More
Greece & Turkey
Iran
Ireland & Scotland
Italy's Cities
Italy's Countryside
Scandinavia
Spain
Travel Extras

BLU-RAY

Celtic Charms
Eastern Europe Favorites
European Christmas
Italy Through the Back Door
Mediterranean Mosaic
Surprising Cities of Europe

PHRASE BOOKS & DICTIONARIES

French
French, Italian & German
German
Italian
Portuguese
Spanish

JOURNALS

Rick Steves' Pocket Travel Journal
Rick Steves' Travel Journal

APPS

Select Rick Steves guides are available as apps in the Apple App Store.

PLANNING MAPS

Britain, Ireland & London
Europe
France & Paris
Germany, Austria & Switzerland
Ireland
Italy
Spain & Portugal

Avalon Travel
a member of the Perseus Books Group
1700 Fourth Street
Berkeley, CA 94710

Printed in Canada by Friesens.
First printing January 2012.

ISBN 978-1-59880-687-8

For the latest on Rick's lectures, guidebooks, tours, public radio show, and public television
series, contact Europe Through the Back Door, Box 2009, Edmonds, WA 98020, 425/771-
8303, fax 425/771-0833, www.ricksteves.com, rick@ricksteves.com.

Europe Through the Back Door Reviewing Editors: Risa Laib, Jennifer Madison Davis
ETBD Editors: Suzanne Kotz, Cathy Lu, Tom Griffin, Cathy McDonald, Gretchen
   Strauch, Claire Burns
Researchers: Amanda Buttinger, Cameron Hewitt, Gene Openshaw
Avalon Travel Senior Editor and Series Manager: Madhu Prasher
Avalon Travel Project Editor: Kelly Lydick
Copy Editor: Amy Scott
Proofreader: Denise Silva
Indexer: Stephen Callahan
Production and Layout: McGuire Barber Design
Cover Design: Kimberly Glyder Design
Graphic Content Director: Laura VanDeventer
Maps and Graphics: David C. Hoerlein, Lauren Mills, Twozdai Hulse, Laura
   VanDeventer, Barb Geisler, Mike Morgenfeld, Brice Ticen, Kat Bennett
Title Page Photo: Cathedral and Giralda Bell Tower © Matej Kastelic/www.123rf.com
Page 129 Photo: view from the front of the cathedral of Granada © Paco Ayala/
www.123rf.com
Cover Photo: Still in the Nazrides Palace © Fanelie Rosier/www.istockphoto.com
Photography: David C. Hoerlein, Rick Steves, Cameron Hewitt, Robert Wright, Steve
Smith, Dominic Bonuccelli, Pat O'Connor, Cathy McDonald

ABOUT THE AUTHOR

RICK STEVES

Since 1973, Rick Steves has spent 100 days every year exploring Europe. Rick produces a public television series (*Rick Steves' Europe*), a public radio show (*Travel with Rick Steves*), and an app and podcast (*Rick Steves Audio Europe*); writes a bestselling series of guidebooks and a nationally syndicated newspaper column; organizes guided tours that take over ten thousand travelers to Europe annually; and offers an information-packed website (www.ricksteves.com). With the help of his hardworking staff of 80 at Europe Through the Back Door—in Edmonds, Washington, just north of Seattle—Rick's mission is to make European travel fun, affordable, and culturally enlightening for Americans.

Want More Spain?
Maximize the experience with Rick Steves as your guide

Planning Maps
Use the map that's in sync with your guidebook

Phrase Books
Rely on Rick's Spanish Phrase Book and Dictionary

Rick's DVDs
Preview your destinations with 8 shows on Spain

Rick's Audio Europe™ App
Hear Spain travel tips from Rick's radio shows

Small-Group Tours
Take a lively Rick Steves tour through Spain